HOLY LIVING

Jeremy Taylor's greatest works, *Holy Living* and *Holy Dying* (1650, 1651) have appeared only once in a critical text, in R. W. Heber's edition of 1822 (revised by C. P. Eden in 1847): but that edition is not accurate, nor is it readily available. Taylor's devotional classics have nevertheless appeared in a variety of popular editions down to the present day, but none of these presents the text in a way that Taylor could have wished. This present edition therefore attempts to recover Taylor's books in the form which he intended.

The texts of both *Holy Living* and *Holy Dying* are based upon the first editions collated with those editions published during Taylor's lifetime. The wish in this present edition is to recover the original texts and those later variants which have Taylor's authority, so far as it can be discovered. A critical apparatus is provided, including all substantive textual variants at the foot of each text page as they occur, and schedules of non-substantive readings at the end of the book. A textual introduction sets out the problems of editing these texts and provides also bibliographic descriptions of the early editions.

There is a general introduction which outlines Taylor's life and works and studies the intellectual background of *Holy Living* and *Holy Dying*. Other sections in the introduction discuss these complementary books from the standpoint of their plan, style, and reception. A full commentary at the end of the volume clarifies archaisms, translates and explains classical and patristic references, and provides guidance for the general reader.

P. G. Stanwood is Professor of English in the University of British Columbia, Vancouver.

1. Taylor's portrait, engraved by P. Lombart, from the painting at All Souls College, Oxford, first appearing in *The Great Exemplar*, 2nd edn., 1653.

JEREMY TAYLOR

HOLY LIVING
AND
HOLY DYING

Volume I: Holy Living

EDITED BY

P. G. STANWOOD

CLARENDON PRESS · OXFORD

1989

Oxford University Press, Walton Street, Oxford OX2 6DP

*Oxford New York Toronto
Delhi Bombay Calcutta Madras Karachi
Petaling Jaya Singapore Hong Kong Tokyo
Nairobi Dar es Salaam Cape Town
Melbourne Auckland
and associated companies in
Berlin Ibadan*

Oxford is a trade mark of Oxford University Press

*Published in the United States
by Oxford University Press (USA)*

British Library Cataloguing in Publication Data

*Taylor, Jeremy, 1613–1667
Holy living and holy dying.—New ed:
1. Anglicans. Christian life—Early works
I. Title II. Stanwood, Paul G.
III. Taylor, Jeremy, 1631–1667 Rule and
exercises of holy living and dying
248.4'83*

*ISBN 0–19–812705–7 v.1
ISBN 0–19–812349–3 v.2*

Library of Congress Cataloging in Publication Data

*Taylor, Jeremy, 1613–1667.
Holy living; and, Holy dying.
(Oxford English texts)
Originally published under titles: The rule and exercises of holy living (1650) and The rule of holy dying (1651).
Bibliography: p. Includes index.
Contents: v. 1. Holy living—v. 2. Holy dying. 1. Christian life—Anglican authors—Early works to 1800.
2. Death—Religious aspects—Christianity—Early works to 1800. I. Rehman, A. A. II. Taylor, Jeremy, 1613–1667. Rule and exercises of holy dying. 1989. III. Title.
BV4500.T28 1989 248.4'83 88–1469*

*ISBN 0–19–812705–7 (v. 1)
ISBN 0–19–812349–3 (v. 2)*

*Typeset by Joshua Associates Ltd., Oxford
Printed and bound in Great Britain by
Courier International Ltd, Tiptree, Essex*

PREFACE

THIS edition, begun about fifteen years ago but frequently interrupted because of academic and other commitments, at last makes readily available a reliable and attractive text of one of the greatest English prose works of the seventeenth century. The late Dame Helen Gardner first suggested that I undertake this edition of Jeremy Taylor's *Rules and Exercises of Holy Living and Holy Dying*, and my conversations with her at the beginning of the work helped to define its editorial plan. I am also generally indebted to her critical and textual scholarship, and, like many other students of the seventeenth century, have been inspired by her knowledge and love of this period.

The purpose of this edition is first of all to provide a text of Jeremy Taylor's two most famous books, *Holy Living* and *Holy Dying*, in a way that reveals their author's intentions as nearly as one can discover them. I have wished, secondly, to give sufficient introductory and other comment to help the modern reader place these works in their seventeenth-century context. Although these books are quite different in their background, tone, and emphasis, they have often been treated as one work. They are best and most properly seen, however, as a complementary pair. In spite of their considerable popularity, especially in the nineteenth and the earlier part of this century, no edition has ever adequately revealed what the originals were like; nor has any edition attempted to annotate fully Taylor's many allusions and citations. Bishop Reginald Heber's 1822 edition of Taylor's complete works was a model of scholarship for its time, but it 'modernized' the texts of *Holy Living* and *Holy Dying*, which were not, in any case, those of the first editions. Charles Page Eden's 'revised and corrected' re-issue of Heber in 1847–54 provided some helpful annotations for *Holy Living* and *Holy Dying*, but he left much unexplained. No further serious work on these texts has been done until this present edition.

This edition seeks to restore the texts of the first editions, but with the addition of Taylor's corrections, in so far as they can be ascertained, in subsequent editions during the author's lifetime. Some other additions have been made, especially the autograph corrections and material of the Wyat presentation copy of the first edition of *Holy Living* in Northern Illinois University (formerly in the possession of Robert Gathorne-Hardy) and the fifth edition of 1656 in the library of

King's College, Cambridge. I have preserved the spelling of these manuscript notes and of the earliest printed texts, as well as the punctuation. Whenever I have made additions or altered an original reading, I give a textual note at the bottom of the appropriate page. I also provide a schedule of emended accidentals at the end of each volume. The textual introductions set out full details of my editorial procedures.

Each volume contains a General Introduction: that to *Holy Living* includes a description of Taylor's life and works and an account of his reputation; and each introduction discusses the tradition, plan, sources, and style of its respective work. The Commentary in each volume seeks to explain Taylor's references, translate his non-English quotations, and clarify whatever might be obscure to a modern reader. I have aimed to be economical in my annotations, providing only such information as I deemed essential for adequate understanding.

I am pleased to record my many obligations in this long task, especially to the pioneering editors, Heber and Eden. Dr A. A. Rehman, the assistant editor of the present edition of *Holy Living*, has kindly permitted me to make full use of his Ph.D. dissertation, 'A Critical Edition of Taylor's *Holy Living*' (University of British Columbia, 1984). I am pleased also to acknowledge the assistance of Dr Tirthankar Bose, who collated a number of the copies of *Holy Dying*, contributed substantially to the writing of the Commentary for that volume, and compiled the index to both volumes. I am very grateful to both Dr Rehman and Dr Bose for their frequent collaboration with me in many details of this edition, but I accept full responsibility for the final results.

Other individuals have been most helpful in answering questions, giving advice, or translating Taylor's notes. My thanks to colleagues at the University of British Columbia: Dr Silvana Carr for help with the Italian proverbs, Dr Elizabeth A. E. Bongie with the Latin, and especially Dr H. G. Edinger for his translations of all the Greek and for his help with all the classical allusions. For their timely assistance with special points in the Commentary of both volumes, I am grateful to the Reverend the Dean of Gonville and Caius College, John Sturdy, and to Professor N. G. L. Hammond of Cambridge University. I am also much indebted to Professor William P. Williams of Northern Illinois University for his invaluable bibliographical studies of Taylor.

I am grateful to the following libraries for permission to consult their books and manuscripts: in the United States, the Folger Shakespeare Library; the Library of Congress; the Henry E. Huntington Library (for the copy-text of the first edition of *Holy Living*); the Beinecke Library, Yale University; the Houghton and Widener libraries, Harvard University; Northern Illinois University Library (and their Jeremy Taylor Collection); in Canada, the University of British Columbia Library; in England, the Bodleian Library, Oxford; the Cambridge University Library, and the libraries of Emmanuel College, King's College, Peterhouse, and Trinity College, Cambridge; the British Library (and North Room); and in Ireland, the Library of Trinity College, Dublin. Illustrations appear by the kind permission of Northern Illinois University Library and the Houghton Library of Harvard University.

This book has been published with the help of a grant from the Canadian Federation for the Humanities, using funds provided by the Social Sciences and Humanities Research Council of Canada (SSHRC). I am also happy to thank the Canada Council for a Leave Fellowship in 1974–5, during the early stages of the work; and the SSHRC for assisting me with an Extended Research Grant for the years 1982–4 and with a second Leave Fellowship in 1984–5 when I completed most of this edition. To the University of British Columbia and the Department of English, I am grateful for the several periods of study leave which they have allowed me. For such generous support over so long a period, I am indeed deeply appreciative.

I have saved for last my particular thanks to Dorothy Stanwood, who has helped me in many matters of detail, including the collation of the copy of the fifth edition of *Holy Dying* in the library of Emmanuel College, Cambridge. Finally, if this work were to bear a dedication, it would be to the memory of the late Professor Austin Warren (1899–1986), formerly of the University of Michigan in Ann Arbor, who first introduced Jeremy Taylor to me more than thirty years ago, and who watched over the development of this edition with special delight.

P. G. Stanwood

Vancouver, Canada
September 1988

CONTENTS

VOLUME I

VOLUME II

LIST OF ILLUSTRATIONS

SIGLA AND ABBREVIATIONS

1	1650	Huntington Library
2	1651	Yale University Library
3	1651	Northern Illinois University Library
4	1654	Cambridge University Library
5	1656	Cambridge University Library
6	1660	Northern Illinois University Library
7	1663	Yale University Library
8	1668	Yale University Library

GH Robert Gathorne-Hardy: the Wyat presentation copy of the first edition in Northern Illinois University Library
KC Library of King's College, Cambridge: copy of the fifth edition
cor correction (corrected)
cw catchword
ed this edition (or editor)
ital italic font
om omitted
rom roman font
~ used to repeat lemma in note
^ used to call attention to absence of punctuation
\+ following the siglum for an edition, refers to a common reading in subsequent editions (as *1*+)

The following abbreviations are commonly used in the Commentary:
BCP *Book of Common Prayer*
CSEL *Corpus Scriptorum Ecclesiasticorum Latinorum.* Vienna, 1866–.
Loeb Loeb Classical Library (London: Heinemann)
Mansi J. D. Mansi, ed. *Sacrorum Conciliorum Nova et Amplissima Collectio.* 31 vols. Florence, 1759–98; rept. 53 vols. Graz: Akademische Druck- u. Verlagsanstalt, 1960–1.
Nauck A. Nauck, *Tragicorum Graecorum Fragmenta.* 2nd edn. Leipzig, 1889.
OED *Oxford English Dictionary*
PG *Patrologia Graeca.* Ed. J. P. Migne. 162 vols. Paris, 1857–66.
PL *Patrologia Latina.* Ed. J. P. Migne. 221 vols. Paris, 1844–64.
Works *The Whole Works of . . . Jeremy Taylor.* Ed. R. Heber (1822); rev. C. P. Eden. 10 vols. London, 1847–54.

2. Engraved title-page, *The Rule and Exercises of Holy Living,* 12th edn. 1680. A. F. Johnson, *Catalogue of Engraved and Etched English Title-pages,* Anon., 154.

GENERAL INTRODUCTION

I. *Taylor's Life and Works*

Of Jeremy Taylor's early life, as indeed of large parts of his later life, very little is known. He was born in Cambridge in 1613, the fourth child of a barber named Nathaniel Taylor and his wife, Mary. The exact date of Taylor's birth is not known, but he was baptized on 15 August 1613, the likely year of his birth. Nathaniel Taylor, though poor, belonged to a respectable family: his father, Edmund Taylor, had been a churchwarden of the parish of Trinity Church in Cambridge; and Nathaniel was reputedly a man of some education, for his son was later to say, according to one tradition, that he had been 'solely grounded . . . in grammar and the mathematics' by his father.[1]

In 1619, Taylor was sent to a free grammar school in Cambridge founded the previous year in accordance with the will of Dr Stephen Perse, Fellow of Gonville and Caius College, who had died in 1615. After spending some seven years at the Perse School, Taylor was admitted in 1626 as a sizar, or 'poor scholar', to Caius College.[2] At Caius, he became a Perse Scholar in 1628, took a BA three years later, and was elected to a Perse Fellowship in 1633. He took holy orders in the same year (below the canonical age, being only about 20 years old). In the following year (1634), he proceeded to an MA, and, evidently in recognition of his considerable rhetorical and speaking skills, was appointed praelector in rhetoric by the Master of Caius.

Beyond these dates and few details, we know little about Taylor's

[1] In a letter to his tutor at Cambridge, quoted by Heber in his *Life of Jeremy Taylor*. The quotation comes from what Heber calls the 'Jones MS', a collection of transcripts made by William Todd Jones from a number of Taylor's autograph letters which were lost after Jones's death in 1818. As to the authenticity of the original papers, Heber had only the word of Jones's sisters. See *The Whole Works of Jeremy Taylor*, ed. Reginald Heber, rev. Charles Page Eden, 10 vols. (London: Longman, 1850–4), vol. i, pp. x–xi (hereafter referred to as *Works*). I am indebted to Heber, whose *Life* is still the fullest and most detailed.

[2] The admission book of Caius records that Taylor was then in his fifteenth year and had been going to school for the past ten years. To account for the apparent inconsistency of dating, Sir James Ware, the Irish historian and antiquarian, suggested that Taylor might have been born in 1611, though baptized in 1613. C. J. Stranks suggests that Taylor was really thirteen at the time of his admission and that his parents misrepresented his age. The claim of ten years' schooling may indicate that Taylor had been educated privately before entering the Perse School. See Stranks, *The Life and Writings of Jeremy Taylor* (London: SPCK, 1952), pp. 30–1.

nine years at Caius. For the first twenty years of his life Taylor may have travelled no further than the Perse, Caius, Petty Cury, and the Cambridge market-place. Although Milton, Fuller, Crashaw, and Herbert were also at Cambridge during this period, there is no evidence, either in oral tradition or in written allusion, that he knew any of them. It is likely that Taylor studied assiduously, acquiring esteem within his own college, which was, like other Cambridge colleges of the early seventeenth century, independent. Henry More, also a Cambridge contemporary, was Taylor's friend in later life, but there is no evidence that Taylor knew More or his 'circle' at Emmanuel. George Rust (afterwards Dean of Connor during Taylor's period as Diocesan) was another near contemporary, later friend, and Taylor's funeral eulogist. What we observe in Taylor's narrow acquaintance simply reflects Cambridge life in his day, when people did not move easily outside their own college, and men whom we would expect to make good companions were not necessarily aware of each other.

The year 1634 saw the event which was to change Taylor's life. At the time, he was praelector and was sharing rooms in college with the Reverend Thomas Risden, who was engaged as a preacher at St Paul's Cathedral. On one occasion, Risden asked Taylor to stand in for him. Taylor did so, and performed so well that he was asked to return a number of times. He preached, according to Rust, 'to the admiration and astonishment of his auditory; and by his florid and youthful beauty, and sweet and pleasant air, and sublime and raised discourses, he made his hearers take him for some young angel newly descended from the visions of glory'.[3] Rust may be too extravagant in his praise (he was, after all, preaching Taylor's funeral sermon); but he is correct in pointing to Taylor's ability to charm and impress the congregation at St Paul's, many of whom would remember their late dean, John Donne. Someone commended Taylor to Archbishop Laud, who arranged for this very young man (of only twenty-two) to preach before him. Laud heard Taylor preach, according to Rust, 'not less to his wonder than satisfaction', but he thought the preacher too young. Taylor asked Laud to pardon the 'fault' of his youth and wittily promised that 'if he lived he would mend it'.[4] Laud was satisfied, and he determined to support Taylor as his protégé.

Taylor may not have returned to Cambridge. We know nothing for certain about how he spent the next two years, his movements being

[3] George Rust, *A Funeral Sermon, preached August 13th, 1667* (London, 1668), in *Works*, vol. i, p. cccxxii.

[4] Ibid.

obscure until he surfaced in Oxford in 1635, when he was incorporated into the university. Soon after, Laud recommended him for a fellowship at All Souls College, and, exercising his visitorial privilege, appointed Taylor in January 1636 over the objections of Gilbert Sheldon, the Warden.

Taylor now seemed well settled as a promising young clergyman with all the advantages of a man of letters. In 1638 he was presented, probably on Laud's commendation, with the rectory of Uppingham in Rutland by Bishop Juxon of London. Meanwhile, he was made a chaplain to Laud and to the King. These additional duties must have necessitated frequent and lengthy absences from All Souls, and he must have spent little time in Oxford. While he kept Uppingham as a place of residence, he was often in London, too, leaving the parish in the care of a curate.

Little is known about his Oxford days. According to Anthony à Wood, Taylor turned his attention to casuistry and sharpened his skills in that art: he later wrote a massive tome entitled *Ductor Dubitantium, or the Rule of Conscience* (1660), which he regarded as his most important study.[5] At Oxford, Taylor certainly knew William Chillingworth, Laud's godson, whose *Religion of Protestants: A Safe Way to Salvation* (1637), with its theme of charity and toleration, deeply affected him. Chillingworth had written his book at Great Tew, near Oxford, the country estate of Lucius Cary, second Viscount of Falkland, where a thoughtful group, including John Hales, Edward Hyde (Earl of Clarendon), and perhaps Jeremy Taylor, too, regularly gathered to discuss issues of religion and politics and the reasonableness of 'latitudinarianism'. We know that Taylor had some connection with Falkland's little circle, for Chillingworth wrote to a friend whom he addresses as 'Harry' that 'Mr. Taylor did much confirme my opinion of his sufficience.' But Chillingworth confides what he sees as a fault in Taylor's character, and recommends a corrective course: 'Let mee tell you in your eare—methinks he wants much of the ethicall part of a discourser, and slights too much many times the arguments of those he discourses with; but this is a fault he would quickly leave, if he had a friend that would discreetly tell him of it. If you . . . would tell him, that you heard one that knows him, magnifye him exceedingly for other things, but censure him for this, you might doe him a very friendly office.'[6] The youthful Taylor may also have been quite impatient in discourse.

[5] Anthony à Wood, *Athenae Oxonienses* (London, 1692), ii. 282.

[6] See P. Des Maiseaux, *An Historical and Critical Account of the Life and Writings of William Chillingworth* (London, 1725), p. 50.

During his Oxford years, Taylor also knew Christopher Davenport, a Franciscan friar known as Franciscus a Sancta Clara (*c.* 1595–1680). Of Merton College, Sancta Clara was a convert to Roman Catholicism; he had been to Douai, had returned to England as a missionary, and had soon been appointed one of Queen Henrietta Maria's chaplains. A learned and moderate man, Sancta Clara wrote a conciliatory (and controversial) work entitled *Deus, Natura, Gratia* (1634). Taylor was on good terms with Sancta Clara, enough to create the suspicion that he had Catholic leanings, which he subsequently took great pains to dispel. In his 'Sermon Preached upon the Anniversary of the Gunpowder Treason' (the earliest of his extant works), delivered before the university at St Mary's Church on 5 November 1638, Taylor laboured to demonstrate his anti-Romanist views and to prove himself a true Anglican; this highly political and intemperate sermon was highly successful in this regard.[7]

Not long after becoming the incumbent at Uppingham, Taylor was married, on 27 May 1639, to Phoebe Landisdale, or Langsdale, probably the sister of Edward Langsdale, a former pupil at Cambridge. Apart from her name, we know little about Phoebe or of the Taylors' domestic life at Uppingham; but the parish register shows that in May 1642 they buried a son, William. Taylor remained altogether a little over three years in Uppingham.

When we next see him, he is at Oxford with King Charles in November 1642 and at the beginning of the most difficult years of his life. By this time, the 'great storm' of seventeenth-century England had finally broken: Laud was in the tower, and King and Parliament were at war. Taylor followed the King to Nottingham, carrying with him the manuscript of his first book, *Of the Sacred Order and Offices of Episcopacy* (1642), which he had begun at Uppingham. Charles read the work before its publication and was pleased enough with it to have Taylor made a Doctor of Divinity at Oxford; but he would not permit Taylor to dedicate the book to him. Thus *Episcopacy Asserted* (as the book is generally known) was dedicated to Christopher Hatton, who became Taylor's patron and friend. The book is polemical, a kind of Royalist answer to such works as Milton's *Of Prelatical Episcopacy* (1641); but it is long and dull, and overloaded with quotations.

While Taylor was with the King in 1642–3, the Parliamentarians

[7] See *Works*, viii. 457–96; also J. B. Dockery, *Christopher Davenport: Friar and Diplomat* (London; Burns and Oates, 1960), pp. 56–61, and Anthony à Wood's biography of Davenport in *Athenae Oxoniensis*, ii. 486.

sequestered his living of Uppingham and gave it to a Presbyterian. In compensation for this loss, the King presented him, in early 1643, with the living of Overstone in Northamptonshire, though Taylor may never have resided there. Taylor remained with the King, now based at Oxford, probably until 1645, when he went to Wales; for his name turns up in connection with the struggle between the Royalist and Parliamentary forces for the possession of Cardigan Castle. Since Taylor was by then a chaplain in the King's army at Oxford, he may have been acting in that capacity when Parliamentary forces, under Rowland Laugharne, took Cardigan, and captured him in February 1645. He seems to have been held prisoner in Cardigan until Laugharne was defeated in April at Newcastle Emlyn; then, in the general exchange of prisoners, he was set free.

Taylor may have been in Wales even before the battles at Cardigan Castle; in fact, he may have been forced to join the Royalist army simply because of its nearness. In *The Liberty of Prophesying* (1647), his epistle dedicatory to Christopher Hatton implies that he had attempted in vain to keep clear of the warring parties:

> In this great Storm which hath dasht the Vessell of the Church all in pieces, I have been cast upon the Coast of *Wales*, and in a little Boat thought to have enjoyed that rest and quietnesse, which in *England* in a greater I could not hope for: Here I cast Anchor, and thinking to ride safely, the Storm followed me with so impetuous violence, that it broke a Cable, and I lost my Anchor: And here again I was exposed to the mercy of the Sea, and the gentlenesse of an Element that could neither distinguish things nor persons. And but that he who stilleth the raging of the Sea, and the noise of his Waves, and the madnesse of his people, had provided a Plank for me, I had been lost to all the opportunities of content or study. But I know not whether I have been more preserved by the courtesies of my friends, or the gentlenesse and mercies of a noble Enemy.[8]

With almost no income since the sequestration of Uppingham (Overstone could not have helped much), and left to fend for himself during the confusion of the King's campaigns, Taylor no doubt had felt the need to seek employment in surroundings safer and more secluded than Oxford.[9] Two friends with Welsh connections, perhaps the friends referred to above, had offered some prospects. In company

[8] *Works*, v. 341; the quotation is taken from the first edition of 1647, pp. 1–2.

[9] With regard to the supposition that Taylor left Oxford to avoid conflict, see Heber's *Life*, in *Works*, vol. i, pp. xxvi–xxviii; Edmund Gosse, *Jeremy Taylor* (London: Macmillan, 1904), pp. 32–4; Stranks, *Life and Writings*, pp. 64–5.

with William Nicholson and William Wyat, he had set up a school at Llanfihangel-Aberbythych in the Royalist centre of Carmarthenshire—perhaps the 'little boat'; but whether the school was established before or after his imprisonment in Cardigan Castle is not clear.

Newton Hall, the house in which Taylor set up his school, was next door to Golden Grove, the seat of Richard Vaughan, second Earl of Carbery. The proximity led to friendship, and soon Carbery became Taylor's patron. He made Taylor chaplain of his household, and took him to live at Golden Grove. When Taylor first came to know him, Carbery was about fifty years of age; he had been the member for Carmarthen in the Parliament of 1624, and had succeeded to his earldom in 1634. At the outbreak of the Civil War, he was considered the wealthiest, as well as one of the most influential, of the landholders in the south of Wales. At the beginning of the war, Carbery declared himself for the King, raised a militia, and was made Commander of the Royalist forces in Wales. He showed little zeal for the business of war, however, and when, in 1644, pitted against a superior general, he was defeated by Laugharne, he made his peace with Parliament and received a pardon. Thereupon he retired to Golden Grove to continue the life of a country gentleman which the war had interrupted. Although accused by some Royalists of having conspired with the Earl of Essex for his own defeat, he managed to keep his influence with his party. At the Restoration, he was made Warden of the Welsh Marches, though whispers accusing him of cowardice and treachery continued to be heard. This man, a 'trimmer' (as Edmund Gosse calls him),[10] who trod a wary path of self-preservation during troubled times, provided Taylor for several years with the means and the 'rest and quietnesse' necessary for him to produce his finest work. Taylor had a patroness, too, in Frances, the Countess Carbery, whose evident piety and other noble virtues he frequently extolled.

The first of the works of Taylor's Golden Grove period was *The Liberty of Prophesying*, published in 1647 in London by Richard Royston, who was to publish almost all his writings from this time on. Obviously influenced by Chillingworth's *Religion of Protestants* (1637), Taylor's book is an earnest plea for toleration, and seeks to show that persuasion, not persecution, is the best way to deal with any unpopular opinion or 'heresy'. Taylor's solution to intemperance is simple: all one needs is a belief in the Creed and a spirit of charity and goodwill.

[10] Gosse, *Jeremy Taylor*, p. 35.

He writes: 'Now if [one] believes his Creed, he believes all that is necessary to all, or of it selfe, and if he doe his morall endeavour beside, he can doe no more toward finding out all the rest, and then he is secured.'[11] But Taylor's plea was not attuned to the times, for by 1647 Presbyterianism had become the official religion, the Church of England had been disestablished, and the rising power of the army was encouraging the growth of Independents. Yet for many years, this book was among Taylor's most popular and most often quoted books, giving comfort even to the hated Anabaptists, to whom Taylor devoted a chapter in which he showed that their opinions could be held by reasonable men. But there were attacks, too, and one of the fiercest was by the Scottish writer Samuel Rutherford, in *A Free Disputation against Pretended Liberty of Conscience* (1649); the story has also persisted that the King himself, taking exception to Taylor's book, ordered Henry Hammond (1605–60), another of his chaplains, to write against it.

Taylor next turned to practical devotion, beginning with *The Great Exemplar* (1649), or, as the full title aptly reads, *The Great Exemplar of Sanctity and Holy Life according to the Christian Institution: described in the history of the Life and Death . . . of Jesus Christ*. An extremely long work, interspersed with numerous prayers and short sermons, and the first of its kind in English, it is divided into three major parts, each dedicated to a different patron: Hatton, the Countess Dowager of Northampton, and the Countess of Carbery. This book was followed by the two works on which Taylor's present fame rests primarily: *The Rule and Exercises of Holy Living* (1650) and *The Rule and Exercises of Holy Dying* (1651). Taylor dedicated them both to Carbery, but it was the Countess of Carbery who encouraged him to write them. *Holy Dying* especially, as Taylor says in its dedication, was 'intended first to minister to her piety'. But before he finished it, Lady Carbery died. So Taylor had the opportunity to pay tribute to her not only in the dedication, but also in a funeral sermon, surely one of his most eloquent works. Taylor's grief was doubly great, for his own wife died about this time, and he writes sadly in his dedication that both he and Carbery have 'lately seen and felt' the 'sorrows of death' and the 'sad departure of friends'.

Taylor next published the first part of *Eniautos*, or *A Course of Sermons for all the Sundays of the Year* (1651), called *The Summer Half*; the

[11] *Works*, v. 355; p. 30 of the first edition.

second part, *The Winter Half*, came out in 1653, and both parts, comprising fifty-two sermons, appeared together in 1654. Now Taylor turned once more to polemical work, this time with an attack on the Roman Catholic doctrine of transubstantiation. Dedicated to Bishop John Warner (1581–1666), *The Real Presence and Spiritual of Christ in the Blessed Sacrament* is an effort to define the 'real presence' of Christ in the Sacrament in 'receptionist' terms—that is, as 'present to our spirits only'. Taylor argues for the doctrine, common among Anglican divines in the seventeenth century, that the bread and wine continue unchanged after the consecration, but that the communicant nevertheless receives them as the true Body and Blood of Christ.

While in London, perhaps to arrange for the publication of this book, Taylor preached at St Gregory's (near St Paul's), a church in which Cromwell's government still permitted Anglican clergy to preach. There, on 15 April, John Evelyn went to hear 'the famous Dr. Jeremy Taylor . . . on Matt. 6: 48, concerning evangelical perfection'.[12] Evelyn was acquainted with Taylor only slightly at this time (he had been at Balliol College when Taylor preached his famous Gunpowder sermon); but the two came to be close friends, and in his diary for 18 May 1655, Evelyn again records hearing 'that excellent preacher', and notes that 'on the 31st, I made a visit to [him], to confer with him about some spiritual matters, using him thenceforward as my ghostly father'. Taylor often appears in Evelyn's *Diary*, and a substantial correspondence reveals many of the concerns and personal attitudes of the two men.

Taylor was nearing the end of his time at Golden Grove, but he busied himself with two more books. The first of these was *The Golden Grove; or A Manual of Daily Prayers and Letanies* (1655). Its title was evidently intended as a compliment not only to his patron's house, but also to *The Golden Grove* (1600), a courtesy book by William Vaughan, Carbery's uncle. A devotional manual, Taylor's little book contains prayers, scriptural passages, and 'Festival Hymns' composed by himself. The hymns are pious and well meaning, but they prove the difficulty of creating religious poetry, even for so gifted a writer. The opening of the hymn for Epiphany is typical in its effort to find appropriate imagery: 'A comet dangling in the air | Presag'd the ruin of death and sin.' The lines limp awkwardly; and Taylor wisely stayed away from verse thereafter.

[12] *The Diary of John Evelyn*, ed. E. S. de Beer (Oxford: Clarendon Press, 1955), iii. 94–5.

In the introduction to *The Golden Grove*, Taylor denounces the policy of the Commonwealth towards religion, maintaining that its seers 'are digging down the foundations' of the church. They have 'destroyed all public forms of ecclesiastical government, discountenanced an excellent liturgy, taken off the hinges of unity, disgraced the articles of religion, polluted public assemblies, taken away all cognizance of schism, by mingling all sects, and giving countenance to that against which all power ought to stand upon their guard'. The time was not auspicious: Cromwell had dissolved Parliament, and he and the army ruled the country; disestablishment of the Church of England was complete, the Prayer Book had been banned, the Laudian policy of uniformity reversed, and

> the people ... fallen under the harrows and saws of impertinent and ignorant preachers, who think all religion is a sermon, and all sermons ought to be libels against truth and old governors, and expound chapters that the meaning may never be understood, and pray, that they may be thought able to talk, but not to hold their peace, they casting not to obtain any thing but wealth and victory, power and plunder. And the people ... grow idle and false, hypocrites and careless, they deny themselves nothing that is pleasant, they despise religion, forget government; and some never think of heaven; and they that do, think to go thither in such paths which all the ages of the church did give men warning of, lest they should that way go to the devil.[13]

Taylor's championing of the Church of England and his condemnation of the government was outspoken and high-pitched, perhaps courageous but probably unwise. But he was steadfast in his loyalty to 'the religion of the church of England, because nothing does more adhere to the word of God, and disregard the crafty advantages of the world'.

This book, with its defiant introduction, was not to cause Taylor so much trouble immediately as *Unum Necessarium, or, The Doctrine and Practice of Repentance*, also published in 1655. The book is dedicated to Carbery, but it contains a preface addressed to his friends Bishop Warner and Brian Duppa (1588–1662), Bishop of Salisbury. With a ringing expansiveness, Taylor deplores the excesses of religious quarrels, surely an ironic touch in the book that led to the most serious controversy of his career. *Unum Necessarium* is Taylor's most comprehensive exposition on the subject of repentance, and especially of his unorthodox belief that repentance on one's death-bed is ineffective. His treatment of original sin, however, was considered the most

[13] *Works*, vii. 589–90.

heterodox and controversial part of the book. In chapter 6, Taylor argues against the doctrine that Adam's sin is transmitted to all mankind; he declares that 'the sin of Adam neither made us (1) Heirs of damnation: nor (2) Naturally and necessarily vicious'.[14] Men inherit from Adam not the actual sin he committed, but only the imperfect nature he acquired after the Fall. By their own choice, men turn their inherited imperfection into corruption and sin; God does not damn anyone solely for Adam's sin. Rather, God judges man on what he does through the exercise of his free will. With regard to infants who die without being baptized, Taylor maintains that they are not consigned to hell:

> Against those that say, the flames of hell is the portion of Adam's heirs, and that infants dying in original sin are eternally tormented . . . I call to witness all the economy of the divine goodness, and justice and truth. . . . Is hell so easy a pain, or are the souls of children so cheap, so contemptible a price, that God should so easily throw them into hell?[15]

In expressing such opinions, Taylor appears to range himself against the ninth of the Thirty-Nine Articles entitled 'Of Original or Birth-sin', and thus falls into a certain kind of Pelagianism—at least, that is how his detractors saw his theological position.

At Oxford Taylor had been able to overcome suspicions of unorthodoxy, but now his plainly expressed views proved more troublesome, especially to Warner and Duppa. Warner wrote to him asking him to reconsider his opinion, and Duppa asked Thomas Barlow (1607–91), of Queen's College, Oxford, later Bishop of Lincoln (1675), to write a refutation. Gilbert Sheldon (1598–1677), former Warden of All Souls, also wrote to Taylor, urging him to recant his views. There was no refutation and no recantation, but Taylor did try to clarify his position.

When the controversy over *Unum Necessarium* erupted, Taylor was in prison, this time in Chepstow Castle, during the summer of 1655. The reason for his imprisonment is not clear: it may have been for political reasons—statements in *The Golden Grove* were obviously unfriendly to the regime—or it may have been for debt, or on account of a zealous Commonwealth official who, anticipating the legislation about to be enacted to silence the Anglican clergy, confined him because he was plainly 'a royalist clergyman still exercising his profession'.[16] While at Chepstow, Taylor wrote *A Further Explication of the*

[14] *Works*, vii. 252.
[15] Ibid., vii. 253.
[16] See Gosse, *Jeremy Taylor*, p. 117, and Stranks, *Life and Writings*, p. 153.

Doctrine of Original Sin, in extenuation of *Unum Necessarium*, and published it in November. Dedicated to Bishop Warner and later incorporated into *Unum Necessarium* as chapter 7, Taylor tries in this brief treatise to clarify and defend his ideas. First, he expresses surprise that what he had earlier written might have given offence:

> It is strange to me that any man should desire to believe God to be more severe and less gentle: that men should be greedy to find out inevitable ways of being damned, that they should be unwilling to have the veil drawn away from the face of God's goodness.... They might have had not only pretences but reasons to be troubled, if I had represented God to be so great a hater of mankind as to damn millions of millions for that which they could not help, or if I had taught that their infants might by chance have gone to hell, and as soon as ever they came for life, descend to an eternal death; if I had told them evil things of God, and hard measures, and evil portions to their children, they might have complained; but to complain because I say God is just to all, and merciful and just to infants ... is a thing that may well be wondered at.[17]

Taylor makes clear that he has not retreated from his position: 'I take a great comfort in this, that my doctrine stands on that side where God's justice and goodness and mercy stand apparently: and they that speak otherwise in this article, are forced by convulsions and violences to draw their doctrine to comply with God's justice and the reputation of His most glorious attributes.'[18] Taylor proceeds to analyse carefully each phrase of the article on original sin, and argues (in what must seem like quibbling to a modern reader) for liberty of interpretation and freedom of opinion, but in effect stretching his meaning to satisfy objections. 'I will not pretend to believe', he says, 'that those doctors who first framed the article did all of them mean as I mean; I am not sure that they did or that they did not; but this I am sure, that they framed the words with much caution and prudence, and so as might abstain from grieving the contrary minds of differing men'.[19] Here is a plea reminiscent of the tolerant spirit of *The Liberty of Prophesying.*

While still imprisoned at Chepstow, Taylor wrote yet another defence of his opinion in a letter to Christiana, dowager Duchess of Devonshire, who had been one of his patrons and also a good friend. She had written to him in prison and, troubled by the attacks being made on him and his book, had asked for an explanation. Taylor's long reply was later published as *Deus Justificatus* (1656). Using somewhat less technical language, he repeats in this letter what he had

[17] *Works*, vii. 301–2. [18] Ibid., vii. 302. [19] Ibid., vii. 331.

already said in *A Further Explication*, but he accuses the Presbyterians of misrepresenting his position on original sin.

When Taylor was released from Chepstow in the autumn of 1655, he did not return to Golden Grove. Instead, he went to Mandinam in Carmarthenshire, about twelve miles from Golden Grove, to the estate of Joanna Bridges, who may have been his wife since shortly before his imprisonment, or at any rate became such soon after his release. She remained his wife until his death.[20] In part because of his marriage, and in part, perhaps, because of a new edict of Cromwell's regime, he never returned to Golden Grove. After November 1655 it became illegal for any Church of England clergyman to exercise his office, and this rule applied to chaplaincies and tutorships. Although the law was not in fact very rigorously enforced, Carbery may have been unwilling to risk Cromwell's displeasure by sheltering Taylor or by continuing to offer him patronage.

Here at Mandinam, in a new domesticity, Taylor remained for almost two years, although leaving occasionally, as we learn from Evelyn's diary, for visits to London. At this time he began *Ductor Dubitantium*, or, as he styled it later, his *Cases of Conscience*, his next long work, which was not published until 1660. But at some time in 1657 Taylor moved to London, perhaps because he felt too far from his friends, perhaps also because part of his wife's property had been sequestered. His move must surely have been in part for economy's sake, for he was becoming increasingly dependent on loans and gifts of money, relying on Evelyn and other friends in London. Employment for dispossessed clergymen was not easy to find; but Taylor may have picked up a number of small jobs, including preaching in private houses (such as Evelyn's, near Deptford) and celebrating Holy Communion, for which he may have received an honorarium, raised by subscription.

Also in 1657, Taylor published *A Discourse of the Nature and Offices of*

[20] In his *Life*, Heber says that Taylor was married three times. According to him, Phoebe Langsdale died at Uppingham in 1642, and Taylor did not marry Joanna Bridges until 1655 or 1656; therefore, the death of a wife which Taylor mentions in a letter of 1650 or 1651 to Dugdale must refer to a 'third intermediate marriage' (see *Works*, vol. i, p. xxiii and note c, and xxxv and note d). But as Stranks points out (*Life and Writings*, pp. 163–4), Heber based this opinion on the untrustworthy Jones MS and was misled regarding the probable date of Phoebe Langsdale's death. Although Stranks, in attempting to show that Taylor's first wife did not die until 1650 or 1651, may place too much reliance on the 'autobiographical' passages in *Holy Living*, the main line of his argument is plausible. There is no good reason for believing that Taylor was married more than twice.

Friendship, in the form of a letter to 'the most ingenious and excellent M.K.P.' Mrs Katherine Philips, whose initials these were, was 'esteemed the most applauded poetess' of the time, according to Anthony à Wood.[21] Known as 'The Matchless Orinda' to her friends, she lived at Cardigan Priory in Wales, and Taylor must have come to know her while he was at Golden Grove. This charming little essay, Taylor's only work on a largely secular theme, is an effort to Christianize classical ideals, notably those expressed by Cicero and Seneca. He is responding to a question from Mrs Philips asking 'how far a dear and perfect friendship is authorized by the principles of Christianity?' Taylor writes:

> The answer is ready and easy. It is warranted to extend to all mankind; and the more we love, the better we are, and the greater our friendships are, the dearer we are to God; let them be as dear, and let them be as perfect, and let them be as many as you can; there is no danger in it; only where the restraint begins, there begins our imperfection; it is not ill that you entertain brave friendships and worthy societies: it were well if you could love, and if you could benefit all mankind; for I conceive that is the sum of all friendship.[22]

The spirit of this work well expresses Taylor's comprehensive generosity, as well as his desire to expound moral points.

It was probably in 1658 that Taylor was in prison again, this time in the Tower, though only briefly. Details of this episode are lacking, and our only knowledge is that provided by a letter from Evelyn to the Lord-Lieutenant of the Tower, in which Evelyn mentions the 'mistake of his printer' as the cause of official displeasure with Taylor, and pleads for his release.[23] The 'mistake' appears to have been the frontispiece that Royston inserted in *A Collection of Offices* (1658), a manual which Taylor hoped might serve in place of the proscribed Book of Common Prayer. The print shows Christ at prayer (see figure 3), the very sort of 'idolatrous' picture which particularly upset the Puritans. But Taylor was soon released, having paid sufficiently for his 'indiscretion'.

While in London and moving in Royalist circles, Taylor had come to know Edward, third Viscount Conway, and his wife Anne, daughter of Sir Henry Finch, whose friendship with Henry More, the Cambridge

[21] Wood, *Athenae Oxoniensis*, ii. 284.

[22] *Works*, i. 77.

[23] The full text of the letter is in the *Diary and Correspondence of John Evelyn*, ed. William Bray (London: Bickers, 1906), iii. 227–8. The letter is dated 14 January 1656/7, perhaps a mistake for 1657/8. See Stranks, *Life and Writings*, p. 170.

3. Engraved frontispiece, *Holy Living*, 6th edn., 1660: figure of Christ in prayer. An earlier, slightly different, version of this plate—now re-engraved—appeared in *A Collection of Offices* (1658).

Platonist, resulted in a long and fascinating correspondence.[24] The Conway family were friends of Evelyn, too, which may have accounted for Taylor's connection. The acquaintance was fortunate, for Viscount Conway soon became to Taylor what Carbery had so long been—a patron and a sincere and thoughtful friend. Conway was a firm Royalist and churchman and the owner of large estates in north-east Ireland. For some time he had been searching for an Anglican clergyman to take charge of the church at Lisnagarvey (or Lisburn), near his great house of Portmore in County Antrim. The incumbent was an Independent to whom Parliament had given the living; but he had offended the local gentry. Conway asked Taylor to take the position of assistant lecturer in order to keep 'sound' doctrine alive in the parish. Reluctant at first, Taylor was ready to accept when Conway offered a chaplaincy as well, and arranged for him to live at Portmore itself. Besides acting as Conway's chaplain, Taylor was also to provide spiritual guidance in the household of Conway's brother-in-law, Major George Rawdon, who was commander of the garrison at Lisnagarvey. Chaplaincies, of course, were still illegal, and perhaps this is why Taylor took on two positions, one official, as assistant lecturer in the parish, one unofficial, as chaplain at Portmore.

The news of Taylor's appointment stirred up opposition in Presbyterian circles in Lisnagarvey, so Conway procured introductions for Taylor to influential people in Ireland and a pass from the Lord-Protector himself, which promised some measure of security from persecution. Taylor arrived in Ireland in June 1658, soon settling in at Portmore with his family. He continued work on *Ductor Dubitantium*; but in June 1659 his settled life was interrupted because of the complaints of an Independent preacher called Tandy, who alleged that Taylor made the sign of the cross during baptism—no doubt he had done so—thereby causing offence. Taylor was put under open arrest, and was told to go to Dublin to answer the charges. Events were moving so rapidly, however, that before Taylor could be prosecuted, Charles II was on his way to England. This meant that it might be best to let a Royalist clergyman alone, and the Irish authorities dropped the charges against Taylor.

[24] Anne Conway suffered from various chronic afflictions, probably of hysterical origin, including terrible headaches. She constantly sought companionship, comfort, and relief, arranging on one occasion for a visit from the 'Irish Stroker', Valentine Greatrakes, to whom healing abilities were attributed. See the *Conway Letters: The Correspondence of Anne, Viscountess Conway, Henry More, and their Friends, 1642–1684*, ed. M. H. Nicolson (New Haven: Yale Univ. Press, 1930).

Taylor was thus free to go to London in March 1660 to arrange for the publication of *Ductor Dubitantium* and to see Charles enter the capital on 29 May. The book over which he had laboured for so many years was finally published in the year of the Restoration, with a dedication to the King. *Ductor Dubitantium, or, The Rule of Conscience in all her general measures; serving as a Great Instrument for the determination of Cases of Conscience* is by far the longest of Taylor's books, being twice the length of its closest competitor, *The Great Exemplar.* It is also one of only a few Protestant works on the subject of conscience, being anticipated only by William Perkins, *The Whole Treatise of the Cases of Conscience* (1606); Joseph Hall, *Resolutions and Decisions of Diverse Practical Cases of Conscience* (1649); and Robert Sanderson, *De Obligate Conscientiae* (1659). Taylor was familiar with these works, his intention being, in part, to add to this body of Protestant literature so that his co-religionists would not need to turn to Roman Catholic works. He considered *Ductor Dubitantium* his *magnum opus*, and he wished to be remembered for it above all else. But the book, though it aroused some interest in his own time (it had gone through four editions by 1696), has remained, in part due to its enormous length, generally unread.[25]

With the Restoration and the general reorganization of the Anglican Church, Taylor hoped for an English preferment; but this was precluded by the fact that his superiors, particularly Sheldon, had not forgotten his *Unum Necessarium.* In August 1660, he was called to take up the Irish bishopric of Down and Connor. Soon after, on the recommendation of the Duke of Ormonde, Lord-Lieutenant of Ireland and Chancellor of Trinity College, he was also made Vice-Chancellor of the University of Dublin, as the college was known.[26] Neither job promised to be easy, for Trinity College was in disarray, and the diocese was full of Presbyterian clergy who had resolved, even before Taylor arrived in Ireland, to resist prelacy and to make trouble.[27]

[25] See James T. Addison, 'Jeremy Taylor, Preacher and Pastor', *Historical Magazine of the Protestant Episcopal Church*, 21 (1952), 181. Also published in 1660, but probably written much earlier, was *The Worthy Communicant.* Dedicated to Princess Mary of Orange, Charles's sister, who was an admirer of Taylor's work, this book deals with the nature of the Blessed Sacrament and the manner in which it is best received.

[26] James Butler, twelfth Earl of Ormonde, had been Lieutenant-General of the King's armies in Ireland until 1650, when he left for France to join Charles II in exile. Immediately after the Restoration, he was put in charge of Irish affairs, but he was not appointed Lord-Lieutenant until November 1661. He was created Duke of Ormonde in March 1661.

[27] See R. B. McDowell and D. A. Webb, *Trinity College Dublin* (Cambridge: Cambridge Univ. Press, 1982), pp. 2–5. See also the letters that Taylor wrote during his episcopacy, which have been reprinted by William P. Williams, 'Eight Unpublished Letters by Jeremy Taylor', *Anglican Theological Review*, 58 (1976), 179–93.

Taylor returned to Ireland later in 1660. In January of the following year, he took the oath as Vice-Chancellor of the University; and immediately, even before travelling to his diocese, he set about re-organizing the College. Trinity College had been founded in 1592, but its fortunes had been various. When Taylor took charge, he found, as he wrote to Ormonde, 'all things in a perfect disorder; indeed so great as can be imagined.... There is indeed a heap of men and boys, but no body of a college.'[28] He appointed new fellows to the College from among men of ability whom he knew, and restored some discipline and order. He also collected, revised, and put together a body of statutes which finally gave the College a workable constitution.

Putting his diocese in order was a task considerably more difficult than reshaping Trinity College. Even before his consecration on 27 January 1661, the Presbyterian clergy of Down and Connor, many of them committed Calvinists from Scotland, had been preaching against episcopacy and the Book of Common Prayer, and some had formed a committee to see what charges could be brought against him. Learning of the Presbyterians' fierce dislike of him, Taylor responded with surprise and bitterness. 'They threaten to murder me,' he wrote to Ormonde in December 1660:

> they have studiously raised reports that I was destroyed by the Scots; they use all the arts they can to disgrace me, and to take the people's hearts from me, and to make my life uncomfortable.... It were better for me to be a poor curate in a village church than a bishop over such intolerable persons; and I will petition your excellency to give me some parsonage in Munster, that I may end my days in peace, rather than abide here, unless I may be enabled with comfort to contest against such violent persons.[29]

In another letter, he asks Ormonde to obtain his removal to Meath, near Dublin, whose bishop is dying.[30] Far from being moved, however, Taylor was given additional responsibility for the nearby small diocese of Dromore. Perhaps with a view to giving him more authority so that he could better deal with the Presbyterian clergy, he was also made a member of the Irish Privy Council.

With all the support he had asked the government for, Taylor went to his diocese in March 1661. Before he held his first visitation, he met with representatives of the Presbyterians at Hillsborough House, near Lisnagarvey, but found them fixed in their beliefs. They believed in ecclesiastical government by a presbytery, and would not take the oath

[28] *Works*, vol. i, p. xciv, note *b*. [29] Ibid., vol. i, p. ci, note *f*.
[30] Ibid., vol. i, p. xcix, note *e*.

of supremacy. So, when Taylor held his first visitation, only two of his clergy attended. Faced with open revolt, he tried meeting again with representatives of the recalcitrant clergy; but, failing to win support, he declared thirty-six clergy removed from their livings.[31] Taylor's decisive action naturally aroused controversy; and certainly it was inconsistent with the ideas of toleration which he had expressed in *The Liberty of Prophesying.* But obviously, the conditions of the time left him no choice but to 'rule or resign', and he had decided to rule.[32]

After this, Taylor continued to take measures against the Presbyterians, with the full support of the secular authorities. The vacant livings were filled, mostly with men from England (among whom was George Rust, who succeeded Taylor as bishop); meanwhile, Taylor struggled to put the Irish church in order. This was clearly not a happy time for Taylor or a pleasant episcopate, for, until the end, he continued to ask for removal to England and release from what he called 'a place of torment' that had 'in it more trouble than all the dioceses in his Majesty's dominions put together'.[33] On 25 May 164, he wrote to Sheldon, now Archbishop of Canterbury:

> I have been informed from a good hand in England, that your grace was pleased once to say, that I myself was the only hindrance to myself of being removed to an English bishopric. If it be by any fault of mine (of which I cannot so much as make a conjecture) I will certainly make amends when I know it, and in the mean time I beg of your grace to pardon it; but if it be only my unworthiness, it is true, I do confess and deplore that; but I know your grace can either find me worthy, or make me so. However, I humbly desire that your grace will not wholly lay me aside, and cast off all thoughts of removing me; for no man shall with a greater diligence, humility, and observance endeavour to make up his other disabilities, than I shall.[34]

This appeal, like all the others, failed; not even Taylor's many influential friends and admirers were able to help him.

In the six years between his return to Ireland and his death, Taylor produced, besides sermons and minor tracts, one long book. This was *A Dissuasive from Popery* (part I appeared in 1664), written at the urging of the Anglican bishops in Ireland and meant to counteract Roman Catholic 'propaganda'. In it, Taylor attacks the Catholic practices of the Irish people, and seeks to show that certain Catholic beliefs such

[31] Patrick Adair, one of those involved, gives an account of this episode in *A True Narrative of the Rise and Progress of the Presbyterian Church in Ireland* (Belfast: Killen, 1866).

[32] See Addison, 'Jeremy Taylor', p. 184.

[33] *Works*, vol. i, p. ci, note *f*.

[34] Ibid., vol. i, p. cxix, note *u*.

as transubstantiation, indulgences, and purgatory are false innovations in true Christian teaching. The book predictably drew rejoinders from Roman Catholics, some of which Taylor answered in part 2 of the *Dissuasive*, written at the end of his life and published posthumously in 1667.

In his last years, Taylor was a public figure, as a Privy Councillor, Vice-Chancellor of the University of Dublin, and a leading churchman. But only a little is known of his domestic and social life. He lost two infant sons at Mandinam; in March 1661, another son, named Edward, died, probably at the age of three. His last surviving son, Charles, died in London only a few days before Taylor himself, in 1667. When he went to Ireland as Bishop, he lived at Hillsborough; but soon after, he moved to Portmore. In 1664 he moved again, because Conway was rebuilding his house. Thereafter he seems to have lived mostly at Lisnagarvey, though he had two or three houses at different places and a farm at Megharalin. His duties took him all over the district, of course, and traditions grew up of the Bishop having 'resided' at many houses in the area. Many friendships endured, but others fell off. He had written to Lord Hatton and received no reply; but he continued to correspond with Evelyn and Henry More. Gosse's sentimental portrait of Taylor in his last years as a man who 'found himself solitary in a strange land' may, indeed, be near the truth.[35]

In 1664, Taylor's health began to fail; and for the next three years he struggled with illness and the duties of his troubled diocese. In the first week of August 1667, he fell ill for the last time. On the 13th he died at Lisnagarvey. He was buried on 3 September at Dromore, as he wished, in the cathedral that he had built.[36]

II. *The Literary and Devotional Tradition of* Holy Living

Although *Holy Living* and *Holy Dying* are printed together traditionally, and appear to be companion volumes, they are in some essential respects quite different from one another, and we must consider them separately.

Holy Living has sometimes been regarded as in the tradition of the

[35] Gosse, *Jeremy Taylor*, p. 204. For further details of Taylor's last days, see Heber, *Life*, vol. i, pp. cxx–cxxiii.

[36] The date of Rust's funeral sermon as given in the title of the published version ('preached August 13, 1667') must actually refer to the date of Taylor's death. See Stranks, *Life and Writings*, pp. 271–3.

'courtesy books' that form a part of post-Renaissance conduct literature, one writer calling it 'the best known example of the religious, moral and domestic branch of the literature of conduct'.[37] Although it does teach day-to-day conduct, and therefore has some affinities with the courtesy book, *Holy Living* also has its roots in the long tradition of devotional literature. Once the staple of the reading public, the hundreds of such books that appeared in the sixteenth and seventeenth century in England are little known today. Popular devotional literature, as distinguished from other religious and theological works, included books of prayers, on the one hand, and books of instruction in Christian ethics, on the other. *Holy Living* belongs to this latter kind of devotional work.[38]

A good example of the devotional book of prayers is the collection published by Michael Sparke, *The Crums of Comfort* (1623), one of the most popular books of its kind in the century. Other important examples are John Cosin's *A Collection of Private Devotions* (1627), a manual of the Book of Hours type, and Lancelot Andrewes's *Preces Privatae* (published posthumously, in 1648). Descended from the Psalters and primers of pre-Reformation days, books of this kind were designed to supplement the official and public forms of worship contained in the Book of Common Prayer. They were designed, that is, to fill the needs of the individual in his own home; and therefore they contain prayers for all kinds of people and for all kinds of occasions. Sparke, in *Crums of Comfort*, for example, includes prayers for different days of the week and times of the day, such as 'at our first rising from sleep' and 'when we wake in the Morning'. To these he adds prayers to be said before and after meals, and before and after hearing a sermon. He provides prayers for servants and for masters of families, for those in poverty and for those in prosperity. Prayers are provided, in short, for nearly every conceivable occasion and condition.

Not all the prayers in books of this kind are original compositions. Many are admittedly borrowed from ancient liturgies and other sources, and some are for the most part compilations. The longer title of Cosin's book is *A Collection of Private Devotions . . . Taken out of the Holy Scriptures, the Ancient Fathers, and the divine Service of our own Church*, and its first aim 'is to continue & preserve the authority of the ancient

[37] Douglas Bush, *English Literature in the Earlier Seventeenth Century*, 2nd edn. (1945; Oxford: Clarendon Press, 1962), p. 331.

[38] See Helen C. White, *English Devotional Literature (Prose), 1600–1640*, Univ. Wisconsin Studies in Language and Literature, 29 (Madison: Univ. Wisconsin, 1931), pp. 9–20.

Lawes, and old godly Canons of the Church, which were made and set forth for this purpose, that men before they set themselves to pray, might know what to pray, and might know what to say'.[39] Likewise, Taylor appends a long section to chapter 4 of *Holy Living* based 'magna ex parte' on the Liturgy of St Basil, and bases a section of chapter 5 of *Holy Dying* on the same source.[40] Comprehensiveness is often regarded as more important than originality in providing prayers for the whole course of the Christian life.

Some devotional manuals offered a series of moral considerations as a supplement to the prayers and as an aid to living a Christian life. The method of these books was to gather scriptural verses around a particular theme, and offer them as subjects for meditation. Sir John Conway's *Meditations and Praiers*, first published in 1569 and again in 1611 as *The Poesie of Floured Prayers*, is this kind of work, and includes prayers as well as meditations. Each of the prayers is preceded by an 'illuminating' thought which serves as the heading or introduction to the prayer. One section is devoted to a phrase-by-phrase reflection on the Lord's Prayer; but the concluding section simply presents 'Sentences out of the Holy Scripture' as subjects for meditation.

A variation of this sort of book is Joseph Hall's *Meditations and Vowes, Divine and Morall, Serving for Direction in Christian and Civil Practice*, published in 1605 in three 'centuries'. Hall's meditations, as he himself says, are 'homely aphorisms', 'naked thoughts' clothed in 'plain and simple words': for example, 'A true friend is not born every day. It is best to be courteous to all, entire with few; so may we perhaps have less cause of joy; I am sure, less occasion of sorrow.'[41] Moralistic and sententious, these *Meditations* are obviously designed for an instructive and practical end. As Hall tells Lady Drury in his dedication to her, 'I made them not for the eye, but for the heart; neither do I commend them to your reading but to your practice.'[42]

Among devotional books concerned primarily with instruction, one with an especially descriptive title must be mentioned. Paul Baynes leaves us in no doubt about his purpose in calling his work *Briefe Directions unto a Godly Life: Wherein every Christian is furnished with most necessary Helps for the furthering of him in a godly course heereupon earth, that so hee may attaine Eternal Happinesse in Heaven* (1618). His aim is clearly to

[39] See Cosin's *Devotions*, ed. P. G. Stanwood (Oxford: Clarendon Press, 1967), p. 11.

[40] See below, pp. 275–79 and p. 218.

[41] See dedications to the first and second 'centuries', in Joseph Hall, *Works*, ed. Philip Wynter (Oxford, 1863), vii. 439, 462; also 468–9.

[42] Ibid., vii. 462.

remind readers that the living of a religious life is not only good in itself, but also a necessity for salvation. As with the collections of prayers that cover the whole range of Christian experience, the advice contained in the works of writers like Baynes ranges widely, from small details of etiquette to large concerns about how to die well. Emphasizing the necessity of devotion and the importance of putting Christianity into practice, he gives explanations of the Christian virtues and opposing vices, and suggests ways in which the former can be acquired and the latter avoided. Complementing such manuals of instruction are books that use the catechetical method to teach the fundamentals of faith; among them may be numbered Henry Hammond's *Practical Catechism* (1644) and William Nicholson's *Plain and Full Exposition of the Catechism* (1655), both of which include commentaries on the Creed and the Ten Commandments and advice on the conduct of daily life.

Prayers and instruction offer two (often overlapping) directions of devotional literature. A third way combines them both. *Holy Living* is probably the best example of such a devotional book that combines prayers and instructions, but two others should be mentioned, especially because of their widespread appeal in the seventeenth century. The earlier of these is Lewis Bayly's *The Practise of Pietie: directing a Christian how to walke that he may please God.* The date of its first publication is unknown, but it was in its third edition by 1613, and its fiftieth by 1673. It was translated into Welsh, French, German, Polish, and even, in 1655, the language of the American Indians of the Massachusetts Bay Colony. Bayly follows the usual practice of providing 'prayers for all occasions'; but he also includes rules and directions of a practical nature. These include directions for reading the Bible with 'profit and ease', for singing the Psalms, and regarding the 'right' manner of 'holy feasting' and observing the Sabbath. The second notable example of such a work is *The Whole Duty of Man*, first published anonymously in 1658, but whose author is now known to have been Richard Allestree.[43] It is more wide-ranging and detailed in its teaching than *The Practise of Pietie*; and, fulfilling the promise of its title, it provides Christian instruction and guidance on every aspect of life, with a simplicity and directness that assured its popularity well into the eighteenth century.[44]

[43] Paul Elmen reviews the reasons for ascribing this work to Allestree in his 'The Authorship of *The Whole Duty of Man*', *The Library*, 5th ser., 6 (1951), 19–27.

[44] See C. J. Stranks, *Anglican Devotion* (London: SCM, 1961), pp. 123–48.

The examples cited so far have been English books by English authors; but in both the sixteenth and the seventeenth centuries Continental works, frequently in translation, were also widely read. Although Roman Catholic works were commonly suppressed or else expurgated, a significant number were nevertheless available. Among them must be mentioned Ignatius Loyola, *Spiritual Exercises* (1533, and frequently translated, or known through other works, such as Tomas de Villacastin, *A Manuall of Devout Meditations and Exercises, ... Drawne for the most part, out of the spirituall Exercises of ... Ignatius* (1618)); Juan de Valdes, *Divine Considerations* (1550), translated and published in 1638 by Nicholas Ferrar (with a prefatory letter by George Herbert); Theodore Beza, *Maister Beza's Houshold Prayers. For the Consolation and Perfection of a Christian Life* (1607); Luis de Granada, *Of Prayer, and Meditation* (1612); Robert Bellarmine, *The Ascent of the Mind to God by a Ladder of Things Created* (1616); Peter Du Moulin, *The Right Way to Heaven, Prayers and Meditations of a Faithful Soule* (1630); and François de Sales, *An Introduction to the Devout Life* (1613). Of the many devotional manuals in print by 1650, the *Introduction* has most relevance to *Holy Living*, for it is the work with which the latter has most in common in terms of tone and style; it is also the only contemporary devotional work from which Taylor quotes. Both Taylor and de Sales emphasize the same methods of devotion, and stress the same virtues. Thematic parallels, such as the common concern for 'the practice of the presence of God', are frequent.[45] General resemblance, however, and Taylor's acknowledged use of one passage from the *Introduction* are inadequate grounds for claiming total dependence on a single source, as some critics have done.[46] Most of the parallels and similarities simply reveal agreement regarding the broad principles of Christian practice. Moreover, many of the topics included in both books are devotional and moral commonplaces. An appropriate conclusion is that Taylor worked

[45] See C. F. Allison, 'The Pastoral Cruelty of Jeremy Taylor's Theology', *Modern Churchman*, NS 15 (1972), 123–31.

[46] Logan Pearsall Smith finds the 'correspondence in method and form of Taylor's *Holy Living* and de Sales's *Introduction à la vie dévote* ... too close to be due to chance' (*The Golden Grove: Selected Passages from the Sermons and Writings of Jeremy Taylor* (Oxford, 1930), p. xxiv). L. Clert-Rolland, in 'François de Sales et Jeremy Taylor', *Revue de Littérature Comparée*, 42 (1968), 557–62, urges that the *Introduction* served as a model for *Holy Living*: 'Il y a plus qu'une simple ressemblance entre les deux auteurs, ... il s'agit, en fait, d'un réel plagiat de la part de Jeremy Taylor.' But Clert-Rolland assigns too much importance to Taylor's single quotation from the *Introduction* (in chap. 4, sect. 10, 262. 13–23 and 28–31), which he clearly acknowledges.

effectively in a well-defined form, borrowing and adapting many sources, finally producing a masterpiece uniquely his own.

The plan of Holy Living

In 1649, the year in which Taylor probably wrote *Holy Living*, the Church of England was in the midst of the most difficult period of its history. The King had been executed that year, four years after Archbishop Laud. Episcopacy had by then been abolished, the Book of Common Prayer banned, and the Church disestablished. Many of the Anglican clergy, having been turned out of their livings, like Taylor himself, were in want and penury. In the aftermath of the Civil War, though the Rump of the Long Parliament still existed, the army and Cromwell in fact exercised all real power. This was the state of affairs, as Taylor says in his dedication, that prompted him to write *Holy Living.* At a time when he has seen 'Religion painted upon Banners, and thrust out of Churches' (p. 5), when men 'prefer a prosperous errour before an afflicted truth', and the 'Ministers of Religion are so scattered that they cannot unite to stop the inundation' of truth by error, he offers the book as a means to help keep the impoverished Church alive. The book presents in 'one body those advices which the severall necessities of many men must use at some time or other, and many of them, daily'. It is a 'collection of holy precepts', or 'rules for conduct of soules', that supplies a need in 'the want of personall and attending Guides' (pp. 5–6). This description of *Holy Living* explains its comprehensive form. Since it is meant to supply a need in the absence of appropriately organized religious teaching (as Taylor believed), the scope of the book extends to all areas in which guidance is necessary, including in its province every concern of the Christian life.

In *Holy Living* Taylor wishes to show that the attainment of salvation is vitally dependent on living a holy and religious life. He makes clear at the very beginning of the book that religion is not confined merely to acts of ritual worship: 'as every man is wholly Gods own portion by the title of creation: so all our labours and care, all our powers and faculties must be wholly imployed in the service of God, even all the dayes of our life, that this life being ended, we may live with him for ever' (p. 17). Religion, in this sense, is the same as a holy life, and each action of a man is a religious duty:

> . . . it becomes us to remember and to adore Gods goodnesse for it, that God hath not onely permitted us to serve the necessities of our nature, but hath

4. Engraved folding-plate, *The Rule and Exercises of Holy Living*, 12th edn., 1680. The plate first appeared in the 4th edn., 1654; here it is re-engraved.

made them to become parts of our duty; that if we by directing these actions to the glory of God intend them as instruments to continue our persons in his service, he by adopting them into religion may turn our nature into grace, and accept our natural actions, as actions of religion. (p. 18)

The structure of *Holy Living* is determined by this understanding of religion.

The opening paragraph of chapter 2 quotes St Paul in the Epistle to Titus: '*For the grace of God bringing salvation hath appeared to all men; teaching us that denying ungodlinesse and worldly lusts, we should live 1. Soberly, 2. Righteously, and 3. Godly in this present world, looking for that blessed hope and glorious appearing of the great God and our Saviour Jesus Christ*' (p. 60). On the basis of this passage, Taylor divides Christian religious practice into the three parts of sobriety, justice, and religion. Taylor defines these three qualities thus: 'The first contains all our deportment in our personal and private capacities, the fair treating of our bodies, and our spirits. The second enlarges our duty in all relations to our Neighbour. The third contains the offices of direct Religion, and entercourse with God' (p. 60). Religion thus has its private, public, and spiritual aspects and consists of man's duties towards himself, towards others, and towards God. This threefold division forms the basis of the structure of *Holy Living.* Of its four chapters, the first introduces the reader to the fundamental requirements of the life of religion and piety, and the subsequent chapters each present one of the three aspects of Christian life.

Taylor begins *Holy Living* with a discussion and enumeration of '*the general instruments, and means serving to a holy life*' (p. 17). These general means—the care of time, purity of intention, and a sense of the nearness and perpetual presence of God—are the habits that are the necessary prerequisites for the practice of all the Christian virtues. The care of time is necessary to avoid the idleness which leads to temptation and sin. It enables a person to order his worldly employment in order to make room for devotion and prayer. Being careful and prudent with regard to time also produces other rewards, for 'He that is choice of his time will also be choice of his company, and choice of his actions, lest the first ingage him in vanity and losse, and the latter by being criminal be a throwing his time and himself away' (p. 19). This effect of the care of time is supplemented by purity of intention. Put very simply, purity of intention means that 'we should intend and designe Gods glory in every action we do' (p. 27). If the end of all a man's actions is the glory and service of God, even the most common actions are sanctified, and evil ones are avoided. To the habit of purity of intention Taylor advises the addition of the practice of the presence of God. A man's actions will be all the more pure and his intentions all the more holy if he reminds himself that he stands in the presence of God at all times and in all places.

The second chapter introduces sobriety as the first important aspect of religion. Christian sobriety, which is concerned with self-governance, is, as Taylor explains, 'all that duty that concerns our selves in the matter of *meat* and *drink* and *pleasures* and *thoughts*' (p. 60), and includes the virtues of temperance, chastity, humility, modesty, and contentedness. Sobriety involves the control of the passions and the practice of moderation in all things: 'It is a using severity, denial, and frustration, of our appetite when it growes unreasonable' (p. 60). In this chapter Taylor treats of such diverse things as the evils of drunkenness, the duties of married people, the follies of inquisitiveness, and the ways of coping with poverty and ill fortune.

In the third chapter, which is short, Taylor discusses Christian justice in traditional terms by dividing it into the two branches of 'commutative justice' and 'distributive justice'. The ideal of commutative justice is based on Matthew 7: 12: 'Whatsoever ye would that men should do to you, even so do to them.' Distributive justice is based on Romans 13: 7: 'Render to all their dues, tribute to whom tribute is due, custome to whome custome. . . . Owe no man anything but to love one another.' Under the first kind of justice, Taylor includes duties of negotiation and restitution; under the second, duties of obedience and provision. The principles of negotiation apply mostly to trade and business dealings. One must honour and uphold private agreements and civil laws; there must be 'honesty in contracts, sincerity in affirming, simplicity in bargaining, and faithfulnesse in performing' (p. 157). Restitution concerns sin involving personal relationships, and has two distinct aspects. One must not only offer reparation for wrongs done, but must seek pardon from God for the sin committed against him. Restitution is, therefore, as Taylor says, quoting Scripture, a part of repentance: '*If the wicked restore the pledge, give again that he had robbed, etc. he shall surely live, he shall not dye*' (p. 162). Obedience and provision, as aspects of distributive justice, apply to personal and familial affairs, as well as to political and ecclesiastical matters. Princes, parents, and spiritual guides are to be obeyed as superiors. They in turn repay obedience by undertaking duties of provision for their charges: the prince must provide for his people, parents for their children, the minister for his flock.

The fourth chapter, the longest in the book, deals with religion. Taylor here uses the word 'religion' in a special sense, defining it through St Paul's use of the word 'godly' in the Epistle to Titus. Religion is 'that part of duty which particularly relates to God in our worshippings and adoration of him, in confessing his excellencies, loving his person, admiring his goodnesse, believing his Word, and doing all that which may in a proper and direct manner do him honour' (p. 174). Having defined religion as worship of God, Taylor divides religious action into two kinds: internal and external. The internal actions of religion are those 'in which the soul onely is imployed' (p. 174), and comprise the virtues of faith, hope, and charity. The external actions of religion are those in which the body as well as the soul is involved (p. 195), and include reading or hearing Scripture, fasting, prayer, the giving of alms, repentance, and receiving the Eucharist. The duties of the worship of God are thus as comprehensive as those which relate to the discipline of a holy life.

In Taylor's scheme of a holy life, repentance has the most important place. Repentance, in both its negative and positive aspects, is an integral part of the life of religion, for it is, on the one hand, a renunciation of sin, and, on the other, a turning towards God. A 'conjugation and society of many duties', as he says, 'it containes in it all the parts of a holy life' (p. 245). The rigidity of his attitude towards repentance is clear in his summing up:

> . . . there is but one repentance in a Mans whole life, if repentance be taken in the proper, and strict Evangelicall Covenant-sense, and not after the ordinary understanding of the word: That is, wee are but once to change our whole state of life, from the power of the Devil and his intire possession, from the state of sin and death, from the body of corruption, to the life of grace, to the possession of Jesus, to the kingdom of the Gospel. (p. 246)

Repentance, thus, is not simply contrition or sorrow for past sin; it is active reform, or change 'from sin to grace, from vitious habits to holy customes' (p. 245). The purpose of repentance is not accomplished solely by a man making a resolution to sin no more, 'For resolution is an imperfect act, a term of relation, and signifies nothing but in order to the action' (p. 250). 'True repentance', he asserts repeatedly, 'is a punishing duty, and acts its sorrow' (p. 248). It is a duty that must 'reduce to act all its holy purposes, and enter into and run through *the state of holy living*' (p. 249). A natural development of this view of repentance is his denial that true repentance can happen near the time of death; for, 'on a Mans death-bed, the day of repentance is past: for repentance being the renewing of a holy life, a living the life of Grace, it is a contradiction to say that a Man can live a holy life upon his death-bed' (p. 251). The inadequacy of death-bed repentance was, as we have already seen, one of Taylor's most deeply held convictions, and he considers the subject in *The Great Exemplar*, *Unum Necessarium*, and *Ductor Dubitantium*, as well as in other works.

Taylor's unyielding disapproval of death-bed repentance has brought him much criticism; and from a traditional Anglican point of view, this is surely fair. Taylor rejects the conventional view that God forgives a sinner even before he demonstrates his repentance; rather, he sees God's forgiveness as a reward which depends on the proven quality of one's repentance. Thus he can say that conversion to a holy life is the only means by which a sinner can obtain God's forgiveness: 'I shall use no other arguments to move a sinner to repentance, but to tell him unlesse he does he shall certainly perish; and if he does repent timely and intirely, that is, live a holy life, he shall be forgiven and be saved' (p. 252).[47]

In his deviation from the usual teaching of his own church, Taylor is following a principle which he recommends to his reader early in *Holy Living*. Under the difficult circumstances of the time, he says in the dedication, 'every Man is to give sentence concerning the state of his own soul by the precepts and rules of our *Lawgiver*, not by the after decrees and usages of the Church, that is, by the essential parts of Religion rather than by the uncertain significations of any exteriour adherencies' (p. 6). That he does not always follow this counsel himself is clear from the number of ecclesiastical authorities he cites throughout *Holy Living*. Indeed, his rules for practical devotion are usually based not only on Scripture, but, as he says in the dedication to *Holy Dying*, on the 'purest channels of the Primitive Church' (p. 13). In his treatment of repentance in *Holy Living*, however, it is obvious that

[47] In the BCP, the Office of Morning Prayer opens on a hopeful note with Ezekiel 18: 27: 'When the wicked man turneth away from his wickedness that he hath committed, and doeth that which is lawful and right, he shall save his soul alive.' The Absolution, following the General Confession, expresses the usual Anglican attitude: 'Wherefore let us beseech him to grant us true repentance, and his Holy Spirit, that those things may please him, which we do at this present; and that the rest of our life hereafter may be pure, and holy.'

he is judging by the 'essential parts of Religion', rather than by the 'after decrees and usages of the Church'. To him, it is clear that if salvation is the reward of religion, of obedience and a holy life, it is unreasonable to expect that a lifelong sinner who repents on his death-bed can gather the same reward merely on the strength of an untried resolution.

III. *Taylor's Use of Religious and Classical Literature*

Taylor is indebted to three main sources in *Holy Living* and *Holy Dying*: the Bible, the Church Fathers, and the classics. The most important of these is obviously the Bible. In common with the learned clergy of his time, Taylor knew the Bible not only in the English Authorized Version of 1611, but also in the Greek and Latin texts. Although he regularly quotes or refers to the Greek New Testament, the Vulgate, and infrequently the Septuagint in most of his works (and occasionally introduces a Hebrew word), he cites the Authorized Version almost exclusively in *Holy Living* and *Holy Dying*, a unique feature of these works.[48] Also, in common with many writers of his time, Taylor frequently quotes the Bible from memory, paraphrases it, and freely alludes to it as one saturated with its language and ideas.

It is possible to distinguish a method in Taylor's use of the Bible, which he describes in his advice regarding the reading of Scripture. While emphasizing its unity and divine origin, he also commends select portions for daily reading. These portions should be those which contain 'most plain and certain duty' (p. 197), especially those which relate the story of the life and death of Christ. 'Read the Gospels, the Psalms of *David*', he says in *Holy Living*, 'especially those portions of Scripture which by the wisdom of the Church are appointed to be publikely read upon Sundayes and holy-dayes, *viz.* the Epistles and Gospels' (p. 197). Taylor's advice is essentially that one should reflect in private on what one hears in public from the eucharistic lectionary.

Taylor's own practice in *Holy Living* conforms to his general advice: though his allusions are wide-ranging and cover the whole of Scripture, including the Apocrypha, his interest centres on the New Testament. Major ethical and doctrinal points are nearly always given some New Testament support, especially from the Epistles: the basic idea of

[48] See Sarah Herndon, 'The Use of the Bible in Jeremy Taylor's Works' (Ph.D. diss., New York Univ., 1945), pp. 58–65.

Holy Living, as we have seen, is contained in St Paul's letter to Titus; and the epistle of St James is important to *Holy Dying*: 'Our life is but a vapor' might, indeed, stand as its motto.[49] Important are the Gospels of Luke (26 references) and especially Matthew (over 30 references). Taylor prefers texts that give direct or binding commands to those containing indirect admonitions through parables, analogies, or metaphors. Thus we find fewer references to the Book of Revelation (12) and to John's Gospel (11): Taylor's intention is primarily to declare man's duty through the Scriptures. For, as he says in *Holy Living*:

> All the doctrine of salvation is plainly set down there, that the most unlearned person by hearing it read, may understand all his duty. What can be plainer spoken than this, *Thou shalt not kill. Be not drunk with wine: Husbands love your wives: whatsoever ye would that men should do to you, do ye so to them.* The wit of man cannot more plainly tell us our duty . . . than the Holy Ghost hath done already. (pp. 196–7)

From such a point of view, the Scriptures are indeed filled with 'most plain and certain duty'.

Taylor is also much affected by the Psalms, which he uses generously in the composition of his prayers. From the Old Testament he generally gives illustrative examples involving well-known figures or events: Abimelech and Isaac, Joseph's bones, Gideon's fleece, God speaking to Job from the whirlwind. Such examples often serve as direct admonitions, as where a succession of Old Testament verses is used to show that repentance must be accompanied by sorrow and weeping (p. 247). But more often, Taylor uses the Old Testament in order to illustrate New Testament precepts.

A second source of inspiration for Taylor is patristic literature, as well as the writings of later commentators, historians, and hagiographers, and conciliar writings and papal decrees. In his use of such an extraordinary variety of non-scriptural and often non-Protestant material, Taylor is following the practice of his contemporaries, who were writing for a church they regarded as reformed, but truly catholic and apostolic. Many Anglican apologists would have agreed with their forebear Bishop John Jewel (1522–71), who declared in his *Apology of the Church of England* (1562) that 'we are come, as near as we possibly could to the Church of Apostles and of the old Catholic bishops and fathers . . . and have directed according to their customs and ordinances not only our Doctrine, but also the Sacraments and the form of

[49] See James 4: 14 and *Holy Dying*, p. 20.

common prayer'.[50] The margins (and often the text) of *Holy Living* and *Holy Dying* are as cluttered with references to the 'old Catholic bishops and fathers' as the sermons of Lancelot Andrewes—that most richly eloquent and witty of King James's court preachers.

Of the Church Fathers, Taylor refers to Augustine and Jerome most frequently, but also commonly cites Gregory the Great, Bernard of Clairvaux, Basil, John Chrysostom, and Cyprian. Respecting and approving of their piety, he considered them, next to the Bible, to be indisputable authorities on religious matters.[51] 'In Christian religion', he told the clergy of his diocese in 1663, 'they that were first were best, because God and not man was the teacher; and ever since that, we have been unlearning the wise notices of pure religion, and mingling them with human notices and human interest.'[52]

Taylor uses the Fathers principally as authorities on moral or doctrinal issues, and for purposes of clarification and amplification of his own arguments. This is how, for example, he uses St Jerome's three signs of faith (*Holy Living*, p. 176) and St Augustine's distinction between faith and hope (ibid., pp. 179–80). He also likes to cite as moral examples small anecdotes extracted from the writings of the Fathers. A notable instance of this is his re-telling of the story of the chaste martyr from St Jerome's 'Life of St. Paul the Hermit' (*Holy Living*, p. 85), which he refers to several times in other works.[53] Similar in nature and origin are his examples of St John 'sporting with a tame partridge' for recreation (*Holy Living*, p. 25) and St Paula Romana's excessive grief for the death of her children (*Holy Living*, p. 131; *Holy Dying*, p. 227). Taylor also treats the Fathers as repositories of beautiful imagery and *sententiae.* The sententious quotation is often not only decorative, but also serves to invoke authority, as when Taylor quotes St John Chrysostom on alms: '*To know the art of almes, is greater than to be crowned with the Diadem of kings. And yet to convert one soul is greater than to poure out ten thousand talents into the baskets of the poor*' (ibid., pp. 233–4).

Taylor's third major source is classical literature, from which he quotes and borrows generously, in quantities next only to the Bible

[50] See *The Works of John Jewel*, ed. John Ayre (Cambridge: Cambridge Univ. Press 1848), iii. 100.

[51] See Lois E. Barr, 'The Non-Biblical Learning of Jeremy Taylor' (Ph.D. diss. Univ. North Carolina, 1954), pp. 110–12. Barr has shown that Taylor's attitude towards the Fathers is decidedly respectful, though he often portrays a consciousness of their limitations.

[52] In 'The Whole Duty of the Clergy', *Works*, viii. 538.

[53] See Barr, 'Non-Biblical Learning', pp. 167–9.

This extraordinarily rich mingling of classical with biblical and patristic sayings was of course common among other writers on Christian conduct, as it was also among contemporary preachers, including Taylor himself. Their sermons appeared to give equal prominence to the Bible and the classics—something that scandalized many Puritans. But Taylor was among those who, in much of his writing, looked for ways to embellish and expand ideas,[54] and quoting the classics often enabled him to express more amply what he saw as essential wisdom. In the preface to *The Great Exemplar*, Taylor writes approvingly 'of those old wise spirits who preserved natural reason and religion in the midst of heathen darkness . . .'

> Homer, Euripides, Orpheus, Pindar, and Anacreon, Aeschylus and Menander, and all the Greek poets; Plutarch and Polybius, Xenophon and all those other excellent persons . . . whose choicest dictates are collected by Stobaeus, Plato and his scholars, Aristotle and after him Porphyry and all his other disciples, Pythagoras and his, especially Hierocles; all the old Academics and Stoics within the Roman schools: . . . And from hence I hope that [the wisest persons] may . . . be invited to love and consider the rare documents of Christianity, which certainly is the great treasure house of those excellent, moral, and perfective discourses, which with much pains and great pleasure, we find respersed and thinly scattered in all the Greek and Roman poets, historians, and philosophers.[55]

Taylor has thus not only listed nearly all the sources he uses most, but has also explained why he uses them.

The range and breadth of Taylor's knowledge of the classics is impressive. His preference for the great didactic writers and moral philosophers is predictable: Plutarch, Epictetus (in Arrian's *Discourses*, as well as the *Enchiridion*), Seneca, Aristotle, and Cicero. Next in importance are the historians: Tacitus, Livy, Lucan, Suetonius, Xenophon, and Herodotus; he quotes also from Aelianus, Diodorus

[54] On the rhetorical practice of seventeenth-century preaching, see W. Fraser Mitchell, *English Pulpit Oratory from Andrewes to Tillotson* (1932; New York: Russell and Russell, 1962), chap. 2, esp. pp. 107–9; see also Irène Simon, *Three Restoration Divines: Barrow, South, Tillotson* (Paris: Société d'Edition 'Les Belles Lettres', 1967), i. 48–62 (on 'The Reform of Pulpit Oratory'). Robert South evidently had Taylor in mind when he preached at St Mary's, Oxford, on 29 July 1660, concerning 'The Scribe Instructed', on a text from Matt. 13: 52: 'For *true Wit* is a severe and a manly Thing. Wit in Divinity is nothing else, but Sacred Truths suitably expressed. 'Tis not shreds of *Latin* or *Greek*, nor a *Deus dixit*, and a *Deus benedixit* . . . or the *Egress*, *Regress*, and *Progress*, and other such Stuff (much like the Style of a Lease) that can properly be called *Wit.* For that is not *Wit*, which consists not with *Wisdom*' (ed. Simon, II [1976], i. 245–6.

[55] *Works*, ii. 36.

Siculus, Josephus, and Procopius. Chief among the poets whom Taylor cites are Ovid and the satirists Horace, Juvenal, and Martial. He quotes frequently from the *Iliad* and the *Odyssey*. Among dramatists, Taylor favours Plautus and Seneca of the Romans, Euripides and Aristophanes of the Greeks. Thus philosophy, history, and poetry—the traditional branches of learning—are all represented in Taylor.

Not all of Taylor's references to classical writings are to the original texts; many for them, especially the little quotations in the margins of his text, have their origin in the commonplace books and collections of moral sayings that were so popular in the late Renaissance. Two such works which Taylor used especially are the *florilegia* of Joannes Stobaeus and Janus Gruter. Taylor also collected lines and phrases from books that he liked; for example, he picked up the quotations from Menander (*Holy Living*, p. 122, note *p*) and Sappho (ibid., p. 235, note *f*) from Plutarch, not from the poets themselves.

Taylor's classical borrowings range from casual references or quotations of a few lines to paraphrases of lengthy passages. Douglas Bush has noticed the curious effect on Taylor's style of his love of classical knowledge:

> Taylor's mind dwells so willingly in the world of the Caesars and the East that casual images, involving no proper names, keep us in a half-ancient atmosphere. It was not in Wales that he thought in terms of consulships and saw 'a wild boar destroy our vineyards', or orchards planted to 'feed our Nephews', a filleted beast bound to the altar, gladiators, pirates, labouring galley-slaves, the tents and triumphal chariots of conquerors.[56]

In *Holy Living* and *Holy Dying*, Taylor indeed leads us into a 'half-ancient atmosphere'; but he also evokes names, some real, many invented. An example of the latter occurs in the section of *Holy Living* on 'The Charge of many Children': 'What difference is it [if one has many children]? *Titius* keeps ten ploughs, *Cornelia* hath ten children' (p. 129). But examples of the former are more common—for example, the following, also from *Holy Living*, from 'Rules of making Restitution':

> And when *Ariarathes* the Cappadocian King had but in wantonesse stopped the mouth of the river *Melanus*, although he intended no evil, yet *Euphrates* being swelled by that means, and bearing away some of the strand of *Cappadocia* did great spoil to the Phrygians and Galatians, he therefore by the Roman Senate was condemned in three hundred talents towards reparation of the damage.
> (p. 163)

[56] Bush, *English Literature in the Earlier Seventeenth Century*, pp. 332–3.

Taylor makes no attempt to balance such examples with others from modern history. Events happening 'in Royal families amongst the *Arsacidæ*, the *Cæsars*, the *Ptolemies*' (p. 101) spring more readily to his mind than any occurrences among people who lived nearer to him in time, hardly excepting such distant figures as Sir Thomas More, Joan of Arc, and Ferdinand of Aragon and Christopher Columbus (*Holy Living*, pp. 25, 184, and 177, respectively), and Henry II of France and Louis XI (*Holy Dying*, pp. 23 and 123 for the former, p. 125 for the latter).

Classical writers are cited by Taylor as authorities on ethical issues and as sources of moral examples, of *sententiae* and decorative images. When enunciating moral principles or rules of conduct, he cites wherever possible a classical source in conjunction with a patristic or scriptural reference. He quotes St Augustine, for example, on the shamefulness of adultery and follows this with a reference to Plutarch on the same subject (*Holy Living*, p. 78 and note *w*). On the duties of parents to their children, in *Holy Living*, Taylor cites Euripides, Ovid, Plutarch, Justinian on the civil law, the Theodosian Code, and Numbers (p. 154 and note *x*). Frequently, Taylor's illustrative scriptural examples are given classical support. In discussing ways of obtaining contentment, Taylor refers to Joseph's being sold to the merchants of Amalek and finally becoming a great lord of Egypt, and continues: 'The case of *Themistocles* was almost like that of *Joseph*, for being banished into *Egypt*, he also grew in favour with the King' (*Holy Living*, p. 123).

Of all the classical writers, Plutarch is the one Taylor uses most extensively, particularly in *Holy Living* (71 references), but also in *Holy Dying* (13).[57] Taylor read Plutarch in the Latin translation of Xylander, which would have been readily available to him when he was writing these books. The references are mostly to the *Moralia*; only ten come from the *Vitae.* Although these references run through most of *Holy Living*, while occurring more sporadically in *Holy Dying*, there are two long portions in each of chapters 2 and 4 of *Holy Living* in which Taylor has used the *Moralia* as a direct, sometimes unacknowledged source. His discussion of modesty, as opposed to curiosity, in chapter 2 (pp. 99–102) is almost entirely based on Plutarch's 'De curiositate'; and the section devoted to 'Instruments or exercises to procure contentednesse' (pp. 109–118), contains many echoes of 'De tranquillitate animi'. In chapter 4, the section on remedies for anger

[57] Seneca is the next most commonly cited classical source, with 18 references in *Holy Living* and 44 in *Holy Dying.*

(pp. 235–8) is indebted to 'De cohibenda ira', and that on covetousness (pp. 240–5) to 'De cupiditate divitiarum'.

In these portions of *Holy Living*, Taylor depends on Plutarch not only for his theme, but also for his content. He lifts small passages from Plutarch with hardly any change and includes them in his own discussion. On the habits of the inquisitive, for example, Plutarch writes in 'De curiositate': 'While treating our own affairs with considerable laxity and neglect, [we] pry into the pedigrees of the rest of the world: our neighbour's grandfather was a Syrian, and his grandmother was a Thracian; and so-and-so owes three talents and has not paid the interest.' And Taylor echoes: 'What is it to me if my Neighbours Grandfather were a Syrian, or his Grandmother illegitimate, or that another is indebted five thousand pounds, or whether his wife be expensive?' (p. 100). Similarly, Plutarch comments on the irritating ways of customs officers: 'We are annoyed and displeased with customs-officials, not when they pick up those articles which we are importing openly, but when in the search for concealed goods they pry into baggage and merchandize which are another's property.' With minor changes, this statement appears in Taylor: 'We are not angry with Searchers and Publicans when they look onely on publick merchandise; but when they break open trunks, and pierce vessels, and unrip packs, and open sealed letters' (p. 101).

Taylor's indebtedness to Plutarch is even more obvious in chapter 4 of *Holy Living.* In much of the section on the remedies for anger, he translates and paraphrases Plutarch's 'De cupiditate divitiarium' as if it were open before him. But noting such verbal correspondences should not lessen our appreciation of Taylor's creative use of his sources, whether Plutarch or others. The organization of the material he selects is his own, and his borrowings blend easily into his own discussion. Sometimes, although indebted to his source for his theme, he elaborates and adapts it. An example is the long passage in chapter 2 on the proper and improper objects of curiosity, developed from Plutarch's similar observations on the same topic (see pp. 101–2 and commentary thereto).

An especially notable instance of Taylor's ability to elaborate on his source is the passage that Coleridge[58] singled out:

> If . . . I am fallen into the hands of Publicans and Sequestrators, and they have taken all from me, what now? let me look about me. They have left me the Sun

[58] See *Coleridge on the Seventeenth Century*, ed. Roberta F. Brinkley (New York: Greenwood Press, 1968), pp. 260–1.

and the Moon, Fire and Water, a loving wife, and many friends to pity me, and some to relieve me, and I can still discourse, and unless I list they have not taken away my merry countenance, and my cheerful spirit, and a good conscience: they still have left me the providence of God, and all the promises of the Gospel, and my Religion, and my hopes of Heaven, and my charity to them too: and still I sleep, and digest, I eat and drink, I reade and meditate, I can walk in my Neighbours pleasant fields, and see the varieties of natural beauties, and delight in all that in which God delights, that is, in vertue and wisdom, in the whole creation, and in God himself. (pp. 113–14)

Here Taylor is amplifying Plutarch's 'De tranquillitate animi' in order to develop a commonplace; he may well feel deeply—even personally—what he says, but his purpose is to establish a mood, a general situation, and a style for expressing them.[59]

IV. *Style*

Taylor's prose style, like that of his contemporary Sir Thomas Browne, has a reputation for ornateness, embellishment, and 'richness'. But Taylor, like Browne, is evidently conscious of the effect he wishes to produce, and also of the kind of prose he means to write. Different topics and occasions demand different treatment; one thus finds a variety of styles in these authors, depending on the subject at hand, with as many examples of simplicity and plainness as of elaborateness.

Taylor has not been well served by modern editors and commentators, who promote the idea that he is the author primarily of ornate prose, a practitioner of 'Ciceronian' copiousness, as opposed to 'Senecan' brevity.[60] A feature of this style most commented on—and hence most familiar—is the long and elaborate simile in which ornamentation seems to appear for its own sake, contributing to a kind of artificiality and a blurring of sense. One such simile (perhaps the most

[59] Some critics detect strong personal feelings in this passage. Logan Pearsall Smith believes that Taylor is referring to his own 'denuded state' in Wales (*The Golden Grove*, p. lvii); Stranks sees the passage as autobiographical evidence that Taylor's first wife was alive when he was writing *Holy Living* (*Life and Writings*, p. 107). But expatiation was Taylor's forte, as Mitchell justly observes in regard to Taylor's sermons (*English Pulpit Oratory*, p. 251). I would maintain that Taylor has here taken an idea from Plutarch, amplified it, and clothed it in evocative language that seems personal.

[60] Regarding these terms, see the influential and classic discussions of the development of seventeenth-century prose by Morris W. Croll: '"Attic Prose" in the Seventeenth Century' and 'The Baroque Style in Prose', in *Style, Rhetoric, and Rhythm: Essays by Morris W. Croll*, ed. J. Max Patrick and others (Princeton: Princeton Univ. Press, 1966), pp. 51–101, 207–33.

famous of his 'purple passages') occurs in his sermon on John 9: 31 entitled 'The Return of Prayers'. The sentence is characteristically anacoluthic, the sentence changing course after its beginning:

> For so have I seen a lark rising from his bed of grass, and soaring upwards, singing as he rises, and hopes to get to heaven, and climb above the clouds; but the poor bird was beaten back with the loud sighings of an eastern wind, and his motion made irregular and unconstant, descending more at every breath of the tempest, than it could recover by the libration and frequent weighing of its wings; till the little creature was forced to sit down and pant, and stay till the storm was over; and then it made a prosperous flight, and did rise and sing, as if it had learned music and motion from an angel as he passed sometimes through the air about his ministries here below: so is the prayer of a good man.[61]

But Taylor reserves such rhetorical flourishes for special moments. And when he uses extended metaphors and similes, he always integrates them into his argument for the purpose of illustration, rather than of mere ornamentation. In fact, it is the relative rarity of such passages which makes them so striking and effective.

Taylor's description of purity of intention in *Holy Living* illustrates his more customary use of figurative language; here he uses a series of similes simply to underscore the point he is making:

> *Holy intention* is to the actions of a man that which the soul is to the body, or form to its matter, or the root to the tree, or the Sun to the World, or the Fountain to a River, or the Base to a Pillar: for without these the body is a dead trunk, the matter is sluggish, the tree is a block, the world is darknesse, the river is quickly dry, the pillar rushes into flatnesse and a ruine; and the action is sinful, or unprofitable and vain. (pp. 28–9)

Similar in purpose and effect are the metaphors that Taylor uses in the opening statements of many sections in both *Holy Living* and *Holy Dying*. Thus: 'Sobriety is the bridle of the passions of desire, and Temperance is the bit and curb of that bridle, a restraint put into a mans mouth' (*Holy Living*, p. 64); '*Modesty* is the appendage of Sobriety, and is to Chastity, to Temperance and to Humility as the fringes are to a Garment' (ibid., p. 99); or '*A Man is a Bubble*', the proverb which begins *Holy Dying* (p. 19), around which Taylor develops his meditation on the brevity and chance nature of life.

Wherever Taylor formulates rules of behaviour or offers advice, he writes in clear, mostly direct statements. Although his sentences are

[61] *Works*, iv. 61–2.

often long and make use of independent clauses linked by conjunctions, there is usually no suspension of syntax. Sometimes there is a little ornamental flourish, as in the following passage from *Holy Living*:

> In the morning, when you awake, accustome your self to *think first upon God*, or something in order to his service; and at night also, let him close thine eyes; and let your sleep be necessary and healthful, not idle and expensive of time, beyond the needs and conveniencies of nature; and sometimes be curious to see the preparation which the sun makes, when he is coming forth from his chambers of the East. (p. 21)

In its multiplication of connectives, Taylor's style is 'loose', freely using 'and', 'or', 'but', often with very little syntactic connection with what has gone before, as in the example above.

Taylor often employs the 'cumulative' period when he feels that his argument needs the aid of rhetorical artifice for greater persuasive force. A typical example occurs near the beginning of *Holy Living*, where Taylor is discussing the necessity of devotion:

> And indeed if we consider how much of our lives is taken up by the needs of nature, how many years are wholly spent before we come to any use of reason, how many years more before that reason is useful to us to any great purposes, how imperfect our discourse is made by our evil education, false principles, ill company, bad examples, and want of experience; how many parts of our wisest and best years are spent in eating and sleeping, in necessary businesses, and unnecessary vanities, in worldly civilities, and lesse useful circumstances, in the learning arts and sciences, languages or trades; that little portion of hours that is left for the practises of piety, and religious walking with God, is so short and trifling, that were not the goodnesse of God infinitely great, it might seem unreasonable or impossible for us to expect of him eternal joyes in heaven, even after the well spending those few minutes which are left for God, and Gods service, after we have served our selves, and our own occasions.
> (pp. 17–18)

Using the common rhetorical figure of climax, the sentence progresses in short clauses from the 'needs of nature' to the 'joyes in heaven'. The grammatical sense is suspended until past the middle of the sentence; but the diction is simple, the language sonorous, the tone earnest.

Not only must one read Taylor in long passages in order to appreciate the undulations and contrasts of his style, but one should also read him in a text as close to his intentions as it is possible to come. Taylor's punctuation, which may seem idiosyncratic and illogical to a modern reader, is an important guide to his thought and style. Our understanding of earlier printed texts has come a long way since Gosse declared (in 1904) that 'to repunctuate Taylor would be an act of real editorial kindness'.[62] But Taylor's sentences, which are sometimes very long, demand punctuation according to the custom of his time. The commas, colons, and semicolons often serve grammatical functions by separating parts of sentences, indicating pauses, and emphasizing sound and rhythm. The punctuation of the first editions needs to be retained for the most part as a reflection of Taylor's whole design.

V. *The Reception of* Holy Living *and* Holy Dying

Taylor has always been best known as a devotional writer. In a letter of 19 February 1654 to William Temple, Dorothy Osborne refers to her reading of *Holy Living* and to 'Dr Taylor (whose devote you must know I am).'[63] But in his own century, his reputation rested not only on *Holy Living* and *Holy Dying*—the only works still widely remembered today—but most especially on *The Great Exemplar*, in its ninth edition in 1694, and *Golden Grove* and *The Worthy Communicant*, in their seventeenth and eleventh editions, respectively, in 1700.[64]

In the first half of the eighteenth century, Taylor's works continued to be printed and were evidently much read. *Holy Living* in particular had become so well known that it was variously imitated, abridged, and adapted for even more popular use. The title (not the contents) of the anonymous *The True Way to Happiness: or the Necessity of Holy Living* (1693) was obviously trading on the familiarity of Taylor's work. Later on, in 1701, there appeared a slim volume called *Rules of Holy Living and Dying, Conformable to Dr. Jeremy Taylor*, compiled by Edward Stacy, a 'Minister of the Church of England', who explains his purpose in the preface:

> In the larger Volumes [that is, Taylor's *Holy Living* and *Holy Dying*] the Paragraphs and Periods are very long, and the *language* generally too deep and

[62] Gosse, *Jeremy Taylor*, p. 226.

[63] See *The Letters of Dorothy Osborne to William Temple*, ed. G. C. Moore Smith (Oxford: Clarendon Press, 1928), pp. 146–7 and n. 2, p. 277, letter 59. Dorothy Osborne quotes from Chap. 3, Sect. 1, 'Of Obedience', p. 146, 13–20.

[64] See Paul Elmen, 'The Fame of Jeremy Taylor', *Anglican Theological Review*, 44 (1962), 389–403. The 1700 edition of *Golden Grove* (the early editions appeared either with this title or as *A Choice Manuall, Containing What is to be Believed, Practised, Desired or Prayed for*) calls itself the twentieth edition, but Gathorne-Hardy and Williams, *Bibliography*, identify only thirteen editions (pp. 63–9 (items 22A–Q)).

learned for mean Capacities, which with the Extravagant price it now bears, makes it neither so useful nor common, as a book of that nature ought to be.

In mine, I have everywhere made my Sentences very short, and used the plainest expressions I could think of.

Stacy's reference to the 'Extravagant price' and his suggestion of the rarity of *Holy Living* and *Holy Dying* is surely disingenuous, for his wretched paraphrase is a commercial venture dependent on Taylor's continued popularity.

An acrimonious dispute over copyright broke out some ten years later, suggesting incidentally how valuable a literary property Taylor's works continued to be. Involved in the dispute were Richard Steele and Royston Meredith. The latter was the grandson and heir of Taylor's publisher, Richard Royston. In 1714 Steele had published, in collaboration with the printer Tonson, a three-volume compilation called *The Ladies Library*, 'written by a Lady'. It consisted of selections from a number of seventeenth-century divines, with large extracts from Taylor, mostly from *Holy Living.* Upon its publication, Meredith, who had inherited the rights to Taylor's works from Royston, wrote to Steele a number of times, accusing him of literary theft and threatening legal proceedings against him. Steele replied that he was only trying to help the 'revered author's grandchild'. Steele did not name this child, but he may have been referring to Lady Wray, who in 1735 wrote a memoir of Taylor. Meredith, still unappeased, published the correspondence in November 1714 as *Mr. Steele detected: Or, the Poor and Oppressed Orphan's Letters to the Great and Arbitrary Mr. Steele.*[65]

Holy Living and *Holy Dying*, which between them had reached seventeen editions by 1700, had gone through nine more editions by 1739, including a Welsh translation in 1701 by E. Wynne. John Wesley read *Holy Living* at Oxford in 1725, and wrote in his journal that he was 'struck particularly with the chapter upon intention' (that is, chapter 1, section 2), which made him feel 'a fixed intention "to give myself up to God"'.[66] *Holy Living* and *Holy Dying* continued to attract Wesley, for, in a letter to his mother of 1730, he is critical of Taylor's definition of hope (*Holy Living*, chapter 4, section 2), but appreciates his discussion of repentance and pardon of sins in *Holy Dying* (chapter 4, sections 6 and 7).[67] The only edition, indeed, of *Holy Living* and *Holy Dying* in the

65 See Gathorne-Hardy and Williams, *Bibliography*, p. 36 (in item 11A).

66 *The Journal of the Rev. John Wesley, A.M.*, ed. Nehemiah Curnock (London: Robert Culley, 1909–16), v. 117.

67 Ibid., viii. 270–1.

latter part of the eighteenth century is Wesley's (in *A Christian Library* (Bristol, 1749–55), vol. 9); for Taylor's general popularity had declined substantially by this time. Nevertheless, Dr Johnson is supposed to have read much of Taylor, and he placed him 'at the head of all the divines that have succeeded the fathers'.[68]

The beginning of the nineteenth century saw Taylor's reputation rise once again. The Romantic writers, especially Coleridge, Lamb, and Hazlitt, praised 'the Shakespeare of divines'.[69] To Coleridge, Taylor had the soul of a poet: 'Is not *The Holy Living and Dying*, a sacred and didactic poem in almost as wide a sense of the word as the *Commedia* of Dante? What Bard of ancient or modern times has surpassed, in richness of language, in fertility of fancy, in majesty of sentiment, in grace of imagery, this Spenser of English prose?'[70] Coleridge introduced Taylor to Lamb, who became an even greater admirer perhaps. 'I love the man', he wrote to Robert Lloyd in 1801, '& I love his paraphernalia [that is, his titles] and I like to name him with all his attributions and additions.' Lamb continues: 'Bishop Taylor has more, and more beautiful imagery . . . more knowledge and description of human life and manners, than any prose book in the language: he has more delicacy, and sweetness, than any mortal, the "gentle" Shakespeare hardly excepted.' In the same letter, Lamb gives us an idea of Taylor's readership at this time:

> He wrote to different classes of people. His Holy Living and Dying and Life of X't were designed to have been used as popular books of family Devotion, and have been thumbed by old women, and laid about in the window seats of old houses in great families, like the Bible. . . . Accordingly in these the *fancy* is perpetually applied to; any slight conceit, allusion or analogy . . . a story true or false, serves for an argument, adapted to women and young persons & 'incompetent judgments'—whereas the Liberty of Prophecy [sic] . . . is a series of severe and masterly reasoning, fitted to great Clerks and learned Fathers, with no more of Fancy than is subordinate and ornamental.[71]

Hazlitt wrote of Taylor with similar approbation. In one of his lectures, he calls *Holy Living* and *Holy Dying* a 'divine pastoral', and

[68] See John Hawkins, *The Life of Samuel Johnson*, ed. Bertram Davis (New York: Macmillan, 1961), p. 243. Boswell complained to Johnson of Taylor's use in his prayers of '"I am the chief of sinners", and other such self-condemning expressions' (*Life of Johnson*, ed. George B. Hill (Oxford: Clarendon Press, 1934), iv. 294).

[69] The expression is William Mason's, in a letter to Thomas Gray of 8 January 1761. See *The Correspondence of Thomas Gray*, ed. P. Toynbee (Oxford: Clarendon Press, 1935), p. 329.

[70] *Coleridge on the Seventeenth Century*, p. 259.

[71] *Lamb as Critic*, ed. Roy Park (London: Routledge and Kegan Paul, 1980), pp. 266, 268.

concludes this lecture with the often quoted comment: 'When the name of Jeremy Taylor is no longer remembered with reverence, genius will have become a mockery and virtue an empty shade.'[72] Hyperbole of this sort is common in the early 1800s and later. Edward Fitzgerald, given a copy of *Holy Living* and *Holy Dying* upon leaving Cambridge, did not at first like the work; but in 1835 he was able to write to his friend John Allen, who had given him the copy:

> What a man [Taylor] is! He has such a knowledge of the nature of man, and such powers of expressing its properties, that I sometimes feel as if he had some exact counterpart of my own individual character under his eye, when he lays open the depth of the heart, or traces some sin to the root. The eye of his portrait expresses this keen intuition: and I think that I should less like to have stood with a tie on my tongue before him than before any other I know of.

Writing again to Allen to ask him to buy another copy, Fitzgerald says that 'Jeremy Taylor's books used to be very common indeed'; the implication is that they are now scarce.[73]

In the United States, Taylor also received some acclaim. Among the first of the works published there under his name was the *Contemplations of the State of Man*, a spurious book now excluded from Taylor's canon; but the 1723 Boston edition of the book called itself the ninth edition, so it must have been something of a success.[74] *The Great Exemplar*, published as *The Life of our Blessed Saviour* in Exeter, New Hampshire, in 1724, seems to have become especially popular later on, for it went through eight editions between 1794 and 1834.[75] In the 1820s and 1830s, Taylor's admirers included a number of literary men: Hawthorne was particularly partial to Taylor's sermons, and had also read Reginald Heber's biography of him. Emerson regularly numbers Taylor among the greatest of English writers, and in his notebooks he often quotes from the sermons, *Holy Living* and *Holy Dying*, *The Great Exemplar*, and other works.[76]

[72] *The Complete Works of William Hazlitt*, ed. P. P. Howe (London: Dent, 1931), vi. 341, 345.

[73] See *The Letters of Edward Fitzgerald*, ed. Alfred M. Terhune and Annabelle B. Terhune (Princeton: Princeton Univ. Press, 1980), i. 163–4.

[74] For an account of the reasons for its exclusion from the canon, see Gathorne-Hardy and Williams, *Bibliography*, p. 137 (item T3).

[75] These editions were published in Greenfield, Mass., 1793; Portsmouth, N.H., 1794; Newburyport, Mass., 1796; Philadelphia, 1809 and 1810; Somerset, Pa., 1818; Philadelphia, 1819; and Pittsburgh, 1834.

[76] See Frederick Asals, 'Jeremy Taylor and Hawthorne's Early Tales', *American Transcendental Quarterly*, 14 (1972), 15–23; and *The Journals and Miscellaneous Notebooks of Ralph Waldo Emerson*, ed. Ralph H. Orth (Cambridge, Mass.: Belknap Press of Harvard

Early nineteenth-century interest in Taylor led to the first edited text of his works by Bishop Heber, which remains the standard text. The many popular editions, selections, and abridgements of his works, especially *Holy Living* and *Holy Dying*, that appeared between 1850 and 1900 testify to Taylor's continued popularity. Among notable editions must be mentioned those of F. A. Malleson (1899, rept. 1894); Henry Morley (1888); and A. R. Waller ('Cambridge English Classics', 1900). Taylor was a 'household classic' at the turn of the century, known especially for *Holy Living* and *Holy Dying*; and in 1904 Gosse could rightly say that Taylor's works were to be found 'where books of any gravity of composition are admitted'.[77]

Much of the twentieth-century response to Taylor, however, seems to reflect the reservations of Arnold in his 'Literary Influence of Academies' (1864). Commenting on part of the notable funeral sermon for Lady Carbery, he noted that 'genius, the ruling divinity of poetry, [is] too busy in it, and intelligence, the ruling divinity of prose, not busy enough. . . . Can any one, with the best models of style in his head, help feeling the note of provinciality there, the want of simplicity, the want of measure, the want of just the qualities that make prose classical?'[78] The statement may say more about Arnold's critical position than it does about Taylor's prose, but the concern with style and the confusion over what it means is fundamental to the inadequacy, or even indifference, of much contemporary reaction. Logan Pearsall Smith's *Golden Grove* (1930), a compilation of purple passages from Taylor's works, could only have reinforced Arnold's dictum. But new editions of Taylor's great devotional classics have been infrequent. Popular editions of *Holy Living* and *Holy Dying* of 1904–6 remained in print until 1910. Longman's issued editions in 1918, 1930, and 1941. In 1956, T. S. Kepler offered a new edition; and in 1970 Anne Lamb edited a much abridged and modernized version of *Holy Living*, which nevertheless had an enormous circulation through one of the religious book clubs in the United States.

Almost all editions of *Holy Living* and *Holy Dying* subsequent to

Univ. Press, 1966), vi. 43–5. Emerson and his contemporaries must have read imported English editions of *Holy Living* and *Holy Dying*, for the earliest nineteenth-century American edition was probably the one that appeared in Amherst in 1831. After this time, the two books, bound together, were issued regularly: in Philadelphia in 1831, 1835, 1843, and 1846; and in New York in 1848, 1856, 1857, 1859, 1865, 1868, 1876, and 1888.

77 See Gosse, *Jeremy Taylor*, p. 69.

78 See Matthew Arnold, *Lectures and Criticism*, ed. R. H. Super (Ann Arbor: Univ. Michigan Press, 1962), pp. 245–6.

Heber's have been based on his, which is modernized to suit the taste of the early 1800s. Thus, no critical edition of these books with old spelling is in print; nor are Taylor's masterpieces currently available in any complete form. The present edition aims to make good this lack, and so to set forth in a suitable way two of the greatest works of seventeenth-century England.

TEXTUAL INTRODUCTION

I. *The Text*

Holy Living was entered in the Stationers' Register by Francis Ash on 7 March 1650. At this time, Ash also held the rights to *The Great Exemplar.* About a year and a half later he died, leaving his title to both books to Richard Royston, according to the entry in the Stationers' Register for 24 November 1651.

The earliest extant form of the text of *Holy Living* is the first edition, which was printed in 1650, in three states. Ash's name appears on the title-page as the publisher of two of these, Royston's on one. Although the title-pages appear in these three different states, all copies in which they appear are part of the same edition, for they are produced from the same setting of type. State I, which appears to be the earliest, reads as follows:

THE RVLE | AND | EXERCISES | OF | HOLY LIVING. | In which are described | The MEANS and INSTRUMENTS | of obtaining every Vertue, and the | Remedies against every Vice, and | Considerations serving to the | resisting all temptations. | Together with | Prayers containing the whole duty of | a Christian, and the parts of Devotion | fitted to all Occasions, and furnish'd | for all Necessities | [rule] | [flower enclosed in a box of fleurs-de-lis ornaments] | [rule] | LONDON, | Printed for *Francis Ash*, Book- | Seller in *Worcester.* | MDCL.

State II differs from the above in two small details: line 6 of the title ('In which are described') is in italics instead of roman type, and the first letter of line 14 ('a Christian') is a capital, not lower case. State III agrees with State II in every detail except the imprint, which reads: 'LONDON, | Printed for *Richard Royston* at the | Angel in *Ivie-Lane.* | MDCL.' Some copies bearing the Royston imprint lack two leaves at the very end (sig. S2 and S3) which contained an 'Appendix' with prayers for the King. All three states have the same colophon: 'LONDON, | Printed by *R. Norton.* | MDCL.'

The reasons for the production of the book with the imprints of two different publishers on the various title-pages have been reconstructed by William P. Williams.[1] The explanation involves Richard Royston and the censorship ordinances which were passed by Parlia-

[1] William P. Williams, 'The First Edition of *Holy Living*: An Episode in the Seventeenth-Century Book Trade', *The Library*, 5th ser., 28 (1973), 99–107.

ment in 1643 and again in 1649, which were intended to suppress 'lying and scandalous' writings against the government.[2] Royston was a devoted Anglican who had been bookseller to Charles I, as he was later to become to Charles II and James II.[3] In 1645 he was arrested and imprisoned, under the ordinances of 1643, on charges of selling and printing scandalous books and pamphlets against Parliament. Later on, in October 1649, after publishing Charles I's *Eikon Basilike*, he was again accused of selling unlicensed and 'scandalous' (meaning Royalist) books, and was bound in a surety of five hundred pounds for good behaviour. He was well known for his Royalist sympathies, and it was probably his attachment to the cause of the King and the Anglican Church that made him decide to publish Taylor's writings. As soon as Taylor had established himself as a Royalist and Anglican apologist, Royston had begun to publish his works. In 1647 he brought out *The Liberty of Prophesying*, and by 1649 had reissued most of Taylor's earlier works after taking over their copyrights. From this time on he would publish nearly everything that Taylor wrote.

Though Royston had become Taylor's exclusive publisher by 1649, it was not he, but Francis Ash, who published Taylor's first popular devotional work, *The Great Exemplar.* Ash entered the book in the Stationers' Register in October 1648, and the first edition, printed by Roger Norton,[4] appeared in 1649 bearing his imprint. How he acquired Taylor's permission to publish *The Great Exemplar* is a mystery. It is inconceivable that Taylor had refused to give Royston the book, for he had by this time given Royston permission to publish everything that he had written. With a shop in London and possibly another in Oxford,[5] Royston was better situated than Ash to be

[2] For a brief account of these ordinances, see Henry R. Plomer, *A Dictionary of Booksellers and Printers who were at work in England, Scotland and Ireland from 1641 to 1667* (London: Bibliographical Society, 1907), pp. xii–xvii.

[3] Royston left his business and copyrights to his granddaughter on condition that she marry a member of the Church of England. See Plomer, *Dictionary*, p. 159.

[4] The title-page of *The Great Exemplar* gives only the initials of the printer, 'R.N.', but this is sufficient to identify Roger Norton, who was to become one of Royston's regular printers. A staunch Royalist, Norton petitioned unsuccessfully at the Restoration to be appointed King's printer, as his father, Bonham Norton, had been. One of the grounds on which he made the petition was that he had been of service to the King during the interregnum by printing Royalist publications. See Plomer, *Dictionary*, p. 139.

[5] Royston had extensive connections with printers and booksellers in Oxford, which makes it likely that he had an establishment there as well as in London. After 1655, he published a number of Henry Hammond's works jointly with Richard Davis, an Oxford bookseller (see Wing H568, H576, and H584). At his death, he left bequests to several Oxford booksellers (Plomer, *Dictionary*, p. 159). It was probably through Oxford circles that Royston became acquainted with Taylor.

Taylor's publisher. For, in the twenty-one years that he had been in business as a bookseller and bookbinder in Worcester, Ash had never published a book.[6] Moreover, his trade had been confined to Worcester and the West Country. It is strange that he should suddenly have ventured into publishing in London and begun with a work by Taylor.

The mystery is deepened by indications that Royston was also involved in the publication of *The Great Exemplar*. Though the title-page of the first edition bears Ash's imprint, the ornament that appears in it belonged to Royston, and was to appear in other works of Taylor's published by him. The use of this ornament shows that Royston had some share in the printing of the book, and must therefore have had some interest in it, even before the transfer of its rights, along with those of *Holy Living*, in November 1651. The fact that Royston reissued a substantial part of *The Great Exemplar* in 1650 together with the *Treatise* of two years earlier is another indication of his interest in it.[7]

The probable explanation is that Taylor offered the book to Royston, but that Royston had just published and was again about to publish some politically sensitive material which made immediate publication of *The Great Exemplar* inadvisable. In 1648 he had brought out, in one volume entitled *Treatises*, some of Taylor's polemical works, including the 'Gunpowder Sermon', *The Liberty of Prophesying*, and *A Discourse concerning Prayer Extempore.* Later that year or early in 1649, he had also brought out an enlarged, revised version of *Prayer Extempore*, retitled *An Apology for Authorised and Set Forms of Liturgie*. These works all dealt with topics that were controversial, and hence politically dangerous. The *Apology*, especially, contained opinions that the government would have found objectionable, for Taylor defends the banned Book of Common Prayer and attacks Parliament's substitute for it, the *Directory of Public Worship*. Royston was also at that time preparing to publish *Eikon Basilike.* Any or all of these works, Royston was aware, might be considered 'scandalous' by Parliament's censors and be subject to seizure, as would *The Great Exemplar* if he recorded his rights to it at this time. Having been in trouble with the censors once before, he must have expected some such reaction. His

[6] Ash took up his freedom of the Stationers' Company on 10 August 1627. See E. Arber, *A Transcript of the Registers of the Company of Stationers, 1554–1640* (London, 1875–95; rept. New York: Peter Smith, 1950), iii. 320b.

[7] See R. Gathorne-Hardy and W. P. Williams, *Bibliography*, p. 33 (item 10A).

apprehensions were subsequently shown to be justified, for, though his properties were not seized, the charges that were brought against him in 1649 may well have been due as much to his publication of Taylor's works as to that of *Eikon Basilike.* It is therefore surmised that, in October 1648, in order to ensure that *The Great Exemplar* would get published, even if the anticipated intervention from the authorities materialized, Royston himself involved Francis Ash in its publication. Instead of recording his own rights to the book, Royston had Ash enter it in the Stationers' Register. By this means *The Great Exemplar* would not be recognized as his property, or be associated with the books he was about to print. The entry in the Register would make Ash legally responsible for it, thereby ensuring that its printing would go ahead, even if Royston's properties were seized by the censors. The expenses of the first edition, when it came to be printed, may have been shared by both men, or, as is more probable, been borne by Royston alone. Ash, in other words, merely acted as a front for Royston, his best qualification for the job being that he was based in Worcester, a city that was still not under Parliament's control. The arrangement was no different from any other collaboration between two or more printers, except that it probably included the understanding that the rights would revert to Royston if all went well and the censors did not intervene.

As it happened, the censors did intervene, and the rights remained with Ash for more than two years. However, the arrangement must have worked well, for it was repeated when *Holy Living* came to be printed. In 1650, Royston was operating under some constraints, being under bond not to publish books that might be considered Royalist and anti-Parliament. Though *Holy Living* was a devotional, not a political, book, its preface was certainly Royalist in tone, and, moreover, it contained prayers for the King (which, at this time, could have been interpreted to mean for Charles II). Taylor's reputation alone could have been a hindrance to Royston's open publication of the book. So, in order to get around the difficulty, Royston again involved Francis Ash. The collaboration, as before, included Roger Norton, the printer. Ash entered the book in the Stationers' Register, and the first copies of the first edition, printed by Norton, bore his imprint. Some copies were produced with Royston's name on the imprint, however, making it appear that, though Ash was the legal owner of the copyright, he had allowed Royston to sell some of the books. Royston must have known that he was taking a risk, for he took a further precaution in the preparation of this edition. He extracted prayers for the King from the body of the text and put them in an appendix at the end. The appendix remained in place in Ash's copies, but in Royston's copies it was removed. It was in this form that the first edition went on sale. Royston's copies circulated in London, and Ash sold his, presumably from Worcester.

Royston's precautions proved to be unnecessary, however, for *Holy Living* did not attract the attention of the censors. When a second edition was issued in 1651, the prayers for the King were incorporated in the text, albeit slightly modified. Following Ash's death that year, Royston took over the copyright and brought out the third edition himself. He continued to reprint *Holy Living* until he died in 1686, bequeathing the copyright to his granddaughter, Elizabeth Maior. The last of the seventeenth-century editions, therefore, bear the imprint of Elizabeth's husband, Luke Meredith.

II. *The Transmission of the Text*

Seven editions of *Holy Living* appeared during Taylor's lifetime, in the years 1650, 1651 (twice), 1654, 1656, 1660, and 1663. Another edition was issued in 1668, the year after Taylor's death. For the purposes of the present text, these first eight editions have been collated; and their bibliographical description appears at the end of this section. Their outstanding features as regards transmission of the text are given below, and their relationship is illustrated in figure 5.

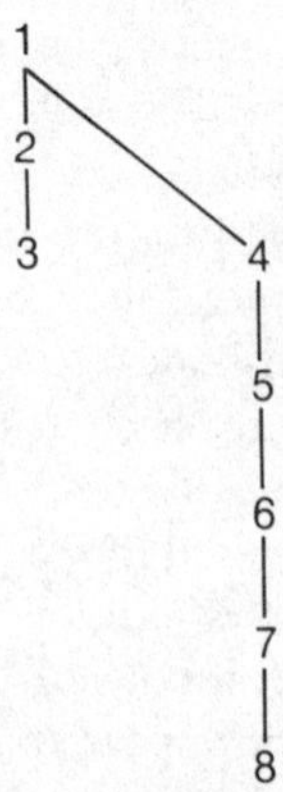

5. Relationship of the editions.

The text of the second edition of 1651 follows that of the first very closely, making it clear that it was set from a copy of the edition of 1650. It contains a number of alterations, however, including authorial corrections and revisions. The major alteration, as mentioned above, is the inclusion in the text of the prayers that were placed in an appendix in the first edition, but with the words 'King' and 'Kingdom' changed to 'Ruler' and 'Dominion'. One of them appears at the end of chapter 1, another at the end of chapter 4, and the rest in their appropriate place at the end of chapter 3. Another restoration in the second edition is a sentence in chapter 2, section 6: 'And when thy little misfortune troubles thee, remember that thou hast known the best of Kings, and the best of Men put to death publickly by his own subjects' (p. 122). This reference to the executed King had been extracted from the text and put in the appendix, for the same reason as the prayers. The second edition also contains a number of revisions and other variants. Most of the latter consist of the addition or substitution of single words or phrases. Some are clearly the result of the compositor's misreading, but a few are obviously authorial. One longer revision, consisting of eleven words inserted in the middle of a sentence in chapter 1, section 1 (19. 27–28), was reprinted only in the third edition, and was not picked up by later editions.

The third edition of *Holy Living*, published in the same year, also describes itself as 'The Second Edition', but is actually a line-for-line resetting of the second edition. It corrects some of the mistakes of the second edition, but adds new mistakes. There is no strong evidence of the author's hand in the corrections. Most of them are corrections of obvious printing errors, and can therefore be ascribed to the compositors. I have consequently treated it as a derived text, whose variants have no independent authority.

The fourth edition, issued in 1654, is an authoritative version of the text, for it was, as its title-page declares, corrected and augmented with 'additionals' by the author. However, though Taylor did go over the text, and even gave attention to the punctuation, neither the corrections nor the additions are very extensive. The corrections include clearer punctuation, the repositioning of a few paragraphs, and rectification of compositor's errors. Apart from a number of new marginal notes, the most substantial additions are two paragraph-length passages, in chapters 2 and 4 (82. 19–21 and 215. 17–25). The prayers for the King, which had been modified in the second edition, revert to their earlier form (but not position) in this edition, with the words

'King' and 'Kingdom' restored. This change was made possible, perhaps, by a relaxation of censorship after 1651.

In punctuation and other accidentals, the fourth edition is closer to the first than to the second or the third. This is one indication that its text does not derive from its immediate predecessors. A further indication is the fact that it does not pick up any of the revisions made in the second edition. For instance, the eleven-word passage inserted in chapter 1, section 1, in the second edition and reprinted in the third, does not appear in it or in any of the subsequent editions that derive from it. These details indicate that, in preparing the fourth edition, Taylor made his corrections and additions in a copy of the first edition. This was then used as printer's copy, and no attempt was made to compare it with copies of either the second or third editions in order to incorporate the earlier revisions.

Of subsequent editions, the fifth carries the claim of corrections and additions on its title-page, although it contains none and is a page-for-page reprint of the fourth. The sixth, likewise, repeats the claim of 'additionals', but is substantially a reprint of its predecessor, although it received some authorial attention, albeit minimal. A copy of the fifth edition in the library of King's College, Cambridge, which was discovered by Robert Gathorne-Hardy, contains a number of corrections in Taylor's hand, a few of which appear in the sixth edition. The most important of these corrections is the change of the term 'communicative justice' in chapter 3 to the appropriate one of 'commutative justice'. The correction of the mistake at this late date shows that, although Taylor had seen and read various earlier editions, he had not at any time proofread them exhaustively. Besides corrections, the sixth edition has other small changes, which reflect an attempt by the printer to normalize Taylor's punctuation and other accidentals. Colons, which Taylor often uses instead of full stops, are turned into full stops; semicolons are changed into colons, and occasionally into commas. Though preserving seventeenth-century spelling for the most part, the edition drops some archaic forms such as the terminal *e* in words like 'drunkenesse'. In general these orthographic changes refect the changing norms of the post-Restoration period.

The seventh edition, of 1660, was issued as an octavo, instead of a duodecimo like the previous six editions. It reproduces the corrections but includes the mistakes and other variants of the sixth edition, thereby showing that it was set from a copy of the latter. The text, however, perhaps because of the changed format, received some attention from both the author and the printer. From the appearance of new marginal notes (though most are no more than documentation of references in the text), it is apparent that Taylor went through at least some parts of the text. However, apart from a few minor corrections, he left it unchanged. The changes in spelling and typography in this edition are probably the work of the printer. The text throughout shows an effort to tidy up its appearance. Italics are more frequent, and some direct quotations and proper names, which previous editions had allowed to stand in roman font, are italicized. This procedure was traditional practice, but the earlier editions, reflecting the oversights of the manuscript, are erratic in their italicization. Capitalization, on the other hand, is less frequent and less idiosyncratic in this edition. Following its predecessor, it normalizes punctuation and some forms of spelling, but also shows a further attempt to get rid of archaisms. For instance, it regularizes Taylor's use of 'eat' as a past participle into 'ate' (see textual notes to 66. 17 and 19). Most of these changes, as in the case of the sixth edition, can be attributed to the compositor. It is possible, nevertheless, that Taylor may have approved some of them. For instance, italicization in some places is very precise, pinpointing quotations and phrases needing emphasis. The author would most likely have isolated such passages, and thus have authorized the change in typography. Such typographical changes have been incorporated in the present edition or else recorded in the textual notes.

The eighth edition, issued after Taylor's death in 1668, is a resetting of the seventh and contributes nothing new. All later editions, like the eighth, are derived from the seventh.

To summarize, the second edition of *Holy Living* was set from a copy of the first edition and contains a number of authorial corrections and revisions which it shares only with its immediate successor. A straight resetting of the second, the third edition is of no textual importance. The fourth edition was set from a copy of the first, and contains new additions and revisions, but omits the revisions of the second edition. The fifth is a line-for-line reprint of the fourth and makes no further contribution to the text. The sixth is a reprint of the fifth, but contains a few authorial corrections. The seventh strays the farthest from the form of the accidentals of previous editions, but substantially preserves the text of its predecessor; however, it contains new marginal notes and some corrections. The eighth edition is a reprint of the seventh. Therefore, the most important editions of the text, after the first, are the second, fourth, sixth, and seventh. Taylor gave his attention, in varying degrees, to all four. With the exception of the sixth edition, he added new material, besides correcting mistakes and revising readings.

Another set of documents used in the preparation of this edition of *Holy Living* remains to be noted. It consists of the copies of the first and the fifth editions described by Gathorne-Hardy in the *Times Literary Supplement* of 20 September 1947 (p. 484). The copy of the first edition that Gathorne-Hardy describes is a presentation copy that Taylor gave to his friend William Wyat. It contains a number of corrections and notes in Taylor's hand, and, on a blank leaf at the end of the text, a long prayer. The copy of the fifth edition, which belongs to the library of King's College, Cambridge, is also a presentation copy and contains a larger number of corrections and revisions in autograph. Apart from the prayer, none of Taylor's revisions in these copies consists of more than a few words. The longest is a sentence in the margin (see p. 210, note *k*). In some places, he corrects or alters punctuation, and corrects or adds biblical references in the margin. In others, he changes the form of small phrases or substitutes single words. Some of these corrections were adopted in later editions of *Holy Living*, but most, including the prayer in the first edition, have not as yet appeared in any printed version of the text. They are incorporated in this one, the autograph prayer being inserted at the end of chapter 1 where it fits best.

III. *The Present Edition*

My purpose in the present edition is to produce a critical text of *Holy Living* and *Holy Dying* using old spelling. For the copy-text of *Holy Living*, I have used the Huntington Library copy of the first edition, which bears the Royston, or state III, imprint. Since this copy lacks the appendix containing prayers for the King, the latter has been taken from a copy bearing the Francis Ash, or state I, imprint in the library of Northern Illinois University. I have compared the Huntington Library copy with other copies of the first edition in the Houghton Library of Harvard University and the library of Cambridge University. While basing my edition on the first edition, I have incorporated revisions and additions that appear in later editions, particularly those in the fourth edition, in which Taylor's interest appears to have been greatest.

6. Taylor's autograph of the prayer beginning 'O Holy and heavenly Father', from Taylor's presentation copy of the first edition of 1650 to William Wyat, written on the blank verso of S3.

All changes to the copy-text are clearly recorded. Substantive notes—that is, notes regarding verbal changes or changes in punctuation which affect the sense—appear at the bottom of the text page on which they occur, beneath Taylor's own notes. The emendation of accidentals in the copy-texts is given in a separate section at the back of each volume. I have ignored the accidentals of later editions, except when I have found it necessary to incorporate them in the text, or when they are of semi-substantive importance. All substantive emendations of the text have the authority of one or more of the later editions—usually the fourth. In the textual notes and the emendation of accidentals, the lemmata are those of the present text. In the emendations, the sigla immediately after the lemmata are those of the editions from which the reading has been adopted; the rest of the note records the readings of the copy-text and other editions. When a siglum does not appear in a note, it indicates agreement with the lemma. A list of the sigla and other abbreviations used in the notes is given on p. xii above.

The Commentary, which appears after the text, contains explanatory notes, documentation of references and allusions, identification of Taylor's sources, and translations of non-English quotations and notes. Quotations and passages that Taylor himself translates are omitted. The notes in the Commentary are keyed to the text by page and line numbers.

Taylor's marginal notes are keyed to the text by complete alphabets, using superscript letters before the quotation or relevant passage. Names of authorities and titles are in roman type, and retain his abbreviations, such as Senec. or Odyss. Scriptural citations are regularized to arabic numerals, but Taylor's abbreviations are preserved: thus, 1 John 3: 4 and 2 Samuel 1: 4, but Joh. 11: 40. Names appear as S. *James*, Taylor's customary practice, not *S. James.* Other abbreviations and contractions are silently expanded, such as 'furnished' for 'furnish'd', and 'weakened' for 'weakned'; and certain words are standardized, such as 'kindred' for 'kinred', 'whether', for 'whither', 'ministering' for 'ministring', 'remembering' for 'remembring', and 'than' for 'then'. 'H.' becomes 'Holy', and the ampersand becomes *et* or and (or etc., but not &c).

Taylor often uses square brackets in conjunction with italic type to designate a quotation, or occasionally to suggest a 'semi-paragraph'. Such brackets have been omitted where inverted commas or italics are sufficient to indicate quoted phrases and passages; but they have been retained where the brackets enclose a rubric, as in some prayers (for example, p. 46). Where Taylor uses inverted commas to call attention to a passage and not to enclose a quotation, they have been silently omitted. The hyphenation of the copy-text is preserved in this edition only when it is not end-of-line; and word divisions, such as 'our selves' or 'him self' are retained in their original form.

Apart from the use of italics, no attempt has been made to reproduce the typography of the copy-text. Ornamental letters and type of different sizes have been normalized. Obvious printing errors, such as turned or transposed letters, wrong fonts, and mis-citations, have been corrected. The long *ſ* has been normalized, and ligatures have been separated where they occur in English (but not in Latin). I give *i* for *j*, *u* for *v*; and I treat Latin like English, omitting the circumflex (as *formâ*). Greek is normalized, with modern breathings supplied; and lines of verse which have been wrongly broken have been corrected. I have also modernized the method of referring to books of the *Iliad* and *Odyssey* by the Greek alphabet: thus *Iliad* χ becomes *Iliad* 22.

When I have emended the text on my own initiative, I have inserted *ed* in the textual note immediately after the lemma; where I have corrected a passage, such as a quotation, I say *cor.* Textual notes employ the swung dash, ~, to stand for a word given in the note immediately before; the caret, ‸, to call attention to missing punctuation; the plus sign, +, to indicate all editions subsequent to the one noted (e.g. *1*+ or *4*+); and editorial comments are italicized.

IV. *Bibliographical Description of Editions Collated*

1. The First Edition. 1650. Wing T371. Huntington Library copy.

Title: THE RVLE | AND | EXERCISES | OF | HOLY LIVING. | *In which are described* | The MEANS and INSTRUMENTS | of obtaining every Vertue, and the | Remedies against every Vice, and | Considerations serving to the | resisting all temptations. | Together with | Prayers containing the whole duty of | A Christian, and the parts of Devotion | fitted to all Occasions, and furnish'd | for all Necessities. | [rule] | [flower enclosed in a box of fleurs-de-lis ornaments] | [rule] | LONDON, | Printed for *Richard Royston* at the | Angel in *Ivie-Lane.* | MDCL.

Coll.: 12mo: ¶^{12} A–R^{12} S^{2}, 218 leaves; plates 1 (Johnson: Vaughan No. 11 before ¶3). Paged A1^{r}–S1^{v}: pp. 1–410.

Contents: ¶1–¶2, blank; ¶3^{r}, title-page (verso blank); ¶4^{r}–¶10^{r}, dedication to the Earl of Carbery; ¶10^{v}–¶12^{v}, the table; A1^{r}–S1^{v}, text; S2^{r}, colophon, '[row of ornaments] | LONDON, | Printed by *R. Norton.* | MDCL. | [row of ornaments]' (verso blank).

2. The Second Edition. 1651. Wing T372. Yale University Library copy.

Title: THE RVLE | AND | EXERCISES | OF | HOLY LIVING. | *In which are described* | The MEANS and INSTRUMENTS | of obtaining every Vertue, and the | Remedies against every Vice, and | Considerations serving to the | resisting all temptations. | Together with | Prayers containing the whole duty of | A Christian, and the parts of Devotion | fitted to all Occasions, and furnish'd | for all Necessities. | [rule] | [ornament] | [rule] | LONDON, | Printed for *Richard Royston* at the | Angel in *Ivie-Lane.* | MDCLI.

Coll.: 12mo: ¶^{12} (–¶1) A–S^{12}, 228 leaves; plates 1 (Johnson: Vaughan No. 11 before ¶2). Paged A1^{r}–S10^{v}: pp. 1–428.

Contents: ¶2^{r}, title-page (verso blank); ¶3^{r}–¶9^{r}, dedication to the Earl of Carbery; ¶9^{v}–¶12^{v}, the table; A1^{r}–S10^{v}, text; S11, blank; S12^{r}, advertisement (verso blank).

Notes: The title-page of this copy omits stating the edition. In other copies of this edition, the statement '*The Seeond* [sic] *Edition*' is added after line 16 of the title.

3. The Third Edition. 1651. Wing T372. Northern Illinois University Library copy.

Title: THE RVLE | AND | EXERCISES | OF | HOLY LIVING. | *In which are described* | The MEANES and INSTRUMENTS | of obtaining every Vertue, and the | Remedies against every Vice, and | Considerations serving to the | resisting all temptations. | Together with | Prayers containing the whole duty of | A Christian, and the parts of Devotion | fitted to all Occasions, and furnish'd | for all Necessities. | *The second Edition.* | [rule] | [ornament] | [rule] | LONDON, | Printed for *Richard Royston* at the | Angel in *Ivie-Lane.* | MDCLI.

Coll.: As in No. 2 above.

Contents: As in No. 2 above.

4. The Fourth Edition. 1654. Wing T373. Cambridge University Library copy.

Title: THE | *RULE* and *EXERCISES* | OF | Holy Living. | *In which are described* | The *Means* and *Instruments* of obtain- | ing every Virtue, and the *Remedies* against | every Vice, and *Considerations* serving | to the resisting all Temptations. | *Together with* | PRAYERS containing the whole duty of a | Christian, and the parts of Devotion fitted to | all Occasions, and furnished for all Necessities. | [rule] | By JER: TAYLOR, D.D. | [rule] | The 4th Edition corrected: | with Additionals. | [double rule] | *LONDON.* | Printed for *Richard Royston* at the Angel | in Ivie-lane. 1654.

Coll.: 12mo: A–T[12] U[6], 234 leaves; plates 1 (before B1). Paged B1[r]–U4[r]: pp. 1–439.

Contents: A1, blank; A2[r], engraved half-title (verso blank); A3[r], title-page (verso blank); A4[r]–A9[v], dedication to the Earl of Carbery; A10[r]–A12[v], the table; B1[r]–U4[r], text; U4[v]–U6[r], advertisement of books published by Royston; U6[v], blank.

5. The Fifth Edition. 1656. Wing T374. Cambridge University Library copy.

Title: THE | *RULE* and *EXERCISES* | OF | Holy Living. | *In which are described* | The *Means* and *Instruments* of obtain- | ing every Virtue, and the *Remedies* against | every Vice, and *Considerations* serving | to the resisting all Temptations. | *Together with* | PRAYERS containing the whole duty of a | Christian, and the parts of Devotion fitted to | all Occasians, and furnished for all Necessities. | [rule] | By JER: TAYLOR, D.D. | [rule] | The 5th Edition corrected: | With Additionals. | [double rule] | *LONDON.* | Printed for *Richard Royston* at the Angel | in Ivie-lane. 1656.

Coll.: As in No. 4 above.

Contents: As in No. 4 above.

Note: This copy lacks leaves C9–C12, pp. 41–8.

6. The Sixth Edition. 1660. No Wing number. Northern Illinois University Library copy.

Title: THE | *RULE* and *EXERCISES* | OF | Holy Living. | *In which are described* | The *Means* and *Instruments* of obtain- | ing every Vertue, and the *Remedies* against | every Vice, and *Considerations* serving | to the resisting all Temptations. | *Together with* | PRAYERS containing the whole duty of a | Christian, and the parts of Devotion fitted to | all Occasions, and furnished for all Necessities. | [rule] | By JER: TAYLOR, D.D. | [rule] | The sixth Edition corrected, | With Additionals. | [double rule] | LONDON, | Printed for *Richard Royston* at the Angel | in Ivie-lane. 1660.

Coll.: 12mo: A–T[12] U[6], 234 leaves; plates 1 (before B1). Paged B1[r]–U4[r]: pp. 1–439.

Contents: A1, blank; A2[r], blank; A2[v], frontispiece; A3[r], title-page (verso blank); A4[r]–A9[v], dedication to the Earl of Carbery; A10[r]–A12[v], the table; B1[r]–U4[r], text; U4[v]–U5[v], advertisement; U6[r], '[band of ornaments] | [rule] | THE | RULE and EXERCISES | OF | Holy Dying. | [rule] | [band of ornaments]' (verso blank).

7. The Seventh Edition. 1663. Wing T375. Yale University Library copy.

Title: [all within double rules] THE | *Rule* and *Exercises* | OF | Holy Living. | *In which are described* | The MEANS and INSTRUMENTS of obtai- | ning every Vertue, and the Remedies against every | Vice, and *Considerations* serving to the resisting | all Temptations. | *Together with* | PRAYERS | *Containing* | The whole duty of a *Christian*, | and the parts of *Devotion* fitted to all Occasions, | and furnished for all Necessities. | [rule] | By JER. TAYLOR, D.D. | [rule] | The Seventh Edition. | [rule] |*LONDON*, | Printed by *James Flesher* for *Richard Royston*, | Bookseller to His most Sacred MAJESTIE. | [centred rule] | MDCLXIII.

Coll.: 8vo: A–Y[8], 176 leaves. Plates 1 (before B1). Pages B1[r]–Y8[r]: pp. 1–335.

Contents: A1[r], half-title 'THE | *Rule* and *Exercises* | OF | Holy Living.'; A1[v], frontispiece; A2[r], title-page (verso blank); A3[r]–A6[v], dedication to the Earl of Carbery; A7[r]–A8[v], contents; B1[r]–Y8[r], text; Y8[v], blank.

8. The Eighth Edition. 1668. Wing T376. Yale University Library copy.

Title: [all within double rules] THE | *Rule* and *Exercises* | OF | Holy Living. | *In which are described* | The MEANS and INSTRUMENTS of obtai- | ning every Vertue, and the *Remedies* against every | Vice, and *Considerations* serving to the resisting | all Temptations. | *Together with* | PRAYERS | Containing | The whole duty of a *Christian*, | and the parts of *Devotion* fitted to all Occasions, | and furnished for all Necessities. | [rule] | By JER. TAYLOR D.D. | [rule] | The Eighth Edition. | [rule] |*LONDON*, | Printed by *Roger Norton* for *Richard Royston*, | Bookseller to His most Sacred Majesty. | MDCLXVIII.

Coll.: As in No. 7 above.

Contents: As in No. 7 above.

7. Engraved title-page of the first edition, 1650. Johnson, *Catalogue*, Vaughan, 11.

THE RVLE
AND
EXERCISES
OF
HOLY LIVING.

In which are described

The MEANS and INSTRUMENTS of obtaining every Vertue, and the Remedies against every Vice, and Considerations serving to the resisting all temptations.

Together with

Prayers containing the whole duty of A Christian, and the parts of Devotion fitted to all Occasions, and furnish'd for all Necessities.

LONDON,
Printed for *Francis Ash*, Book-Seller in *Worcester*.
MDCL.

8. Printed title-page of the first edition, 1650, the State II imprint.

THE RULE
AND
EXERCISES
OF
HOLY LIVING

In which are described
The Means and Instruments
of obtaining every Vertue, and the
Remedies against every Vice, and
Considerations serving to the
resisting all temptations

Together with
Prayers containing the whole duty of
A Christian, and the parts of Devotion
fitted to all Occasions and furnished
for all Necessities.

LONDON,
Printed for *Richard Royston* at the
Angel in *Ivie-Lane.*
MDCL.

The Epistle Dedicatory.

To the right Honourable and truly Noble
Richard Lord Vaughan,
Earl of *Carbery*, Baron of *Emlin*, and
Molingar, Knight of the honourable
Order of the Bath.

My Lord,

I have lived to see Religion painted upon Banners, and thrust out of Churches, and the Temple turned into a Tabernacle, and that Tabernacle made ambulatory, and covered with skins of Beasts and torn Curtains, and God to be worshipped not as he is the *Father of our Lord Jesus* (an afflicted Prince, the King of sufferings) nor, as *the God of peace* (which two appellatives God newly took upon him in the New Testament, and glories in for ever:) but he is owned now rather as the *Lord of Hosts*, which title he was pleased to lay aside when the Kingdom of the Gospel was preached by the Prince of peace. But when Religion puts on Armor, and God is not acknowledged by his New Testament titles, Religion may have in it the power of the Sword, but not the power of Godliness; and we may complain of this to God, and amongst them that are afflicted, but we have no remedy, but what we must expect from the fellowship of Christs sufferings, and the returns of the God of peace. In the mean time, and now that Religion pretends to stranger actions upon new principles; and men are apt to prefer a prosperous errour before an afflicted truth; and some will think they are religious enough if their worshippings have in them the prevailing ingredient; and the Ministers of Religion are so scattered that they cannot unite to stop the inundation, and from Chaires or Pulpits, from their Synods or Tribunals, chastise the iniquity of the errour and the ambition of evil Guides, and the infidelity of the willingly seduced multitude; and that those few good people who have no other plot in their religion but to serve God and save their soules, do want such assistances of ghostly counsel as may serve their emergent needs, and assist their endeavours in the acquist of vertues, and relieve their dangers when they are tempted to sinne and death, I thought I had reasons enough inviting me to draw into one body those advices which the severall necessities

4–5 Baron of *Emlin*, and *Molingar*,] *om* 4+

of many men must use at some time or other, and many of them, daily: that by a collection of holy precepts they might lesse feel the want of personall and attending Guides, and that the rules for conduct of soules might be committed to a Book which they might alwayes have; since they could not alwayes have a Prophet at their needs, nor be suffered to go up to the house of the Lord to inquire of the appointed Oracles.

I know, my Lord, that there are some interested persons who adde scorn to the afflictions of the Church of ENGLAND, and because she is afflicted by Men, call her *forsaken of the Lord*, and because her solemn assemblies are scattered, think that the Religion is lost, and the Church divorced from God, supposing CHRIST (who was a Man of sorrows) to be angry with his Spouse when she is like him, (for that's the true state of the Errour) and that he who promised his Spirit to assist his servants in their troubles, will, because they are in trouble take away the *Comforter* from them, who cannot be a comforter, but while he cures our sadnesses, and relieves our sorrowes, and turnes our persecutions into joyes, and Crowns, and Scepters. But concerning the present state of the Church of *England*, I consider, that because we now want the blessings of external communion in many degrees, and the circumstances of a prosperous and unafflicted people, we are to take estimate of our selves with single judgements, and every Man is to give sentence concerning the state of his own soul by the precepts and rules of our *Lawgiver*, not by the after decrees and usages of the Church, that is, by the essential parts of Religion rather than by the uncertain significations of any exteriour adherencies: for though it be uncertain, when a Man is the Member of a Church, whether he be a Member of Christ or no, because in the Churches Net there are fishes good and bad; yet we may be sure that if we be Members of Christ, we are of a Church to all purposes of spiritual religion and salvation: and in order to this give me leave to speak this great truth.

That Man does certainly belong to God, who 1 Believes and is baptized into all the Articles of the Christian faith, and studies to improve his knowledge in the matters of God, so as may best make him to live a holy life. 2 He that in obedience to Christ worships God diligently, frequently, and constantly with natural Religion, that is, of prayer, praises, and thanksgiving. 3 He that takes all opportunities to remember Christs death by a frequent Sacrament (as it can be had) or else by inward acts of understanding, will, and memory (which is the spiritual communion) supplies the want of the external rite. 4 He that lives chastly. 5 And is merciful. 6 And despises the World, using it as a Man, but never suffering it to rifle a duty. 7 And is just in his dealing, and diligent in his calling. 8 He that is humble in his spirit. 9 And obedient to Government. 10 And content in his fortune and imployment. 11 He that does his duty because he loves God. 12 And especially if after all this he be afflicted, and patient, or prepared to suffer affliction for the cause of God. The Man that hath these twelve signes of grace and predestination does as certainly belong to *God*, and is his Son, as surely as he is his creature.

And if my brethren in persecution, and *in the bands of the Lord Jesus* can truly shew these markes, they shall not need be troubled that others can shew a prosperous outside, great revenues, publick assemblies, uninterrupted successions of Bishops, prevailing Armies, or any arme of flesh, or lesse certain circumstance. These are the markes of the Lord Jesus, and the characters of a Christian: This is a good Religion: and these things Gods grace hath put into our powers, and Gods Lawes have made to be our duty, and the nature of Men, and the needs of Common-wealths have made to be necessary: the other accidents and pomps of a Church are things without our power, and are not in our choice; they are good to be used when they may be had, and they help to illustrate or advantage it: but if any of them constitute a Church in the being of a society and a Government, yet they are not of its constitution as it is Christian, and hopes to be saved.

And now the case is so with us that we are reduced to that Religion which no Man can forbid; which we can keep in the midst of a persecution; by which the Martyrs in the dayes of our Fathers went to Heaven; that by which we can be servants of God, and receive the Spirit of Christ, and make use of his comforts, and live in his love, and in charity with all men; and they that do so cannot perish.

My Lord, I have now described some general lines and features of that Religion which I have more particularly set down in the following pages: in which I have neither served nor disserved the interest of any party of Christians as they are divided by uncharitable names from the rest of their brethren; and no Man will have reason to be angry with me for refusing to mingle in his unnecessary or vitious quarrels: especially while I study to doe him good by conducting him in the narrow way to Heaven, without intricating him in the Labyrinths and wilde turnings of Questions, and uncertaine talkings. I have told what Men ought to do; and by what means they may be assisted; and in most cases I have also told them why; and yet with as much quicknesse as I could thinke necessary to establish a Rule, and not to ingage in Homily or Discourse. In the use of which Rules (although they are plain, useful, and fitted for the best, and for the worst understandings, and for the needs of all men, yet) I shall desire the Reader to proceed with the following advices.

1. They that will with profit make use of the proper instruments of vertue, must so live, as if they were alwayes under the Physicians hand. For the Counsels of Religion are not to be applyed to the distempers of the soul, as men use to take Hellebore; but they must dwell together with the Spirit of a man, and be twisted about his understanding for ever: They must be used like nourishment; that is, by a daily care and meditation; not like a single medicine, and upon the actual pressure of a present necessity. For counsels and wise discourses applyed to an actual distemper, at the best are but like strong smels to an Epileptick person, sometimes they may raise him, but they never cure him. The following rules if they be made familiar to our natures, and the thoughts of every day, may make Vertue and Religion become easy and habitual: but when the temptation is present, and hath already seized upon some portions of our consent, we are not so apt to be counselled, and we finde no gust or relish in the Precept: the lessons are the same, but the instrument is unstrung, or out of tune.

2. In using the instruments of vertue we must be curious to distinguish instruments from duties; and prudent advices from necessary injunctions; and if by any other means the duty can be secured, let there be no scruples stirred concerning any other helps; onely, if they can in that case strengthen and secure the duty, or help towards perseverance, let them serve in that station in which they can be placed. For there are some persons in whom the Spirit of God hath breathed so bright a flame of love, that they do all their acts of vertue by perfect choice, and without objection; and their zeal is warmer than that it will be allayed by temptation: and to such persons mortification by Philosophical instruments, as fasting, sack cloth, and other rudenesses to the body is wholly useless: It is alwayes a more uncertain means to acquire any vertue, or secure any duty; and if love hath filled all the corners of our soul, it alone is able to do all the work of God.

3. Be not nice in stating the obligations of Religion; but where the duty is necessary, and the means very reasonable in it self, dispute not too busily whether in all Circumstances it can fit thy particular; but *super totam materiam*, upon the whole, make use of it. For it is a good signe of a great Religion, and no imprudence when we have sufficiently

considered the substance of affairs, than to be easy, humble, obedient, apt and credulous in the circumstances which are appointed to us in particular by our spiritual Guides, or in general, by all wise men in cases not unlike. He that gives Almes, does best, not alwayes to consider the minutes and strict measures of his ability, but to give freely, incuriously and abundantly. A man must not weigh grains in the accounts of his repentance; but for a great sinne have a great sorrow, and a great severity; and in this take the ordinary advices; though it may be, a lesse rigour might not be insufficient: ἀκϱιβοδίκαιον, or Arithmeticall measures, especially of our own proportioning, are but arguments of want of Love, and of forwardnesse in Religion; or else are instruments of scruple, and then become dangerous. Use the rule heartily and enough, and there will be no harme in thy errour, if any should happen.

4. If thou intendest heartily to serve God, and avoid sinne in any one instance, refuse not the hardest and most severe advice that is prescribed in order to it, though possibly it be a stranger to thee; for whatsoever it be, custome will make it easy.

5. When many instruments for the obtaining any vertue or restraining any vice are propounded, observe which of them fits thy person, or the circumstances of thy need, and use it rather than the other: that by this means thou mayest be engaged to watch and use spiritual arts and observation about thy soul. Concerning the managing of which as the interest is greater, so the necessities are more, and the cases more intricate, and the accidents and dangers greater and more importunate; and there is greater skill required than in the securing an estate, or restoring health to an infirme body. I wish all men in the world did heartily believe so much of this as is true; it would very much help to do the work of God.

Thus (My Lord) I have made bold by your hand to reach out this little scroll of cautions to all those who by seeing your honoured name set before my Book, shall by the fairnes of such a Frontispiece be invited to look into it. I must confess it cannot but look like a designe in me, to borrow your name and beg your Patronage to my book, that if there be no other worth in it, yet at least it may have the splendour and warmth of a burning glasse, which borrowing a flame from the Eye of Heaven, shines and burns by the rayes of the Sun its patron. I will not quit my self from the suspicion: for I cannot pretend it to be a present either of it self fit to be offered to such a Personage, or any part of a just return, (but I humbly desire you would own it for an acknowledgement) of those great endearments, and noblest usages you have past upon me: But so, men in their Religion, give a piece of Gum, or the fat of a cheap Lamb in Sacrifice to him that gives them all that they have or need: and unlesse He who was pleased to imploy your Lordship as a great Minister of his Providence in making a Promise of his good to me, the meanest of his servants (*that he would never leave me nor forsake me*) shall enable me by greater services of Religion to pay my great Debt to your Honour, I must still increase my score; since I shall now spend as much in my needs of pardon for this boldnesse, as in the reception of those favours by which I stand accountable to your Lordship in all the bands of service and gratitude; though I am in the deepest sense of duty and affection——

My most Honoured Lord,
Your Honours most obliged and
Most Humble Servant
TAYLOR.

13 *Honoured*] *Honorable* 2 3   17 *TAYLOR*] *JER*: ~ 4+

THE TABLE

3 and means] *om 2 3*   6 our] *om 4 5 6*

13 *The 19*] *ed, The 18 1+*

The
Rule and Exercises
of
Holy Living, etc.

CHAP. I.

Consideration of the general instruments, and means serving to a holy life: by way of introduction.

IT IS necessary that every Man should consider, that since God hath given him an excellent nature, wisdom and choice, an understanding soul, and an immortal spirit, having made him Lord over the Beasts, and but a little lower than the Angels; he hath also appointed for him a work and a service great enough to imploy those abilities, and hath also designed him to a state of life after this, to which he can onely arrive by that service and obedience. And therefore as every man is wholly Gods own portion by the title of creation: so all our labours and care, all our powers and faculties must be wholly imployed in the service of God, even all the dayes of our life, that this life being ended, we may live with him for ever.

Neither is it sufficient that we think of the service of God as a work of the least necessity, or of small imployment; but that it be done by us as God intended it; that it be done with great earnestnesse and passion, with much zeal and desire: that we refuse no labour, that we bestow upon it much time, that we use the best guides, and arrive at the end of glory by all the wayes of grace, of prudence and religion.

And indeed if we consider how much of our lives is taken up by the needs of nature, how many years are wholly spent before we come to any use of reason, how many years more before that reason is useful to us to any great purposes, how imperfect our discourse is made by our evil education, false principles, ill company, bad examples, and want of experience; how many parts of our wisest and best years are spent in eating and sleeping, in necessary businesses, and unnecessary vanities, in worldly civilities, and lesse useful circumstances, in the learning arts and sciences, languages or trades; that little portion of hours that is left for the practises of piety, and religious walking with God, is so short and trifling, that were not the goodnesse of God infinitely great, it might seem unreasonable or impossible for us to expect of him eternal joyes in heaven, even after the well spending those few minutes which are left for God, and Gods service, after we have served our selves, and our own occasions.

And yet it is considerable, that the fruit which comes from the many dayes of recreation and vanity is very little, and although we scatter much, yet we gather but little profit: but from the few hours we spend in prayer and the exercises of a pious life, the return is great and profitable; and what we sowe in the minutes and spare portions of a few years, grows up to crowns and scepters in a happy and a glorious eternity.

1. Therefore, although it cannot be enjoyned, that the greatest part of our time be spent in the direct actions of devotion and religion, [a]yet it will become, not onely a duty, but also a great providence to lay aside for the services of God, and the businesses of the Spirit as much as we can: because God rewards our minutes with long and eternal happinesses; and the greater portion of our time we give to God, the more we treasure up for our selves; and *No man is a better Merchant than he that layes out his time upon God, and his money upon the Poor.*

2. Onely it becomes us to remember and to adore Gods goodnesse for it, that God hath not onely permitted us to serve the necessities of our nature, but hath made them to become parts of our duty; [b]that if we by directing these actions to the glory of God intend them as instruments to continue our persons in his service, he by adopting them into religion may turn our nature into grace, and accept our natural actions, as actions of religion. [c]God is pleased to esteem it for a part of his service, if we eat or drink; so it be done temperately, and as may best preserve our health, that our health may enable our services towards him: And there is no one minute of our lives (after we are come to the use of reason) but we are, or may be doing the work of God, even then when we most of all serve our selves.

3. [d]To which if we adde, that in these and all other actions of our

[a] Care to set apart Time for Gods service.

[b] To intend and direct Our Actions to Gods glorie and service.

[c] *Πυθομένου τινὸς, πῶς ἔστιν ἐσθίειν ἀρεστῶς θεοῖς; εἰ δικαίως ἐστὶν, ἔφη, καὶ εὐγνωμόνως, καὶ ἴσως, καὶ ἐγκρατῶς, καὶ κοσμίως, οὐκ ἔστι καὶ ἀρεστῶς τοῖς θεοῖς;* Arrian. Epict. l. 1. c. 13.

[d] Consider we are always in Gods providence.

---

15 [a]] *KC, om 1+* 24 [b]] *KC, om 1+* 34 [d]] *KC, om 1+*

lives we always stand before God, acting, and speaking and thinking in his presence, and that it matters not that our conscience is sealed with secresie, since it lies open to God, it will concern us to behave our selves carefully, as in the presence of our Judge.

These three considerations rightly managed, and applyed to the several parts and instances of our lives, will be like *Elisha* stretched upon the childe, apt to put life and quicknesse into every part of it, and to make us live the life of grace, and do the work of God.

I shall therefore by way of introduction reduce these three to practise, and shew how every Christian may improve all and each of these to the advantage of piety, in the whole course of his life: that if he please to bear but one of them upon his spirit, he may feel the benefit, like an universal instrument, helpful in all spiritual and temporal actions.

SECT. I.

The first general instrument of holy living: Care of our time.

He that is choice of his time will also be choice of his company, and choice of his actions, lest the first ingage him in vanity and losse, and the latter by being criminal be a throwing his time and himself away, and a going back in the accounts of eternity.

God hath given to man a short time here upon earth, and yet upon this short time eternity depends: but so, that for every hour of our life (after we are persons capable of laws, and know good from evil) we must give account to the great Judge of Men and Angels. And this is it which our blessed Saviour told us, that we must account for *every idle word*; not meaning, that every word which is not designed to edification, or is less prudent, shall be reckoned for a sin, but that besides our sinful and hurtful, our tempting or malicious language, even the time which we spend in our idle talking and unprofitable discoursings, that time which might and ought to have been imployed to spiritual and useful purposes, that is to be accounted for.

For we must remember, that we have a great work to do, many enemies to conquer, many evils to prevent, much danger to run through, many difficulties to be mastered, many necessities to serve, and much good to do, many children to provide for, or many friends to

27–8 besides our sinful and hurtful, our tempting or malicious language, even] *23, om 14+*

support, or many poor to relieve, or many diseases to cure, besides the needs of nature, and of relation, our private and our publick cares, and duties of the world, which necessity and the Providence of God hath adopted into the family of *Religion.*

And that we need not fear this instrument to be a snare to us, or that the duty must end in scruple, vexation, and eternal fears, we must remember, that the life of every man may be so ordered (and indeed must,) that it may be a perpetual serving of God: The greatest trouble and most busy trade, and worldly incombrances, when they are necessary or charitable, or profitable in order to any of those ends, which we are bound to serve whether publick or private, being a doing Gods work. For God provides the good things of the world to serve the needs of nature, by the labours of the Plowman, the skill and pains of the Artisan, and the dangers and traffick of the Merchant: These men are in their callings the Ministers of the Divine providence, and the stewards of the creation, and servants of the great family of God, *the World*, in the imployment of procuring necessaries for food and clothing, ornament and Physick. In their proportions also, a King and a Priest, and a Prophet, a Judge and an Advocate, doing the works of their imployment according to their proper rules, are doing the work of God, because they serve those necessities which God hath made, and yet made no provisions for them but by their Ministery. So that no man can complain, that his calling takes him off from religion, his calling itself and his very worldly imployment, in honest trades and offices, is a serving of God, and if it be moderately pursued, and according to the rules of Christian prudence, will leave void spaces enough for prayers and retirements of a more spiritual religion.

God hath given every man work enough to do, that there shall be no room for idlenesse, and yet hath so ordered the world, that there shall be space for devotion. He that hath the fewest businesses of the world, is called upon to spend more time in the dressing of his soul, and he that hath the most affairs, may so order them, that they shall be a service of God; whilst at certain periods they are blessed with prayers and actions of religion, and all day long are hallowed by a holy intention.

However, so long as Idlenesse is quite shut out from our lives, all the sins of wantonnesse, softnesse and effeminacy are prevented, and

16–17 the great] a great 5+

there is but little room left for temptation: and therefore to a busie man temptation is fain to climbe up together with his businesses, and sins creep upon him onely by accidents and occasions; whereas to an idle person they come in a full body, and with open violence, and the impudence of a restlesse importunity.

Idlenesse is called [e] *the sin of Sodom and her daughters*, and indeed is [f] *the burial of a living man*, an idle person being so uselesse to any purposes of God and man, that he is like one that is dead, unconcerned in the changes and necessities of the world: and he onely lives to spend his time, and eat the fruits of the earth, like vermin or a wolf, when their time comes they dye and perish, and in the mean time do no good; they neither plow nor carry burdens: all that they do, either is unprofitable, or mischievous.

Idlenesse is the greatest prodigality in the world: it throwes away that, which is invaluable in respect of its present use, and irreparable when it is past, being to be recovered by no power of art or nature. But the way to secure and improve our time we may practise in the following rules.

Rules for imploying our Time.

1. In the morning, when you awake, accustome your self to *think first upon God*, or something in order to his service; and at night also, let him close thine eyes; and let your sleep be necessary and healthful, not idle and expensive of time, beyond the needs and conveniencies of nature; and sometimes be curious to see the preparation which the sun makes, when he is coming forth from his chambers of the East.

2. Let every man that hath a calling, be *diligent* in pursuance of its imployment, so as not lightly, or without reasonable occasion to neglect it in any of those times, which are usually and by the custome of prudent persons and good husbands imployed in it.

3. Let all the *Intervals*, or void spaces of time be imployed in prayers, reading, meditating, works of nature, recreation, charitie, friendlinesse and neighbourhood, and means of spiritual and corporal health: ever remembering, so to work in our calling, as not to neglect the work of our *high calling*; but to begin and end the day with God, with such forms of devotion, as shall be proper to our necessities.

4. The resting dayes of Christians, and *Festivals* of the Church must

[e] Ezekiel 16: 49. [f] Seneca.

10 vermin] a ~ *4*+

in no sense be dayes of idlenesse: for it is in itself better to plow upon holy dayes, than to do nothing, or to do vitiously; but let them be spent in the works of the day; [g]that is, of Religion and Charity, according to the rules appointed.

5. Avoid the company of *Drunkards* and *busie-bodies*, and all such as are apt to talk much to little purpose: for no man can be provident of his time, that is not prudent in the choice of his company: and if one of the Speakers be vain, tedious and trifling, he that hears, and he that answers in the discourse are equal losers of their time.

6. Never talk with any man, or undertake any trifling imployment *meerly to passe the time away*: for [h]every day well spent may become a *day of salvation*, and time rightly employed is *an acceptable time*. And remember, that the time thou triflest away was given thee to repent in, to pray for pardon of sins, to work out thy salvation, to do the work of grace, to lay up against the day of Judgement, a treasure of good works, that thy time may be crowned with Eternity.

7. In the midst of the works of thy calling [i]often retire to God in *short prayers* and ejaculations, and those may make up the want of those larger portions of time, which it may be thou desirest for devotion, and in which thou thinkest other persons have advantage of thee: for so thou reconcilest the outward work, and thy inward calling, the Church and the Commonwealth, the imployment of thy body and the interest of thy soul; for be sure, that God is present at thy breathings and hearty sighings of prayer assoon, as at the longer offices of lesse busied persons; and thy time is as truely sanctified by a trade, and devout, though shorter prayers, as by the longer offices of those whose time is not filled up with labour and useful businesse.

8. Let your imployment be such as may become a reasonable person; and not be a businesse fit for children or distracted people; but fit *for your age and understanding*. For a man may be very idlely busy, and take great pains to so little purpose, that in his labors and expence of time he shall serve no end but of folly, and vanity. There are some Trades, that wholly serve the ends of idle persons and fools; and such as are fit to be seized upon by the severity of laws, and banisht from

[g] See Chap. 4. Sect. 6.

[h] S. Bern. de triplici custodia.

[i] Laudatur Augustus Cæsar apud Lucanum.

—media inter prælia semper
Stellarum cœlique plagis, superisque vacabat.

1 in itself] *2 3, om 1 4+* 22–3 thy body] the body *5+*

under the sun: and there are some people who are busy, but it is as *Domitian* was, in catching flyes.

9. Let your imployment be fitted to *your person and calling.* Some there are that imploy their time in affairs infinitely below the dignity of their person, and being called by God, or by the Republick to help to bear great burdens, and to judge a people, do enfeeble their understandings, and disable their persons by sordid and bruitish businesse. Thus *Nero* went up and down *Greece*, and challenged the Fidlers at their trade. *Æropus* a Macedonian King made Lanterns. *Harcatius* the King of *Parthia* was a Mole-catcher: and *Biantes* the Lydian filed needles. He that is appointed to minister in holy things, must not suffer secular affairs and sordid arts to eat up great portions of his imployment: a Clergy man must not keep a Tavern, nor a Judge be an Inne-keeper; and it was a great idlenesse in *Theophylact* the Patriarch of C. P. to spend his time in his stable of horses, when he should have been in his study, or the Pulpit, or saying his holy offices. Such imployments are the diseases of labour, and the rust of time which it contracts, not by lying still, but by dirty imployment.

10. Let your imployment be such *as becomes a Christian*, that is, in no sence mingled with sin; for he that takes pains to serve the ends of covetousnesse, or ministers to anothers lust, or keeps a shop of impurities or intemperance, is idle in the worse sence; for every hour so spent runs him backward, and must be spent again in the remaining and shorter part of his life, and spent better.

11. Persons of *great quality*, and *of no trade*, are to be most prudent and curious in their imployment and traffick of time. They are miserable, if their education hath been so loose and undisciplined, as to leave them unfurnished of skill to spend their time: but most miserable are they, if such misgovernment and unskilfulnesse make them fall into vitious and baser company, and drive on their time by the sad minutes and periods of sin and death. They that are *learned* know the worth of time, and the manner how well to improve a day; and they are to prepare themselves for such purposes, in which they may be most useful in order to arts and arms: to counsel in publick, or government in their Countrey: But for others of them that are *unlearned*, let them choose good company, such as may not tempt them to a vice, or joyn with them in any; but that may supply their defects by counsel and discourse, by way of conduct or conversation. Let them learn easy and

19 your] our 5+ 38 or] and 5+

useful things, read history, and the laws of the Land, learn the customs of their Countrey, the condition of their own estate, profitable and charitable contrivances of it: let them study prudently to govern their families, learn the burdens of their Tenants, the necessities of their neighbours, and in their proportion supply them, and reconcile their enmities, and prevent their Law-suits, or quickly end them and in this glut of leisure and disimployment, let them set apart greater portions of their time for religion, and the necessities of their Souls.

12. Let the *women of noble birth* and great fortunes do the same things in their proportions and capacities, nurse their children, look to the affairs of the house, visit poor cottages, and relieve their necessities, be curteous to the neighbourhood, learn in silence of their husbands, or their spiritual Guides, read good books, pray often, and speak little, and *learn to do good works for necessary uses*, for by that phrase S. *Paul* expresses the obligation of Christian women to good houswifery, and charitable provisions for their family and neighbourhood.

13. Let all persons of *all conditions* avoid all delicacy and nicenesse in their *clothing* or *diet*, because such softnesse engages them upon great mispendings of their time, while they dresse and combe out all their opportunities of their morning devotion, and half the dayes severity, and sleep out the care and provision for their Souls.

14. Let every one of every condition avoid *curiosity*, and all enquiry into things that concern them not. For all businesse in things that concern us not, is an imploying our time to no good of ours, and therefore not in order to a happy Eternity. In this account our neighbours necessities are not to be reckoned; for they concern us as one member is concerned in the grief of another; but going from house to house, tatlers, and busie-bodies, which are the canker and rust of idlenesse, as idlenesse is the rust of time, are reprooved by the Apostle in severe language, and forbidden in order to this exercise.

15. As much as may be, cut off all *impertinent and uselesse imployments* of your life, unnecessary and phantastick visits, long waitings upon great personages, where neither duty nor necessity, nor charity obliges us, all vain meetings, all laborious trifles, and whatsoever spends much time to no real, civil, religious, or charitable purpose.

16. Let not your *recreations* be lavish spenders of your time, but choose such which are healthful, short, transient, recreative, and apt to refresh you; but at no hand *dwell* upon them, or make them your

24 concern] *4+*, concerns *1 2 3*

great imployment: for he that spends his time in sports, and calls it recreation, is like him, whose garment is all made of fringes, and his meat nothing but sawces, they are healthlesse, chargeable and uselesse. And therefore avoid such games which require much time or long attendance; or which are apt to steal thy affections from more severe imployments. For to whatsoever thou hast given thy affections, thou wilt not grudge to give thy time. Natural necessity and the example of [j]S. *John* (who recreated himself with sporting with a tame Partridge) teach us that it is lawful to relax and unbend our bow, but not to suffer it to be unready or unstrung.

17. Set apart some portions of every day for *more solemn devotion* and religious imployment, which be *severe* in *observing*: and if variety of imployment or prudent affairs, or civil society presse upon you, yet so order thy *rule*, that the necessary parts of it be not omitted; and though just occasions may make your prayers shorter, yet let nothing but a violent, sudden and impatient necessity make thee upon any one day wholly to omit thy morning and evening devotions; which if you be forced to make very short, you may supply and lengthen with ejaculations and short retirements in the day time in the midst of your imployment, or of your company.

18. [k]Do not the *work of God negligently* and idlely: let not thy heart be upon the world, when thy hand is lift up in prayer: and be sure to prefer an action of religion in its place and proper season before all worldly pleasure, letting secular things (that may be dispensed with in themselves,) in these circumstances wait upon the other; not like the Patriarch who ran from the Altar in S. *Sophia* to his stable in all his Pontificals, and in the midst of his office, to see a Colt newly fallen from his beloved and much valued Mare *Phorbante.* More prudent and severe was that of Sir *Thomas More*, who being sent for by the King when he was at his prayers in publick, returned answer, he would attend him when he had first performed his service to the KING of Kings. And it did honour to [l]*Rusticus*, that when Letters from *Cæsar* were given to him, he refused to open them, till the Philosopher had done his Lecture. In honouring God and doing his work, put forth all thy strength, for of that time onely thou mayest be most confident that it is gained, which is prudently and zealously spent in Gods Service.

[j] Cassian. Collat. 24. c. 21.
[k] Jerem. 48: 10.
[l] Plutarch. de Curiosit.

15 your] our 5+

19. When the *Clock strikes*, or however else you shall measure the day, it is good to say a short ejaculation every hour, that the parts and returns of devotion may be the measure of your time; and do so also in all the *breaches* of thy sleep, that those spaces which have in them no direct businesse of the world may be filled with religion.

20. If by thus doing you have not secured your time by an early and forehanded care, [m]yet be sure by a timely diligence *to redeem the time*, that is, to be pious and religious in such instances in which formerly you have sinned, and to bestow your time especially upon such graces, the contrary whereof you have formerly practised, doing actions of chastity and temperance with as great a zeal and earnestnesse as you did once act your uncleannesse: and then, by all arts to watch against your present and future dangers, from day to day securing your standing; this is properly *to redeem your time*, that is, to buy your security of it at the rate of any labour and honest arts.

21. Let him that is most busied [n]set apart some *solemn time every year*, in which, for the time quitting all worldly businesse, he may attend wholly to fasting and prayer, and the dressing of his soul by confessions, meditations and attendances upon God; that he may make up his accounts, renew his vows, make amends for his carelessenesse, and retire back again from whence levity and the vanities of the world, or the importunity of temptations, or the distraction of secular affairs have carried him.

22. In this we shall be much assisted, and we shall finde the work more easie, if before we sleep every night we [o]*examine the actions of the past day* with a particular scrutiny, if there have been any accident extraordinary: as, long discourse, a Feast, much businesse, variety of company: If nothing but common hath happened, the lesse examination will suffice: only let us take care that we sleep not without such a recollection of the actions of the day, as may represent any thing that is remarkable, and great, either to be the matter of sorrow or thanksgiving: for other things, a general care is proportionable.

23. Let all these things be done *prudently and moderately*; not with

[m] *Οἱ ἐν αὐτοῖς εὐδοκιμοῦντες οἷς ἥμαρτον, εὐπρεπεστέραν τὴν ἀπολογίαν εἰσαεὶ φέρονται*. Procop. 2. Vandal.

[n] 1 Cor. 7: 5.

[o] *Μηδ᾽ ὕπνον μαλακοῖσιν ἐπ᾽ ὄμμασι προσδέξασθαι,*
Πρὶν τῶν ἡμερινῶν ἔργων τρὶς ἕκαστον ἐπελθεῖν·
Πῇ παρέβην; τί δ᾽ ἔρεξα; τί μοι δέον οὐκ ἐτελέσθη; Pythag. Carm.

---

4 those spaces which] those which spaces *2*   22 importunity] importunities *3*, opportunity *5*+

scruple and vexation. For these are good advantages, but the particulars are not divine commandements; and therefore are to be used as shall be found expedient to every ones condition. For, provided that our duty be secured; for the degrees and for the instruments, every man is permitted to himself and the conduct of such who shall be appointed to him. He is happy, that can secure every hour to a sober or a pious imployment: but the duty consists not scrupulously in minutes and half hours, but in greater portions of time; provided, that no minute be imployed in sin, and the great portions of our time be spent in sober imployment; and all the appointed dayes and some portions of every day be allowed for Religion. In all the lesser parts of time we are left to our own elections and prudent management, and to the consideration of the great degrees and differences of glory that are laid up in Heaven for us, according to the degrees of our care and piety and diligence.

The benefits of this Exercise.

This exercise, besides that it hath influence upon our whole lives, it hath a special efficacy for the preventing of 1. Beggerly sins, that is, those sins which idlenesse and beggery usually betray men to; such as are lying, flattery, stealing, and dissimulation. 2. It is a proper antidote against carnal sins, and such as proceed from fulnesse of bread and emptinesse of imployment. 3. It is a great instrument of preventing the smallest sins and irregularities of our life, which usually creep upon idle, disimployed, and incurious persons. 4. It not onely teaches us to avoid evil, but ingages us upon *doing good*, as the proper businesse of all our dayes. 5. It prepares us so against *sudden changes*, that we shall not easily be surprized at the sudden coming of the day of the Lord: For he that is curious of his time, will not easily be unready and unfurnished.

SECT. II.

The second general instrument of Holy Living: Purity of intention.

That we should intend and designe Gods glory in every action we do, whether it be natural or chosen, is expressed by [p]S. *Paul, Whether ye eat*

[p] 1 Cor. 10: 31.

24 incurious] curious *4*+

or drink, do all to the glory of God: Which rule, when we observe; every action of nature becomes religious, and every meal is an act of worship, and shall have its reward in its proportion, as well as an act of prayer. Blessed be that goodnesse and grace of God, which out of infinite desire to glorifie and save mankinde, would make the very works of nature capable of becoming acts of vertue, that all our life time we may do him service.

This grace is so excellent, that it sanctifies the most *common action* of our life, and yet so necessary, that without it the very best actions of our devotion are imperfect and vitious. For he that prayes out of custome, or gives almes for praise, or fasts to be accounted religious, is but a Pharisee in his devotion, and a beggar in his alms, and an hypocrite in his fast. But a holy end sanctifies all these, and all other actions which can be made holy and gives distinction to them and procures acceptance.

For, as to know the end, distinguishes a Man from a Beast: so to chuse a good end, distinguishes him from an evil man. *Hezekiah* repeated his good deeds upon his sick bed, and obtained favour of God; but the Pharisee was accounted insolent [q]for doing the same thing: because this man did it to upbraid his brother, the other to obtain a mercy of God. *Zecharias* questioned with the Angel about his message, and was made speechlesse for his incredulity; but the blessed Virgin *Mary* questioned too, and was blamelesse; for she did it to enquire after the *manner* of the thing; but he did not believe the *thing it self*: He doubted of Gods power, or the truth of the Messenger; but she onely of her own incapacity. This was it which distinguished the mourning of *David* from the exclamation of *Saul*: the confession of *Pharaoh* from that of *Manasses*; the tears of *Peter* from the repentance of *Judas*: [r] 'For the praise is not in the deed done, but in the manner of its doing. If a man visits his sick friend, and watches at his pillow for charity sake, and because of his old affection we approve it: but if he does it in hope of legacy, he is a Vulture, and onely watches for the carkasse. The same things are honest and dishonest: the *manner of doing them*, and the *end* of the designe makes the separation.'

Holy intention is to the actions of a man that which the soul is to the body, or form to its matter, or the root to the tree, or the Sun to the

[q] Atticus eximie si cœnat, lautus habetur,
Se Rutilus, demens — Juven. Sat. 11.

[r] Seneca.

19 [q]] *4+*, *om 1 2 3*

World, or the Fountain to a River, or the Base to a Pillar: for without these the body is a dead trunk, the matter is sluggish, the tree is a block, the world is darknesse, the river is quickly dry, the pillar rushes into flatnesse and a ruine; and the action is sinful, or unprofitable and vain. The poor Farmer that gave a dish of cold water to *Artaxerxes* was rewarded with a golden goblet; and he that gives the same present to *a Disciple in the name of a Disciple* shall have a Crown: but if he gives water in despite when the Disciple needs wine or a Cordial, his reward shall be to want that water to cool his tongue. But this duty must be reduced to rules.

Rules for our intentions.

1. In every action reflect upon *the end*; and in your undertaking it, consider *why* you do it, and what you propound *to your self for a reward*, and *to your action as its end.*

2. Begin every action in the Name of the Father, of the Son, and of the Holy Ghost: the meaning of which is, 1. that we be careful, that we do not the action without the permission or warrant of God. 2. That we designe it to the glory of God, if not in the direct action, yet at least in its consequence; if not in the particular, yet at least in the whole order of things and accidents. 3. That it may be so blessed, that what you intend for innocent and holy purposes, may not by any chance or abuse, or misunderstanding of men be turned into evil, or made the occasion of sin.

3. Let every action of concernment be *begun with prayer*, that God would not onely blesse the action, but sanctifie your purpose; and make an oblation of the action to God: holy and well intended actions being the best oblations and presents we can make to God; and when God is entitled to them, he will the rather keep the fire upon the Altar bright and shining.

4. In the prosecution of the action, renew and re-inkindle your purpose by *short ejaculations* to these purposes. *Not unto us, O Lord, not unto us, but unto thy Name let all praise be given*: and consider, *Now I am working the work of God: I am his servant, I am in a happy imployment, I am doing my Masters businesse; I am not at my own dispose, I am using his talents, and all the gain must be his*: for then be sure, as the glory is his, so the reward shall be thine. If thou bringest his goods home with increase, he will make thee ruler over Cities.

6 present] *om 7 8* 15 action] day *3* 16 1.] *7 8, om 1 2 3 4 5 6*

5. Have a care that while the Altar thus sends up a holy fume, thou doest not suffer the birds to come and carry away the Sacrifice: that is, let not that which began well, and was intended for Gods glory, *decline*, and end in thy owne praise, or temporal satisfaction, or a sin. A story told to represent the vilenesse of unchastity is well begun; but if thy female auditor be pleased with thy language, and begins rather to like thy person for thy story, than to dislike the crime: be watchful, lest this goodly head of gold descend in silver and brasse, and end in iron and clay, like *Nebuchadnezzars* image; [s]for from the *end* it shall have its name and reward.

6. If any *accidental event* which was not first intended by thee can come to passe, let it not be taken into thy purposes, nor at all be made use of; as if by telling a true story you can do an ill turn to your enemy, by no means do it; but when the temptation is found out, turn all thine enmity upon that.

7. In every more solemne action of Religion, joyn together *many good ends*, that the consideration of them may entertain all your affections, and that when any one ceases, the purity of your intention may be supported by another supply. He that fasts onely to tame a rebellious body, when he is provided of a remedy either in Grace or Nature, may be tempted to leave off his fasting. But he that in his fast intends the mortification of every unruly appetite, an accustoming himself to bear the yoke of the Lord, a contempt of the pleasures of meat and drink, humiliation of all wilder thoughts, obedience, and humility, austerity and charity, and the convenience and assistance to devotion, and to do an act of repentance; whatever happens, will have reason enough to make him to continue his purpose, and to sanctifie it. And certain it is, the more good ends are designed in an action, the more degrees of excellency the man obtains.

8. If any temptation to spoil your purpose happens in a religious duty, do not presently *omit the action*, but rather strive to rectifie your intention and to mortifie the temptation. S. *Bernard* taught us this rule. For when the Devil observing him to preach excellently, and to do much benefit to his hearers, tempted him to vain glory, hoping that the good man to avoid that, would cease preaching, he gave this answer onely, *I neither began for thee, neither for thee will I make an end.*

9. In all actions which are of *long continuance*, deliberation and

[s] Qui furatur ut mœchetur, mœchus est magis quam fur. Arist. Eth.

14 thine] thy *6+* 22 an] and *6+*

abode, let your holy and pious intention be *actual*, that is, that it be by a special prayer, or action, by a peculiar act of resignation or oblation be given to God: but in smaller actions, and little things, and indifferent, fail not to secure a pious *habitual* intention, that is, that it be included within your general care, that no action have an ill end; and that it be comprehended in your general prayers, whereby you offer your self and all you do to Gods glory.

10. Call not *every temporal end*, a defiling of thy intention, but onely, 1. When it contradicts any of the ends of God, or 2. When it is principally intended in an action of religion. For sometimes a temporal end is part of our duty: and such are all the actions of our calling, whether our imployment be religious or civil. We are commanded to provide for our family: but if the Minister of Divine offices shall take upon him that holy calling for covetous or ambitious ends, or shall not designe the glory of God principally and especially, he hath polluted his hands and his heart; and the fire of the Altar is quenched, or it sends forth nothing but the smoak of mushromes, or unpleasant gums. And it is a great unworthinesse to prefer the interest of a creature before the ends of God the Almighty Creator.

But because many cases may happen in which a mans *heart may deceive him*, and he may not well know what is in his own spirit; therefore by these following signes we shall best make a judgement *whether our intentions be pure, and our purposes holy.*

Signes of purity of intention.

1. It is probable our hearts are right with God, and our intentions innocent and pious, [f]if we set upon actions of religion or civil life with an *affection proportioned* to the quality of the work; that we act our temporal affairs with a desire no greater than our necessity; and that in actions of religion we be zealous, active, and operative, so far as prudence will permit; but in all cases, that we value a religious designe before a temporal; when otherwise they are in equal order to their several ends: that is, that whatsoever is necessary in order to our souls health be higher esteemed than what is for bodily; and the necessities, the indispensable necessities of the spirit be served before the needs of nature, when they are required in their several circumstances: Or plainer yet; when we choose any temporal inconvenience, rather than

[f] See Sect. 1 of this Chapt. Rule 18.

2 oblation] ~ it *2 3* 3 be] *om 5+*

commit a sin, and when we choose to do a duty rather than to get gain. But he that does his recreation, or his merchandise cheerfully, promptly, readily and busily, and the works of religion slowly, flatly, and without appetite, and the spirit moves like *Pharaohs* chariots when the wheels were off, it is a signe that his heart is not right with God, but it cleaves too much to the world.

2. It is likely our hearts are pure, and our intentions spotlesse, when we are *not solicitous* of the *opinion* and censures of men; but onely that we do our duty, and be accepted of God. For our eyes will certainly be fixed there from whence we expect our reward: and if we desire that God should approve us, it is a signe we do his work, and expect him our pay-Master.

3. He that does as well *in private* between God and his own soul *as in publick*, in Pulpits, in Theatres, and Market-places, hath given himself a good testimony that his purposes are full of honesty, noblenesse and integrity. For what *Helkanah* said to the Mother of *Samuel*, *Am not I better to thee than ten sons*? is most certainly verified concerning God: that he, who is to be our Judge, is better than ten thousand witnesses. But he, that would have his vertue published, studies not vertue, but glory. [u]He is not just, that will not be just without praise: but he is a righteous man that does justice, when to do so, is made infamous: and he is a wise man who is delighted with *an ill name* that is *well gotten*. [v]And indeed that man hath a strange covetousnesse, or folly, that is not contented with this reward, that, *He hath pleased God.* And see what he gets by it? [w]He that does good works for praise, or secular ends sells an inestimable jewel for a trifle; and that which would purchase Heaven for him, he parts with for the breath of the people, which at the best is but aire, and that not often wholsome.

4. It is well also when we are not sollicitous or troubled concerning the *effect and event* of all our actions; but that being first by Prayer recommended to him, is left at his dispose: for then in case the event be not answerable to our desires, or to the efficacy of the instrument, we have nothing left to rest in, but the honesty of our purposes; which it is the more likely we have secured, by how much more we are indifferent concerning the successe. S. *James* converted but eight persons when he preached in *Spain*; and our blessed Saviour converted fewer than his own Disciples did: And if thy labours prove unprosperous, it

[u] Seneca. Ep. 113. [v] S. Chrys. l. 2 de compan. cordis.
[w] S. Greg. Moral. 8. cap. 43.

note *w* cap. 43] *cor*, cap. 25 *1*+

thou beest much troubled at that, it is certain thou didst not think thy self secure of a reward for your intention, which you might have done if it had been pure and just.

5. He loves *vertue* for Gods sake and its own, that loves and honours it *wherever* it is to be seen; but he that is *envious* or *angry* at a vertue that is not his own, at the perfection or excellency of his Neighbour, is not covetous of the vertue, but of its reward and reputation, and then his intentions are polluted. It was a great ingenuity in *Moses*, that wished *all the people* might be *prophets*; but if he had designed his own honour, he would have prophecyed alone. But he that desires onely that the work of God and religion shall go on, is pleased with it, who ever is the instrument.

6. He that *despises the world* and all its appendant vanities is the best Judge, and the most secured of his intentions, because he is the furthest removed from a temptation. Every degree of mortification is a testimony of the purity of our purposes, and in what degree we despise sensual pleasure, or secular honours, or worldly reputation, in the *same degree* we shall conclude our heart right to religion and spiritual designes.

7. When we are *not sollicitous* concerning the *instruments* and *means* of our actions, but use those means which God hath laid before us, with resignation, indifferency and thankfulnesse, it is a good signe that we are rather intent upon the ends of Gods glory, than our own conveniency or temporal satisfaction. He that is indifferent whether he serve God in riches or in poverty is rather a seeker of God, than of himself; and he that will throw away a good book, because it is not curiously guilded, is more desirous to please his eye, than to inform his understanding.

8. When a temporal end consisting with a spiritual and pretended to be subordinate to it happens to *fail* and be defeated, if we can *rejoyce* in that, so Gods glory may be secured, and the interests of religion, it is a great signe our hearts are right, and our ends prudently designed and ordered.

When our *intentions* are thus *ballanced*, regulated and discerned, we may consider, 1. That *this exercise* is of so universal efficacy in the whole course of a holy life, that it is like the *soul to every* holy *action*, and must be provided for in every undertaking; and is of it self alone sufficient to make all natural and indifferent actions to be adopted into the family of religion.

18 heart] hearts *3*   31 may] *4+*, *om 1 2 3*

2. That there are some actions, which are usually reckoned as parts of our religion, which yet of themselves are so relative and imperfect, that without the purity of intention they degenerate: and unlesse they be directed and proceed on to those purposes which God designed them to, they return into the family of common, secular, or sinful actions. Thus *almes* are for *charity*: *fasting* for *temperance*: *prayer* is for *religion*: *humiliation* is for *humility*: *austerity* or *sufferance* is in order to the vertue of *patience*; and when these actions fail of their several ends, or are not directed to their own purposes, *alms* are mispent; *fasting* is an impertinent trouble; *prayer* is but lip-labour; *humiliation* is but hypocrisie; *sufferance* is but vexation; for such were the *alms* of the Pharisee, the *fast* of *Jezabel*, the *prayer* of *Judah* reproved by the Prophet *Isaiah*, the *humiliation* of *Ahab*, the *martyrdome* of *Hereticks*; in which nothing is given to God but the body, or *the forms of religion*, but the soul, and *the power of godlinesse* is wholly wanting.

3. We are to consider that *no intention* can *sanctifie* an *unholy* or unlawful action: *Saul* the King disobeyed Gods commandment, and spared the cattel of *Amalek* to reserve the best for sacrifice: and *Saul* the Pharisee persecuted the Church of God with a designe to do God service: and they that kild the Apostles had also good purposes, but they had unhallowed actions: [x]When there is both truth in election and charity in the intention; when we go to God in wayes of his own choosing, or approving, then *our eye is single*, and our hands are clean, and our hearts are pure. But when a man does evil that good may come of it, or good to an evil purpose, that man does like him that rowls himself in thorns that he may sleep easily: he rosts himself in the fire, that he may quench his thirst with his own sweat; he turns his face to the East that he may go to bed with the Sun. I end this with the saying of a wise Heathen. [y]'He is to be called evil that is good onely for his own sake: Regard not how full hands you bring to God, but how pure: Many cease from sin out of fear alone, not out of innocence or love of vertue, and they (as yet) are not to be called innocent, but timerous'.

[x] S. Bern. lib. de præcept.
[y] Publius Mimus.

SECT. III.

The third general instrument of holy living: or the practise of the presence of God.

That God is present in all places, that he sees every action, hears all discourses, and understands every thought, is no strange thing to a Christian ear, who hath been taught this doctrine, not onely by *right reason*, and the consent of all the wise men in the world, but also by God himself in holy Scripture. [z] *Am I a God at hand (saith the Lord) and not a God afar off? Can any hide himself in secret places that I shall not see him? (saith the Lord) Do not I fill heaven and earth?* [a] *Neither is there any creature that is not manifest in his sight: but all things are naked and open to the eyes of him with whom we have to do;* [b] *for in him we live and move and have our being.* [c] God is wholly in every place, included in no place, not bound with cords (except those of love) not divided into parts, not changeable into several shapes, filling heaven and earth with his present power, and with his never absent nature. So S. *Augustine* expresses this article. So that we may imagine God to be as the Aire and the Sea, and we all inclosed in his circle, wrapt up in the lap of his infinite nature, or as infants in the wombs of their pregnant Mothers: and we can no more be removed from the presence of God, than from our own being.

Several manners of the divine presence.

The presence of God is understood by us in several manners and to several purposes.

1. God is present *by his essence*, which because it is infinite cannot be contained within the limits of any place: and because he is of an essential purity, and spiritual nature, he cannot be undervalued by being supposed present in the places of unnatural uncleannesse: because as the sun reflecting upon the mud of strands and shores is unpolluted in its beams: so is God not dishonoured when we suppose him in every of his Creatures, and in every part of every one of them, and is still as unmixt with any unhandsome adherence, as is the soul in the bowels of the body.

[z] Jer. 23: 23, 24.
[a] Hebr. 4: 13.
[b] Acts 17: 28.
[c] Lib. 7. de Civit. cap. 30.

note *z* Jer. 23: 23, 24] *KC*, Jer. 23. 24 *1*+

2. [d]God is every where present *by his power.* He roules the Orbs of Heaven with his hand, he fixes the Earth with his Foot, he guides all the Creatures with his Eye, and refreshes them with his influence: He makes the powers of Hell to shake with his terrours, and binds the Devils with his Word, and throws them out with his command; and sends the Angels on Embassies with his decrees: He hardens the joynts of Infants, and confirms the bones when they are fashioned beneath secretly in the earth: He it is that assists at the numerous productions of fishes, and there is not one hollownesse in the bottom of the sea, but he shows himself to be Lord of it, by sustaining there the Creatures that come to dwell in it: And in the wildernesse, the Bittern and the Stork, the Dragon and the Satyr, the Unicorn and the Elk live upon his provisions, and revere his power, and feel the force of his Almightinesse.

3. God is *more specially present* in some places by the several and more special manifestations of himself to extraordinary purposes. 1. *By glory*: Thus his seat is in Heaven; because there he sits incircled with all the outward demonstrations of his glory, which he is pleased to show to all the inhabitants of those his inward and secret Courts. And thus *they that die in the Lord* may be properly said to be *gone to God*; with whom although they were before, yet now they enter into his Courts, into the secret of his Tabernacle, into the retinue and splendor of his glory. *That* is called *walking* with God, but *this* is dwelling or being with him. *I desire to be dissolved and to be with Christ*, so said *Paul.* But this manner of the Divine presence is reserved for the elect people of God and for their portion in their countrey.

4. [e]God is *by grace and benediction* specially present *in holy places*, anc in the solemn assemblies of his servants. If holy people meet in grots and dens of the earth, when persecution or a publick necessity disturbs the publick order, circumstance, and convenience, God fails no to come thither to them: but God is also by the same or a greate reason present there where they meet *ordinarily, by order, and public authority*: There God is present ordinarily, that is, at every such meeting. God will go out of his way to meet his Saints, when themselves ar forced out of their way of order by a sad necessity: but else, [f]Gods *usua*

[d] *Θεὸς περιέχει τῇ βουλήσει τὸ πᾶν, . . . μείζων τοῦ παντὸς ὥσπερ τῇ οὐσίᾳ, οὕτω καὶ τῇ ἀξίᾳ.* Resp. ad orthod.

[e] Matt. 18: 20. Heb. 10: 25.

[f] 1 King 5: 9. Psal. 138: 1, 2.

---

1 [d]] *4+, om 1 2 3*

way is to be present in those places where his servants are appointed *ordinarily* to meet. But his presence there signifies nothing but his *readinesse* to hear their prayers, to blesse their persons, to accept their offices, and to like even the circumstance of orderly and publick meeting. For thither, the prayers of consecration, the publick authority separating it, and Gods love of order, and the reasonable customes of Religion, have in ordinary, and in a certain degree fixed this manner of his presence; and he loves to have it so.

5. God is *especially present* in the hearts of his people *by his holy Spirit*: and indeed the hearts of holy men are Temples in the truth of things, and in type and shadow they are of Heaven it self. For God *reigns* in the hearts of his servants. *There is his Kingdom.* The power of grace hath *subdued* all his enemies. There is, *his power.* They *serve* him night and day and give him thanks and praise; that is, *his glory*: This is the religion and worship of God in the Temple. [g]The temple it self is the heart of man; Christ is the High Priest, who from thence sends up the incense of prayers and joyns them to his own intercession, and presents all together to his Father; and the Holy Ghost by his dwelling there, hath also consecrated it into a Temple; and God dwels in our hearts by faith, and Christ by his Spirit, and the Spirit by his purities; so that we are also Cabinets of the Mysterious Trinity; and what is this short of Heaven it self, but as infancy is short of manhood, and letters of words? The same state of life it is, but not the same age. It is *Heaven in a Looking-glasse*, (dark, but yet true) representing the beauties of the soul, and the graces of God, and the images of his eternal glory by the reality of a special presence.

6. God is especially present in the *consciences* of all persons *good and bad, by way of testimony* and *judgement*: that is, he is there a remembrancer to call our actions to minde, a witnesse to bring them to judgement, and a Judge to acquit or to condemne. And although this manner of presence is in this life after the manner of this life, that is, imperfect, and we forget many actions of our lives; yet the greatest changes of our state of grace or sin, our most considerable actions are alwayes present, like Capital Letters to an aged and dim eye: and at the day of judgement God shall draw aside the cloud and manifest this manner of his presence more notoriously, and make it appear, that he was an observer of our very thoughts; and that he onely laid those

[g] 1 Cor. 3: 16. 2 Cor. 6: 16.

11 are of Heaven] are Heaven *4+*

things by which because we covered with dust and negligence they were not then discerned. But when we are risen from our dust and imperfection, they all appear plain and legible.

Now the consideration of this great truth is of a very universal use in the whole course of the life of a Christian. All the consequents and effects of it are universal. [h]He that remembers that God stands *a witnesse* and *a judge*, beholding every secrecy; besides his impiety, must have put on impudence if he be not much restrained in his temptation to sin. For the greatest part of sinnes is taken away, if a man have a witnesse of his conversation: And he is a great despiser of God who sends a Boy away when he is going to commit fornication, and yet will dare to do it, though he knows God is present, and cannot be sent off: as if the eye of a little Boy were more awful, than the all-seeing eye of God. He is to be feared in publick, he is to be feared in private: if you go forth he spies you: if you go in he sees you: when you light the candle he observes you: when you put it out, then also God marks you: Be sure that while you are in his sight you behave your self as becomes so holy a presence. But if you will sin, retire your self wisely, and go where God cannot see: For no where else can you be safe. And certainly, if men would alwayes actually consider, and really esteem this truth, that God is the *great Eye* of the World, alwayes watching over our actions, and an *ever open ear* to hear all our words, and an *unwearied arm* ever lifted up to crush a sinner into ruine, it would be the readiest way in the world to make sin to cease from amongst the children of men, and for men to approach to the blessed estate of the Saints in Heaven, who cannot sin, for they alwayes walk in the presence and behold the face of God. This instrument is to be reduced to practise according to the following Rules.

Rules of exercising this consideration.

1. Let this actual thought often return, that God is omnipresent, filling every place, and say with *David*, [i] *Whither shall I go from thy Spirit, or whither shall I flee from thy presence? If I ascend up into heaven, thou art there. If I make my bed in hell, thou art there, etc.* This thought by being frequent will make an *habitual dread* and reverence towards God, and fear in all

[h] S. Aug. de Verbis Domin. c. 2.

[i] Psal. 139: 7–13.

9 sinnes] sin *78* note *h* Domin.] *cor*, Domic. *1*+; c. 2] *cor*, c. 3 *1*+ note *i* Psal. 139: 7–13.] *KC*, Psal. 137. 7, 8. *1 2 3 4*, Psal. 13. 75. *5*, Psal. 13, 7, 8. *6*

thy actions: [j]For it is a great necessity and ingagement to do unblameably, when we act before that Judge, who is *infallible* in his sentence, *all knowing* in his information, *severe* in his anger, *powerful* in his providence, and *intolerable* in his wrath and indignation.

2. In the beginning of actions of Religion, make an *act of adoration*, that is, solemnly worship God, and place thy self in Gods presence, and behold him with the eye of faith, and let thy desires actually fix on him as the object of thy worship, and the reason of thy hope, and the fountain of thy blessing. For when thou hast placed thy self before him, and kneelest in his presence, it is most likely, all the following parts of thy devotion will be answerable to the wisdom of such an apprehension, and the glory of such a presence.

3. Let *every thing you see*, represent to your spirit the presence, the excellency and the power of God, and let your conversation with the creatures lead you unto the Creator; for so shall your actions be done more frequently with an actual eye to Gods presence, by your often seeing him in the glasse of the creation. In the face of the Sun you may see Gods beauty: In the fire you may feel his heat warming, in the water his gentleness to refresh you: he it is that comforts your spirit when you have taken Cordials: it is the dew of Heaven that makes your field give you bread; and the breasts of God are the bottles that minister drink to your necessities. This Philosophy which is obvious to every mans experience, is a good advantage to our piety, and by this act of understanding, our wills are checked from violence and misdemeanour.

4. In your retirement make *frequent colloquies* or short discoursings between God and thy own soul. *Seven times a day do I praise thee: and in the night season also I thought upon thee when I was waking.* So did *David*: and every act of complaint or thanksgiving, every act of rejoycing or of mourning, every petition and every return of the heart in these entercourses, is a going to God, an appearing in his presence, and a representing him present to thy spirit and to thy necessity. And this was long since by a spiritual person called, *a building to* [illegible] *a Chappel in our heart.* It reconciles *Martha's* imployment with *Maries* Devotion, Charity, and Religion; the necessities of our calling, and the imployments of devotion. For thus in the midst of the works of your Trade, you may retire into your Chappel (your Heart) and converse with GOD by frequent addresses and returns.

[j] Boeth. l. 5. de consol.

2 that] the 5+

5. Represent and offer to GOD, *acts of love and fear*, which are the proper effects of this apprehension, and the proper exercise of this consideration. For as GOD is every where present by his *power*, he calls for *reverence* and godly fear: As he is present to thee in all thy *needs*, and relieves them, he deserves thy *love*; and since in every accident of our lives we finde one or other of these apparent, and in most things we see both, it is a proper and proportionate return, that to every such demonstration of God, we expresse our selves sensible of it by admiring the Divine goodnesse, or trembling at his presence, ever obeying him because we love him, and ever obeying him because we fear to offend him. This is that which *Enoch* did, who thus *walked with God.*

6. Let us remember that *God is in us*, and that we are in him: we are his workmanship, let us not deface it: we are in his presence, let us not pollute it by unholy and impure actions. [k] *God hath also wrought all our works in us*: and because he rejoyces in his own workes, if we defile them, and make them unpleasant to him, we walk perversly with GOD, and he will walk crookedly toward us.

7. *God is in the bowels of thy brother*; refresh them when he needs it, and then you give your almes *in the presence of God*, *and to God*, and he feels the relief which thou providest for thy brother.

8. *God is in every place*; suppose it therefore to be a Church: and that decency of deportment and piety of carriage, which you are taught by religion or by custome, or by civility and publick manners to use in Churches, the same *use in all places*: with this difference onely, that in Churches let your deportment be religious in external forms and circumstances also; but there and every where let it be religious in abstaining from spiritual undecencies, and in readinesse to do good actions: that it may not be said of us, as God once complained of his people; [l] *Why hath my beloved done wickednesse in my house*?

9. *God is in every creature*: be cruel towards none, neither abuse any by intemperance. Remember that the creatures and every member of thy own body is one of the lesser cabinets and receptacles of God. They are such which God hath blessed with his presence, hallowed by his touch, and separated from unholy use by making them to belong to his dwelling.

10. He walks as in the presence of God, that converses with him in frequent prayer and frequent communion, that runs to him in all his necessities: that asks counsel of him in all his doubtings, that opens all

[k] Isa. 26: 12. [l] Jerem. 11: 15. Secund. vulg. Edit.

his wants to him, that weeps before him for his sins; that asks remedy and support for his weaknesse, that fears him as a Judge, reverences him as a Lord, obeyes him as a Father, and loves him as a Patron.

The Benefits of this exercise.

The benefit of this consideration and exercise being universal upon all the parts of piety, I shall lesse need to specifie any particulars; but yet most properly this exercise of considering the divine presence is, 1. an excellent *help to prayer*, producing in us reverence and awfulnesse to the divine Majesty of God, and actual devotion in our offices. 2. It produces a *confidence in God*, and fearlessenesse of our enemies, patience in trouble, and hope of remedie, since God is so nigh in all our sad accidents, he is a disposer of the hearts of men, and the events of things, he proportions out our tryals, and supplyes us with remedie, and where *his rod strikes us, his staffe supports us:* To which we may adde this, that God who is alwayes with us, is especially *by promise* with us in *tribulation*, to turn the misery into a mercy, and that our greatest trouble may become our advantage by intitling us to a new manner of the Divine presence. 3. It is apt to produce *joy and rejoycing in God*; we being more apt to delight in the partners and witnesses of our conversation; every degree of mutual abiding and conversing being a relation and an endearment: we are of the same houshold with God; he is with us in our natural actions to preserve us, in our recreations to restrain us, in our publick actions to applaud or reprove us, in our private to observe us, in our sleeps to watch by us, in our watchings to refresh us: and if we walk with God in *all his wayes* as he walks with us in *all ours*, we shall finde perpetual reasons to enable us to keep that rule of God, *Rejoyce in the Lord alwayes, and again I say rejoyce.* And this puts me in minde of a saying of an old religious person, [m] *There is one way of overcoming our ghostly enemies, spiritual mirth, and a perpetual bearing of God in our mindes.* This effectively resists the Devil, and suffers us to receive no hurt from him. 4. This exercise is apt also to *enkindle holy desires of the enjoyment* of God, because it produces joy when we do enjoy him; The same desires that a weak man hath for a Defender, the sick man for a Physitian, the poor for a Patron, the childe for his Father, the espoused Lover for her betrothed. 5. From the same fountain are apt to issue *humility of spirit*, apprehensions of our great distance and our great needs, our daily wants, and hourly supplies, admiration of Gods

[m] In vitam S. Anton.

unspeakable mercies: It is the cause of great modesty and decency in our actions; it helps to recollection of minde, and restrains the scatterings and loosnesse of wandring thoughts; it establishes the heart in good purposes, and leadeth on to perseverance; it gains purity and perfection, (according to the saying of God to *Abraham*, *Walk before me and be perfect*) holy fear, and holy love, and indeed every thing that pertains to holy living: when we see our selves placed in the *Eye of God* who sets us on work and will reward us plenteously, to serve him with an *Eye-service* is very pleasing; for he also sees the heart: and the want of this consideration was declared to be the cause why Israel sinned so grievously, [n] *For they say the Lord hath forsaken the earth, and the Lord seeth not: therefore the land is full of blood, and the city full of perversenesse.* What a childe would do in the eye of his Father, and a Pupil before his Tutor, and a Wife in the presence of her Husband, and a servant in the sight of his Master, let us alwayes do the same: for *we are made a spectacle to God, to Angels, and to men*; we are alwayes in the sight and presence of the Allseeing and Almighty God, who also is to us a Father, and a Guardian, a Husband, and a Lord.

Ad Chap. I.

Prayers and Devotions according to the religion and purposes of the foregoing Considerations.

I.
For grace to spend our time well.

O Eternal God who from all eternity doest behold and love thy own glories and perfections infinite, and hast created me to do the work of God, after the manner of men, and to serve thee in this generation, and according to my capacities; give me thy grace, that I may be a curious and prudent spender of my time, so as I may best prevent or resist all temptations, and be profitable to the Christian Common-wealth, and by discharging all my duty may glorifie thy Name. Take from me all slothfulnesse and give me a diligent and an active spirit, and wisdom to choose my imployment, that I may do works proportionable to my person, and to the dignity of a Christian, and may fill up all the spaces

[n] Ezek. 9: 9. Psal. 10: 11.

19 *Ad* Chap. I.] *ed, om 1+*

of my time with actions of religion and charity, that when the Devil assaults me, he may not find me idle; and my dearest Lord, at his sudden coming may finde me busie in lawful, necessary, and pious actions, improving my talent intrusted to me by thee my Lord, that I may enter into the joy of my Lord to partake of his eternal felicities, even for thy mercie sake, and for my dearest Saviours sake. *Amen.*

Here follows the devotion of ordinary dayes; for the right imployment of those portions of time which every day must allow for religion.

The first prayers in the Morning as soon as we are dressed.

Humbly and reverently compose your self, with heart lift up to God and your head bowed, and meekly kneeling upon your knees, say the Lords Prayer: after which use the following Collects, or as many of them as you shall choose.

Our Father which art in Heaven, etc.

I.

An act of adoration being the song that the Angels sing in Heaven.

[o]Holy, Holy, Holy, Lord God Almighty, which was, and is, and is to come: [p]Heaven and Earth, Angels and Men, the Aire and the Sea give glory, and honour, and thanks to him that sitteth on the throne, who liveth for ever and ever. [q]All the blessed spirits and souls of the righteous cast their crowns before the throne, and worship him that liveth for ever and ever. Thou art worthy, O Lord, to receive glory and honour, and power, for thou hast created all things, and for thy pleasure they are and were created. [r]Great and marvellous are thy works, O Lord God Almighty: Just and true are thy wayes, thou King of Saints. Thy wisdom is infinite, thy mercies are glorious; and I am not worthy O Lord to appear in thy presence before whom the Angels hide their faces. O Holy and Eternal Jesus, Lamb of God who wert slain from the beginning of the world, thou hast redeemed us to God by thy blood out of every nation, and hast made us unto our God Kings and Priests, and we shall reigne with thee for ever. Blessing, honour, glory and power be unto him that sitteth on the throne, and to the Lamb for ever and ever. *Amen.*

[o] Rev. 11: 17. [p] and 5: 10, 13. [q] and 4: 10. [r] Revel. 15: 3.

16 [o]] *om 2 3* 17 [p]] *om 2 3* 19 [q]] *7 8, om 1 2 3 4 5 6*

II.

An act of thanksgiving being the song of David *for the Morning.*

Sing praises unto the Lord, O ye saints of his, and give thanks to him for a remembrance of his holinesse. For his wrath indureth but the twinkling of an eye, and in his pleasure is life: heaviness may endure for a night, but joy cometh in the morning. Thou Lord hast preserved me this night from the violence of the spirits of darknesse, from all sad casualtyes, and evil accidents, from the wrath which I have every day deserved: thou hast brought my soul out of hell, thou hast kept my life from them that go down into the pit: thou hast shewed me marvellous great kindnesse and hast blessed me for ever: the greatnesse of thy glory reacheth unto the heavens, and thy truth unto the clouds. Therefore shall every good man sing of thy praise without ceasing, O my God I will give thanks unto thee for ever. *Allelujah.*

III.

An act of oblation or presenting our selves to God for the day.

Most Holy and Eternal God, Lord and Soveraigne of all the creatures, I humbly present to thy divine Majesty, my self, my soul and body, my thoughts and my words, my actions and intentions, my passions and my sufferings to be disposed by thee to thy glory, to be blessed by thy providence, to be guided by thy counsel, to be sanctified by thy spirit, and afterwards that my body and soul may be received into glory: for nothing can perish which is under thy custody; and the enemy of souls cannot devour what is thy portion, nor take it out of thy hands. This day, O Lord, and all the dayes of my life I dedicate to thy honour; and the actions of my calling to the uses of grace, and the religion of all my dayes to be united to the merits and intercession of my holy Saviour Jesus, that in him and for him I may be pardoned and accepted. *Amen.*

IV.

An act of repentance or contrition.

For as for me, I am not worthy to be called thy servant, much lesse am I worthy to be thy son, for I am the vilest of sinners and the worst of men, a lover of the things of the world, and a despiser of the things of God, *proud and envious, lustful and intemperate*, greedy of sin, and im-

3 thanks to] thanks unto *2 3*   32 the vilest] *1*+, not of ~ ~ *KC*

patient of reproof, desirous to seem holy, and negligent of being so, transported with interest, fooled with presumption and false principles, disturbed with anger, with a peevish and unmortified spirit, and disordered by a whole body of sin and death. Lord pardon all my sins for my sweetest Saviours sake; thou who didst dye for me, Holy Jesus, save me and deliver me, O reserve not my sins to be punished in the day of wrath and eternal vengeance; but wash away my sins, and blot them out of thy remembrance, and purifie my soul with the waters of repentance and the bloud of the crosse, that for what is past thy wrath may not come out against me, and for the time to come I may never provoke thee to anger or to jealousie. O just and dear God be pitiful and gracious to thy servant. *Amen.*

V.
The prayer or petition.

Blesse me gracious God in my calling to such purposes as thou shalt choose for me, or imploy me in: Relieve me in all my sadnesses, make my bed in my sicknesse, give me patience in my sorrows, confidence in thee and grace to call upon thee in all temptations. O be thou my Guide in all my thoughts, words and actions, my protector in all dangers: give me a healthful body, and a clear understanding, a sanctified, and just, a charitable, and humble, a religious and a contented spirit; let not my life be miserable or wretched, nor my name stained with sin or shame, nor my condition lifted up to a tempting and dangerous fortune; but let my condition be blessed, my conversation useful to my Neighbours and pleasing to thee, that when my body shall lie down in its bed of darknesse, my soul may passe into the Regions of light, and live with thee for ever through Jesus Christ. *Amen.*

VI.
An act of intercession or prayer for others to be added to this, or any other office, as our devotion, or duty, or their needs shall determine us.

O God of infinite mercy, who hast compassion on all men, and relievest the necessities of all that call to thee for helpe, hear the prayers of

6 O] *2 3, om 1 4+*   19 thoughts, words and] *KC, om 1+*   protector in] *illegible word after 'protector' in KC (perhaps '& deliverer')*   20 dangers:] *illegible word follows in KC*   22 or] *KC, om 1+*   23 or] *KC, om 1+*

thy servant who is unworthy to ask any petition for himself, yet in humility and duty is bound to pray for others.

[s]O let thy mercie descend upon the whole Church, preserve her in truth and peace, in unity and safety, in all stormes, and against all temptations and enemies, that she offering to thy glory the never ceasing sacrifice of prayer and thanksgiving may advance the honour of her Lord, and be filled with his Spirit, and partake of his Glory. *Amen.*

[t]In mercy remember the King, preserve his person in health and honour, his crown in wealth and dignity, his kingdoms in peace and plenty, the Churches under his protection in piety and knowledge, and a strict and holy religion: keep him perpetually in thy fear and favour, and crown him with glory and immortality. *Amen.*

[u]Remember them that minister about holy things, let them be clothed with righteousnesse, and sing with joyfulnesse. *Amen.*

[v]Blesse thy servant [my Wife or Husband] with health of body and of spirit. O let the hand of thy blessing be upon his [or her] head night and day, and support him in all necessities, strengthen him in all temptations, comfort him in all his sorrows, and let him be thy servant in all changes, and make us both to dwell with thee for ever in thy favour, in the light of thy countenance, and in thy glories. *Amen.*

[w]Blesse my children with healthful bodies, with good understandings, with the graces and gifts of thy Spirit, with sweet dispositions and holy habits, and sanctifie them throughout in their bodies and souls and spirits, and keep them unblameable to the coming of the Lord Jesus. *Amen.*

[x]Be pleased, O Lord, to remember my friends, all that have prayed for me, and all that have done me good [*here name such whom you would specially recommend*:] Do thou good to them, and return all their kindnesse double into their own bosome, rewarding them with blessings, and sanctifying them with thy graces, and bringing them to glory.

[y]Let all my family and kindred, my neighbours and acquaintance [*here name what other relation you please*] receive the benefit of my prayers, and the blessings of God; the comforts and supports of thy providence, and the sanctification of thy Spirit.

[s] For the Church. [t] For the King. [u] For the Clergy.
[v] For wife or husband. [w] For our children.
[x] For Friends and Benefactors. [y] For our family.

9–13 In mercy. . . . *Amen.*] *2+, in appendix at end of chapter 4 1* 9 King] Ruler *2 3* 10 crown] power *2 3* kingdoms] *6+*, dominions *2, 3*, kingdom *1 4 5* note *t* King] Ruler *2 3*

[z]Relieve and comfort all the persecuted and afflicted: speak peace to troubled consciences: strengthen the weak: confirm the strong: instruct the ignorant: deliver the oppressed from him that spoileth him, and relieve the needy that hath no helper, and bring us all by the waters of comfort, and in the wayes of righteousnesse to the kingdom of rest and glory, through Jesus Christ our Lord. *Amen.*

To God the Father of our Lord Jesus Christ, To the eternal Son that was incarnate and born of a Virgin, To the Spirit of the Father and the Son, be all honour and glory, worship and thanksgiving now and forever. Amen.

Another form of prayer for the Morning.

In the Name of the Father, and of the Son, and of the Holy Ghost. Our Father, etc.

I.

Most glorious and eternal God, Father of mercy, and God of all comfort, I worship and adore thee with the lowest humility of my soul and body, and give thee all thanks and praise for thy infinite and essential glories and perfections, and for the continual demonstration of thy mercies upon me, upon all mine, and upon thy holy Catholick Church.

II.

I acknowledge dear God that I have deserved the greatest of thy wrath and indignation; and that if thou hadst dealt with me according to my deserving, I had now at this instant been desperately bewailing my miseries in the sorrows and horrours of a sad eternity. But thy mercy triumphing over thy justice and my sins, thou hast still continued to me life and time of repentance; thou hast opened to me the gates of grace and mercy, and perpetually callest upon me to enter in and to walk in the paths of a holy life, that I may glorifie thee and be glorified of thee eternally.

III.

Behold, O God, for this thy great and unspeakable goodnesse; for the preservation of me this night, and for all other thy graces and blessings I

[z] For all in misery.

27 may] *KC*, might *1*+

offer up my soul and body, all that I am, and all that I have as a Sacrifice to thee and thy service; humbly begging of thee to pardon all my sins, to defend me from all evil, to lead me into all good, and let my portion be amongst thy redeemed ones in the gathering together of the Saints, in the Kingdom of grace and glory.

IV.

Guide me, O Lord, in all the changes and varieties of the world, that in all things that shall happen, I may have an evennesse and tranquillity of spirit; that my soul may be wholly resigned to thy Divinest will and pleasure, never murmuring at thy gentle chastisements and fatherly correction, never waxing proud or insolent though I feel a torrent of comforts or prosperous successes.

V.

Fix my thoughts, my hopes and my desires upon Heaven and heavenly things; teach me to despise the world, to repent me deeply for my sins; give me holy purposes of amendment, and ghostly strength and assistances to perform faithfully whatsoever I shall intend piously. Enrich my understanding with an eternal treasure of Divine truths, that I may know thy will, and thou who workest in us to will and to do of thy good pleasure; teach me to obey all thy Commandments, to believe all thy Revelations, and make me partaker of all thy gracious promises.

VI.

Teach me to watch over all my wayes, that I may never be surprized by sudden temptations or a carelesse spirit, nor ever return to folly and vanity. Set a watch, O Lord, before my mouth, and keep the door of my lips, that I offend in my tongue neither against piety nor charity. Teach mee to think of nothing but thee and what is in order to thy glory and service; to speak nothing but thee and thy glories; and to do nothing but what becomes thy servant whom thy infinite mercy by the graces of thy holy Spirit hath sealed up to the day of Redemption.

VII.

Let all my passions and affections be so mortified and brought under the dominion of grace, that I may never by deliberation and purpose,

11–12 proud or . . . comforts or] *KC*, ~ and . . . ~ and *1*+ 26 offend] ~ not *6*+

nor yet by levity, rashnesse, or inconsideration offend thy Divine Majesty. Make me such as thou wouldest have me to bee: strengthen my faith, confirm my hope, and give me a daily increase of charity, that this day and ever I may serve thee according to all my opportunities and capacities; growing from grace to grace, till at last by thy mercies I shall receive the consummation and perfection of grace, even the glories of thy Kingdom in the full fruition of the face and excellencies of God the Father, the Son and the holy Ghost: to whom be glory and praise, honour and adoration given by all Angels and all Men, and all Creatures, now and to all eternity. *Amen.*

To this may be added the prayer of intercession for others whom we are bound to remember; which is at the end of the foregoing prayer: or else you may take such special prayers which follow at the end of the third or fourth Chapter, [for parents, for children, etc.].

After which conclude with this ejaculation.

Now and in all tribulation and anguish of spirit, in all dangers of soul and body, in prosperity and adversity, in the hour of death, and in the day of judgement, holy and most blessed Saviour Jesus, have mercy upon me, save me and deliver me and all faithful people. *Amen.*

Between this and Noon usually are said the publick prayers appointed by Authority: to which all the Clergy are obliged; and other devout persons that have leisure do accompany them.

Afternoon, or at any time of the day, when a devout person retires into his closet for private prayer, or spiritual exercises, he may say the following devotions.

An exercise to be used at any time of the day.

In the name of the Father, and of the Son, etc. Our Father, etc.

The hymn collected out of the Psalms, recounting the excellencies and greatnesse of God.

[a]O be joyful in God all ye lands: sing praises unto the honour of his Name, make his Name to be glorious. O come hither and behold the works of God, how wonderful he is in his doings toward the children of men. He ruleth with his power for ever.

[a] Psal. 66: 1, 5, 7.

13 *third or*] 2, ~ *and 3, om 1 4*+ 16 Now and in] Now in *7 8* 22 *do*] *to 4*+ 31 toward] towards *3 7 8* Notes *a* to *p* *These notes all appear for the first time in* 7 *and are reprinted in subsequent editions.*

[b]He is the Father of the fatherlesse, and defendeth the cause of the widow, even God in his holy habitation. He is the God that maketh men to be of one minde in a house, and bringeth the prisoners out of captivity: but letteth the runnagates continue in scarcenesse.

[c]It is the Lord that commandeth the waters; it is the glorious God that maketh the thunder. It is the Lord that ruleth the sea; the voice of the Lord is mighty in operation, the voice of the Lord is a glorious voice.

[d]Let all the Earth fear the Lord, stand in awe of him all ye that dwell in the world: [e]Thou shalt shew us wonderful things in thy righteousnesse, O God of our salvation, thou that art the hope of all the ends of the Earth, and of them that remaine in the broad sea.

Glory be to the Father, etc.

Or this,

[f]O Lord, thou art my God, I will exalt thee: I will praise thy Name, for thou hast done wonderful things: thy counsels of old are faithfulnesse and truth.

[g]Thou in thy strength setst fast the Mountains, and art girded about with power. Thou stillest the raging of the Sea, and the noise of his waves, and the madnesse of his people.

They also that remain in the uttermost parts of the Earth shall be afraid at thy tokens: thou that makest the out-goings of the morning and evening to praise thee.

[h]O Lord God of Hosts, who is like unto thee: thy truth most mighty Lord is on every side. [i]Among the gods there is none like unto thee, O Lord, there is none that can do as thou doest. For thou art great and doest wondrous things: thou art God alone.

[j]God is very greatly to be feared in the counsel of the Saints: and to be had in reverence of all them that are round about him.

Righteousnesse and equity is in the habitation of thy seat: mercy and truth shall go before thy face. [k]Glory and worship are before him: power and honour are in his Sanctuary.

[l]Thou Lord art the thing I long for: thou art my hope even from my youth: through thee have I been holden up ever since I was born: thou

[b] Psal. 68: 5, 6.
[c] Psal. 29: 3–4.
[d] Psal. 33: 8.
[e] Psal. 65: 5.
[f] Isa. 25: 1.
[g] Psal. 65: 6–8.
[h] Psal. 89: 9.
[i] Psal. 86: 8–9.
[j] Psal. 89: 7, 15.
[k] Psal. 96: 6.
[l] Psal. 71: 5–6.

art he that took me out of my mothers womb: my praise shall be alwayes of thee.

Glory be to the Father, etc.

After this may be read some portion of holy Scripture out of the New Testament, or out of the sapiential bookes of the Old. viz. *Proverbs, Ecclesiastes, etc. because these are of great use to piety and to civil conversation. Upon which, when you have a while meditated; humbly composing your self upon your knees, say as followeth.*

Ejaculations.

[m]My help standeth in the Name of the Lord: who hath made Heaven and Earth.

[n]Shew the light of thy countenance upon thy servant: and I shall be safe.

[o]Do well, O Lord, to them that be true of heart: and evermore mightily defend them.

[p]Direct me in thy truth and teach me: for thou art my Saviour and my great Master.

Keep me from sin and death eternal: and from my enemies visible and invisible.

Give me grace to live a holy life: and thy favour that I may dye a godly and happy death.

Lord hear the prayer of thy servant: and give me thy holy Spirit.

The prayer.

O Eternal God, mercifull and gracious, vouchsafe thy favour and thy blessing to thy servant: let the love of thy mercies, and the dread and fear of thy Majesty, make me careful and inquisitive to search thy will, and diligent to perform it, and to persevere in the practises of a holy life, even till the last of my dayes.

II.

Keep me, O Lord, for I am thine by creation; guide me, for I am thine by purchase, thou hast redeemed me by the blood of thy Son: and love me with the love of a Father; for I am thy childe by adoption and grace: let thy mercy pardon my sins, thy providence secure me from the

[m] Psal. 124: 8. [n] Psal. 80: 3: [o] Psal. 125:4. [p] Psal. 25: 5.

punishments and evils I have deserved, and thy care watch over me; that I may never any more offend thee: make me in malice to be a childe; but in understanding, piety, and the fear of God, let me be a perfect man in Christ, innocent and prudent, readily furnished and instructed to every good work.

III.

Keep me, O Lord, from the destroying Angel, and from the wrath of God: let thy anger never rise against mee; but thy rod gently correct my follies and guide me in thy ways, and thy staffe support me in all sufferings and changes. Preserve me from fracture of bones, from noisome, infectious, and sharp sicknesses, from great violences of Fortune and sudden surprizes; keep all my senses intire till the day of my death; and let my death be neither sudden, untimely, nor unprovided: let it be after the common manner of men, having in it nothing extraordinary, but an extraordinary piety, and the manifestation of thy great and miraculous mercy.

IV.

Let no riches ever make me forget myself; no poverty ever make me to forget thee: Let no hope or fear, no pleasure or pain, no accident without, no weaknesse within, hinder or discompose my duty, or turn me from the wayes of thy Commandements. O let thy Spirit dwell with me for ever, and make my soul just and charitable, full of honesty, full of religion, resolute and constant in holy purposes, but inflexible to evil. Make me humble and obedient, peaceable and pious; let me never envy any mans good, nor deserve to be despised my self; and if I be, teach me to bear it with meekness and charity.

V.

Give me a tender conscience; a conversation discreet, and affable modest and patient, liberal and obliging; a body chaste and healthful competency of living according to my condition, contentednesse in al estates, a resigned will and mortified affections, that I may be as thou wouldst have me, and my portion may be in the lot of the righteous, in the brightnesse of thy countenance, and the glories of eternity. *Amen*

29 obliging; a body chaste] *GH4*+, obliging body; a chaste *1*, obliging, a body chast *2 3*

Holy is our God. Holy is the Almighty. Holy is the Immortal. Holy, holy, holy, Lord God of Sabbaoth, have mercy upon me.

A form of Prayer for the evening, to be said by such who have not time, or opportunity to say the publick prayers appointed for this office.

I.
Evening Prayer

O Eternal God, Great Father of Men and Angels, who hast established the Heavens and the Earth in a wonderful order, making day and night to succeed each other: I make my humble addresse to thy Divine Majesty, begging of thee mercy and protection this night and ever. O Lord pardon all my sins, my light and rash words, the vanity and impiety of my thoughts, my unjust and uncharitable actions, and whatsoever I have transgressed against thee this day, or at any time before. Behold, O God, my soul is troubled in the remembrance of my sins, in the frailty and sinfulnesse of my flesh exposed to every temptation, and of it self not able to resist any: Lord God of mercy, I earnestly beg of thee to give me a great portion of thy grace; such as may be sufficient, and effectual for the mortification of all my sins and vanities and disorders; that as I have formerly served my lust and unworthy desires, so now I may give my self up wholly to thy service, and the studies of a holy life.

II.

Blessed Lord, teach me frequently and sadly to remember my sins; and be thou pleased to remember them no more: let me never forget thy mercies, and do thou still remember to do me good. Teach me to walk alwayes as in thy presence: Ennoble my soul with great degrees of love to thee, and consigne my spirit with great fear, religion and veneration of thy holy Name and laws; that it may become the great imployment of my whole life to serve thee, to advance thy glory, to root out all the accursed habits of sin, that in holinesse of life, in humility, in charity, in chastity, and all the ornaments of grace, I may by patience wait for the coming of our Lord Jesus. *Amen.*

III.

Teach me, O Lord to number my dayes that I may apply my heart unto wisdom; ever to remember my last end, that I may not dare to sin against thee: Let thy holy Angels be ever present with me to keep me in all my wayes from the malice and violence of the spirits of darknesse; from evil company, and the occasions and opportunities of evil, from perishing in popular judgements, from all the wayes of sinful shame, from the hands of all mine enemies; from a sinful life, and from despair in the day of my death: Then, O brightest Jesu, shine gloriously upon me, let thy mercies and the light of thy Countenance sustain me in all my agonies, weaknesses and temptations. Give me opportunity of a prudent and spiritual Guide, and of receiving the holy Sacrament; and let thy loving spirit so guide me in the wayes of peace and safety, that with the testimony of a good conscience, and the sense of thy mercies and refreshment, I may depart this life in the unity of the Church, in the love of God, and a certain hope of salvation through Jesus Christ our Lord and most blessed Saviour. *Amen.*

Our Father, etc.

Another form of Evening Prayer, which may also be used at bed-time.

Our Father, etc.

[q]I will lift up my eyes unto the hills from whence cometh my help.

My help cometh of the Lord which made heaven and earth.

He will not suffer thy foot to be moved: he that keepeth thee will not slumber.

Behold, he that keepeth Israel shall neither slumber nor sleep.

The Lord is thy keeper, the Lord is thy shade upon thy right hand.

The sun shall not smite thee by day: neither the moon by night.

The Lord shall preserve thee from all evil: he shall preserve thy soul.

The Lord shall preserve thy going out and thy coming in: from this time forth for evermore. Glory be to the Father, etc.

[q] Psal. 121: 1 etc.

I.

Visit I beseech thee, O Lord, this habitation with thy mercy, and me with thy grace and salvation. Let thy holy Angels pitch their tents round about and dwell here, that no illusion of the night may abuse me, the spirits of darknesse may not come neer to hurt me, no evil or sad accident oppresse me: and let the eternal spirit of the Father dwell in my soul and body, filling every corner of my heart with light and grace. Let no deed of darknesse overtake me; and let thy blessing most blessed God be upon me for ever, through Jesus Christ our Lord. *Amen.*

II.

Into thy hands most blessed Jesu, I commend my soul and body, for thou hast redeemed both with thy most precious blood. So blesse and sanctifie my sleep unto me, that it may be temperate, holy, and safe, a refreshment to my wearied body to enable it so to serve my soul, that both may serve thee with a never failing duty. O let me never sleep in sin or death eternal, but give me a watchful and a prudent spirit, that I may omit no opportunity of serving thee, that whether I sleep or wake, live or die, I may be thy servant and thy childe: that when the work of my life is done, I may rest in the bosom of my Lord, till by the voice of the Archangel, the trump of God, I shall be awakened and called to sit down and feast in the eternal supper of the Lamb. Grant this O Lamb of God, for the honour of thy mercies and the glory of thy name, O most merciful Saviour and Redeemer Jesus. *Amen.*

III.

Blessed be the God and Father of our Lord Jesus, who hath sent his Angels, and kept me this day from the destruction that walketh at noon, and the arrow that flyeth by day: and hath given me his Spirit to restrain me from those evils to which my own weaknesses, and my evil habits, and my unquiet enemies would easily betray me. Blessed and for ever hallowed be thy name for that never ceasing showre of blessing by which I live, and am content, and blessed, and provided for in all necessities, and set forward in my duty and way to heaven. Blessing, honour, glory and power, be unto him that sitteth on the throne, and to the Lamb for ever and ever. *Amen.*

8 let] *6+*, *om 1 2 3 4 5*

Holy is our God, Holy is the Almighty, Holy is the Immortal. Holy, holy, holy, Lord God of Sabbaoth, have mercy upon me.

Ejaculations and short meditations to be used in the Night when we wake.

[r]Stand in awe and sin not: commune with your own heart upon your bed, and be still. I will lay me down in peace and sleep: for thou Lord only makest me dwell in safety.

O Father of Spirits and the God of all flesh, have mercy and pity upon all sick and dying Christians, and receive the souls which thou hast redeemed returning unto thee.

[s]Blessed are they that dwell in the heavenly Jerusalem: where there is no need of the Sun, neither of the Moon to shine in it: for the glorie of God does lighten it, and the Lamb is the light thereof. [t]And there shall be no night there, and they need no candle, for the Lord God giveth them light, and they shall reign for ever and ever.

Meditate on *Jacobs* wrastling with the Angel all night: be thou also importunate with God for a blessing, and give not over till he hath blessed thee.

Meditate on the Angel passing over the children of Israel, and destroying the Egyptians, for disobedience and oppression. Pray for the grace of obedience and charity and for the divine protection.

Meditate on the Angel who destroyed in a night the whole army of the Assyrians for fornication. Call to minde the sins of thy youth, the sins of thy bed; and say with *David*, *My reins chasten me in the night season, and my soul refuseth comfort.* Pray for pardon and the grace of chastity.

Meditate on the agonies of Christ in the garden, his sadnesse and affliction all that night; and thank and adore him for his love that made him suffer so much for thee: and hate thy sins which made it necessary for the Son of God to suffer so much.

Meditate on the four last things. 1. The certainty of death. 2. The terrours of the day of judgement. 3. The joyes of Heaven. 4. The pains of Hell, and the eternity of both.

Think upon all thy friends which are gone before thee, and pray that God would grant to thee to meet them in a joyful resurrection.

[u]The day of the Lord will come as a thiefe in the night, in the which the heavens shal passe away with a great noise, and the elements shal

[r] Psal. 4: 4, 8. [s] Rev. 21: 23. [t] Rev. 22: 5. [u] 2 Pet. 3: 10–11

note *r* Psal. 4: 4, 8] *78*, Psal. 4. *123456*

melt with fervent heat, the earth also and the works that are therein shall be burnt up. Seeing then that all these things shall be dissolved, what manner of persons ought we to be in all holy conversation and godlinesse, looking for and hastening unto the coming of the day of God?

Lord, in mercy remember thy servant in the day of Judgement.

Thou shalt answer for me, O Lord my God. In thee, O Lord have I trusted: let me never be confounded. *Amen.*

I desire the Christian Reader to observe that all these offices or forms of prayer (if they should be used every day) would not spend above an hour and a halfe: but because some of them are double (and so but one of them to be used in one day) it is much lesse: and by affording to God one hour in 24. thou mayest have the comforts and rewards of devotion. But he that thinks this is too much, either is very busie in the world, or very carelesse of heaven. However, I have parted the prayers into smaller portions that he may use which, and how many he please in any one of the forms.

Ad Sect. II.

A prayer for holy Intention in the beginning and pursuit of any considerable action, as Study, Preaching, etc.

O Eternal God, who hast made all things for man, and man for thy glory, sanctifie my body and soul, my thoughts and my intentions, my words and actions, that whatsoever I shall think or speak, or do, may be by me designed to the glorification of thy Name, and by thy blessing it may be effective and successeful in the work of God, according as it can be capable. Lord turn my necessities into vertue, the works of nature into the works of grace, by making them orderly, regular, temperate, subordinate and profitable to ends beyond their own proper efficacy: And let no pride or self-seeking, no covetousnesse or revenge, no impure mixture or unhandsome purposes, no little ends or low imaginations pollute my Spirit, and unhallow any of my words or actions: but let my body be a servant of my spirit, and both body and spirit servants of Jesus, that doing all things for thy glory here, I may be partaker of thy glory hereafter thorough Jesus Christ our Lord. *Amen.*

Ad Sect. III.

A prayer meditating and referring to the divine presence.

This prayer is especially to be used in temptation to private sins.

O Almighty God infinite and eternal, thou fillest all things with thy presence; thou art every where by thy essence and by thy power, in heaven by Glory, in holy places by thy grace and favour, in the hearts of thy servants by thy Spirit, in the consciences of all men by thy testimony and observation of us: Teach me to walk alwayes as in thy presence, to fear thy Majesty, to reverence thy wisdom and omniscience, that I may never dare to commit any undecency in the eye of my Lord and my Judge, but that I may with so much care and reverence demean my self, that my Judge may not be my accuser, but my Advocate: that I expressing the belief of thy presence here by careful walking, may feel the effects of it in the participation of eternal glory thorough Jesus Christ. *Amen.*

An additional prayer.

O Holy and heavenly Father who art seated in inaccessible light, where no mortall eye can approach and live, whose word alone is of an infinite force, in whom we all live and move and have our being, and yet art mercifully pleased to admitt into thy presence sinfull man clothed upon with all his weakenesses, to accept and encourage his boldnesse of addresse and to account it to him for righteousnesse. Mercifully looke down upon me the unworthiest of all thy Creatures, yet one, for whom Christ dyed, and descended into the torments of the grave.

Pardon, O Lord, the sins and offences of my youth, that what has been committed by me, before thou hadst touchd my heart with thy sanctifying grace, may never rise up in judgement against me to condemne me, forgive the errours of my understanding, the vanity of my affections, and all the faults and offences of my former life, and imprint in my heart such a deep sense of them and make the remembrance of my death so presentiall to my thoughts, that I may never returne into the same sins againe. Send thy saving grace into my heart to be a centinell against all appearance of evill: Let the remembrance of thy goodnesse and gloryes make me feare to offend, but bold to lay

16 *An additional prayer.*] *GH, om 1+; title and paragraph divisions added by ed*

my necessities at thy feet. Lord inflame my heart with great degrees of love to thee that the fondnesse of my affection may spend it selfe wholly upon thy beauties, having first thrown away the love of all worldly things. Let all my actions be so holy and innocent, that they may teame with blessings upon me.

Lord pardon the sins of this day, and let their remembrance dwell with me, till I have forgot to returne to them. Thy mercies toward me have been infinite, and like the divine essence incomprehensible. Particularly in defending me this day from all dangers, notwithstanding the guilt of my greivous sins engraven upon my soule in largest characters.

Lord also defend me this night, and for ever be my protectour, for I fly unto thee for help, I am not able to promise my selfe one minute of life, all I doe is in thy name and power. Thou restrainest the spirits of darknesse, and keepest them from hurting us. Lord also make their temptation void, and take away the evill of my affections, that I may be a fit temple of the Holy Ghost defended and inhabited by thee. Make me alwayes to remember that my soule is in thy hand, that whatsoever thou layest upon me is for my good, that thou carest for me, and in order to my preservation numberest the haires of my head.

And make me wholly to resigne my selfe up to thy desposure in all the affaires of my life, that being adopted into the number of thy Elect, I may hereafter come to make one in that blessed quire, whom thou shalt choose to sing thy praises to all eternitye. Heare thy servant O Merciful Father at the intercession of thy deare son Jesus.

9 day] *ed, om MS* 15 hurting] *ed*, hurtest *MS* 24 servant] *ed, om MS*

Chap. II.

Of Christian Sobriety.

Sect. I.

Of sobriety in the general sense.

CHRISTIAN Religion in all its moral parts is nothing else but the Law of Nature and great Reason, complying with the great necessities of all the world, and promoting the great profit of all relations, and carrying us through all accidents of variety of chances to that end which God hath from eternal ages purposed for all that lived according to it, and which he hath revealed in Jesus Christ: and according to the Apostles Arithmetik hath but these three parts of it. 1. Sobriety. 2. Justice. 3 Religion. [a] *For the grace of God bringing salvation hath appeared to all men; teaching us that denying ungodlinesse and worldly lusts, we should live 1. Soberly, 2. Righteously, and 3. Godly in this present world, looking for that blessed hope and glorious appearing of the great God and our Saviour Jesus Christ.* The first contains all our deportment in our personal and private capacities, the fair treating of our bodies, and our spirits. The second enlarges our duty in all relations to our Neighbour. The third contains the offices of direct Religion, and entercourse with God.

Christian sobriety is all that duty that concerns our selves in the matter of *meat* and *drink* and *pleasures* and *thoughts*, and it hath within it, the duties of 1. *Temperance.* 2. *Chastity.* 3. *Humility.* 4. *Modesty.* 5. *Content.*

It is a using severity, denial, and frustration, of our appetite when it growes unreasonable in any of these instances: the necessity of which we shall to best purpose understand, by considering the evil consequences of sensuality, effeminacy or fondnesse after carnal pleasures.

Evil consequents of voluptuousnesse.

1. A longing after sensual pleasures is a dissolution of the spirit of a man, and makes it loose, soft, and wandering, unapt for noble, wise, or

[a] Tit. 2: 11, 12.

12 [a]] *om 7 8*

spiritual imployments; because [b]the principles upon which pleasure is chosen and pursued, are sottish, weak, and unlearned, such as prefer the body before the soul, the appetite before reason, sense before the Spirit, the pleasures of a short abode, before the pleasures of eternity.

2. The nature of sensual pleasure is vain, empty, and unsatisfying, biggest alwayes in expectation, and a meer vanity in the enjoying, and leaves a sting and thorn behinde it, when it goes off. Our laughing if it be loud and high commonly ends in a deep sigh, and all the instances of pleasure have a sting in the tayl, though they carry beauty on the face and sweetnesse on the lip.

3. Sensual pleasure is a great abuse to the Spirit of a man; being a kind of fascination or witchcraft, blinding the understanding and enslaving the will. [c]And he that knowes he is free-born or redeemed with the blood of the Sonne of God, will not easily suffer the freedom of his soul to be entangled and rifled.

4. It is most contrary to the state of a Christian, whose life is [d]a perpetual exercise, a wrastling and a warfare, to which, sensual pleasure disables him, by yeilding to that enemy with whom he must strive if ever he will be crowned. And this argument the Apostle intimated: [e]*He that striveth for masteries is temperate in all things: Now they do it to obtain a corruptible crown, but we an incorruptible.*

5. It is by a certain consequence the greatest impediment in the world to martyrdom; that being a fondnesse, this being a cruelty to the flesh: to which a Christian man arriving by degrees must first have crucified the lesser affections: for he that is overcome by little arguments of pain, will hardly consent to lose his life with torments.

Degrees of sobriety.

Against this voluptuousnesse, sobriety is opposed *in three degrees.*

1. *A despite or disaffection to pleasures*, or a resolving against all entertainment of the instances and temptations of sensuality, and it consists in the internal faculties of will and understanding, decreeing and

[b] Tu si animum vicisti potius quam animus te, est quod gaudeas: Qui animum vincunt, quam quos animus, semper probiores cluent. Trinum.

[c] *Μόνον σκέψαι, πόσου πωλεῖς τὴν σεαυτοῦ προαίρεσιν, ἄνθρωπε· εἰ μηδὲν ἄλλο, μὴ ὀλίγου αὐτὴν πωλήσῃς.* Arrian. l. 1. c. 2.

[d] *Θέλεις ὀλύμπια νικῆσαι; . . . δεῖ σ' εὐτακτεῖν, ἀναγκοτροφεῖν, ἀπέχεσθαι πεμμάτων, γυμνάζεσθαι πρὸς ἀνάγκην, κ.τ.λ.* Epict. c. 29.

[e] 1 Cor. 9: 25.

---

1 [b]] *4+*, *om 1 2 3*   17 and a warfare] and warfare *5+*   note *d* Epict.] *7 8*, Epist. *1 4 5 6*, Ep. *2 3*   c. 29] *cor*, cap. 34 *1+*

declaring against them, disapproving and disliking them upon good reason, and strong resolution.

2. *A fight and actual war* against all the temptations and offers of sensual pleasure in all evil instances and degrees; and it consists in prayer, in fasting, in cheap diet, and hard lodging, and laborious exercises, and avoiding occasions, and using all arts and industry of fortifying the Spirit, and making it severe, manly, and Christian.

3. *Spiritual pleasure* is the highest degree of *Sobriety*, and in the same degree in which we relish and are in love with spiritual delights, [f]*the hidden Manna*, with the sweetnesses of devotion, with the joyes of thanksgiving, with rejoycings in the Lord, with the comforts of hope, with the delitiousnesse of charity and almes-deeds, with the sweetnesse of a good conscience, with the peace of meeknesse, and the felicities of a contented spirit: in the same degree we disrelish and loath the husks of swinish lusts, and the parings of the apples of Sodom: and the taste of sinful pleasures is unsavoury as the Drunkards vomit.

Rules for suppressing voluptuousnesse.

The precepts and advices which are of best and of general use in the curing of sensuality are these.

1. Accustom thy self to cut off all superfluity in the provisions of thy life: for our desires will enlarge beyond the present possession so long as all the things of this world are unsatisfying: if therefore you suffer them to extend beyond the measures of necessity or moderated conveniency, they will still swell: but you reduce them to a little compasse, when you make nature to be your limit. [g]We must more take care that our desires should cease, than that they should be satisfied: and therefore reducing them to narrow scantlings and small proportions is the best instrument to redeem their trouble and prevent the dropsie, because that is next to an universal denying them: it is certainly a paring off from them all unreasonablenesse and irregularity. [h]*For whatsoever covets unseemly things, and is apt to swell to an inconvenient bulk, is to be chastened and tempered and such are sensuality, and a Boy*, said the Philosopher.

2. [i]Suppress your sensuall desires in their first approach: for ther

[f] Apoc. 2: 17.
[g] Desideria tua parvo redime, hoc enim tantum curare debes ut desinant. Senec.
[h] L. 3. Eth. c. 12.
[i] Facilius est initia affectum prohibere, quam impetum regere. Senec. ep. 85.

note *i* ep. 85] *cor*, ep. 86 *1*+

they are least, and thy faculties and election are stronger; but if they in their weaknesse prevail upon thy strengths, there will be no resisting them when they are increased, and thy abilities lessened. *You shall scarce obtain of them to end, if you suffer them to begin.*

3. Divert them with some laudable imployment, and take off their edge by inadvertency, or a not attending to them. For since the faculties of a man cannot at the same time with any sharpnesse attend to two objects, if you imploy your spirit upon a book or a bodily labour, or any innocent and indifferent imployment, you have no room left for the present trouble of a sensual temptation. For to this sense it was that *Alexander* told the Queen of *Caria*, that his Tutor *Leonidas* had provided two Cooks for him. [j] *Hard marches all night, and a small dinner the next day*: these tamed his youthful aptnesses to dissolution, so long as he eat of their provisions.

4. Look upon pleasures, not upon that side that is next the Sunne, or where they look beauteously, that is, as they come towards you to be enjoyed; for then they paint, and smile, and dresse themselves up in tinsel and glasse, gems and counterfeit imagery: [k] but when thou hast rifled and discomposed them with enjoying their false beauties, and that they begin to go off, then behold them in their nakednesse and wearinesse: See what a sigh and sorrow, what naked unhandsome proportions and a filthy carkasse they discover; and the next time they counterfeit, remember what you have already discovered, and be no more abused. And I have known some wise persons have advised to cure the passions and longings of their children by letting them taste of every thing they passionately fancied: for they should be sure to find lesse in it than they looked for, and the impatience of their being denied would be loosened and made slack; and when our wishings are no bigger than the thing deserves, and our usages of them according to our needs (which may be obtained by trying what they are, and what good they can do us) we shall finde in all pleasures so little entertainment, that the vanity of the possession will soon reprove the violence of the appetite. And if this permission be in innocent instances, it may be of good use: But *Solomon* tried it in all things, taking his fill of all pleasures: and soon grew weary of them all. The same thing we may do by reason which we do by experience, if either we will look upon

[j] *Νυκτοποϱίαν καὶ ὀλιγαϱιστίαν.*

[k] Voluptates abeuntes fessas et pœnitentia plenas, animis nostris natura subjecit, quo minus cupide repetantur. Senec.

Læta venire Venus, tristis abire solet.

pleasures as we are sure they will look when they go off, after their enjoyment, or if we will credit the experience of those men who have tasted them and loathed them.

5. Often consider, and contemplate the joyes of heaven, that when they have filled thy desires, which are the sails of the soul, thou mayest steer onely thither, and never more look back to *Sodom.* And when thy soul dwels above, and looks down upon the pleasures of the World, they seeme like things at distance, little and contemptible, and men running after the satisfaction of their sottish appetites seem foolish as fishes, thousands of them running after a rotten worme that covers a deadly hook; or at the best but like children with great noise pursuing a bubble rising from a wallnut shell, which ends sooner than the noise.

6. To this, the example of Christ and his Apostles, of *Moses* and all the Wise men of all ages of the world will much help: who understanding how to distinguish good from evil, did choose a sad and melancholy way to felicitie, rather than the broad, pleasant and easie path to folly and misery.

But this is but the general. Its first particular is Temperance.

SECT. II.

Of Temperance in Eating and Drinking.

[1]Sobriety is the bridle of the passions of desire, and Temperance is the bit and curb of that bridle, a restraint put into a mans mouth, a moderate use of meat and drink, so as may best consist with our health, and may not hinder but help the works of the soul by its necessary supporting us, and ministering cheerfulnesse and refreshment.

Temperance consists in the actions of the soul principally: for it is a grace that chooses natural means in order to proper and natural and holy ends: It is exercised about eating and drinking, because they are necessary: but therefore it permits the use of them onely as they minister to lawful ends: It does not eate and drink for pleasure but for need, and for refreshment, which is a part or a degree of need. I deny not but eating and drinking *may be*, and in healthful bodies *alwayes is* with pleasure: because there is in nature no greater pleasure, than that all the appetites which God hath made should be satisfied: and a man may choose a morsel that is pleasant, the lesse pleasant being rejected

[1] *Ἐγκράτεια, ἀπὸ τοῦ ἐν κράτει ἔχειν ἐπιθυμίαν.*

as being lesse useful, lesse apt to nourish, or more agreeing with an infirm stomach, or when the day is festival, by order, or by a private joy. In all these cases it is permitted to receive a more free delight, and to designe it too, as the lesse principal: that is, that the chief reason why we choose the more delicious, be the serving that end for which such refreshments and choices are permitted. But when delight is the only end and rests in it self, and dwells there long, then, eating and drinking is not a serving of God, but an inordinate action; because it is not in the way to that end whether God directed it. But the choosing of a delicate before a more ordinary dish is to be done as other humane actions are, in which there are no degrees and precise natural limits described, but a latitude is indulged: it must be done moderately, prudently, and according to the accounts of wise, religious, and sober men; and then God who gave us such variety of creatures, and our choice to use which we will, may receive glorie from our temperate use, and thanksgiving, and we may use them indifferently without scruple, and a making them to become snares to us, either by too licentious and studied use of them, or too restrained and scrupulous fear of using them at all, but in such certain circumstances in which no man can be sure he is not mistaken.

But temperance in meat and drink is to be estimated by the following measures.

Measures of Temperance in eating.

1. *Eat not before the time*, unless necessity, or charity, or any intervening accident, which may make it reasonable and prudent, should happen. Remember it had almost cost *Jonathan* his life because he tasted a little hony before the sun went down, contrary to the Kings commandment, and although a great need which he had, excused him from the sin of gluttony, yet it is inexcusable when thou eatest before the usual time, and thrustest thy hand into the dish unseasonably, out of greedinesse of the pleasure, and impatience of the delay.

2. *Eat not hastily and impatiently*, but with such decent and timely action, that your eating be a humane act, subject to deliberation and choice, and that you may consider in the eating: whereas he that eats hastily, cannot consider particularly of the circumstances, degrees, and little accidents and chances that happen in his meale; but may contract many little undecencies, and be suddenly surprised.

7 in] *om* 5+

3. *Eat not delicately, or nicely*, that is, be not troublesome to thy self or others in the choice of thy meats, or the delicacy of thy sauces. It was imputed as a sin to the sons of Israel, that they loathed Manna and longed for flesh: *the quails stuck in their nostrills, and the wrath of God fell upon them.* And for the manner of dressing, the sons of *Eli* were noted of indiscreet curiosity: they would not have the flesh boiled, but raw that they might *rost it with fire.* Not that it was a sin to eat it, or desire meat rosted; but that when it was appointed to be boiled, they refused it; which declared an intemperate and a nice palate. It is lawful in all senses to comply with a weak and a nice stomach: but not with a nice and curious palate. When our health requires it, that ought to be provided for; but not so, our sensuality and intemperate longings. *Whatsoever is set before you, eat*; if it be provided for you, you may eat it be it never so delicate; and be it plain and common, so it be wholsom and fit for you, it must not be refused upon curiosity; for every degree of that is a degree of intemperance. [m]Happy and innocent were the ages of our forefathers, who eat herbs and parched corne, and drank the pure stream, and broke their fast with nuts and roots; and when they were permitted flesh, eat it only dressed with hunger and fire; and the first sauce they had was bitter herbs, and sometimes bread dipt in vinegar. But in this circumstance moderation is to be reckoned in proportion to the present customs, to the company, to education, and the judgement of honest and wise persons, and the necessities of nature.

4. *Eat not too much*: load neither thy stomach nor thy understanding. *If thou sit at a bountiful table, be not greedy upon it, and say not there is much meat on it. Remember that a wicked Eye is an evil thing: and what is created more wicked than an eye? Therefore it weepeth upon every occasion. Stretch not thy hand whithersoever it looketh, and thrust it not with him into the dish. A very little is sufficient for a man well nurtured, and he fetcheth not his winde short upon his bed.*

Signes and effects of Temperance.

We shall best know that we have the grace of temperance by the following signes, which are as so many arguments to engage us also upon its study and practise.

[m] Fœlix initium prior ætas contenta dulcibus arvis,
Facili quæ sera solebat jejunia solvere glande.
Arbuteos fœtus, montanaque fraga legebant. Boeth. l. 2 de consol.

17 eat] ate *78* 19 eat] ate *78* note *m* fraga] *cor*, fragra *1*+ l. 2] *2*+, 1 *1*

1. A temperate man is modest; greedinesse is unmannerly and rude. And this is intimated in the advice of the son of *Sirach.* [n] *When thou sittest amongst many reach not thy hand out first of all. Leave off first for manners sake, and be not unsatiable lest thou offend.* 2. [o]Temperance is accompanied with gravity of deportment: greedinesse is garish, and rejoyces loosely at the sight of dainties. 3. Sound, but moderate sleep is its signe and its effect. [p] *Sound sleep cometh of moderate eating: he riseth early and his wits are with him.* 4. A spiritual joy and a devout prayer. 5. A suppressed and seldom anger. 6. A command of our thoughts and passions. 7. A seldom returning and a never prevailing temptation. 8. To which adde, that a temperate person is not curious of sauces and deliciousnesse. He thinks not much, and speaks not often of meat and drink; hath a healthful body, and long life, unlesse it be hindered by some other accident; whereas to gluttony, [q] *the pain of watching and choler, the pangs of the belly* are continual company: And therefore [r]*Stratonicus* said handsomely concerning the luxury of the Rhodians, 'They built houses as if they were immortal, but they feasted as if they meant to live but a little while.' And *Antipater* by his reproach of the old glutton *Demades* well expressed the basenesse of this sin, saying, that *Demades* now old and alwayes a glutton, was like a spent sacrifice, nothing left of him but his belly and his tongue, all the man besides, is gone.

Of Drunkennesse.

But I desire that it be observed; that because intemperance in eating is not so soone perceived by others as immoderate drinking, and the outward visible effects of it are not either so notorious or so ridiculous, therfore gluttony is not of so great disreputation amongst men as drunkennesse: yet according to its degree it puts on the greatnesse of the sin before God, and is most strickly to be attended to, least we be surprized by our security and want of diligence; and the intemperance is alike criminal in both, according as the affections are either to the meat or drinke. Gluttony is more uncharitable to the body, and drunkennesse to the soule, or the understanding part of man; and therefore in Scripture is more frequently forbidden and declaimed against, than the other: and sobriety hath by use obtained to signify Temperance in drinking.

[n] Ecclus. 31: 17, 18.

[o] Cicero vocat temperantiam ornatum vitæ, in quo decorum illud et honestum situm est.

[p] Ecclus. 31. Verse 20.

[q] Ibid.

[r] Plutarch. de cupid. divit.

14 *of watching*] *watching 3+, om 1 2* — note *p* Verse 20] Verse 22 *2 3, om 5+*

Drunkennesse is an immoderate affection, and use of drink. That I call immoderate, that is besides or beyond that order of good things, for which God hath given us the use of drink. The ends are; digestion of our meat, cheerfulnesse and refreshment of our spirits, or any end of health; *besides* which, if we go, or at any time *beyond* it, it is inordinate and criminal, it is the vice of drunkennesse. It is forbidden by our blessed Saviour in these words. [s] *Take heed to your selves lest at any time your hearts be overcharged with surfetting and drunkennesse. Surfetting*, that is the evil effects, the sottishnesse and remaining stupidity of habitual, or of the last nights *drunkennesse.* For Christ forbids both the actual and the habitual intemperance; not onely the effect of it, but also the affection to it: for in both there is sinne. [t]He that drinks but little, if that little makes him drunk, and if he know beforehand his own infirmity, is guilty of *surfetting*, not of *drunkennesse.* But he that drinks much and is strong to bear it, and is not deprived of his reason violently, is guilty of the sin of *drunkennes.* It is a sin not to prevent such uncharitable effects upon the body and understanding: And therefore a man that loves not the drink is guilty of *surfetting*, if he does not watch to prevent the evil effect: and it is a sin, and the greater of the two, inordinately to love or to use the drink, though the *surfetting*, or violence do not follow. Good therefore is the counsel of the son of *Syrach*: [u] *Shew not thy valiantnesse in wine; for wine hath destroyed many.*

Evil consequents to drunkennesse.

The evils and sad consequents of drunkennesse (the consideration of which are as so many arguments to avoyd the sin) are to this sence reckoned by the writers of holy Scripture, and other wise personages of the world. 1. [v]It causeth woes and mischiefe, [w]wounds and sorrow, sin and shame; it maketh bitternesse of spirit, brawling and quarrelling, it increaseth rage and lesseneth strength, it maketh red eyes, and a loose and babling tongue. 2. It particularly ministers to lust, and yet disables the body; so that in effect it makes a man wanton as a Satyr, and impotent as age: And *Solomon* in enumerating the evils of this vice

[s] Luke 21: 34.

[t] *Κραιπάλη ἀπὸ προτεραίας* aut *ἀπὸ χθιζῆς οἰνοποσίας*. Schol. in Aristoph Idem fere apud Plutarch. Vinolentia animi quandam remissionem et levitatem, ebrietas futilitatem significat. Plutarch. de garrul.

[u] Ecclus. 31: 25. [v] Prov. 23: 29. Ecclus. 31: 26.

[w] Multa faciunt ebrii, quæ post a sobrios pudet. Senec.

19 and[1]] but *23*

adds this to the account: [x] *Thine eyes shall behold strange women; and thy heart shall utter perverse things*: as if the drunkard were onely desire, and then impatience, muttering and enjoying like an Eunuch imbracing a woman. 3. It besots and hinders the actions of the understanding, making a man brutish in his passions, and a fool in his reason; and [y] differs nothing from madnesse, but that it is voluntary, and so is an equal evil in nature, and a worse in manners. 4. It takes off all the guards, and lets loose the reins of all those evils to which a man is by his nature, or by his evil customs inclined, and from which he is restrained by reason and severe principles. Drunkennesse calls off the Watch men from their towers, and then all the evils that can proceed from a loose heart, and an untied tongue, and a dissolute spirit, and an unguarded, unlimited will, all that we may put upon the accounts of drunkennesse. 5. It extinguisheth and quenches the Spirit of God: for no man can be filled with the Spirit of God and with wine at the same time; And therefore Saint *Paul* makes them exclusive of each other. [z] *Be not drunk with wine wherein is excesse, but be filled with the Spirit*: And since *Josephs* cup was put into *Benjamins* sack, no man hath a divining goblet. 6. It opens all the Sanctuaries of Nature, and discovers the nakednesse of the soul, all its weaknesses and follies; it multiplies sins and discovers them; it makes a man uncapable of being a private friend, or a publick Counseller. 7. [a] It taketh a mans soul into slavery and imprisonment more then any vice whatsoever, because it disarms a man of all his reason and his wisdom, wherby he might be cured, and therefore commonly grows it upon him with age: a drunkard being still more a fool and lesse a man. I need not adde any sad examples, since all story and all ages have too many of them. *Amnon* was slain by his brother *Absalom*, when he was warm and high with wine. *Simon* the High Priest and two of his sons were slain by their brother at a

[x] Prov. 23: 33.

[y] Insaniæ comes est ira, contubernalis ebrietas. Plutarch.

—Corpus onostum
Hesternis vitiis animum quoque prægravat. Horat.

Ebrietas est voluntaria insania. Senec.

[z] Ephes. 5: 18.
Οἶνός σε τρώει μελιήδης, ὅς τε καὶ ἄλλους
Βλάπτει, ὅς ἄν μιν χανδὸν ἕλῃ, μηδ' αἴσιμα πίνῃ. Homer.

[a] Prov. 31: 4.
. . . *Οὐδεὶς δὲ μεθύων, ἄν σκοπῇς,*
ὅς οὐχὶ δοῦλός ἐστι τοῦ πεπωκέναι. Philem.

---

25 grows it] it grows *2 3 7 8* note *y* Horat.] *4+*, *om 1 2 3* note *z* *Οἶνος . . .* Homer.] *4+*, *om 1 2 3*

drunken feast. *Holofernes* was drunk when *Judith* slew him: [b] and all the great things that *Daniel* spake of *Alexander* were drowned with the surfet of one nights intemperance: and the drunkennesse of *Noah* and *Lot* are upon record to eternal ages, that in those early instances, and righteous persons and lesse criminal drunkennesse than is that of Christians in this period of the world, God might show that very great evils are prepared to punish this vice; no lesse than shame, and slavery, and incest, the first upon *Noah*, the second upon one of his sons, and the third in the person of *Lot.*

Signes of drunkennesse.

But if it be enquired concerning the periods and distinct significations of this crime, and when a man is said to be drunk? to this I answer, That drunkennesse is in the same manner to be judged as sicknesse. As every illnesse or violence done to health in every part of its continuance is a part or degree of sicknesse: so is every going off from our natural and common temper and our usual severity of behaviour, a degree of drunkennesse. He is not onely drunk that can drink no more; for few are so; but he hath sinned in a degree of drunkennesse who hath done any thing towards it beyond his proper measure. But its parts and periods are usually thus reckoned. 1. Apish gestures. 2. Much talking. 3. Immoderate laughing. 4. Dulnesse of sence. 5. Scurrility, that is, wanton, or jeering, or abusive language. 6. An useless understanding. 7. Stupid sleep. 8. Epilepsies, or fallings, and reelings and beastly vomitings. The least of these, even when the tongue begins to be untyed, is a degree of drunkennesse.

But that we may avoyd the sin of intemperance in meats and drinks, besides the former rules of measures, these counsels also may be useful.

Rules for obtaining Temperance.

1. Be not often present at feasts, nor at all in dissolute company, when it may be avoyded; for variety of pleasing objects steals away the heart of man: and company is either violent or enticing; and we are weak or complying, or perhaps desirous enough to be abused. But if you be unavoidably or indiscreetly ingaged, let not mistaken civilitie or good

[b] Alexandrum intemperantia bibendi, et ille Herculanus ac fatalis Scyphus perdidit.

12 drunk; to] *6+*, drunk? To *1 2 3 4 5*

nature engage thee, either to the temptation of staying (if thou understandest thy weaknesse) or the sin of drinking inordinately.

2. Be severe in your judgement concerning your proportions, and let no occasion make you enlarge far beyond your ordinary. For a man is surprized by parts; and while he thinks one glass more will not make him drunk; that one glasse hath disabled him from well discerning his present condition and neighbour danger: *while men think themselves wise they become fools*: [c]they think they shall tast the aconite and not dye, or crown their heads with juice of poppy and be not drowsie; and if they drink off the whole vintage, still they think they can swallow another goblet. But remember this, when ever you begin to consider whether you may safely take one draught more, it is then high time to give over: let that be accounted a signe late enough to break off: for every reason to doubt, is a sufficient reason to part the company.

3. Come not to table but when thy need invites thee: and if thou beest in health leave something of thy Appetite unfilled, something of thy natural heat unimployed, that it may secure thy digestion, and serve other needs of nature or the spirit.

4. Propound to thy self (if thou beest in a capacity) a constant rule of living, of eating and drinking; which though it may not be fit to observe scrupulously, lest it become a snare to thy conscience, or indanger thy health upon every accidental violence: yet let not thy rule be broken often nor much, but upon great necessity and in small degrees.

5. [d]Never urge any man to eat or drink beyond his own limits, and his own desires. He that does otherwise is drunke with his brothers surfet, and reeles and falls with his intemperance, that is, the sin of drunkennesse is upon both their scores, they both lye wallowing in the guilt.

6. Use S. *Pauls* instruments of Sobriety. *Let us who are of the day be sober, putting on the brestplate of faith and love, and for an helmet the hope of Salvation.* Faith, Hope, and Charity are the best weapons in the world to fight against intemperance. The faith of the Mahometans forbids them to drink wine, and they abstain religiously, as the sons of *Rechab*: and the faith of Christ forbids drunkennesse to us; and therefore is infinitely more powerful to suppresse this vice, when we remember that *we are Christians*, and to abstain from drunkennesse and gluttony is part of the Faith and Discipline of Jesus, and that with these vices,

[c] Senec. Ep. 83.
Chi ha bevuto tutto il mare può bere anchor un tratto.

[d] Nil interest, faveas sceleri an illud facias. Senec.

neither our love to God, nor our hopes of heaven can possibly consist; and therefore when these enter the heart, the others go out at the mouth: for this is the Devil that is cast out by fasting and prayer, which are the proper actions of these graces.

7. As a pursuance of this rule, it is a good advice, that as we begin and end all our times of eating with prayer and thanksgiving: so at the meal we remove and carry up our minde and Spirit to the Coelestiall table, often thinking of it, and often desiring it; that by enkindling thy desire to heavenly banquets, thou mayest be indifferent and lesse passionate for the Earthlie.

8. Mingle discourses pious, or in some sence profitable, and in all sences charitable and innocent, with thy meal, as occasion is ministered.

9. Let your drink so serve your meat, as your meat doth your health; that it be apt to convey and digest it, and refresh the spirits; but let it never go beyond such a refreshment as may a little lighten the present load of a sad or troubled spirit; never to inconvenience, lightnesse, sottishnesse, vanity, or intemperance: and know that the loosing the bands of the tongue, and the very first dissolution of its duty, is one degree of the intemperance.

10. In all cases be carefull that you bee not brought under the power of such things which otherwise are lawful enough in the use. *All things are lawful for me, but I will not be brought under the power of any thing*, said Saint *Paul.* And to be perpetually longing, and impatiently desirous of any thing, so that a man cannot abstaine from it, is to lose a mans liberty, and to become a servant of meat and drink, or *smoke*: And I wish this last instance were more considered by persons who little suspect themselves guilty of intemperance, though their desires are strong and impatient, and the use of it perpetual and unreasonable to all purposes, but that they have made it habitual, and necessary as intemperance it self is made to some men.

11. Use those advices which are prescribed as instruments to suppresse voluptuousnesse in the foregoing Section.

2 others go] *5*+, other goes *1 2 3 4*

SECT. III.
Of Chastity.

Reader stay, and reade not the advices of the following Section, unlesse thou hast a chaste spirit, or desirest to be chaste, or at least, art apt to consider whether you ought or no. For there are some spirits so Atheistical, and some so wholly possessed with a spirit of uncleannesse, that they turn the most prudent and chaste discourses into dirt and filthy apprehensions: like cholerick stomacks changing their very Cordials and medicines into bitternesse; and in a literal sense turning the grace of God into wantonnesse: *They study cases of conscience in the matter of carnal sins, not to avoid, but to learn wayes how to offend God and pollute their own spirits: and search their houses with a Sunbeam that they may be instructed in all the corners of nastinesse. I have used all the care I could, in the following periods, that I might neither be wanting to assist those that need it, nor yet minister any occasion of fancy or vainer thoughts to those that need them not. If any man will snatch the pure taper from my hand, and hold it to the Devil, he will onely burn his own fingers, but shall not rob me of the reward of my care and good intention, since I have taken heed how to expresse the following duties, and given him caution how to reade them.*

Chastity is that duty which was mystically intended by GOD in the Law of Circumcision. It is the circumcision of the heart, the cutting off *all superfluity of naughtinesse*, and a suppression of all irregular desires in the matter of sensual or carnal pleasure. I call all desires irregular and sinful that are not sanctified; 1. By the holy institution or by being within the protection of marriage. 2. By being within the order of nature. 3. By being within the moderation of Christian modesty. *Against the first* are, fornication, adultery, and all voluntary pollutions of either sex. *Against the second* are all unnatural lusts, and incestuous mixtures. *Against the third* is all immoderate use of permitted beds; concerning which, judgement is to be made as concerning meats and drinks; there being no certain degree of frequency or intention prescribed to all persons, but it is to be ruled as the other actions of a man, by proportion to the end, by the dignity of the person in the honour and severity of being a Christian, and by other circumstances, of which I am to give account.

Chastity is that grace which forbids and restrains all these, keeping the body and soul pure in that state in which it is placed by God, whether of the single or of the married life. Concerning which our

1 SECT. III.] *4+*, *om 1 2 3*

duty is thus described by S. *Paul.*[e] *For this is the will of God, even your sanctification, that ye should abstain from fornication: that every one of you should know how to possesse his vessel in sanctification and honour*: *Not in the lust of concupiscence, even as the Gentiles which know not God.*

Chastity is either *abstinence* or *continence. Abstinence* is that of Virgins or Widows: *Continence* of married persons. *Chaste marriages* are honourable and pleasing to God: *Widowhood* is pitiable in its solitarinesse and losse, but amiable and comely when it is adorned with gravity and purity, and not sullied with remembrances of the passed license, nor with present desires of returning to a second bed. [f]But *Virginity* is a life of Angels, the enamel of the soul, the huge advantage of religion, the great opportunity for the retirements of devotion: and being empty of cares, it is full of prayers: being unmingled with the World, it is apt to converse with God: and by not feeling the warmth of a too forward and indulgent nature, flames out with holy fires, till it be burning like the Cherubim and the most extasied order of holy and unpolluted Spirits.

Natural virginity of it self is not a state more acceptable to God: but that which is chosen and voluntary in order to the conveniences of Religion and separation from worldly incombrances, is therefore better than the married life; not that it is more holy, but that it is a freedom from cares, an opportunity to spend more time in spiritual imployments; it is not allayed with businesses and attendances upon lower affairs: and if it be a chosen condition to these ends; it containeth in it a victory over lusts, and greater desires of Religion, and self-denial, and therefore is more excellent than the married life, in that degree in which it hath greater religion, and a greater mortification, a lesse satisfaction of natural desires, and a greater fulnesse of the spiritual: and just so is to expect that little coronet or special reward which God hath prepared (extraordinary and besides the great Crown of all faithful souls) for those [g] *who have not defiled themselves with women, but follow the* Virgin *Lamb forever.*

But some married persons even in their marriage do better please God than some Virgins in their state of virginity: They by giving great example of conjugal affection, by preserving their faith unbroken, by

[e] 1 Thes. 4: 3–5.

[f] Virginitas est in carne corruptibili incorruptionis perpetua meditatio. S. Aug. 1. de virg. c. 13.

[g] Apoc. 14: 4. Isa. 56: 45.

---

19 conveniences] conveniencies *2*   note *e* 1 Thes. 4: 3–5.] *6*+, 1 Thes. 3. 4, 5. *1 2 3 4*, 5 Thess. 3. 4, 5. *5*

educating children in the fear of God, by patience and contentednesse, and holy thoughts and the exercise of vertues proper to that state, do not onely please God, but do it in a higher degree than those Virgins whose piety is not answerable to their great opportunities and advantages.

However, married persons, and Widows, and Virgins are all servants of God and coheirs in the inheritance of Jesus, if they live within the restraints and laws of their particular estate, chastely, temperately, justly, and religiously.

The evil consequents of Uncleannesse.

The blessings and proper affects of chastity we shall best understand by reckoning the evils of uncleannesse and carnality.

1. Uncleannesse of all vices is the most shameful. [h] *The eye of the adulterer waiteth for the twilight, saying; No eye shall see me: and disguiseth his face. In the dark they dig through houses which they had marked for themselves in the day time: they know not the light: for the morning is to them as the shadow of death. He is swift as the waters; their portion is cursed in the earth, he beholdeth not the way of the vineyards.* [i]Shame is the eldest daughter of Uncleannesse.

2. The appetites of uncleannesse are full of cares and trouble, and in its fruition is sorrow and repentance. [j] *The way of the adulterer is hedged with thorns*: [k]full of fears and jealousies, burning desires and impatient waitings, tediousnesse of delay, and sufferance of affronts, and amazements of discovery.

3. Most of its kindes are of that condition, that they involve the ruine of two souls: and he that is a fornicatour or adulterous, steals the soul as well as dishonours the body of his Neighbour: and so it becomes like the sin of falling *Lucifer*, who brought a part of the stars with his tail from heaven.

4. Of all carnal sins it is that alone which the Devil takes delight to imitate and counterfeit; communicating with Witches and impure persons in no corporal act, but in this onely.

5. Uncleannesse with all its kindes is a vice which hath a professed enmity against the body. [l] *Every sin which a man doth is without the body, but he that committeth fornication sinneth against his own body.*

[h] Job 24: 15–18. Prov. 6: 23. [i] *ἄτιμα πάθη.* [j] Hos. 2: 6.
[k] Appetitus fornicationis anxietas est, satietas vero penitentia. S. Hieron.
[l] 1 Cor. 6: 18.

3 it] *om 5+* 32 no] the *5+* note *h* Prov. 6: 23] *om 6+*

6. Uncleannesse is hugely contrary to the spirit of Government by [m]embasing the spirit of a man, making it effeminate, sneaking, soft, and foolish, without courage, without confidence. [n]*David* felt this after his folly with *Bathsheba*: he fell to unkingly arts and stratagems to hide the crime, and he did nothing but increase it; and remained timorous and poor spirited, till he prayed to God once more to establish him with a free and a *Princely spirit.* And no superiour dare strictly observe discipline upon his charge, if he hath let himself loose to the *shame of incontinence.*

7. The Gospel hath added two arguments against uncleannesse which were never before used, nor indeed could be, since GOD hath given the holy Spirit to them that are baptized, and rightly confirmed, and entered into covenant with him, our bodies are made temples of the holy Ghost in which he dwels: and therfore uncleanness is Sacriledge and defiles a Temple. It is S. *Pauls* argument: [o]*Know ye not that your body is the temple of the holy Ghost?* and *He that defiles a Temple, him will God destroy.* Therfore *Glorifie God in your bodies*, that is, *flee fornication.* To which for the likeness of the argument adde, *That our bodies are members of Christ*, and therefore *God forbid* that we should *take the members of Christ and make them members of a harlot.* So that uncleannesse dishonours Christ, and dishonours the holy Spirit: it is a sin against God, and in this sence a sin against the Holy Ghost.

8. [p]The next special argument which the Gospel ministers especially against adultery, and for preservation of the purity of marriage, is that Marriage is by Christ hallowed into a mystery to signifie the Sacramental and mystical union of Christ and his Church. He therefore that breaks this knot, which the Church and their mutual faith hath tyed, and Christ hath knit up into a mystery, dishonours a great rite of Christianity, of high, spiritual and excellent signification.

9. [q]S. *Gregory* reckons uncleannesse to be the parent of these monsters: Blindnesse of minde, inconsideration, precipitancy or giddinesse in actions, self love, hatred of God, love of the present pleasures, a despite or despair of the joyes of religion here, and of Heaven hereafter. Whereas a pure minde in a chast body is the Mother of wisdom and deliberation, sober counsells, and ingenuous actions, open deportment, and sweet carriage, sincere principles, and unprejudicate understanding, love of God, and self denyall, peace and confidence,

[m] φθαρτικαὶ τῶν ἀρχῶν. [n] Spiritu principali me confirma. Ps. 51.
[o] 1 Cor. 6: 19. 1 Cor. 3: 17. [p] Ephes. 5: 32. [q] Moral. 31.

35 deliberation] deliberations *2 3*

holy prayers and spiritual comfort, and a pleasure of Spirit infinitely greater then the sottish and beastly pleasures of unchastity. [r]*For to overcome pleasure is the greatest pleasure, and no victory is greater than that which is gotten over our lusts and filthy inclinations.*

10. Adde to all these, the publick dishonesty and disreputation that all the Nations of the world have cast upon adulterous and unhallowed embraces. *Abimelech* to the men of *Gerar* made it death to meddle with the wife of *Isaac*: and *Judah* condemned *Thamar* to be burnt for her adulterous conception: [s]and God, besides the Law made to put the adulterous person to death, did constitute a setled and constant miracle to discover the adultery of a suspected woman, that her bowels should burst with drinking the waters of Jealousie. The Egyptian Law was to cut off the nose of the adulteresse, and the offending part of the adulterer. The Locrians put out the adulterers both eyes. The Germanes (as *Tacitus* reports) placed the Adulteresse amidst her kindred naked, and shaved her head, and caused her husband to beat her with clubs thorough the city. The Gortinaeans crowned the man with wool to shame him for his effeminacy: and the Cumani caused the woman to ride upon an asse naked and hooted at: and for ever after called her by an appellative of scorn: [t]*a rider upon the asse.* All nations barbarous and civil agreeing in their general designe of rooting so dishonest and shameful a vice from under heaven.

[u]The middle ages of the Church were not pleased that the Adulteresse should be put to death: [v]but in the primitive ages the civil Lawes by which Christians were then governed, gave leave to the wronged husband to kill his adulterous wife, if he took her in the fact: but because it was a priviledge indulged to men, rather then a direct detestation of the crime, a consideration of the injury rather than of the uncleannesse, therefore it was soon altered: but yet hath caused an inquiry, *whether is worse, the Adultery of the man or the woman.*

The resolution of which case in order to our present affair, is thus, 1. *In respect of the person*, the fault is greater in a man than in a woman, who is of a more plyant and easie spirit, and weaker understanding, and hath nothing to supply the unequal strengths of men, but the

[r] S. Cyprian. de bono pudicitiæ.
[s] Numb. 5: 14.
[t] ʼΟνόβατις.
[u] Concil. Tribur. c. 46. Concil. Aurel. 1. sub Clodovaco.
[v] Cod. de adulteriis. ad legem Juliam, l. 1. et Cod. Theod. de adulteriis c. placuit.

22 a] *7 8, om 1 2 3 4 5 6*

defensative of a passive nature and armour of modesty, which is the natural ornament of that sex. [w] *And it is unjust that the man should demand chastity and severity from his wife, which himself will not observe towards her*, said the good Emperour *Antoninus*: It is as if the man should perswade his wife to fight against those enemies to which he had yielded himself a prisoner. 2. *In respect of the effects and evil consequents*, the adultery of the woman is worse, as bringing bastardy into a family, and disinherisons or great injuries to the Lawful children, and infinite violations of peace, and murders, and divorces, and all the effects of rage and madnesse. 3. *But in respect of the crime*, and as relating to God they are equal, intollerable, and damnable: and since it is no more permitted to men to have many wives, than to women to have many husbands, and that in this respect their privilege is equal, their sin is so too. And this is the case of the question in Christianity. And the Church anciently refused to admit such persons to the holy Communion, until they had done seven yeers penances in fasting, in sackcloth, in severe inflictions and instruments of chastity and sorrow, according to the discipline of those ages.

Acts of chastity in general.

The actions and proper offices of the grace of chastity in general are these.

1. *To resist all unchast thoughts*; at no hand entertaining pleasure in the unfruitful fancies and remembrances of uncleannesse; although no definite desire or resolution be entertained.

2. [x] *At no hand to entertain any desire*; or any phantastick, imaginative loves, though by shame, or disability, or other circumstance they be restrained from act.

3. [y] *To have a chast eye and hand*: for it is all one with what part of the body we commit adultery: and if a man lets his eye loose, and enjoys the lust of that, he is an adulterer. *Look not upon a woman to lust after her.* And supposing all the other members restrained, yet if the eye be permitted to lust, the man can no otherwise be called chast, than he can

[w] Apud. Aug. de adulter. conjug.
Plut. conjug. præcept.

[x] —Casso saltem delectamine
Amare quod potiri non licet. Poeta.

[y] Patellas luxuriæ oculos, dixit *Isidorus*. Ἀλγηδόνας ἀνθρώπων, alius quidam. Time videre unde possis cadere, et noli fieri perversa simplicitate securus. S. Aug.

11–14 and since . . . Christianity.] *4+*, *om 1 2 3* 32 than] that *2 3*

be called severe and mortified, that sits all day seeing playes and revellings, and out of greedinesse to fill his eye, neglects his belly: There are some vessels which if you offer to lift by the belly or bottom you cannot stir them, but are soon removed if you take them by the ears. It matters not with which of your members you are taken and carried off from your dutie and severity.

4. *To have a heart and minde chast and pure*: that is, detesting all uncleannesse; disliking all its motions, past actions, circumstances, likenesses, discourses: and this ought to be the chastity of Virgins and Widows, of old persons and Eunuchs especially, and generally of all men according to their several necessities.

5. [z] *To Discourse chastly and purely*, with great care declining all undecencies of language, chastening the tongue, and restraining it with grace, as vapours of wine are restrained with a bunch of myrrhe.

6. *To disapprove by an after act all involuntary and natural pollutions*: for if a man delights in having suffered any natural pollution, and with pleasure remembers it, he chooses that which was in it self involuntary: and that which being natural was innocent, becoming voluntary is made sinful.

7. They that have performed these duties and parts of Chastity, will certainly abstain from all exterior actions of uncleannesse: those noon-day and mid-night Devils, those lawlesse and ungodly worshippings of shame and uncleannesse; whose birth is in trouble, whose growth is in folly, and whose end is in shame.

But besides these general acts of Chastity which are common to all states of men and women, there are some few things proper to the severals.

Acts of virginal Chastity.

1. Virgins must remember that the virginitie of the bodie is onely excellent in order to the puritie of the soul: who therefore must consider that since they are in some measure in a condition like that of angels, it is their duty to spend much of their time in Angelical imployment: for in the same degree that Virgins live more spiritually than other persons, in the same degree is their virginity a more excellent state: But else it is no better than that of involuntary or constrained

[z] Sp. Minucius Pontifex Posthumiam monuit, ne verbis vitæ castimoniam non æquantibus uteretur. Plut. de cap. ex inim. utilit.

17 remembers] *6+*, remember *12345*   note *z* Posthumiam] *cor*, Posthumium *1+*

Eunuchs; a misery and a trouble, or else a mere privation, as much without excellency as without mixture.

2. Virgins must contend for a singular modesty; whose first part must be an ignorance in the distinction of sexes, or their proper instruments: or if they accidentally be instructed in that, it must be supplied with an inadvertency or neglect of all thoughts and remembrances of such difference: and the following parts of it, must be pious and chast thoughts, holy language, and modest carriage.

3. Virgins must be retired and unpublick: for all freedom and loosenesse of society is a violence done to virginity; not in its natural, but in its moral capacity: that is, it looses part of its severity, strictnesse and opportunity of advantages by publishing that person, whose work is religion, whose company is Angels, whose thoughts must dwell in heaven, and separate from all mixtures of the world.

4. Virgins have a peculiar obligation to charity: for this is the virginity of the soul; as puritie, integrity, and separation is of the body, which doctrine we are taught by Saint *Peter.*[a] *Seeing ye have purified your souls in obeying the truth thorough the spirit unto unfaigned love of the brethren: see that ye love one another with a pure heart fervently.* For a Virgin that consecrates her body to God, and pollutes her spirit with rage, or impatience, or inordinate anger, gives him what he most hates, a most foul and defiled soul.

5. These rules are necessary for Virgins that offer that state to God, and mean not to enter into the state of marriage: for they that onely wait the opportunity of a convenient change, are to steer themselves by the general rules of Chastity.

Rules for Widows or vidual Chastity.

For Widows, the fontinel of whose desires hath been opened by the former permissions of the marriage-bed, they must remember:

1. That God hath now restrained the former license, bound up their eyes, and shut up their heart into a narrower compasse, and hath given them sorrow to be a bridle to their desires. A Widow must be a mourner; and she that is not, cannot so well secure the chastity of her proper state.

2. It is against publick honesty to marry another man so long as she is with childe by her former Husband: and of the same fame it is in a lesser proportion, to marry within the year of mourning: but anciently

[a] 1 Pet. 1: 22.

it was infamous for her to marry, till by common account the body was dissolved into its first principle of earth.

3. A Widow must restrain her memory and her fancy: not recalling or recounting her former permissions and freer licenses with any present delight: for then she opens that sluce which her Husbands death and her own sorrow have shut up.

4. A Widow that desires her widowhood should be a state pleasing to God, must spend her time as devoted Virgins should, in fastings and prayers, and charity.

5. A Widow must forbid her self to use those temporal solaces, which in her former estate were innocent, but now are dangerous.

Rules for married persons, or matrimonial chastity.

[b]Concerning married persons; besides the keeping of their mutual faith, and contract with each other, these particulars are useful to be observed.

1. Although their mutual endearments are safe within the protection of marriage, yet they that have Wives or Husbands must be as though they had them not; that is, they must have an affection greater to each other than they have to any person in the world, but not greater than they have to God: but that they be ready to part with all interest in each others person rather than sin against God.

2. In their permissions and license they must be sure to observe the order of Nature, and the ends of God. [c]*He is an ill Husband that uses his Wife as a man treats a Harlot*, having no other end but pleasure. Concerning which our best rule is, that although in this, as in eating and drinking there is an appetite to be satisfied, which cannot be done without pleasing that desire, yet since that desire and satisfaction was intended by Nature for other ends, they should never be separate from those ends, but alwayes be joyned with all or one of these ends; *with a desire of children, or to avoyd fornication, or to lighten and ease the cares and sadnesses of houshold affairs, or to endear each other*: but never with a purpose either in act or desire to separate the sensuality from these ends which hallow it. *Onan* did separate his act from its proper end, and so ordered his embraces that his Wife should not conceive, and God punished him.

[b] Nisi fundamenta stirpis jacta sint probe,
Miseros necesse est esse deinceps posteros. Eurip.

[c] Non debemus eodem amico uti et adulare; nec eadem uti uxore et scorto. Plut. conjug. præcept.

29 *a*] *the* 2 3

3. [d]Married persons must keep such modesty and decency of treating each other, that they never force themselves into high and violent lusts, with arts and misbecoming devices: alwayes remembering that those mixtures are most innocent which are *most simple*, and *most natural, most orderly and most safe.*

4. It is a duty of matrimonial chastity to be restrained and temperate in the use of their lawful pleasures: concerning which although no universal Rule can antecedently be given to all persons, any more than to all bodies one proportion of meat and drink: yet married persons are to estimate the degree of their license according to the following proportions. 1. That it be moderate so as to consist with health. 2. That it be so ordered as not to be too expensive of time, that precious opportunity of working out our salvation. 3. That when duty is demanded it be alwayes payed (so far as is in our powers and election) according to the foregoing measures. 4. That it be with a temperate affection, without violent transporting desires, or too sensuall applications. Concerning which a man is to make judgement by proportion to other actions, and the severities of his religion, and the sentences of sober and wise persons, alwaies remembering that marriage is a provision for supply of the natural necessities of the body; not for the artificial and procured appetites of the mind. And it is a sad truth, that many married persons thinking that the floodgates of liberty are set wide open without measures or restraints (so they sail in that channel) have felt the final rewards of intemperance and lust, by their unlawful using of lawful permissions. Onely let each of them be temperate, and both of them be modest. [e]*Socrates* was wont to say, that those women to whom Nature had not been indulgent in good features and colours, should make it up themselves with excellent manners; and those who were beautiful and comely, should be careful that so fair a body be not polluted with unhandsome usages. To which *Plutarch* addes; that a wife if she be unhandsome, should consider, how extreamly ugly she should be, if she wanted modesty: but if she be handsome, let her think how gracious that beauty would be if she superads chastity.

[d] Non recte est ab Herodoto dictum, simul cum tunica mulierum verecundiam exuere. Quæ enim casta est, posita veste, verecundiam ejus loco induit, maximaque verecundia conjuges tessera maximi invicem amoris utuntur. Plut. conjug. præcept.

[e] De conjug. præcept.

---

15 4.] *2 3 6 7 8, om 1 4 5* 19–21 alwaies remembering . . . mind.] *4+, om 1 2 3*
21 And] *4+*, For *1 2 3*

5. Married persons by consent are to abstain from their mutual entertainments at solemn times of devotion: not as a duty of it self necessary, but as being the most proper act of purity which in their condition they can present to God: and being a good advantage for attending their preparation to the solemn duty, and their demeanour in it. It is S. *Pauls* counsel, [f]that *by consent for a time they should abstain, that they may give themselves to fasting and prayer.* And though when Christians did receive the holy Communion every day, it is certain they did not abstain, but had children: [g]yet when the Communion was more seldom, they did with religion abstain from the marriage-bed during the time of their solemn preparatory devotions, as anciently they did, from eating and drinking till the solemnity of the day was past.

6. It were well if married persons would in their penitential prayers, and in their general confessions suspect themselves, and accordingly ask a general pardon for all their undecencies and more passionate applications of themselves in their offices of marriage: that what is lawful and honourable in its kinde may not be sullied with imperfect circumstances; or if it be, it may be made clean again by the interruption and recallings of such a repentance of which such uncertain parts of action are capable.

But because of all the dangers of a Christian, none more pressing and troublesome than the temptations to lust, no enemy more dangerous than that of the flesh, no accounts greater than what we have to reckon for at the audit of Concupiscence, therefore it concerns all that would be safe from this death to arme themselves by the following rules to prevent, or to cure all the wounds of our flesh made by the poysoned arrows of Lust.

Remedies against uncleannesse.

1. [h]When a temptation of lust assaults thee, do not resist it by heaping up arguments against it, and disputing with it, considering its offers,

[f] 1 Cor. 7: 5.

[g] Hoc etiam ex more Christianorum. Tertul. Suadens fœminis Christianis ne Paganis nubant ait, Quis denique solennibus Paschæ abnoctantem securus sustinebit? Tertul. ad uxor. 2. 4. Et ex more etiam Gentilium. Plut. sympos. 3. qu. 6. Nobis autem, si leges civitatis recte colimus, cavendum est, ne ad templa et sacrificia accedamus, Paulo ante re venerea usi. Atque expedit, nocte et somno interjecto, justoque intervallo adhibito, mundos rursum quasi de integro, et ad novum diem nova cogitantes (ut ait Democritus) surgere.

[h] Contra libidinis impetum apprehende fugam si vis obtinere victoriam. S. Aug.
Nella guerra d'amor chi fugge vince.

and its danger, but *flie from it*, that is, think not at all of it; lay aside all consideration concerning it, and turn away from it, by any severe and laudable thought or businesse. S. *Hierome* very wittily reproves the Gentile superstition, who pictured the Virgin Deityes armed with a sheild and lance, as if chastity could not be defended without war and direct contention. No; this enemy is to be treated otherwise. If you hear it speak, though but to dispute with it, it ruines you; and the very arguments, you go about to answer, leave a relish upon the tongue. A man may be burned if he goes neer the fire, though but to quench his house; and by handling pitch, though but to draw it from your cloths, you defile your fingers.

2. Avoid *idlenesse*, and fill up all the spaces of thy time with severe and usefull imployment: for lust usually creepes in at those emptinesses, where the soul is unimployed and the body is at ease. For no easy, healthfull, and idle person was ever chast, if he could be tempted. But of all imployments, *bodily labour* is most usefull and of greatest benefit for the driving away this Devill.

3. Give no entertainment to the *beginnings*, the *first motions* and secret whispers of the spirit of impurity. [i]For if you totally suppress it, it dyes: if you permit the furnace to breath its smoke and flame out at any vent, it will rage to the consumption of the whole. This cockatrice is soonest crushed in the shell, but if it growes, it turns to a serpent, and a Dragon, and a Devill.

4. *Corporal mortification* and hard usages of our body hath by all ages of the Church bin accounted a good instrument and of some profit against the spirit of fornication. A spare diet, and a thin course table, seldome refreshment, frequent fasts, not violent and interrupted with returns to ordinary feeding, but constantly little, unpleasant, of wholesome but sparing nourishment: For by such cutting off the provision of victual wee shall weaken the strengths of our Enemy. To which if we adde, lyings upon the ground, painfull postures in prayer, reciting our devotions with our armes extended at full length, like *Moses* praying against *Amalek*, or our blessed SAVIOUR hanging upon his painful bed of sorrowes, the Crosse; and (if the lust be upon us and sharply tempting) by inflicting any smart to overthrow the strongest passion by the most

[i] —Quisquis in primo obsitit
Pepulitque amorem, tutus ac victor fuit.
Qui blandiendo dulce nutrivit malum,
Sero recusat ferre quod subiit jugum. Senec. Hippol.

19 [i]] *4*+, *om 1 2 3* 25 accounted . . . some profit] *4*+, an approved remedy *1 2*

violent paine, we shall finde great ease for the present, and the resolution and apt sufferance against the future danger. And this was Saint *Pauls* remedy, *I bring my body under*; he used some rudenesses towards it. But it was a great noblenesse of chastity which S. *Hierome* [j]reports of a Son of the King of *Nicomedia*, who being tempted upon flowers and a perfumed bed with a soft violence, but yet tyed down to the temptation, and sollicited with circumstances of Asian Luxury by an impure Curtesan; least the easinesse of his posture should abuse him, spit out his tongue into her face: to represent that [k]no vertue hath cost the Saints so much, as this of Chastity.

5. [l]*Fly from all occasions*, temptations, loosenesses of company, Balls and Revellings, undecent mixtures of wanton dancings, idle talke, private society with stranger women, starings upon a beauteous face, the company of women that are singers, amorous gestures, garish and wanton dressings, feasts and liberty, banquets and perfumes, wine and strong drinks, which are made to persecute chastity; [m]some of these being the very Prologues to lust, [n]and the most innocent of them being but like condited or pickled Mushroms, which if carefully corrected, or seldom tasted, may be harmlesse, but can never do good: Ever remembering that it is easier to die for chastity, than to live with it; and the Hangman could not extort a consent from some persons, from whom a Lover would have intreated it. For the glory of chastity will easily overcome the rudenesse of fear and violence; but easinesse and softnesse, and smooth temptations creep in, and like the Sun make a mayden lay by her vail and robe, which persecution like the Northern winde, made her hold fast and clap close about her.

[j] In vita S. Pauli.

[k] Benedictus in spinis se volutavit. S. Martinianus faciem et manus ussit. S. Johannes cognomento Bonus, calamos acutos inter ungues et carnem digitorum intrusit. S. Theoctiste in silvis more ferarum vixit, ne inter Arabes pollueretur.

[l] *Στέφος πλέκων ποθ' εὗρον*
ἐν τοῖς ῥόδοις Ἔρωτα,
καὶ τῶν πτερῶν κατασχὼν
ἐβάπτισ' εἰς τὸν οἶνον,
λαβὼν δ' ἔπιον αὐτόν·
καὶ νῦν ἔσω μελῶν μου
πτεροῖσι γαργαλίζει. Julian.

Venus rosam amat propter fabellam quam recitat. Libanius.

[m] Venter mero æstuans cito despumatur in libidines. S. Hieron.

[n] Il fuoco che non mi scalda non voglio che mi Scotti.

---

11 [l]] *4+*, *om 1 2 3* 13 stranger] strange *5+* 15–16 wine and strong drinks,] *4+*, *om 1 2 3* 16 [m]] *4+*, *om 1 2 3*

6. [o]He that will secure his chastity, must *first cure his pride and his rage.* For oftentimes lust is the punishment of a proud man, to tame the vanity of his pride by the shame and affronts of unchastity: and the same intemperate heat that makes anger, does enkindle lust.

7. If thou beest assaulted with an unclean Spirit, trust not thy self alone, but runne forth into company, whose reverence and modesty may suppresse, or whose society may divert thy thoughts: and a perpetual witnesse of thy conversation is of especial use against this vice, which evaporates in the open air like Camphyre, being impatient of light and witnesses.

8. Use frequent and earnest prayer to the King of Purities, the first of Virgins, the eternal GOD, who is of an essential purity; that hee would be pleased to reprove and cast out the unclean Spirit. For besides the blessings of prayer by way of reward, it hath a natural vertue to restrain this vice: because a prayer against it, is an unwillingnesse to act it; and so long as we heartily pray against it, our desires are secured, and then this Devil hath no power. This was S. *Pauls* other remedy. *For this cause I besought the Lord thrice.* [p]And there is much reason and much advantage in the use of this instrument; because the main thing that in this affair is to be secured is a mans minde. He that goes about to cure lust by *bodily exercises* alone (as Saint *Pauls* phrase is) or mortifications, shall find them sometimes instrumental to it, and incitations of sudden desires, but alwaies insufficient and of *little profit*: but he that hath a chaste mind shall find his body apt enough to take laws; and let it doe its worst; it cannot make a sinne; and in its greatest violence can but produce a little natural uneasiness, not so much trouble as a severe fasting day, or a hard nights lodging upon boords. If a man be hungry he must eat, and if he be thirsty he must drink in some convenient time; or else he dies: but if the body be rebellious, so the minde be chaste, let it doe its worst, if you resolve perfectly not to satisfie it, you can receive no great evil by it. Therefore the proper cure is by applications to the Spirit, and securities of the minde; which can no way so well be secured as by frequent and fervent prayers, and sober resolutions, and severe discourses.

[o] —numquid ego a te
Magno prognatum deposco consule—
Velatamque stola, mea cum conferbuit ira? Horat. Serm. lib. I. Sat. 2.

[p] Mens impudicam facere; non corpus solet.

---

1 [o]] *4+, om 1 2 3* 18 [p]] *4+, om 1 2 3* 18–34 And there is . . . discourses.] *4+, om 1 2 3*

9. Therefore, hither bring in succour from consideration of the *Divine presence*, and of his holy Angels, *meditation of Death*, and the passions of CHRIST upon the Crosse, *imitation of his purities*, and of the Virgin *Mary* his unspotted and holy Mother, and of such eminent Saints who in their generations were burning and shining lights, unmingled with such uncleannesses which defile the soul, and who now follow the Lambe whithersoever he goes.

10. These remedies are of universal efficacy in all cases extraordinary and violent: but in ordinary and common, [q]the remedy which GOD hath provided, that is, *Honourable marriage*, hath a natural efficacy, besides a vertue by Divine blessing, to cure the inconveniences which otherwise might afflict persons temperate and sober.

SECT. IV.
Of Humility.

Humility is the great Ornament and Jewel of Christian Religion; that whereby it is distinguished from all the wisdome of the world; it not having been taught by the wise men of the Gentiles; but first put into a discipline, and made part of a religion by our Lord Jesus Christ, who propounded himselfe imitable by his Disciples so signally in nothing, as in the twinne sisters of Meeknesse and Humility. *Learne of me for I am meek and humble, and ye shall finde rest unto your souls.*

For all the World, all that we are, and all that we have; our bodies and our souls, our actions and our sufferings, our conditions at home, our accidents abroad, our many sinnes, and our seldome vertues are as so many arguments to make our souls dwell low in the deep valleys of Humility.

Arguments against Pride by way of Consideration.

1. *Our Body* is weak and impure, sending out more uncleannesses from its several sinkes than could be endured if they were not necessary and natural: and we are forced to passe that through our mouthes, which as soon as we see upon the ground, we loathe like rottennesse and vomiting.

2. *Our strength* is inferiour to that of many Beasts, and our infirmities

[q] Danda est opera ut matrimonio divinciantur, quod est tutissimum juventutis vinculum. Plut. de educ. lib.

1 Therefore, hither] *4+*, Hither *1 2 3*

so many that we are forced to dresse and tend Horses and Asses, that they may help our needs, and relieve our wants.

3. *Our beauty* is in colour inferiour to many flowers, and in proportion of parts it is better than nothing. For even a Dog hath parts as well proportioned and fitted to his purposes, and the designes of his nature, as we have: and when it is most florid and gay, three fits of an ague can change it into yellownesse and leanness, and the hollowness and wrinkles of deformity.

4. *Our learning* is then best when it teaches most humility: but to be proud of Learning is the greatest ignorance in the World. For our learning is so long in getting, and so very imperfect, that the greatest Clerke knowes not the thousand part of what hee is ignorant; and knowes so uncertainly what he seemes to know, and knowes no otherwise than a Fool, or a Childe, even what is told him, or what he guesses at, that except those things which concerne his duty, and which God hath revealed to him, which also every Woman knowes so far as is necessary; the most Learned Man hath nothing to bee proud of, unlesse this be a sufficient argument to exalt him, that he uncertainly guesses at some more unnecessary things than many others, who yet know all that concernes them, and minde other things more necessary for the needs of life and Common-wealths.

5. *Hee that is proud of riches is a Foole.* For if he be exalted above his Neighbours because hee hath more gold, how much inferiour is hee to a Gold Mine? How much is he to give place to a chain of Pearl, or a knot of Diamonds? For certainly that hath the greatest excellence from whence he derives all his gallantry and preheminence over his Neighbours.

6. If a man be exalted by reason of any *excellence* in his soul, he may please to remember, that all souls are equal; and their differing operations are because their instrument is in better tune, their body is more healthful, or better tempered: which is no more praise to him, than it is that he was born in *Italy*.

7. *He that is proud of his birth* is proud of the blessings of others, not of himself: for if his parents were more eminent in any circumstance than their Neighbours, he is to thank God, and to rejoyce in them; but still he may be a Fool, or unfortunate, or deformed; and when himself was born, it was indifferent to him whether his Father were a King or Peasant; for he knew not any thing, nor chose any thing: and most commonly it is true, that he that boasts of his Ancestors, who were the founders and raisers of a Noble Family, doth confesse that he hath i

himself a lesse vertue and a lesse honour, and therefore that he is degenerated.

8. Whatever other difference there is between thee and thy Neighbour, if it be bad, it is thine own, but thou hast no reason to boast of thy misery and shame: if it be good, thou hast received it from God; and then thou art more obliged to pay duty and tribute, use and principal to him: and it were a strange folly for a man to be proud of being more in debt than another.

9. Remember what thou wert before thou wert begotten? Nothing. What wert thou in the first regions of thy dwelling, before thy birth? Uncleannesse. What wert thou for many years after? Weaknesse. What in all thy life? A great sinner. What in all thy excellencies? A mere debter to God, to thy parents, to the earth, to all the creatures. [r]But we may if we please use the method of the Platonists, who reduce all the causes and arguments for humility which we can take from ourselves, to these seven heads. 1. The spirit of a man is light and troublesome. 2. His body is brutish and sickly. 3. He is constant in his folly and errour, and inconstant in his manners and good purposes. 4. His labours are vain, intricate, and endlesse. 5. His fortune is changeable, but seldome pleasing, never perfect. 6. His wisdom comes not till he be ready to die, that is, till he be past using it. 7. His death is certain, alwayes ready at the door, but never far off. Upon these or the like meditations if we dwell, or frequently retire to them, we shall see nothing more *reasonable* than to be *humble*, and nothing more *foolish* than to be *proud.*

Acts or offices of humility.

The grace of humility is exercised by these following rules.

1. Think not thy self better for any thing that happens to thee from without. For although thou mayest by gifts bestowed upon thee be better than another, as one horse is better than another, that is, of more use to others; yet as thou art a man, thou hast nothing to commend thee to thy self, but that onely by which thou art a man; that is, by what thou choosest and refusest.

2. Humility consists not in railing against thy self, or wearing mean clothes, or going softly and submissely; but in a hearty and real evil or mean opinion of thy self. Believe thy self an unworthy person,

[r] Apuleius de Demon. Socratis.

3 Whatever] Whatsoever *3 5+* 35 a] *om 7 8*

heartily, as thou believest thy self to be hungry, or poor, or sick, when thou art so.

3. Whatsoever evil thou sayest of thy self to be content that others should think to be true: and if thou callest thy self *fool*, be not angry if another say so of thee: For if thou thinkest so truely, all men in the world desire other men to be of their opinion; and he is an hypocrite that accuses himself before others, with an intent not to be believed. But he that calls himself intemperate, foolish, lustful, and is angry when his neighbours call him so, is both a false and a proud person.

4. [s]Love to be concealed, and little esteemed: be content to want praise, never being troubled when thou art slighted or undervalued: for thou canst not undervalue thy self, and if thou thinkest so meanly as there is reason, no contempt will seem unreasonable, and therefore it will be very tolerable.

5. [t]Never be ashamed of thy birth, or thy parents, or thy trade, or thy present imployment, for the meannesse or poverty of any of them: and when there is an occasion to speak of them, such an occasion as would invite you to speak of any thing that pleases you, omit it not; but speak as readily and indifferently of thy meannesse, as of thy greatnesse. *Primislaus* the first King of *Bohemia* kept his countrey shooes alwayes by him, to remember from whence he was raised: and *Agathocles* by the furniture of his Table confessed, that from a Potter he was raised to be the King of *Sicily*.

6. Never speak any thing directly tending to thy praise or glorie: that is, with a purpose to be commended, and for no other end. If other ends be mingled with thy honour, as if the glory of God, or charity, or necessity, or any thing of prudence be thy end, you are not tyed to omit your discourse, or your designe that you may avoid praise, but pursue your end, though praise come along in the Company. Onely let not praise be the designe.

7. When thou hast said or done any thing for which thou receivest praise or estimation, take it indifferently, and return it to God, reflecting upon him as the Giver of the gift, or the blesser of the action, or the aid of the designe: and give God thanks for making thee an instrument of his glory, or the benefit of others.

8. Secure a good name to thy self by living vertuously and humbly:

[s] Ama nesciri et pro nihilo reputari. Gerson.

[t] Il villan nobilitado non cognosce il suo parentado.
Chi del' arte sua si vergogna sempre vive con vergogna.

---

note *t* il suo] *cor, om 1+*

but let this good name be nursed abroad, and never be brought home to look upon it: let others use it for their own advantage: let them speak of it if they please, but do not thou at all use it, but as an instrument to do God glory, and thy neighbour more advantage. Let thy face like *Moses* shine to others, but make no looking glasses for thy self.

9. Take no content in praise when it is offered thee: but let thy rejoycing in Gods gift be allayed with feare, lest this good bring thee to evill. Use the praise as you use your pleasure in eating and drinking: if it comes, make it do drudgery, let it serve other ends, and minister to necessities, and to caution, lest by pride you lose your just praise which you have deserved; or else by being praised unjustly, you receive shame into your self, with God and wise men.

10. Use no stratagems and devices to get praise. [u]Some use to enquire into the faults of their own actions or discourses on purpose to hear that it was well done or spoken, and without fault: others bring the matter into talk, or thrust themselves into company, and intimate and give occasion to be thought or spoke of. These men make a bait to perswade themselves to swallow the hook, till by drinking the waters of vanity they swell and burst.

11. Make no suppletories to thy self, when thou art disgraced or slighted, by pleasing thy self with supposing thou didst deserve praise, though they understood thee not, or enviously detracted from thee: [v]neither do thou get to thy self a private theatre and flatterers, in whose vain noises, and phantastick praises thou mayet keep up thy own good opinion of thy self.

12. Entertain no fancies of vanity and private whispers of this Devil of pride: such as was that of *Nebuchodonosor*; *Is not this great Babylon which I have built for the honour of my name, and the might of my majesty, and the power of my kingdom*? Some phantastick spirits will walk alone, and dream waking, of greatnesses, of palaces, of excellent orations, full theatres, loud applauses, sudden advancement, great fortunes: and so will spend an hour with imaginative pleasure, all their imployment being nothing but fumes of pride, and secret, indefinite desires, and significations of what their heart wishes: In this, although there is nothing of its own nature directly vitious, yet it is either an ill mother,

[u] *Τί οὖν ὀβελίσκον καταπιὼν περιπατεῖς; ἤθελον ἵνα με καὶ οἱ ἀπαντῶντες θαυμάζωσι, καὶ ἐπακολουθοῦντες ἐπικραυγάζωσιν, ὦ μεγάλου φιλοσόφου.* Arrian. l. 1, cap. 21.

[v] Alter alteri satis amplum theatrum sumus; satis unus, satis nullus. Senec.

or an ill daughter, an ill signe or an ill effect; and therefore at no hand consisting with the safety and interests of humility.

13. Suffer others to be praised in thy presence: and entertain their good and glory with delight: but at no hand disparage them or lessen the report, or make an objection: and think not the advancement of thy brother is a lessening of thy worth. But this act is also to extend further.

14. Be content that he should be imployed, and thou laid by as unprofitable; his sentence approved, thine rejected; he be preferred, and thou fixed in a low imployment.

15. Never compare thy self with others, unlesse it be to advance them and to depresse thy self. To which purpose we must be sure in some sence or other to think our selves the worst in every company where we come: one is more learned than I am; another is more prudent; a third, honourable; a fourth more chast; or he is more charitable, or lesse proud. For the humble man observes their good and reflects onely upon his own vilenesse; or considers the many evils of himself certainly known to himself, and the ill of others but by uncertain report: or he considers that the evils done by another are out of much infirmity, or ignorance, but his own sins are against a clearer light; and if the other had so great helps, he would have done more good and lesse evil; or he remembers that his old sins before his conversion were greater in the nature of the thing, or in certain circumstances, than the sins of other men (So S. *Paul* reckoned himself the chiefest of sinners, because formerly he had acted the chiefest sin of persecuting the Church of God.) But this rule is to be used with this caution: That though it be good alwayes to *think* meanest of our selves, yet it is not ever safe to *speak* it, because those circumstances and considerations which determine thy thoughts, are not known to others as to thy self; and it may concern others that they hear thee give God thanks for the graces he hath given thee. But if thou preservest thy thoughts and opinion of thy self truely humble, you may with more safety give God thanks in publick for that good which cannot, or ought not to be concealed.

16. Be not alwayes ready to excuse every oversight, or indiscretion, or ill action: but if thou beest guilty of it, confesse it plainly; for vertue scorns a lye for its cover; but to hide a sin with it, is like a crust of leprosie drawn upon an ulcer: if thou beest not guilty (unless it be

37 to hide] *2*+, hide to *1*

scandalous) be not over earnest to remove it: but rather use it as an argument to chastise all greatnesse of fancy and opinion in thy self; and accustome thy self to bear reproof patiently and contentedly, and the harsh words of thy enemies, as knowing that the anger of an enemy is a better Monitor, and represents our faults or admonishes us of our duty with more heartinesse, than the kindnes does, or precious balms of a friend.

17. Give God thanks for every weaknesse, deformity, and imperfection, and accept it as a favour and grace of God, and an instrument to resist pride and nurse humility; ever remembering that when God by giving thee a crooked backe, hath also made thy spirit stoop or lesse vain, thou art more ready to enter the narrow gate of Heaven, than by being strait, and standing upright, and thinking highly. Thus the Apostles *rejoyced in their infirmities*, not moral, but natural, and accidental, in their being beaten and whipt like slaves, in their nakednesse and poverty.

18. [w]Upbraid no mans weaknesse to him to discomfort him; neither report it to disparage him; neither delight to remember it to lessen him, or to set thy self above him. Be sure never to praise thy self, or to dispraise any man else, unlesse GODS glory, or some holy end doe hallow it. [x]And it was noted to the praise of *Cyrus*, that amongst his equals in age he would never play at any sport, or use any exercise in which he knew himself more excellent than they: but in such in which he was unskilful he would make his challenges, lest he should shame them by his victory, and that himself might learn something of their skill, and do them civilities.

19. Besides the foregoing parts and actions, humility teaches us to submit ourselves and all our faculties to GOD: *To believe all things, to do all things, to suffer all things* which his will enjoynes us; to bee content in every estate or change, knowing we have deserved worse than the worst we feel: And (as *Anytus* said to *Alcibiades*) he hath taken but half, when he might have taken all: to adore his goodnesse, to fear his Greatnesse, to worship his eternall and infinite excellencies, [y]and to submit our selves to all our superiours in all things according to Godliness: and to be meek and gentle in our conversation towards others.

[w] Ama l'amico tuo con il difetto suo.

[x] In colloquiis pueri invisi aliis non fient, si non omnino in disputationibus victoriam semper obtinere laborent. Non enim tantum egregium est scire vincere, sed etiam posse vinci pulchrum est, ubi victoria est damnosa. Plut. de educ. liber.

[y] Nihil ita dignum est odio ut eorum mores qui compellantibus se difficiles præbent. Plut.

Now although according to the Nature of every grace, this begins as a gift, and is increased like a habit, that is, best by its own acts, yet besides the former acts and offices of humility, there are certain other exercises and considerations, which are good helps and instruments for the procuring and increasing this grace, and the curing of pride.

Meanes and exercises of obtaining and increasing the grace of Humility.

1. Make confession of thy sins often to God; and consider what all that evil amounts to, which you then charge upon your self. Look not upon them as scattered in the course of a long life: now, an intemperate anger, then, too full a meal: now, idle talking, and another time impatience: but unite them into one continued representation, and remember, that he whose life seems fair, by reason that his faults are scattered at large distances, in the severall parts of his life, yet if all his errours and follies were articled against him; the man would seem vitious and miserable: and possibly this exercise, really applyed upon thy Spirit, may be usefull.

2. Remember that we usually disparage others upon slight grounds, and little instances; and towards them one fly is enough to spoil a whole box of ointment: and if a man be highly commended, we think him sufficiently lessened, if we clap one sin or folly, or infirmity into his account: Let us therefore be just to ourselves, since we are so severe to others, and consider, that whatsoever good, any one can think or say of us, we can tell him of hundreds of base and unworthy, and foolish actions, any one of which were enough (we hope) to destroy anothers reputation: Therefore let so many be sufficient to destroy our over high thoughts of our selves.

3. When thy Neighbour is cryed up by publike fame, and popular noises; that we may disparage and lessen him, we cry out that the people is a Heard of unlearned and ignorant persons, ill judges, loud trumpets, but which never give certain sound: [z]let us use the same art to humble our selves, and never take delight and pleasure in publike reports, and acclamations of assemblies, and please our selves with their judgement, of whom in other the like cases we affirm that they are mad.

4. We change our opinion of others by their Kindnesse or

[z] *Οὐχ οὗτοί εἰσι περὶ ὧν εἴωθας λέγειν ὅτι μαίνονται; τί οὖν, ὑπὸ τῶν μαινομένων θέλεις θαυμάζεσθαι;* Arrian. lib. 1. cap. 21.

unkindnesse towards us. If he be my Patron and bounteous, he is wise, he is noble, his faults are but warts, his vertues are mountainous: but if he proves unkinde or rejects our importunate suite, then he is ill natured, covetous, and his free meal is called gluttony; that which before we called *civility*, is now very *drunkennesse*, and all he speakes is flat and dull, and ignorant as a swine: This indeed is unjust towards others, but a good instrument, if we turn the edge of it upon our selves: we use our selves ill, abusing our selves with false principles, cheating our selves with lies and pretences, stealing the choice and election from our wils, placing voluntary ignorance in our understandings, denying the desires of the Spirit, setting up a faction against every noble and just desire; the least of which because we should resent up to reviling the injurious person, it is but reason we should at least not flatter our selves with fond and too kinde opinions.

5. Every day call to minde some one of thy foulest sinnes, or the most shameful of thy disgraces, or the indiscreetest of thy actions, or any thing that did then most trouble thee, and apply it to the present swelling of thy spirit and opinion, and it may help to allay it.

6. Pray often for this grace with all humility of gesture and passion of desire, and in thy devotion interpose many acts of humility by way of confession and addresse to God, and reflection upon thy self.

7. [a]Avoid great Offices and imployments, and the noises of worldly honour. For in those states many times, so many ceremonies and circumstances will seeme necessary, as will destroy the sobriety of thy thoughts. If the number of thy servants be fewer, and their observances lesse, and their reverences lesse solemn, possibly they will seeme lesse than thy dignity: and if they bee so much and so many, it is likely they will be too big for thy spirit. And here bee thou very carefull, lest thou bee abused by a pretence that thou wouldest use thy great Dignity as an opportunity of doing great good. For supposing it might be good for others, yet it is not good for thee: they may have encouragement in noble things from thee, and by the same instrument thou mayest thy self be tempted to pride and vanity: And certaine it is, GOD is as much glorified by thy example of humility in a low or temperate condition, as by thy bounty in a great and dangerous.

8. Make no reflexe acts upon thy owne humility, nor upon any other grace with which GOD hath enriched thy soul. For since GOD oftentimes hides from his Saints and Servants the sight of those excellent

[a] Fabis abstine, dixit Pythagoras. Nam olim Magistratus per suffragia fabis lata creabantur. Plut.

things by which they shine to others (though the dark side of the Lanterne be towards themselves) that hee may secure the grace of humility, it is good that thou doe so thy self: and if thou beholdest a grace of GOD in thee, remember to give him thanks for it, that you may not boast in that which is none of thy own: and consider how thou hast sullyed it, by handling it with dirty fingers, with thy own imperfections, and with mixture of unhandsome circumstances. Spiritual pride is very dangerous, not onely by reason, it spoiles so many graces by which wee drew nigh to the Kingdome of GOD, but also because it so frequently creeps upon the spirit of holy persons. For it is no wonder for a Beggar to call himself poor; or a Drunkard to confesse that he is no sober person: But for a holy person to be humble; for one whom all men esteeme a Saint, to fear lest himselfe become a Devil, and to observe his own danger, and to discern his own infirmities, and make discovery of his bad adherencies, is as hard as for a Prince to submit himself to be guided by Tutors, and make himself subject to discipline like the meanest of his servants.

9. Often meditate upon the effects of Pride on one side, and Humility on the other. First, That Pride is like a Canker, and destroyes the beauty of the fairest flowers, the most excellent gifts and graces: but humility crownes them all. Secondly, That [b]Pride is a great hinderance to the perceiving the things of GOD, and Humility is an excellent preparative and instrument of spiritual wisdom. Thirdly, That Pride hinders the acceptation of our prayers, but *Humility pierceth the clouds, and will not depart till the most High shall regard.* Fourthly, That Humility is but a speaking truth, and all Pride is a lye. Fifthly, That Humility is the most certain way to reall honour, and pride is ever affronted or despised. Sixthly, That Pride turned *Lucifer* into a Devil, and Humility exalted the Son of God above every Name, and placed him eternally at the right hand of his Father. Seventhly, That [c]*GOD resisteth the proud*, professing open defiance and hostility against such persons, but *giveth grace to the humble*, Grace and pardon, remedy and relief against misery and oppression, content in all conditions, tranquillity of spirit patience in afflictions, love abroad, peace at home, and utter freedom from contention and the sin of censuring others, and the trouble of being censured themselves. For the humble man will not *judge his brother for the mote in his eye*, being more troubled at *the beam in*

[b] Mat. 11: 25. [c] James 4: 6.

4 you may] thou may *3 4 5*, thou mayest *6+*

his own eye; and is patient and glad to be reproved, because himself hath cast the first stone at himself, and therefore wonders not that others are of his minde.

10. [d]Remember that the blessed Saviour of the world hath done more to prescribe, and transmit, and secure *this grace* than any other: his whole life being a great continued example of humility: a vast descent from the glorious bosom of his Father to the womb of a poor mayden, to the form of a servant, to the miseries of a sinner, to a life of labour, to a state of poverty, to a death of malefactors, to the grave of death, and the intolerable calamities which we deserved: and it were a good designe and yet but reasonable, that we should be as humble in the midst of our greatest imperfections and basest sins as Christ was in the midst of his fulnesse of the spirit, great wisdom, perfect life and most admirable vertues.

11. Drive away all flatterers from thy company, and at no hand endure them; for he that endures himself so to be abused by another is not onely a fool for entertaining the mockery, but loves to have his own opinion of himself to be heightened and cherished.

12. Never change thy imployment for the sudden coming of another to thee: But if modesty permits or discretion, appear to him that visits thee the same that thou wert to God and thy self in thy privacy. But if thou wert walking or sleeping, or in any other innocent imploiment or retirement, snatch not up a book to seem studious, nor fall on thy knees to seem devout, nor alter any thing to make him believe thee better imployed than thou wert.

13. To the same purpose it is of great use that he who would preserve his humilitie, should choose some spiritual person to whom he shall oblige himself to discover his very thoughts, and fancies; every act of his and all his entercourse with others in which there may be danger; that by such an opennesse of spirit, he may expose every blast of vain glory, every idle thought to be chastened and lessened by the rod of spiritual discipline: and he that shall finde himself tyed to confesse every proud thought, every vanity of his spirit, will also perceive they must not dwell with him, nor finde any kindnesse from him: and besides this, the nature of pride is so shameful, and unhandsome, that the very discovery of it is a huge mortification and means of suppressing it. A man would be ashamed to be told that he enquires after the faults of his last Oration or action on purpose to be commended: and

[d] John 13: 15.

therefore when the man shall tell his spiritual Guide the same shameful story of himself, it is very likely he will be humbled, and heartily ashamed of it.

14. Let every man suppose what opinion he should have of one that should spend his time in playing with drumsticks and cockle-shells, and that should wrangle all day long with a little boy for pins, or should study hard and labour much to cozen a childe of his gauds, and who would run into a river deep and dangerous with a great burden upon his back, even then when he were told of the danger and earnestly importuned not to do it: and let him but change the Instances and the person, and he shall finde that he hath the same reason to think as bad of himself, who pursues trifles with earnestnesse, spending his time in vanity, and his *labour for that which profits not*; who knowing the laws of God, the rewards of vertue, the cursed consequents of sin, that it is an evil spirit that tempts him to it, a Devil, one that hates him, that longs extreamly to ruine him, that it is his own destruction that he is then working, that the pleasures of his sin are base and bruitish, unsatisfying in the enjoyment, soon over, shameful in their story, bitter in the memory, painful in the effect here, and intolerable hereafter, and for ever: yet in despite of all this, he runs foolishly into his sin and his ruine, meerly because he is a fool, and winks hard, and rushes violently like a horse into the battel, or like a mad man to his death. He that can think great and good things of such a person, the next step may court the rack for an instrument of pleasure, and admire a swine for wisdom, and go for counsel to the prodigall and trifling grashopper.

After the use of these and such like instruments and considerations, if you would try how your soul is grown; you shall know that humility like the root of a goodly tree is thrust very farre into the ground by these goodly fruits which appeare above ground.

Signes of Humility.

1. The humble man trusts not to his own discretion, but in matters of concernment relyes rather upon the judgement of his friends, counsellers, or spiritual guides. 2. He does not pertinaciously pursue the choice of his own will, but *in all things* lets God choose for him, and his Superiours in those things which concern them. 3. [e]He does not

[e] Assai commanda, chi ubidisce al saggio.

7 much] *om 4+*

murmur against commands. 4. He is not inquisitive into the reasonableness of *indifferent and innocent* commands, but believes their command to be reason enough in such cases to exact his obedience. 5. He lives according to a rule, and with compliance to publick customs, without any affectation or singularity. 6. He is meek and indifferent in all accidents and chances. 7. [f]He patiently bears injuries. 8. He is alwayes unsatisfied in his own conduct, resolutions, and counsels. 9. He is a great lover of good men, and a praiser of wise men, and a censurer of no man. 10. He is modest in his speech, and reserved in his laughter. 11. He fears when he hears himself commended, lest God make another judgment concerning his actions than men do. 12. He gives no pert or saucy answers when he is reproved, whether justly or unjustly. 13. He loves to sit down in private, and if he may, he refuses the temptation of offices and new honours. 14. He is ingenuous, free and open in his actions and discourses. 15. He mends his fault and gives thanks when he is admonished. 16. He is ready to do good offices to the murderers of his fame, to his slanderers, backbiters and detractors, as Christ washed the feet of *Judas*. 17. And is contented to be suspected of Indiscretion, so, before God he may be really innocent, and not offensive to his neighbour, nor wanting to his just and prudent interest.

SECT. V.
Of Modesty.

Modesty is the appendage of Sobriety, and is to Chastity, to Temperance and to Humility as the fringes are to a Garment. It is a grace of God that moderates the overactiveness and curiosity of the minde, and orders the passions of the body, and external actions, and is directly opposed to *Curiosity*, to *Boldnesse*, to *Undecency*. The practise of Modesty consists in these following rules.

Acts and duties of Modesty as it is opposed to [g] *Curiosity.*

1. [h]Inquire not into the secrets of God, but be content to learn thy duty according to the quality of thy person or imployment: that is plainly, if thou beest not concerned in the conduct of others: but if

[f] Verum humilem patientia ostendit. S. Hier.
[g] *Εὐσχημοσύνη.* [h] Ecclus. 3: 21–23.

thou beest a teacher, learne it so as may best enable thee to discharge thy office. Gods commandments were proclaimed to all the world, but Gods counsels are to himself and to his secret ones, when they are admitted within the veil.

2. [i]Inquire not into the things which are too hard for thee, but learn modestly to know thy infirmities and abilities, and raise not thy mind up to inquire into mysteries of State, or the secrets of Government, or difficulties Theological, if thy imployment really be, or thy understanding be judged to be of a lower rank.

3. Let us not inquire into the affairs of others that concerne us not, but be busied within our selves and our own spheres; ever remembering that to pry into the actions or interests of other men not under our charge, may minister to pride, to tyranny, to uncharitablenesse, to trouble, but can never consist with modesty, unlesse where duty or the mere intentions of charity, and relation do warrant it.

4. [j]Never listen at the doors or windows: for besides that it contains in it danger and a snare, it is also an invading my neighbours privacy, and a laying that open which he therfore inclosed, that it might not be open. Never ask what he carries covered so curiously; for it is enough that it is covered curiously. Hither also is reducible that we never open letters without publick authority, or reasonably presumed leave, or great necessity, or charity.

Every man hath in his own life sins enough, in his own minde trouble enough, in his own fortune evils enough, and in performance of his offices failings more than enough to entertain his own enquiry so that curiositie after the affairs of others, cannot be without envy and an evil minde. What is it to me if my Neighbours Grandfather were a Syrian, or his Grandmother illegitimate, or that another is indebted five thousand pounds, or whether his wife be expensive? But commonly curious persons, (or as the Apostles phrase is) *busie-bodies* are not sollicitous, or inquisitive into the beauty and order of a well governed family, or after the vertues of an excellent person; but if there be any thing for which men keep locks and bars and porters, thing

[i] Qui scrutatur est Majestatis opprimetur a gloria. Prov. 25.
Αὔτη ἀρχὴ τοῦ φιλοσοφεῖν, αἴσθησις τοῦ ἰδίου ἡγεμονικοῦ, πῶς ἔχει· μετὰ γὰρ τ γνῶναι ὅτι ἀσθενῶς, οὐκέτι θελήσει χρῆσθαι αὐτῷ πρὸς τὰ μέγιστα. Arrian. lib. c. 26.
Et plus sapere interdum vulgus quod quantum opus est sapiat. Lactant.
[j] Eccles. 7: 21.
Ne occhi in lettera, ne mano in tasca, ne orecchi in secreti altrui.

---

14 where] their *2 3*

that blush to see the light, and either are shameful in manners, or private in nature, these things are their care and their businesse. But if great things will satisfie our enquiry, the course of the Sun and Moon, the spots in their faces, the Firmament of Heaven, and the supposed Orbs, the ebbing and flowing of the Sea, are work enough for us: or if this be not, let him tell me, whether the number of the stars be even or odde, and when they began to be so? since some ages have discovered new stars which the former knew not, but might have seen, if they had bin where now they are fixed. If these be too troublesome, search lower, and tell me, why this turfe this year brings forth a Daisie, and the next year a Plantane: why the apple bears his seed in his heart, and wheat bears it in his head: let him tell, why a graft taking nourishment from a crab-stock shall have a fruit more noble than its nurse and parent: let him say, why the best of oyl is at the top, the best of wine in the middle, and the best of hony at the bottom, otherwise than it is in some liquors that are thinner, and in some that are thicker? But these things are not such as please busie bodies. They must feed upon Tragedies, and stories of misfortunes and crimes; and yet tell them ancient stories of the ravishment of chast maidens, or the debauchment of nations, or the extream poverty of learned persons, or the persecutions of the old Saints, or the changes of government, and sad accidents happening in Royal families amongst the *Arsacidæ*, the *Cæsars*, the *Ptolemies*, these were enough to scratch the itch of knowing sad stories. But unlesse you tell them something *sad and new*, something that is done within the bounds of their own knowledge or relation, it seems tedious and unsatisfying; which showes plainly it is an evil spirit: envie and idlenesse married together, and begot curiosity. Therefore *Plutarch* rarely well compares curious and inquisitive ears to the execrable gates of cities, out of which onely Malefactors, and hangmen and tragedies passe, nothing that is chast or holy. If a Physitian should go from house to house unsent for and enquire what woman hath a Cancer in her bowels, or what man hath a fistula in his colick gut, though he could pretend to cure it, he would be almost as unwelcome as the disease it self: and therefore it is inhumane to enquire after crimes and disasters without pretence of amending them, but onely to discover them. We are not angry with Searchers and Publicans when they look onely on publick merchandise; but when they break open trunks, and pierce vessels, and unrip packs, and open sealed letters.

Curiosity is the direct incontinency of the spirit: and adultery it self in its principle is many times nothing but a curious inquisition after, and envying of another mans inclosed pleasures: and there have been many who refused fairer objects that they might ravish an inclosed woman, from her retirement and single possessour. But these inquisitions are seldom without danger, never without basenesse; they are neither just nor honest, nor delightful, and very often uselesse to the curious inquirer. For men stand upon their guards against them, as they secure their meat against Harpyes and Cats, laying all their counsels and secrets out of their way; or as men clap their garments close about them when the searching and saucy winds would discover their nakednesse: as knowing that what men willingly hear, they do willingly speak of. Knock therefore at the door before you enter upon your neighbours privacy; and remember that there is no difference between entering into his house, and looking into it.

Acts of Modesty as it is opposed to [k] *boldnesse.*

1. Let us alwayes bear about us such impressions of reverence and fear of God as to tremble at his voice, to expresse our apprehensions of his greatnesse in all great accidents, in popular judgements, loud thunders, tempests, earth quakes, not onely for fear of being smitten our selves, or that we are concerned in the accident, but also that we may humble our selves before his Almightinesse, and expresse that infinite distance between his infinitenesse and our weaknesses, at such times especially when he gives such visible arguments of it. He that is merry and ayry at shore when he sees a sad and a loud tempest on the sea, or dances briskly when God thunders from heaven, regards not when God speaks to all the world, but is possessed with a firm immodesty.

2. Be reverent, modest, and reserved in the presence of thy betters, giving to all according to their quality their titles of honour, keeping distance, speaking little, answering pertinently, not interposing without leave or reason, not answering to a question propounded to another; and ever present to thy superiours the fairest side of thy discourse, of thy temper, of thy ceremony, as being ashamed to serve excellent persons with unhandsome entercourse.

3. [l]Never lye before a King, or a great person, nor stand in a lye

[k] *Αἰσχύνη.*

[l] Quem Deus tegit verecundiæ pallio, hujus maculas hominibus non ostendit. Maimon. Can. Eth.

Πρῶτον ἀγαθῶν ἀναμάρτητον, δεύτερον δ᾽ αἰσχῦναι. Meliss.

when thou art accused, nor offer to justifie what is indeed a fault, but modestly be ashamed of it, ask pardon and make amends.

4. [m]Never boast of thy sin, but at least lay a vail upon thy nakednesse and shame, and put thy hand before thine eyes that thou mayest have this beginning of repentance, to believe thy sin to be thy shame. For he that blushes not at his crime, but addes shamelessenesse to his shame, hath no instrument left to restore him to the hopes of vertue.

5. Be not confident and affirmative in an uncertain matter, but report things modestly, and temperately according to the degree of that persuasion, which is, or ought to be begotten in thee by the efficacy of the authority, or the reason inducing thee.

6. [n]Pretend not to more knowledge than thou hast, but be content to seem ignorant where thou art so, lest thou beest either brought to shame, or retirest into shamelessnesse.

Acts of Modesty as it is opposed to [o] *undecency.*

1. In your prayers, in churches, and places of religion use reverent postures, great attention, grave ceremony, the lowest gestures of humility; remembering that we speak to God, in our reverence to whom we cannot possibly exceed; but that the expression of this reverence be according to law or custom, and the example of the most prudent and pious persons: that is, let it be the best in its kinde to the best of essences.

2. In all publick meetings, private addresses, in discourses, in journeyes use those forms of salutation, reverence and decency, which the custom prescribes, and is usual amongst the most sober persons; giving honour to whom honour belongeth, taking place of none of thy betters, and in all cases of question concerning civil precedency, giving it to any one that will take it, if it be onely thy own right that is in question.

3. Observe the proportion of affections in all meetings and to all persons: be not merry at a funeral, nor sad upon a festival, but *rejoyce with them that rejoyce, and weep with them that weep.*

[m] A Chione saltem vel ab Helide disce pudorem,
Abscondunt spurcas hæc monumenta lupas. Mart. l. 1, ep. 34.

Obstare primum est velle nec labi via:
Pudor est secundus nosse peccandi modum. Senec. Hip.

[n] Ecclus. 3: 25.

[o] *Κοσμιότης, εὐταξία*, or *εὐπρέπεια.*

---

note *m* Obstare primum . . . Senec. Hip.] *4+*, *om 1 2 3*

4. Abstain from wanton and dissolute laughter, petulant and uncomely jests, loud talking, jeering, and all such actions which in civil account are called undecencies, and incivilities.

5. Towards your parents use all modesty of duty and humble carriage: towards them and all your kindred be severe in the modesties of chastity: ever fearing, lest the freedoms of natural kindenesse should enlarge into any neighbourhood of unhandsomenesse. For all incestuous mixtures, and all circumstances and degrees towards it, are the highest violations of modesty in the world: for therefore incest is grown to be so high a crime, especially in the last periods of the world, because it breaks that reverence which the consent of all nations and the severity of humane laws hath enjoyned towards our parents and neerest kindred, in imitation of that law which God gave to the Jewes in prosecution of Modestie in this instance.

6. [p]Be a curious observer of all those things which are of good report, and are parts of publick honesty. For publick fame, and the sentence of prudent and publick persons, is the measure of good and evil in things indifferent: and charity requires us to comply with those fancies and affections which are agreable to nature, or the analogie of vertue, or publick laws, or old customs. It is against Modesty for a woman to marry a second husband as long as she bears a burden by the first, or to admit a second love while her funeral tears are not wiped from her cheeks. [q]It is against publick honesty to do some lawful actions of privacy in publick theatres, and therefore in such cases retirement is a duty of modesty.

7. Be grave, decent and modest in thy clothing and ornament: never let it be above thy condition, not alwayes equal to it, never light or amarous, never discovering a nakednesse through a thin vail, which thou pretendest to hide: never to lay a snare for a soul, but remember what becomes a Christian professing holinesse, chastity, and the discipline of the holy Jesus: and the first effect of this let your servants feel by your gentleness and aptness to be pleased with their usual diligence, and ordinary conduct: [r]For the man or woman that is

[p] Phil. 4: 8.

[q] At meretrix abigit testem veloque seraque,
Raraque Summœni fornice rima patet. Mart.

[r] Tuta sit ornatrix: odi quae sauciat ora
Unguibus, et rapta brachia figit acu.
Devovet, et tangit dominae caput illa, simulque
Plorat ad invisas sanguinolenta comas. Ovid.

31–105. 2 and the first . . . immodesty above.] *4+*, *om 1 2 3* 33 [r]] *4+*, *om 1 2 3*

dressed with anger and impatience, wears pride under their robes, and immodesty above.

8. Hither also is to be reduced singular and affected walking, proud, nice and ridiculous gestures of body, painting and lascivious dressings, all which together God reprooves by the Prophet: [s] *The Lord saith, because the daughters of Sion are haughty, and walk with stretched forth necks and wanton eyes, walking and mincing as they go, and make a tinkling with their feet, therefore the Lord will smite her with a scab of the crown of the head, and will take away the bravery of their tinkling ornaments.* And this duty of modesty in this instance is expresly enjoyned to all Christian women by Saint *Paul*, [t] *That women adorn themselves in modest apparel with shamefastnesse and sobriety, not with broidered hair, or gold or pearl, or costly array, but (which becometh women professing godlinesse) with good works.*

9. As those meats are to be avoided which tempt our stomacks beyond our hunger, so also should prudent persons decline all such spectacles, relations, Theatres, loud noyses and out-cryes which concern us not, and are besides our natural or moral interest. [u] Our senses should not like petulant and wanton Girles wander into Markets and Theatres without just imployment; but when they are sent abroad by reason, return quickly with their errand, and remain modestly at home under their guide, till they be sent again.

10. Let all persons be curious in observing modesty towards themselves in the handsome treating their own body, and such as are in their power, whether living or dead. Against this rule they offend who expose to others their own, or pry into others nakednesse beyond the limits of necessity, or where a leave is not made holy by a permission from God. It is also said that God was pleased to work a miracle about the body of *Epiphanius* to reprove the immodest curiosity of an unconcerned person who pryed too neer when charitable people were composing it to the grave. In all these cases and particulars, although they seem little, yet our duty and concernment is not little. Concerning which, I use the words of the Son of *Sirach*, *He that despiseth little things, shall perish by little and little.*

[s] Isaiah 3: 16–18. Prov. 6: 13.
[t] 1 Tim. 2: 9.
[u] Oedipum curiositas in extremas conjecit calamitates. Plut.

note *s* Isaiah 3: 16–18] *7 8*, Isa. 3. 15. *1 2 3 4 5 6* Prov. 6: 13] *om 7 8*

SECT. VI.

Of Contentednesse in all estates and accidents.

Vertues and Discourses are like Friends, necessary in all fortunes; but those are the best which are Friends in our sadnesses, and support us in our sorrows, and sad accidents: and in this sense, no man that is vertuous can be friendlesse; nor hath any man reason to complain of the Divine Providence, or accuse the publick disorder of things, or his own infelicity, since God hath appointed one remedy for all the evils in the World, and that is, a contented spirit: For this alone makes a man passe through fire and not be scorched, through Seas and not be drowned, through hunger and nakednesse and want nothing. For since all the evil in the World consists in the disagreeing between the object and the appetite, as when a man hath what he desires not, or desires what he hath not, or desires amisse; he that composes his spirit to the present accident, hath variety of instances for his vertue, but none to trouble him, because his desires enlarge not beyond his present fortune: and a wise man is placed in the variety of chances like the Nave or Centre of a wheel, in the midst of all the circumvolutions and changes of posture, without violence or change, save that it turns gently in complyance with its changed parts, and is indifferent which part is up and which is down; for there is some vertue or other to be exercised what ever happens, either patience or thanksgiving, love or fear, moderation or humility, charity or contentednesse, and they are every one of them equally in order to this great end, and immortal felicity: and beauty is not made by white or red, by black eyes and a round face, by a strait body and a smooth skin; but by a proportion to the fancy: No rules can make amability, our mindes and apprehensions make that; and so is our felicity; and we may be reconciled to poverty and a low fortune, if we suffer contentednesse and the grace of God to make the proportions. [v]For no man is poor that does not think himself so: But if in a full fortune, with impatience he desires more, he proclaims his wants and his beggerly condition.

But because this grace of contentednesse was the sum of all the old moral Philosophy, and a great duty in Christianity, and of most universal use in the whole course of our lives, and the onely instrument to

[v] Non facta tibi est, si dissimules, injuria.

24 and immortal] *4+*, an ~ *123* 33 But because this] *part of preceding paragraph 4+*

ease the burdens of the World and the enmities of sad chances, it will not be amisse to presse it by the proper arguments by which God hath bound it upon our spirits, it being fastened by Reason and Religion, by duty and interest, by necessity and conveniency, by example, and by the proposition of excellent rewards, no lesse than peace and felicity.

1. Contentednesse in all estates is a duty of Religion: it is the great reasonablenesse of complying with the Divine Providence which governes all the World, and hath so ordered us in the administration of his great Family. He were a strange fool that should be angry because Dogs and Sheep need no shoes, and yet himself is full of care to get some: God hath supplyed those needs to them by natural provisions, and to thee by an artificial: for he hath given thee reason to learn a trade, or some means to make or buy them, so that it onely differs in the manner of our provision; and which had you rather want, shoes or reason? And my Patron that hath given me a Farm is freer to me than if he gives a loafe ready baked. But however, all these gifts come from him, and therefore it is fit he should dispense them as he please; and if we murmure here, we may at the next melancholy be troubled that God did not make us to be Angels, or Stars. For if that which we are or have, do not content us, we may be troubled for every thing in the World, which is besides our being, or our possessions.

God is the Master of the Scenes, we must not choose which part we shall act; it concerns us onely to be careful that we do it well, alwayes saying, [w] *If this please God let it be as it is*: and we who pray that Gods will may be done in Earth as it is in Heaven must remember that the Angels do whatsoever is commanded them, and go where ever they are sent, and refuse no circumstances: and if their imployment be crossed by a higher decree, they sit down in peace and rejoyce in the event; [x] and when the Angel of *Judea* could not prevail in behalf of the people committed to his charge, because the Angel of *Persia* opposed it, he onely told the story at the command of God, and was as content, and worshipped with as great an extasie in his proportion, as the prevailing Spirit. Do thou so likewise: keep the station where God hath placed you, and you shall never long for things without, but sit at home feasting upon the *Divine Providence* and thy own *reason*, by which we are taught that it is necessary and reasonable to submit to God.

For, is not all the World Gods family? Are not we his creatures? Are we not as clay in the hand of the Potter? Do we not live upon his meat,

[w] *Εἰ τοῦτο τῷ Θεῷ φίλον, τοῦτο γενέσθω.* [x] Dan. 10: 13.

and move by his strength and do our work by his light? Are we any thing but what we are from him? And shall there be a mutiny among the flocks and herds, because their Lord or their Shepherd chooses their pastures, and suffers them not to wander into Deserts and unknowne wayes? If we choose, we do it so foolishly that we cannot like it long, and most commonly not at all: but God who can do what he please, is wise to choose safely for us, affectionate to comply with our needs, and powerful to execute all his wise decrees. Here therefore is the wisdome of the contented man, to let God choose for him: for when we have given up our wills to him, and stand in that station of the battel where our great General hath placed us, our spirits must needs rest while our conditions have for their security the power, the wisdom, and the charity of God.

2. Contentednesse in all accidents brings great peace of spirit, and is the great and onely instrument of temporal felicity. It removes the sting from the accident, and makes a man not to depend upon chance, and the uncertain dispositions of men for his well being, but onely on GOD and his own Spirit. [y]Wee our selves make our fortunes good or bad, and when God lets loose a Tyrant upon us, or a sicknesse, or scorne, or a lessened fortune, if we fear to dye, or know not to be patient, or are proud, or covetous, then the calamity sits heavy on us. But if we know how to manage a noble principle, and fear not Death so much as a dishonest action, and think impatience a worse evil than a Feaver, and Pride to be the biggest disgrace, and poverty to be infinitely desirable before the torments of covetousnesse; then we who now think vice to be so easie, and make it so familiar, and think the cure so impossible, shall quickly be of another minde, and reckon these accidents amongst things eligible.

But no man can be happy that hath great hopes and great fears of things without, and events depending upon other men, or upon the chances of Fortune. The rewards of Vertue are certain, and our provisions for our natural support are certain, or if we want meat till we dye, then we dye of that disease, and there are many worse than to dye with an *atrophy* or Consumption, or unapt and courser nourishment: But he that suffers a transporting passion concerning things within the power of others, is free from sorrow and amazement no longer than his enemy shall give him leave; and it is ten to one but he shall be smitten then and there where it shall most trouble him: for so the Adder

[y] *Ὁ θεὸς τέθεικε, καί φησιν, εἴ τι ἀγαθὸν θέλεις, παρὰ σεαυτοῦ λαβέ.* Arrian. Ep.

teaches us where to strike, by her curious and fearfull defending of her head. The old Stoicks when you told them of a sad story would still answer *τί πρός με; What is that to me*? Yes; for the Tyrant hath sentenced you also to prison. Well? What is that? He will put a chain upon my leg, but he cannot binde my soul. No: but he will kill you. Then Ile dye. If presently, let me go that I may presently be freer than himself: but if not till anon or to morrow, I will dine first, or sleep, or do what reason and nature calls for, as at other times. This in Gentile Philosophy is the same with the discourse of S. *Paul*, [z] *I have learned in whatsoever state I am therewith to be content. I know both how to be abased, and I know how to abound, every where and in all things I am instructed, both how to be full and to be hungry, both to abound and suffer need.*

[a] We are in the world like men playing at Tables, the chance is not in our power, but to play it, is; and when it is fallen we must manage it as we can, and let nothing trouble us, but when we do a base action, or speak like a fool, or think wickedly: these things God hath put into our powers: but concerning those things which are wholly in the choice of another, they cannot fall under our deliberation, and therefore neither are they fit for our passions. My fear may make me miserable, but it cannot prevent what another hath in his power and purpose: and prosperities can onely be enjoyed by them who fear not at all to lose them, since the amazement and passion concerning the future takes off all the pleasure of the present possession. Therefore if thou hast lost thy land, do not also lose thy constancy: and if thou must die a little sooner, yet do not die impatiently. For no chance is evil to him that is content, [b] *and to a man nothing is miserable, unless it be unreasonable.* No man can make another man to be his slave, unless he hath first enslaved himself to life and death, to pleasure or pain, to hope or fear: command these passions, and you are freer than the Parthian kings.

Instruments or exercises to procure contentednesse.

Upon the strength of these premises we may reduce this vertue to practise by its proper instruments first, and then by some more special considerations or arguments of content.

1. When any thing happens to our displeasure, let us endeavour to take off its trouble by turning it into spiritual or artificial advantage,

[z] Philip. 4: 11, 12. 1 Tim. 6: 6. Hebr. 13: 5.
[a] Chi ben e mal può soffrire a grand honor non puo venir.
[b] *Πᾶν τὸ εὔλογον, φορητόν.*

note *z* 1 Tim. 6: 6] *7 8*, 1 Tim. 6. 8 *1 2 3 4 5 6*

and handle it on that side, in which it may be useful to the designes of reason. For there is nothing but hath a double handle, or at least we have two hands to apprehend it. When an enemy reproaches us, let us look on him as an impartial relator of our faults, for he will tell thee truer than thy fondest friend will, and thou mayest call them *precious balms*, though *they break thy head*, and forgive his anger while thou makest use of the plainnesse of his declamation. *The Ox when he is weary treads surest*, and if there be nothing else in the disgrace but that it makes us to walk warily, and tread sure for fear of our enemies, that is better than to be flattered into pride and carelessenesse. This is the charity of Christian Philosophy, which expounds the sence of the divine providence fairly, and reconciles us to it by a charitable construction: and we may as well refuse all physick if we consider it onely as unpleasant in the tast, and we may finde fault with the rich valleys of Thasus, because they are circled with sharp mountains: but so also we may be in charity with every unpleasant accident, because though it tast bitter it is intended for health and medicine.

If therefore thou fallest from thy imployment in publick, take sanctuary in an honest retirement, being indifferent to thy gain abroad, or thy safety at home: If thou art out of favour with thy Prince, secure the favour of the KING of Kings, and then there is no harm come to thee: and when *Zeno Citiensis* lost all his goods in a storm, he retired to the studies of Philosophy, to his short cloak, and a severe life, and gave thanks to fortune for his prosperous mischance. When the North-winde blows hard, and it rains sadly, none but fools sit down in it and cry: wise people defend themselves against it with a warm garment, or a good fire, and a dry roof: when a storm of a sad mischance beats upon our spirits, turn it into some advantage by observing where it can serve another end, either of religion or prudence, of more safety or lesse envy: it will turn into something that is good, if we list to make it so: at least it may make us weary of the worlds vanity, and take off our confidence from uncertain riches, and make our spirits to dwell in those regions, where content dwells essentially: if it does any good to our souls, it hath made more than sufficient recompence for all the temporal affliction. He that threw a stone at a dog, and hit his cruel stepmother, said, that although he intended it otherwise, yet the stone was not quite lost: and if we fail in the first designe, if we bring it home to another equally to content us, or more to profit us, then we have put

15 with] by *78* 20–1 the favour] thy ~ *23*

our conditions past the power of chance; and this was called in the old Greek Comedy *a being revenged on fortune by becoming Philosophers* and turning the chance into reason or religion: for so a wise man shall overrule his stars, and have a greater influence upon his own content, than all the constellations and planets of the firmament.

2. Never compare thy condition with those above thee; but to secure thy content look upon those thousands with whom thou wouldest not for any interest change thy fortune and condition. A souldier must not think himself unprosperous, if he be not successeful as the son of *Philip*, or cannot grasp a fortune as big as the Roman Empire: Be content that thou art not lessened as was *Pyrrhus*: or if thou beest, that thou art not routed like *Crassus*: and when that comes to thee, it is a great prosperity, that thou art not caged and made a spectacle like *Bajazet*: or thy eyes were not pulled out like *Zedekiahs*: or that thou wert not flead alive like *Valentinian.* If thou admirest the greatnesse of *Xerxes*, look also on those that digged the mountain *Atho*, or whose ears and noses were cut off, because the Hellespont carried away the bridge. It is a fine thing (thou thinkest) to be carried on mens shoulders: but give God thanks that thou are not forced to carry a rich fool upon thy shoulders: as those poor men do whom thou beholdest. There are but a few Kings in mankinde, but many thousands who are very miserable, if compared to thee. However it is a huge folly rather to grieve for the good of others, than to rejoyce for that good which God hath given us of our own.

And yet there is no wise or good man that would change persons or conditions intirely with any man in the world. It may be he would have one mans wealth added to himself, or the power of a second, or the learning of a third, but still he would receive these into his own person, because he loves that best, and therefore esteems it best, and therefore overvalues all that which he is, before all that which any other man in the world can be. Would any man be *Dives* to have his wealth, or *Judas* for his office, or *Saul* for his kingdom, or *Absalom* for his beauty, or *Achitophel* for his policy? It is likely he would wish all these, and yet he would be the same person still. For every man hath desires of his own, and objects just fitted to them, without which he cannot be, unlesse he were not himself. And let every man that loves himself so well as to love himself before all the world, consider, if he have not something for which, in the whole he values himself far more

33 beauty] bounty *7 8 see Commentary*

than he can value any man else. There is therefore no reason to take the finest feathers from all the winged nation to deck that bird, that thinks already she is more valuable than any the inhabitants of the ayre. Either change all or none. Cease to love your self best, or be content with that portion of being and blessing for which you love your self so well.

3. It conduces much to our content, if we passe by those things which happen to our trouble, and *consider that which is pleasing and prosperous*, that by the representation of the better the worse may be blotted out: and at the worst you have enough to keep you alive, and to keep up, and to improve your hopes of Heaven. If I be overthrown in my suit at Law, yet my house is left me still and my land: or I have a vertuous wife, or hopeful children, or kinde friends, or good hopes: If I have lost one childe, it may be I have two or three still left me; *or else reckon the blessings which already you have received*, and therefore be pleased in the change and variety of affairs to receive *evil from the hand of God as well as good. Antipater* of Tarsus used this art to support his sorrows on his death bed, and reckoned the good things of his past life, not forgetting to recount it as a blessing, and argument that God tooke care of him, that he had a prosperous journey from Cilicia to Athens. [c] *Or else please thy self with hopes of the future*: for we were not born with this sadnesse upon us; and it was a change that brought us into it, and a change may bring us out again. [d] *Harvest will come, and then every farmer is rich, at least for a moneth or two.* It may be thou art entered into the cloud which will bring a gentle shower to refresh thy sorrows.

Now suppose thy self in as great a sadnesse, as ever did load thy spirit, wouldest thou not beare it cheerfully and nobly, if thou wert sure that within a certain space some strange excellent fortune would relieve thee, and enrich thee, and recompence thee so as to overflow all thy hopes and thy desires, and capacities? Now then, when a sadnesse lies heavy upon thee, remember that thou art a Christian designed to the inheritance of Jesus: and what dost thou think concerning thy great fortune, thy lot and portion of eternity? Doest thou think thou shalt be saved or damned? Indeed if thou thinkest thou shalt perish, I cannot blame thee to be sad, sad till thy heart-strings

[c] La speranza è il pan de' poveri.

—Non si male nunc et olim
Sic erit.

[d] Ἀεὶ γεωργὸς εἰς νέωτα πλούσιος.

---

4 or be] or to be *2 3* 19 and] an *4+*

crack: but then why art thou troubled at the losse of thy money? what should a damned man do with money, which in so great a sadnesse it is impossible for him to enjoy? Did ever any man upon the rack, afflict himself because he had received a crosse answer from his Mistresse? or call for the particulars of a purchase upon the gallows? If thou doest really believe thou shalt be damned, I do not say it will *cure* the sadnesse of thy poverty, but it will *swallow* it up. But if thou believest thou shalt be saved, consider how great is that joy, how infinite is that change, how unspeakable is the glory, how excellent is the recompence for all the sufferings in the world, if they were all laden upon thy spirit? So that let thy condition be what it will, if thou considerest thy own present condition, and compare it to thy future possibility, thou canst not feel the present smart of a crosse fortune to any great degree, either because thou hast a far bigger sorrow, or a far bigger joy. Here thou art but a stranger travelling to thy Countrey where the glories of a Kingdom are prepared for thee, it is therefore a huge folly to be much afflicted because thou hast a lesse convenient Inne to lodge in by the way.

But these arts of *looking forwards and backwards* are more than enough to support the spirit of a Christian: there is no man but hath blessings enough in present possession to outweigh the evils of a great affliction. Tell the joynts of thy body, and do not accuse the universal providence for a lame leg, or the want of a finger, when all the rest is perfect: and you have a noble soul, a particle of Divinity, the image of GOD himself: and by the want of a finger you may the better know how to estimate the remaining parts, and to account for every degree of the surviving blessings. *Aristippus* in a great suit at law lost a Farm, and to a Gentleman who in civility pitied and deplored his losse, He answered, I have two Farms left still, and that is more than I have lost, and more than you have by one. If you misse an Office for which you stood Candidate, then besides that you are quit of the cares and the envy of it, you still have all those excellencies which rendered you capable to receive it, and they are better than the best Office in the Commonwealth. If your estate be lessened, you need the lesse to care who governs the Province, whether he be rude or gentle. I am crossed in my journey, and yet I scaped robbers; and I consider, that if I had been set upon by Villanes I would have redeemed that evil by this which I now suffer, and have counted it a deliverance: or if I did fall into the hands

10–11 thy spirit] the ~ 5+

of theeves, yet they did not steal my land: or I am fallen into the hands of Publicans and Sequestrators, and they have taken all from me, what now? let me look about me. They have left me the Sun and the Moon, Fire and Water, a loving wife, and many friends to pity me, and some to relieve me, and I can still discourse, and unless I list they have not taken away my merry countenance, and my cheerful spirit, and a good conscience: they still have left me the providence of God, and all the promises of the Gospel, and my Religion, and my hopes of Heaven, and my charity to them too: and still I sleep, and digest, I eat and drink, I reade and meditate, I can walk in my Neighbours pleasant fields, and see the varieties of natural beauties, and delight in all that in which God delights, that is, in vertue and wisdom, in the whole creation, and in God himself: and he that hath so many causes of joy, and so great, is very much in love with sorrow and peevishness, who loses all these pleasures, and chooses to sit down upon his little handful of thorns: such a person were fit to bear *Nero* company in his funeral sorrow for the losse of one of *Poppeas* hairs, or help to mourn for *Lesbia's* sparrow: and because he loves it, he deserves to starve in the midst of plenty, and to want comfort while he is encircled with blessings.

4. Enjoy the present whatsoever it be, and be not sollicitous for the future: for if you take your foot from the present standing, and thrust it forward toward to morrows event, you are in a restlesse condition: [e]it is like refusing to quench your present thirst by fearing you shall want drink the next day. If it be well today, it is madnesse to make the present miserable by fearing it may be ill to morrow, when your belly is full of to dayes dinner to fear you shall want the next dayes supper: for it may be you shall not, and then to what purpose was this dayes affliction? But if to morrow you shall want, your sorrow will come time enough, though you do not hasten it; let your trouble tarry till its own

[e] Quid sit futurum cras, fuge quaerere, et
Quem sors dierum cunque dabit lucro
Appone. Hor. l. 1. Od. 9.

Prudens futuri temporis exitum
Caliginosa nocte premit Deus,
Ridetque, si mortalis ultra
Fas trepidet: quod adest, memento
Componere aequus. Hor. l. 3. Od. 29.

Τὸ σήμερον μέλει μοι·
Τὸ δ' αὔριον τίς οἶδεν; Anacr. Od. xv.

---

note *e* Od. 9.] *6+*, Od. 4. *1 2 3 4 5*

day comes. But if it chance to be ill to day do not increase it by the care of to morrow. Enjoy the blessings of this day, if God sends them, and the evils of it bear patiently and sweetly: for this day is only ours, we are dead to yesterday, and we are not yet born to the morrow. He therefore that enjoyes the present, if it be good, enjoyes as much as is possible: and if onely that dayes trouble leans upon him, it is singular and finite. *Sufficient to the day* (said Christ) *is the evil thereof. Sufficient*, but *not intolerable*: but if we look abroad and bring into one dayes thoughts the evil of many, certain and uncertain, what will be, and what will never be, our load will be as intolerable as it is unreasonable. To reprove this instrument of discontent, the Ancients fained that in Hell stood a man twisting a rope of Hay, and still he twisted on suffering an Asse to eat up all that was finished: so miserable is he who thrusts his passions forward towards future events, and suffers all that he may enjoy to be lost and devoured by folly and inconsideration, thinking nothing fit to be enjoyed but that which is not, or cannot be had. Just so, many young persons are loath to dye, and therefore desire to live to old age, and when they are come thither, are troubled that they are come to that state of life to which before they were come, they were hugely afraid they should never come.

5. Let us prepare our mindes against changes, alwayes expecting them, that we be not surprized when they come: For nothing is so great an enemy to tranquillity and a contented spirit, as the amazement and confusions of unreadinesse and inconsideration: and when our fortunes are violently changed, our spirits are unchanged, if they alwayes stood in the Suburbs and expectation of sorrowes. *O Death, how bitter art thou to a man that is at rest in his possessions*: and to the Rich Man who had promised to himself ease and fulnesse for many years, it was a sad arrest that his soul was surprized the first night: but the Apostles who every day knockt at the gate of death, and looked upon it continually, went to their Martyrdom in peace and evennesse.

6. Let us often frame to our selves and represent to our considerations the images of those blessings we have, just as we usually understand them when we want them. Consider how desirable health is to a sick man, or liberty to a prisoner; and if but a fit of the toothach seizes us with violence, all those troubles which in our health afflicted us, disband instantly and seem inconsiderable. He that in his health is troubled that he is in debt, and spends sleeplesse nights, and refuses

14 forward] forwards *5*+

meat because of his infelicity, let him fall into a fit of the Stone or a high Feaver, he despises the arrest of all his first troubles, and is as a man unconcerned. Remember then that God hath given thee a blessing, the want of which is infinitely more trouble than thy present debt, or poverty or losse; and therefore is now more to be valued in the possession, and ought to out-weigh thy trouble. The very privative blessings, the blessings of immunity, safeguard, liberty and integrity which we commonly enjoy, deserve the thanksgiving of a whole life. If God should send a Cancer upon thy face, or a Wolfe into thy side, if he should spread a crust of Leprosie upon thy skin, what wouldst thou give to be but as now thou art? Wouldest thou not on that condition be as poor as I am? or as the meanest of thy brethren? Would you not choose your present losse or affliction as a thing extremely eligible, and a redemption to thee if thou mightest exchange the other for this? Thou art quit from a thousand calamities, every one of which if it were upon thee would make thee insensible of thy present sorrow: and therefore let thy joy (which should be as great for thy freedom from them, as is thy sadnesse when thou feelest any of them) do the same cure upon thy discontent. For if we be not extremely foolish or vain, thanklesse or sencelesse, a great joy is more apt to cure sorrow and discontent, than a great trouble is. I have known an affectionate wife when she hath been in fear of parting with her beloved Husband, heartily desire of God his life or society upon any conditions that were not sinful; and choose to beg with him, rather than to feast without him: and the same person hath upon that consideration born poverty nobly, when God hath heard her prayer in the other matter: What wise man in the world is there who does not prefer a small fortune with peace before a great one with contention, and war and violence? and then he is no longer wise if he alters his opinion when he hath his wish

7. If you will secure a contented spirit, you must measure your desires by your fortune and condition, not your fortunes by your desires. That is, [f]be governed by your needs not by your fancy; by Nature, not by evil customes and ambitious principles. He that would shoot an arrow out of a Plow, or hunt a Hare with an Elephant, is not unfortunate for missing the mark or prey; but he is foolish for choosing such unapt instruments: and so is he that runs after his content with appetites not springing from natural needs, but from artificial, phantastical and violent necessities: These are not to be satisfied; or if they

[f] Assai basta per chi non è ingordo.

2 he] *6+*, *om 1 2 3 4 5*

were, a man hath chosen an evill instrument towards his content: Nature did not intend rest to a Man by filling of such desires. Is that Beast better that hath two or three Mountains to graze on, than a little Bee that feeds on Dew or Manna, and lives upon what falls every morning from the Store-houses of Heaven, *Clouds and Providence*: [g]Can a Man quench his thirst better out of a River than a full Urn, or drink better from the Fountain when it is finely paved with Marble, than when it swels over the green Turfe? Pride and artificial gluttonies do but adulterate Nature, making our diet healthlesse, our appetites impatient and unsatisfiable, and the taste mixt, phantastical, and meretricious. But that which we miscal poverty, is indeed Nature: and its proportions are the just measures of a Man, and the best instruments of content: But when we create needs that God or Nature never made, we have erected to our selves an infinite stock of trouble that can have no period.

Sempronius complained of want of clothes, and was much troubled for a new suit, being ashamed to appear in the Theatre with his Gown a little thread-bare: but when he got it and gave his old clothes to *Codrus*, the poor man was ravisht with joy, and went and gave God thanks for his new purchase: and *Codrus* was made richly fine and cheerfully warm by that which *Sempronius* was ashamed to wear; and yet their natural needs were both alike, the difference onely was, that *Sempronius* had some artificial and phantastical necessities superinduced, which *Codrus* had not; and was harder to be relieved, and could not have joy at so cheap a rate; because the one lived according to Nature, the other by Pride and ill customes, and measures taken by other mens eyes and tongues, and artificial needs. He that propounds to his fancy things greater than himself, or his needs, and is discontent and troubled when he fails of such purchases, ought not to accuse Providence, or blame his fortune but his folly. God and Nature made

[g] —Quanto præstantius esset
Numen aquæ, viridi si margine clauderet undas
Herba, nec ingenuum violarent marmora tophum.

—me pascunt olivæ
Me cichorea, levesque malvæ.
Frui paratis et valido mihi,
Latoc, dones. Horat. l. 1. Od. 31.

Amabo levem cupressum,
Omissis Cretæ pascuis:
Terræ mihi datum est parum;
Careo interim doloribus. Pindar.

25 the one] he only *5+*

no more needs than they mean to satisfie: and he that will make more must look for satisfaction where he can.

8. [h]In all troubles and sadder accidents, let us take sanctuary in Religion, and by innocence cast out anchors for our souls to keep them from shipwrack, though they be not kept from storm. For what Philosophy shall comfort a Villane that is haled to the rack for murdering his Prince; or that is broken upon the wheele for Sacriledge? His cup is full of pure and unmingled sorrow: His body is rent with torment, his name with ignominy, his soul with shame and sorrow which are to last eternally: but when a man suffers in a good cause, or is afflicted and yet walks not perversly with his God, then, *Anytus and Melitus may kill me, but they cannot hurt me*; then S. *Pauls* character is engraved in the forehead of our fortune: [i] *We are troubled on every side, but not distressed, perplexed, but not in despair, persecuted, but not forsaken, cast down, but not destroyed:* [j] *and who is he that will harm you if ye be followers of that which is good*? For indeed every thing in the World is indifferent but sin: and all the scorchings of the Sun are very tolerable in respect of the burnings of a Feaver or a Calenture. The greatest evils are from within us: and from our selves also we must look for our greatest good; for God is the Fountain of it, but reaches it to us by our own hands; and when all things look sadly round about us, then only we shall finde how excellent a fortune it is to have God to friend; and of all friendships that onely is created to support us in our needs. For it is sin that turns Ague into a Feaver, and a Feaver to the Plague, fear into despair, anger into rage, and losse into madnesse, and sorrow to amazement and confusion: but if either we were innocent, or else by the sadnesse are made penitent, we are put to School, or into the Theatre, either to learn how, or else actually to combat for a Crown; the accident may serve an end of mercy, but is not a Messenger of wrath.

Let us not therefore be governed by *external* and *present*, *and seeming things*; nor let us make us the same judgement of things, that common and weak understandings do; nor make other men, and they not the wisest, to be judges of our felicity, so that we be happy or miserable as they please to think us; but let reason and experience, and religion, and hope relying upon the Divine promises be the measure of our

[h] Vacare culpa in calamitatibus maximum solatium.
[i] 2 Cor. 4: 8.
[j] 1 Pet. 3: 13. 1 Pet. 4: 15, 16.

---

2 where] when *7 8*   31 make us the] make the *4+*

judgement. [k]No *wise man* did ever describe felicity without vertue: and no *good man* did ever think vertue could depend upon the variety of a good or bad fortune. It is no evil to be poor, but to be vitious and impatient.

Means to obtain content by way of consideration.

To these exercises and spiritual instruments if we adde the following considerations concerning the nature and circumstances of humane chance, wee may better secure our peace. For as to children who are afraid of vain Images, we use to perswade confidence by making them to handle and look neerer such things, that when in such a familiarity they perceive them innocent, they may overcome their fears: so must timorous, phantastical, sad and discontented persons be treated; they must be made to consider and on all sides to look upon the accident, and to take all its dimensions, and consider its consequences, and to behold the purpose of God, and the common mistakes of men, and their evil sentences they usually passe upon them; For then we shall perceive that like Colts and unmanaged Horses we start at dead bones and livelesse blocks, things that are unactive as they are innocent. But if we secure our hopes and our fears, and make them moderate and within government, we may the sooner overcome the evil of the accident: *for nothing that we feel is so bad as what we fear.*

1. Consider that the universal providence of God hath so ordered it, that the good things of Nature and Fortune are divided, that we may know how to bear our own and relieve each others wants and imperfections. [l]It is not for a Man, but for a God to have all excellencies and all felicities. He supports my poverty with his wealth, I counsel and instruct him with my learning and experience. He hath many friends, I many children: He hath no Heir, I have no inheritance: and any one great blessing together with the common portions of Nature and necessity is a fair fortune, if it be but health or strength, or the swiftnesse of *Ahimaaz.* For it is an unreasonable discontent to be troubled that I have not so good Cocks, or Dogs, or Horses as my Neighbour,

[k] Beatitudo pendet a rectis consiliis in affectionem animi constantem desinentibus. Plut.

[l] Non te omnia ad læta genuit,
O Agamemnon, Atreus;
Opus est te gaudere et mœrere:
Mortalis enim natus es, et, ut haud velis,
Superi sic constituerunt.

being more troubled that I want one thing that I need not, than thankfull for having received all that I need. *Nero* had this disease, that he was not content with the fortune of the whole Empire, but put the Fidlers to death for being more skilful in the trade than he was: and *Dionysius* the elder, was so angry at *Philoxenus* for singing, and with *Plato* for disputing better than he did, that he sold *Plato* a Slave into *Ægina*, and condemned the other to the Quarries.

This consideration is to be enlarged by adding to it that there are some instances of fortune and a fair condition that cannot stand with some others, but if you desire this, you must lose that, and unlesse you be content with one, you lose the comfort of both. If you covet Learning, you must have leisure and a retired life: if to be a Polititian, you must go abroad and get experience and do all businesses, and keep all company, and have no leisure at all. If you will be rich, you must be frugal: If you will be popular, you must bee bountiful: If a Philosopher, you must despise riches. The Greek that designed to make the most exquisite picture that could be imagined fancyed the eye of *Chione*, and the hair of *Pægnium*, and *Tarsia's* lip, and *Philenium's* chinne, and the forehead of *Delphia*, and set all these upon *Milphidippa's* neck, and thought that he should out do both Art and Nature. But when he came to view the proportions he found that what was excellent in *Tarsia* did not agree with the other excellency of *Philenium*; and although singly they were rare pieces, yet in the whole they made a most ugly face. The dispersed excellencies and blessings of many men, if given to one would not make a handsome, but a monstrous fortune. Use therefore that faculty which Nature hath given thee, and thy education hath made actual, and thy calling hath made a duty: but if thou desirest to be a Saint, refuse not his persecution: If thou wouldest be famous as *Epaminondas* or *Fabricius* accept also of their poverty, for that added lustre to their persons and envy to their fortune, and their vertue without it could not have been so excellent. Let *Euphorion* sleep quietly with his old rich Wife: and let *Medius* drink on with *Alexander*: and remember, thou canst not have the riches of the first, unlesse you have the old Wife too; [m] nor the favour which the second had with his Prince, unlesse you buy it at his price, that is, pay thy sobriety down at first, and thy health a little after; and then their condition though it looked splendidly, yet when you handle it on all sides, it will prick your fingers.

2. Consider how many excellent personages in all Ages have suffered as great or greater calamities than this which now tempts thee t

[m] Prandet Aristoteles, quandet Philippo lubet, Diogenes quando Diogeni.

impatience. *Agis* was the most noble of the Greeks, and yet his Wife bore a Childe by *Alcibiades*: and *Philip* was Prince of *Iturea*, and yet his Wife ran away with his Brother *Herod* into Galilee: and certainly in a great fortune that was a great calamity. But these are but single instances. Almost all the ages of the world have noted that their most eminent Scholers were most eminently poor, some by choice, but most by chance, and an inevitable decree of providence: And in the whole sex of women God hath decreed the sharpest pains of childe-birth, to show that there is no state exempt from sorrow, and yet that the weakest persons have strengths more than enough to bear the greatest evil: and the greatest Queens and the Mothers of Saints and Apostles, have no charter of exemption from this sad sentence. But the Lord of men and Angels was also the King of sufferings; and if thy course robe trouble thee, remember the swadling clothes of Jesus: if thy bed be uneasy, yet it is not worse than his Manger; and it is no sad-nesse to have a thin table, if thou callest to minde that the King of heaven and earth was fed with a little breast milk; and yet besides this he suffered all the sorrows which we deserved. We therefore have great reason to sit down upon our own hearths, and warme our selves at our own fires, and feed upon content at home: for it were a strange pride to expect to be more gently treated by the Divine providence than the best and wisest men, than Apostles and Saints, nay, than the son of the Eternal God, the heir of both the worlds.

This Consideration may be enlarged by surveying all the states and families of the world: and [n]he that at once saw *Ægina* and *Megara*, *Pyræus* and *Corinth* lye gasping in their ruines, and almost buried in their own heaps had reason to blame *Cicero* for mourning impatiently the death of one woman. In the most beauteous and splendid fortune there are many cares and proper interruptions and allayes: In the fortune of a Prince there is not the course robe of beggery; but there are infinite cares: and the Judge sits upon the Tribunal with great ceremony and ostentation of fortune, and yet at his house, or in his breast there is something that causes him to sigh deeply. [o]*Pittacus* was

[n] Servius Sulpitius.

[o] Hic in foro beatus esse creditur,
Cum foribus apertis sit suis miserrimus;
Imperat mulier, jubet omnia, semper litigat.

Ferre quam sortem patiuntur omnes,
Nemo recusat.

3 ran] *5*+, run *1 2 3 4*

a wise and valiant man, but his wife overthrew the Table when he had invited his friends: upon which the good man to excuse her incivility and his own misfortune said, that every man had one evil, and he was most happy that had but that alone: And if nothing else happens, yet sicknesses so often do imbitter the fortune and content of a family, that a Physician in a few years, and with the practise upon a very few families, gets experience enough to minister to almost all diseases. And when thy little misfortune troubles thee, remember that thou hast known the best of Kings, and the best of Men put to death publickly by his own subjects.

3. There are many accidents which are esteemed great calamities, and yet we have reason enough to bear them well and unconcernedly; for they neither touch our bodies nor our souls: our health and our vertue remains intire, our life and our reputation. It may be I am slighted, or I have received ill language, but my head akes not for it, neither hath it broke my thigh, nor taken away my vertue, unlesse I lose my charity or my patience. Inquire therefore what you are the worse either in your soul or in your body, for what hath happened: for upon this very stock many evils will disappeare, [p] since the body and the soul make up the whole man: and when the daughter of *Stilpo* proved a wanton, he said it was none of his sin, and therefore there was no reason it should be his misery: And if an enemy hath taken all that from a Prince whereby he was a King; he may refresh himself by considering all that is left him, whereby he is a man.

4. Consider that sad accidents and a state of affliction is a School of vertue: it reduces our spirits to sobernesse, and our counsels to moderation; it corrects levity, and interrupts the confidence of sinning. [q] *It is good for me* (said *David*) that *I have been afflicted, for thereby I have learned thy Law.* And *I know (O Lord) that thou of very faithfulnesse hast caused me to be troubled.* For God, who in mercy and wisdom governs the world, would never have suffered so many sadnesses, and have sent them especially to the most vertuous and the wisest men, but that he intends they should be the seminary of comfort, the nursery of vertue,

[p] Si natus es tu, Trophime, solus omnium hac lege,
Ut semper eant tibi res arbitrio tuo,
Felicitatem hanc si quis promisit Deum,
Irascereris jure, nam mala is fide
Et improbe egisses. Menan.

[q] 119. Psalm. 10. part. v. 3.

8–10 And when . . . own subjects.] *2+, in appendix at end of chap. 4 1* note *p* tu] *cor, om 1+* nam] *cor*, non *1+*

the exercise of wisdom, the tryal of patience, the venturing for a crown, and the gate of glory.

5. Consider that afflictions are oftentimes the occasions of great temporal advantages: and we must not look upon them as they sit down heavily upon us, but as they serve some of Gods ends, and the purposes of universal Providence: And when a Prince fights justly, and yet unprosperously, if he could see all those reasons for which God hath so ordered it, he would think it the most reasonable thing in the world, and that it would be very ill to have it otherwise. If a man could have opened one of the pages of the Divine counsel, and could have seen the event of *Josephs* being sold to the Merchants of Amalek, he might with much reason have dried up the young mans tears: and when Gods purposes are opened in the events of things, as it was in the case of *Joseph*, when he sustained his Fathers family and became Lord of Egypt, then we see what ill judgement we made of things, and that we were passionate as children, and transported with sence and mistaken interest. The case of *Themistocles* was almost like that of *Joseph*, for being banished into Egypt, he also grew in favour with the King, and told his wife, *He had been undone, unlesse he had been undone.* For God esteems it one of his glories that he brings good out of evil, and therefore it were but reason we should trust God to govern his own world as he pleases: and that he should patiently *wait till the change cometh*, or the reason be discovered.

And this consideration is also of great use to them who envy at the prosperity of the wicked, and the successe of Persecutors, and the baits of fishes, and the bread of dogs. God fails not to sow blessings in the long furrows which the plowers plow upon the back of the Church: and this successe which troubles us will be a great glory to God, and a great benefit to his Saints and servants, and a great ruine to the Persecutors, who shall have but the fortune of *Theramenes*, one of the thirty Tyrants of Athens, who scaped when his house fell upon him, and was shortly after put to death with torments by his Collegues in the Tyranny.

To which also may be added that the great evils which happen to the best and wisest men are one of the great arguments, upon the strength of which we can expect felicity to our souls, and the joyes of another world. And certainly they are then very tolerable and eligible, when with so great advantages they minister to the faith and hope of a Christian. But if we consider what unspeakable tortures are provided for the wicked to all eternity, we should not be troubled to see them prosperous here, but rather wonder that their portion in this life is not bigger, and that ever they should be sick, or crossed, or affronted, or troubled with the contradiction and disease of their own vices, since if they were fortunate beyond their own ambition it could not make them recompence for one houres torment in Hell, which yet they shall have for their eternall portion.

After all these considerations deriving from sence and experience, grace and reason, there are two remedies still remaining, and they are *Necessity* and *Time.*

6. For it is but reasonable to bear that accident patiently which God sends, [r]since impatience does but intangle us like the fluttering of a bird in a net, but cannot at all ease our trouble, or prevent the accident: it must be run thorough, and therefore it were better we compose our selves to a patient, than to a troubled and miserable suffering.

7. But however, if you will not otherwise be cured, time at last will do it alone; and then consider, do you mean to mourne *alwayes*, or but *for a time*? If alwayes; you are miserable and foolish. If for a time; then why will you not apply those reasons to your grief at first, with which you will cure it at last: or if you will not cure it with reason, see how little of a man there is in you, that you suffer time to do more with you than reason or religion: you suffer your selves to be cured just as a beast, or a tree is; let it alone and the thing will heal it self; but this is neither honourable to thy person, nor of reputation to thy religion. However be content to bear thy calamity, because thou art sure in a little time it will sit down gentle and easy: For to a mortal man no evil is immortal: And here let the worst thing happen that can, it will end in death, and we commonly think that to be neer enough.

8. Lastly, of those things which are reckoned amongst evils, some are better than their contraries; and to a good man the very worst is tolerable.

Poverty or a low Fortune.

1. Poverty is better than riches, and a mean fortune to be chosen before a great and splendid one. It is indeed despised and makes men contemptible: it exposes a man to the insolence of evil persons, and leaves a man defencelesse: it is alwayes suspected: its stories are accounted lies, and all its counsells follyes: it puts a man from all imployment: it makes a mans discourses tedious, and his society

[r] Nemo recusat ferre, quod necesse est pati.

troublesome. This is the worst of it: and yet all this and farre worse than this the Apostles suffered for being Christians; and Christianitie it selfe may be esteemed an affliction as well as poverty, if this be all that can be said against it; for the Apostles and the most eminent Christians were really poor, and were used contemptuously: and yet, [s]that poverty is despised may be an argument to commend it, if it be despised by none but persons vitious and ignorant. However, certain it is that a great fortune is a great vanity, and riches is nothing but danger, trouble, and temptation; like a garment that is too long, and bears a train; not so useful to one, but it is troublesome to two; to him that bears the one part upon his shoulders, and to him that bears the other part in his hands: But poverty is the sister of a good minde, the parent of sober counsels and the nurse of all vertue.

For, what is it that you admire in the fortune of a great King? Is it that hee alwayes goes in a great company? You may thrust your self into the same croud, or goe often to Church, and then you have as great a company as he hath, and that may upon as good ground please you as him, that is, justly neither: [t]for so impertinent and uselesse pomp, and the other circumstances of his distance, are not made for him, but for his Subjects, that they may learne to separate him from common usages, and be taught to be governed. But if you looke upon them as fine things in themselves, you may quickly alter your opinion when you shall consider that they cannot cure the toothach, nor make one wise, or fill the belly, or give one nights sleep, (though they help to break many) nor satisfying any appetite of Nature, or Reason, or Religion: but they are states of greatnesse which onely makes it possible for a Man to be made extremely miserable. And it was long agoe observed by the Greeke Tragedians, and from them by *Arrianus*, saying, That [u]all our Tragedies are of Kings and Princes, and rich or ambitious personages, but you never see a poor man have a part, unlesse it be as a Chorus, or to fill up the Scenes, to dance or to be

[s] Alta fortuna alto travaglio apporta. [t] Da autorità la ceremonia al' atto.

[u] *Οὐδείς δὲ πένης τραγῳδίαν συμπληροῖ, εἰ μὴ ὡς χορευτής.*

Bis sex dierum mensura consero ego agros,
Berecynthia arva.

. . . .

Animusque meus sursum usque evectus ad polum
Decidit humi, et me sic videtur alloqui;
Disce haud nimis magni facere mortalia. Tantal. in Tragœd.

29 or] and *2 3*

derided: but the Kings and the great Generals; First (sayes he) they begin with joy *στέψατε δώματα*, 'crown the houses': but about the third or fourth Act, they cry out, O *Citheron* why didst thou spare my life to reserve me for this more sad calamity? And this is really true in the great Accidents of the World: for a great estate hath great crosses, and a mean fortune hath but small ones. It may be the poor man loses a Cow (for if his Childe dyes he is quit of his biggest care) but such an accident in a rich and splendid Family doubles upon the spirits of the parents: Or it may be the poor man is troubled to pay his rent, and that's his biggest trouble: but it is a bigger care to secure a great fortune in a troubled estate, or with equal greatnesse, or with the circumstances of honour, and the nicenesse of reputation to defend a Law-suit: and that which will secure a common mans whole estate, is not enough to defend a great mans honour.

[v]And therefore it was not without mystery observed among the Ancients, that they who made gods of gold and silver, of hope and fear, peace and fortune, Garlick and Onions, Beasts and Serpents, and a quartan Ague, yet never deified money: meaning, that however wealth was admired by common or abused understandings; yet from riches, that is, from that proportion of good things which is beyond the necessities of Nature, no moment could be added to a mans real content or happinesse. [w]Corn from *Sardinia*, herds of *Calabrian* cattel, meadows through which pleasant *Liris* glides, silkes from *Tyrus*, and golden Chalices to drown my health in, are nothing but instruments of vanity or sinne, and suppose a disease in the soul of him that longs for them, or admires them: [x]And this I have otherwhere represented more largely; to which I here adde, that riches have very *great dangers* to their souls, not onely *who covet them*, but to all *that have them.* For if a great personage undertakes an action passionately, and upon great interest, let him manage it indiscreetly, let the whole designe be unjust, let it be acted with all the malice and impotency in the World, he shall have enough to flatter him, but not enough to reprove him. He had need be a bold man that shall tell his Patron, he is going to Hell; and that Prince had need be a good man that shall suffer such a Monitor: And though it bee a strange kinde of civility and an evil dutifulnesse in Friends and Relatives to suffer him to perish without reproofe or

[v] —funesta pecunia, Templo
Nondum habitas, nullas nummorum ereximus aras
Ut colitur pax atque fides.

[w] Horat. Od. 31. lib. 1.

[x] Chap. 4. Sect. 8. Title of Covetousness.

medicine, rather than to seem unmannerly to a great sinner, yet it is none of their least infelicities, that their wealth and greatnesse shall put them into sinne, and yet put them past reproof. I need not instance in the habitual intemperance of rich Tables, nor the evil accidents and effects of fulnesse; pride and lust, wantonnesse and softnesse of disposition, huge talking, and an imperious spirit, despite of Religion, and contempt of poor persons: At the best, [y] *it is a great temptation for a man to have in his power whatsoever he can have in his sensual desires*; and therefore riches is a blessing like to a present made of a whole Vintage to a Man in a Hectick Feaver; he will be much tempted to drink of it, and if he does he is inflamed, and may chance to dye with the kindnesse.

Now besides what hath been already noted, in the state of poverty there is nothing to be accounted for, but *the fear of wanting necessaries*, of which if a man could be secured, that he might live free from care, all the other parts of it might be reckoned amongst the advantages of wise and sober persons, rather than objections against that state of fortune.

But concerning this I consider, that there must needs be great security to all Christians, since CHRIST not onely made expresse promises that we should have sufficient for this life; but also took great pains and used many arguments to create confidence in us: and such they were which by their own strength were sufficient, though you abate the authority of the Speaker. The Sonne of GOD told us, his Father takes care of us: Hee that knew all his Fathers counsels and his whole kindnesse towards mankinde, told us so. How great is that truth, how certain, how necessary, which CHRIST himself proved by arguments! The excellent words and most comfortable sentences which are our Bills of Exchange, upon the credit of which we lay our cares down, and receive provisions for our need, are these. [z] *Take no thought for your life what ye shall eat or what ye shall drink, nor yet for your body what ye shall put on. Is not the life more than meat, and the body than raiment? Behold the fowls of the air, for they sow not neither do they reap, nor gather into barns, yet your heavenly Father feedeth them. Are ye not much better than they? Which of you by taking thought can adde one cubit to his stature? And why take ye thought for raiment? Consider the Lillies of the field, how they grow: They toil not, neither do they spin, and yet I say unto you, that even* Solomon *in all his glory, was not arayed like one of these. Therefore if God so clothe the grasse of the field which to day is, and to morrow is cast into the oven, shall he not much more clothe*

[y] James 2: 5–7. [z] Mat. 6: 25.

you, O ye of little faith? Therefore take no thought, saying, what shall we eat, or what shall we drink, or wherewithall shall we be clothed? (for after all these things do the Gentiles seek.) For your heavenly Father knoweth that ye have need of all these things. But seek ye first the kingdom of God, and his righteousnesse, and all these things shall bee added unto you. Take therefore no thought for the morrow: for the morrow shall take thought for the things of it self: sufficient to the day is the evil thereof. [a]The same discourse is repeated by S. *Luke*: and accordingly our duty is urged and our confidence abetted by the Disciples of our Lord, in divers places of holy Scripture. So S. *Paul*, [b]*Be careful for nothing, but in every thing by prayer and supplication with thanksgiving, let your request be made known unto God*: And againe, [c]*Charge them that are rich in this world that they bee not high minded, nor trust in uncertaine riches, but in the living* GOD, *who giveth us richly all things to enjoy*: and yet again, [d]*Let your conversation be without covetousnesse, and be content with such things as ye have; for he hath said, I will never leave thee nor forsake thee: So that we may boldly say, the Lord is my helper.* And all this is by S. *Peter* summed up in our duty, thus: *Cast all your care upon him, for he careth for you*: Which words he seems to have borrowed out of the 55 Psalm, verse 23. where *David* saith the same thing almost in the same words. To which I onely adde the observation made by him, and the argument of experience; *I have been young and now am old, and yet saw I never the righteous forsaken, nor his seed begging their bread.* And now after all this, a fearlesse confidence in God and concerning a provision of necessaries is so reasonable that it is become a duty; and he is scarce a Christian whose faith is so little as to be jealous in God and suspitious concerning meat and clothes: that man hath nothing in him of the noblenesse or confidence of Charity.

Does not God provide for all the birds and beasts and fishes? Do not the sparrows fly from their bush, and every morning finde meat where they laid it not? Do not the young ravens call to God and he feeds them? and were it reasonable that the sons of the family should fear the Father would give meat to the chickens and the servants, his sheep and his dogs, but give none to them? He were a very ill Father that should do so: or he were a very foolish son that should think so of a good Father. But besides the reasonablenesse of this faith and this hope; we have infinite experience of it. How innocent, how carelesse how secure is Infancy? and yet how certainly provided for! We have

[a] Luke 12: 22 to the 31 verse. [b] Phil. 4: 6. [c] 1 Tim. 6: 17.
[d] Heb. 13: 5, 6.

14 [d]] *7, 8, om 1 2 3 4 5 6*

ived at Gods charges all the dayes of our life, and have (as the Italian roverb sayes) set down to meat at the sound of a bell; and hitherto he ath not failed us: we have no reason to suspect him for the future; we lo not use to serve men so; and lesse time of tryal creates great con-idences in us towards them who for twenty years together never broke heir word with us: and God hath so ordered it that a man shall have ad the experience of many years provision, before he shall under-tand how to doubt: that he may be provided for an answer against the emptation shall come, and the mercies felt in his childehood, may nake him fear lesse when he is a man. Adde to this that God hath iven us his holy Spirit; he hath promised heaven to us; he hath given s his son; and we are taught from Scripture to make this inference rom hence, *How should not he with him give us all things else?*

The Charge of many Children.

Ve have a title to be provided for as we are Gods creatures: another itle as we are his Children: another because God hath promised: and very of our children hath the same title; and therefore it is a huge folly nd infidelity to be troubled and full of care because we have many hildren. Every childe we have to feed is a new revenue, a new title to iods care and providence; so that many children are a great wealth: nd if it be said they are chargeable, it is no more than all wealth and reat revenues are. For what difference is it? *Titius* keeps ten ploughs, *ornelia* hath ten children: He hath land enough to imploy, and to feed ll his hindes; she blessings, and promises, and the provisions and the uth of God to maintain all her children. His hindes and horses eat up ll his corn, and her children are sufficiently maintained with her ttle. They bring in and eat up; and she indeed eats up, but they also ring in from the store houses of heaven, and the granaries of God: nd my children are not so much mine as they are Gods: he feeds them the womb by wayes secret and insensible; and would not work a erpetual miracle to bring them forth, and then to starve them.

Violent necessities.

ut some men are highly tempted, and are brought to a strait, that ithout a miracle they cannot be relieved, what shall they do? It may e their pride or vanity hath brought the necessity upon them, and it is

4 lesse] least *2 3* 10 fear lesse] fearlesse *2 3 8* 22 *Titius*] *Titia 2 3*

not a need of Gods making; and if it be not they must cure it themselves by lessening their desires, and moderating their appetites; and yet if it be innocent though unnecessary, God does usually relieve such necessities; and he does not onely upon our prayers grant us more than he promised of temporal things: but also he gives many times more than we ask. This is no object for our faith, but ground enough for a temporal and prudent hope: and if we fail in the particular, God will turn it to a bigger mercy, if we submit to his dispensation, and adore him in the denyal. But if it be a matter of necessity, let not any man by way of impatience cry out, that God will not work a miracle; for God by miracle did give meat and drink to his people in the wilderness, of which he had made no particular promise in any Covenant: and if all natural means fail, it is certain that God will rather work a miracle than break his word: He can do that, He cannot do this. Onely we must remember that our portion of temporal things is but *food and raiment*: God hath not promised us coaches and horses, rich houses and jewels, Tyrian silks and Persian carpets, neither hath he promised to minister to our needs in such circumstances as we shall appoint, but such as himself shall choose. God will enable either thee to pay thy debt (if thou beggest it of him) or else he will pay it for thee, that is, take thy desire as a discharge of thy duty, and pay it to thy Creditor in blessings, or in some secret of his providence. It may be he hath laid up the corn that shall feed thee, in the granary of thy Brother, or will clothe thee with his wool; he enabled Saint *Peter* to pay his Gabel, by the ministery of a fish; and *Elias* to be waited on by a crow, who was both his minister, and his steward for provisions: and his Holy Son rode in triumph upon an asse that grazed in another mans pastures. And if God gives to him the dominion and reserves the use to thee, thou hast the better half of the two; but the charitable man serves God and serves thy need; and both joyn to provide for thee, and God blesses both. But if he takes away the flesh-pots from thee, he can also alter the appetite, and he hath given thee power and commandment to restrain it: and if he lessens the revenue, he will also shrink the necessity; or if he gives but a very little, he will make it go a great way: or if he sends thee but course diet, he will blesse it and make it healthful, and can cure all the anguish of thy povertie by giving thee patience and the grace of contentednesse. For the grace of God secures you of provisions, and yet the grace of God feeds and supports the spirit in the want of provisions: and if a thin table be apt to enfeeble the spirit of one used to feed better, yet the cheerfulnesse of a spirit that is blessed will make a thin table become a delicacy, if the man was as well taught as he was fed, and learned his duty when he received the blessing. Poverty therefore is in some sences eligible and to be preferred before riches, but in all sences it is very tolerable.

Death of Children, or neerest Relatives and Friends.

There are some persons who have been noted for excellent in their lives and passions, rarely innocent, and yet hugely penitent for indiscretions and harmelesse infirmities, such as was *Paulina*, one of the ghostly children of S. *Hierom*, and yet when any of her children dyed she was arrested with a sorrow so great as brought her to the margent of her grave. And the more tender our spirits are made by Religion, the more easy we are to let in grief, if the cause be innocent, and be but in any sence twisted with piety and due affections. To cure which we may consider that al the world must die, and therfore to be impatient at the death of a person concerning whom it was certain and known that he must die, is to mourn because thy friend or childe was not born an Angel, and when thou hast a while made thy self miserable by an importunate and uselesse grief, it may be thou shalt die thy self, and leave others to their choice whether they will mourn for thee or no: but by that time it will appear how impertinent that grief was which served no end of life, and ended in thy own funeral. But what great matter is it, if sparks fly upward, or a stone falls into a pit, if that which was combustible be burned, or that which was liquid be melted, or that which is mortal do die? It is no more than a man does every day; for every night death hath gotten possession of that day, and we shall never live that day over again; and when the last day is come there are no more dayes left for us to die. And what is sleeping and waking, but living and dying? what is Spring and Autumne, youth and old age, morning and evening, but real images of life and death, and really the same to many considerable effects and changes?

Untimely death.

But it is not mere dying that is pretended by some as the cause of their impatient mourning; but that the childe died young, before he knew good and evil; his right hand from his left, and so lost all his portion of this world, and they know not of what excellency his portion in the next shall be. If he dyed young, he lost but little, for he understood but little, and had not capacities of great pleasures, or great cares: but yet he dyed innocent and before the sweetnesse of his soul was defloured and ravished from him by the flames and follies of a forward age: he went out from the dining-rooms before he had fallen into errour by the intemperance of his meat or the deluge of drink: and he hath obtained this favour of God, that his soul hath suffered a lesse imprisonment and her load was sooner taken off that he might with lesser delayes goe and converse with immortal spirits: and the babe is taken into Para- dise before he knows good and evil, (For that knowledge threw ou great Father out) and this ignorance returns the childe thither. [e]Bu (as concerning thy own particular) remove thy thoughts back to thos days in which thy childe was not born, and you are now but as ther you was, and there is no difference but that you had a son born, and i you reckon that for evil, you are unthankful for the blessing; if it b good, it is better that you had the blessing for a while than not at al and yet if he had never been born, this sorrow had not been at all: bu be no more displeased at God for giving you the blessing for a while than you would have been if he had not given it at all; and reckon tha intervening blessing for a gain, but account it not an evil; and if it be good, turn it not into a sorrow and sadnesse. But if we have grea reason to complain of the calamities and evils of our life, then we hav the lesse reason to grieve that those whom we loved, have so small portion of evil assigned to them. And it is no small advantage, that ou children dying young receive: for their condition of a blessed immor tality is rendered to them secure by being snatcht from the dangers o an evil choice and carried to their little cells of felicity, where they ca weep no more. And this the wisest of the Gentiles understood wel when they forbade any offerings or libations to be made for dea infants, as was usual for their other dead; as believing they we entered into a secure possession, to which they went with no othe condition, but that they passed into it thorough the way of mortalit and for a few moneths wore an uneasy garment. And let weepin parents say, if they do not think that the evils their little babes hav suffered are sufficient. If they be, why are they troubled that they we taken from those many and greater, which in succeeding years a great enough to try all the reason and religion which art and natur

[e] Iidem si puer parvulus occidat, æquo animo ferendum putant: si vero in cunis, querendum quidem: atqui ab hoc acerbius exegit natura quod dederat. At id quide ipsum in cæteris rebus melius putatur, aliquam partem quam nullam attingere. Sen

9 [e]] *4+*, *om 1 2 3* 17 at] *om 7* note *e* ab] *cor, om 4+* dederat] *c* dederit 4+

and the grace of God hath produced in us, to enable us for such sad contentions. And possibly we may doubt concerning men and women, but we cannot suspect that to infants death can be such an evil, but that it brings to them much more good, than it takes from them in this life.

Death unseasonable.

But others can well bear the death of infants: but when they have spent some years of childehood or youth, and are entered into arts, and society, when they are hopeful and provided for, when the parents are to reap the comfort of all their fears and cares, then it breaks the spirit to loose them. This is true in many; but this is not love to the dead, but to themselves: for they misse what they had flattered themselves into by hope and opinion: and if it were kindnesse to the dead, they may consider, that since we hope he is gone to God and to rest, it is an ill expression of our love to them, that we weep for their good fortune. For that life is not best which is longest: and when they are descended into the grave, it shall not be inquired how long they have lived, but how well. [f]And yet this shortening of their dayes is an evil wholly depending upon opinion. For if men did naturally live but twenty years, then we should be satisfied if they dyed about sixteen, or eighteen: and yet eighteen years now are as long as eighteen years would be then; and if a man were but of a dayes life, it is well if he lasts till even song, and then says his compline an hour before the time: and we are pleased and call not that death immature if he lives till seventy: and yet this age is as short of the old periods, before and since the flood, as this youths age (for whom you mourn) is of the present fulnesse. Suppose therefore a decree passed upon this person (as there have been many upon all mankinde) and God hath set him a shorter period; and then we may as well bear the immature death of the young man, as the death of the oldest men: for they also are immature and unseasonable in respect of the old periods of many generations. And why are we troubled that he had arts and sciences before he dyed? or are we troubled that he does not live to make use of them? The first is cause of joy, for they are excellent in order to certain ends: And the second cannot be cause of sorrow, because he hath no need to use them as the case now stands, being provided for with the provisions of an Angel, and the manna of Eternity. However, the sons and the parents, friends

[f] Juvenis relinquit vitam quem Dii diligunt. Menand.

3 from them] *4*+, them from *1 2 3* 36 manna] *KC*, maner *1*+

and relatives are in the world, like hours and minutes to a day. The hour comes and must passe; and some stay but minutes, and they also passe, and shall never return again. But let it be considered, that from the time in which a man is conceived, from that time forward to Eternitie he shall never cease to be: and let him dye young or old, still he hath an immortal soul, and hath laid down his body onely for a time, as that which was the instrument of his trouble and sorrow, and the scene of sicknesses and disease. But he is in a more noble manner of being, after death, than he can be here: and the childe may with more reason be allowed to cry for leaving his mothers womb for this world, than a man can for changing this world for another.

Sudden deaths or violent.

Others are yet troubled at the manner of their childes or friends death. He was drowned, or lost his head, or dyed of the plague, and this is a new spring of sorrow: but no man can give a sensible account, how it shall be worse for a childe to dye with drowning in half an hour, than to endure a feaver of one and twenty dayes. And if my friend lost his head, so he did not lose his constancy, and his religion, he dyed with huge advantage.

Being Childelesse.

But by this means I am left without an Heir: Well, suppose that: Thou hast no Heir, and I have no inheritance; and there are many Kings and Emperors that have died childlesse: many Royal lines are extinguished: And *Augustus Cæsar* was forced to adopt his wives son to inherit all the Roman greatnesse. And there are many wise persons that never marryed; and we read no where that any of the children of the Apostles did survive their Fathers: and all that inherit any thing of Christs kingdom come to it by Adoption, not by natural inheritance and to dye without an natural heir is no intolerable evil, since it was sanctified in the person of Jesus who dyed a Virgin.

Evil, or unfortunate Children.

And by this means we are freed from the greater sorrows of having a fool, a swine, or a goat to rule after us in our families: [g] and yet even this

[g] Κρεῖττον τὸν παῖδα κακὸν εἶναι, ἤ σε κακοδαίμονα. Epict.

12 deaths] death 4+

condition admits of comfort. For all the wilde *Americans* are supposed to be the sons of *Dodonaim*; and the sons of *Jacob* are now the most scattered and despised people in the whole world. The son of *Solomon* was but a silly weak man; and the son of *Hezekiah* was wicked: and all the fools and barbarous people, all the thieves and pirates, all the slaves and miserable men and women of the world are the sons and daughters of *Noah*; and we must not look to be exempted from that portion of sorrow which God gave to *Noah*, and *Adam*, to *Abraham*, to *Isaack* and to *Jacob*: I pray God send us into the lot of *Abraham.* [h]But if any thing happens worse to us, *it is enough for us that we bear it evenly.*

Our own death.

And how if you were to die your self? you know you must. [i]Onely be ready for it, by the preparations of a good life; and then it is the greatest good that ever happened to thee: else there is nothing that can comfort you. But if you have served God in a holy life, send away the women and the weepers, tell them it is as much intemperance to weep too much, as to laugh too much: and when thou art alone, or with fitting company, dye as thou shouldest; but do not dye impatiently and like a fox catched in a trap. For if you fear death you shall never the more avoid it, but you make it miserable. *Fannius* that kild himself for fear of death, dyed as certainly, as *Portia* that eat burning coals, or *Cato* that cut his own throat. To dye is necessary and natural, and it may be honourable: [j]but to dye poorly, and basely, and sinfully, that alone is it, that can make a man unfortunate. No man can be a slave, but he that fears pain, or fears to die. To such a man nothing but chance and peaceable times can secure his duty, and he depends upon things without, for his felicity; and so is well but during the pleasure of his enemy, or a Thief, or a Tyrant, or it may be, of a dog, or a wilde bull.

[h] *Σοὶ δ᾽ ἀϱκεέτω τὸ εὐσταθεῖν.*
[i] Ad fines cum perveneris ne revertito. Pythag.
[j] *Οὐ κατθανεῖν γάϱ*, etc.

Ad Chap. II.

Prayers for the several Graces and parts of Christian Sobriety.

A Prayer against Sensuality.

O Eternal Father, thou that sittest in Heaven invested with essential Glories and Divine perfections, fill my soul with so deep a sence of the excellencies of spiritual and heavenly things, that my affections being weaned from the pleasures of the world, and the false allurements of sin, I may with great severity and the prudence of a holy discipline and strict desires, with clear resolutions and a free spirit have my conversation in Heaven and heavenly imployments; that being in affections as in my condition a Pilgrim and a stranger here, I may covet after and labour for an abiding city, and at last may enter into and for ever dwell in the Coelestial Jerusalem which is the mother of us all, through Jesus Christ our Lord. *Amen.*

For Temperance.

O Almighty God and gracious Father of Men, and Angels, who openest thy hand and fillest all things with plenty, and hast provided for thy servant sufficient to satisfie all my needs: teach me to use thy creatures soberly and temperately, that I may not with loads of meat or drink make the temptations of my enemy to prevail upon me, or my spirit unapt for the performance of my duty, or my body healthlesse, or my affections sensual and unholy. O my God, never suffer that the blessings which thou givest me may either minister to sin or sicknesse, but to health and holinesse, and thanksgiving, that in the strength of thy provisions I may cheerfully and actively and diligently serve thee: that I may worthily feast at thy table here, and be accounted worthy through thy grace to be admitted to thy table hereafter at the Eternal supper of the Lamb to sing an Allelujah to God the Father, the Son and the Holy Ghost for ever and ever. *Amen.*

For Chastity: to be said especially by unmarried persons.

Almighty God, our most holy and eternal Father, who art of pure eyes, and canst behold no uncleannesse; [k]let thy gracious and holy Spirit

[k] The petition.

1 *Ad* Chap. II.] *ed, om 1+* 32 [k]] *GH, om 1+*

descend upon thy servant, and reprove the spirit of Fornication and Uncleannesse, and cast him out, [l]that my body may be a holy Temple, and my soul a Sanctuary to entertain the Prince of purities, the holy and eternal Spirit of God. [m]O let no impure thoughts pollute that soul which God hath sanctified; no unclean words pollute that tongue which God hath commanded to be an Organ of his praises; no unholy and unchaste action rend the vail of that Temple where the holy JESUS hath been pleased to enter, and hath chosen for his habitation: [n]but seal up all my senses from all vain objects, and let them be intirely possessed with Religion, and fortified with prudence, watchfulnesse and mortification: that I possessing my vessel in holiness, may lay it down with a holy hope, and receive it again in a joyful resurrection through Jesus Christ our Lord. *Amen.*

A Prayer for the love of God, to be said by Virgins and Widows professed or resolved so to live: and may be used by any one.

O Holy and purest Jesus who wert pleased to espouse every holy soul and joyn it to thee with a holy union, and mysterious instruments of religious society and communications, O fill my soul with Religion and desires, holy as the thoughts of Cherubim, passionate beyond the love of women, that I may love thee as much as ever any creature loved thee, even with all my soul, and all my faculties, and all the degrees of every faculty; let me know no loves but those of duty and charity, obedience and devotion, that I may for ever run after thee who art the King of Virgins, and with whom whole kingdoms are in love, and for whose sake Queens have dyed; and at whose feet Kings with joy have laid their Crowns and Scepters: My soul is thine O dearest Jesu, thou art my Lord, and hast bound up my eyes and heart from all stranger affections; give me for my dowry purity and humility, modesty and devotion, charity and patience, and at last bring me into the Bride-chamber to partake of the felicities and to lye in the bosome of the Bridegroom to eternal ages, O holy and sweetest Saviour Jesus. *Amen.*

[l] The order or reason of it.
[m] The petition repeated with arguments.
[n] The means turned into petitions.

2 [l]] *GH, om 1+* 4 [m]] *GH, om 1+* 8 [n]] *GH, om 1+*

A Prayer to be said by married persons in behalf of themselves and each other.

O Eternal and gracious Father who hast consecrated the holy estate of marriage to become mysterious, and to represent the union of Christ and his Church, let thy holy Spirit so guide me in the doing the duties of this estate, that it may not become a sin unto me; nor that liberty which thou hast hallowed by the holy Jesus, become an occasion of licentiousnesse by my own weaknesse and sensuality: and do thou forgive all those irregularities and too sensual applications which may have in any degree discomposed my spirit and the severity of a Christian. Let me in all accidents and circumstances be severe in my duty towards thee, affectionate and dear to my wife [or Husband] a guide and good example to my family, and in all quietnesse, sobriety, prudence and peace a follower of those holy pairs who have served thee with godlinesse and a good testimony: and the blessings of the eternal God, blessings of the right hand, and of the left be upon the body and soul of thy servant my Wife [or Husband] and abide upon her [or him] till the end of a holy and happy life; and grant that both of us may live together for ever in the embraces of the holy and eternal Jesus, our Lord and Saviour. *Amen.*

A Prayer for the grace of Humility.

O Holy and most gracious Master and Saviour Jesus, who by thy example and by thy precept, by the practise of a whole life and frequent discourses didst command us to be meek and humble in imitation of thy incomparable sweetnesse and great humility: be pleased to give me the grace as thou hast given me the commandment: enable me to do whatsoever thou commandest, and command whatsoever thou pleasest: O mortifie in me all proud thoughts, and vain opinions of my self: let me return to thee the acknowledgement and the fruits of all those good things thou hast given me, that by confessing I am wholly in debt to thee for them, I may not boast myself for what I have received and for what I am highly accountable: and for what is my own, teach me to be ashamed and humbled, it being nothing but sin and misery, weaknesse and uncleannesse. Let me go before my brethren in nothing but in striving to do them honour and thee glory; never to seek my own praise; never to delight in it when it is offered; that despising my self I may be accepted by thee in the honours with which thou shalt crown thy humble and despised servants for Jesus's sake in the kingdom of eternal glory. *Amen.*

Acts of Humility and modesty by way of prayer and meditation.

1.

Lord I know that my spirit is light and thorny, my body is bruitish and exposed to sicknesse; I am constant to folly, and inconstant in holy purposes: My labours are vain and fruitlesse; my fortune full of change and trouble, seldome pleasing, never perfect: My wisdom is folly; being ignorant even of the parts and passions of my own body: and what am I, O Lord, before thee, but a miserable person, hugely in debt, not able to pay?

2.

Lord I am nothing, and I have nothing of my self, I am lesse than the least of all thy mercies.

3.

What was I before my birth? First nothing, and then uncleannesse. What during my childehood? weaknesse and folly. What in my youth? folly still and passion, lust and wildenesse. What in my whole life? a great sinner, a deceived and abused person. Lord pity me, for it is thy goodnesse that I am kept from confusion and amazement when I consider the misery and shame of my person, and the defilements of my nature.

4.

Lord what am I, and Lord what art thou? What is man that thou art mindeful of him, and the son of Man that thou so regardest him?

5.

How can Man be justified with God? or how can he be clean that is born of a Woman? Behold even to the Moon and it shineth not, yea the Stars are not pure in his sight. [o]How much lesse man that is a Worm, and the son of Man which is a Worm?

[o] Job 25.

1 Jesus's] Jesus his *2*+

A Prayer, for a contented spirit, and the grace of moderation and patience.

O Almighty God, Father and Lord of all the Creatures, who hast disposed all things and all chances so as may best glorifie thy wisdom, and serve the ends of thy justice, and magnifie thy mercy, by secret and undiscernable wayes bringing good out of evil; I most humbly beseech thee to give me wisdom from above that I may adore thee and admire thy wayes, and footsteps which are in the great Deep and not to be searched out; teach me to submit to thy providence in all things, to be content in all changes of person and condition, to be temperate in prosperity, and to reade my duty in the lines of thy mercy, and in adversity to be meek, patient and resigned, and to look through the cloud, that I may wait for the consolation of the Lord, and the day of redemption; in the mean time doing my duty with an unwearied diligence, and an undisturbed resolution, having no fondnesse for the vanities or possessions of this World, but laying up my hopes in Heaven and the rewards of holy living, and being strengthened with the Spirit in the inner man, through Jesus Christ our Lord. *Amen.*

CHAP. III.

Of Christian Justice.

JUSTICE is by the Christian Religion enjoyned in all its parts by these two propositions in Scripture. *Whatsoever yee would that men should do to you, even so do to them.* This is the measure of a *commutative justice*, or of that justice which supposes exchange of things profitable, for things profitable: that as I supply your need, you may supply mine, as I do a benefit to you, I may receive one by you: and because every man may be injured by another, therefore his security shall depend upon mine: if he will not let me be safe, he shall not be safe himself, (onely the manner of his being punished, is upon great reason both by God and all the World taken from particulars, and committed to a publick dis-interested person, who will do justice without passion, both to him and to me.) If he refuses to do me advantage, he shall receive none when his needs require it. And thus *God gave necessities* to men, that all men might need; and *several abilities* to severall persons, that each Man might help to supply the publick needs, and by joyning to fill up all wants, they may be knit together by justice, as the parts of the world are by nature: and *he hath made us all obnoxious* to injuries, and made every little thing strong enough to do us hurt by some instrument or other; and hath given us all a sufficient stock of self love, and desire of self preservation, to be as the chain to tye together all the parts of society, and to restrain us from doing violence, lest we be violently dealt withall our selves.

The other part of justice is commonly called *distributive*, and is commanded in this rule, [a] *Render to all their dues, tribute to whom tribute is due, custome to whom custome, fear to whom fear, honour to whom honour. Owe no man any thing, but to love one another.* This justice is distinguished from the first, because the obligation depends not upon contract or express bargain, but passes upon us by vertue of some command of God, or of our Superiour, by nature or by grace, by piety or religion, by trust or by office, according to that Commandment: [b] *As every man hath*

[a] Rom. 13: 7.
[b] 1 Pet. 4: 10.

5 a] *KC, om 1+*   *commutative*] 6+, *communicative 1 2 3 4 5*   7 as$_\wedge$] is, *5*

received the gift, so let him minister the same one to another, as good stewards of the manifold grace of God. And as the first considers an equality of persons in respect of the contract or particular necessity: this supposes a difference of persons, and no particular bargains, but such necessary entercourses, as by the Laws of God or man are introduced. But I shall reduce all the particulars of both kindes to these four heads. 1. Obedience. 2. Provision. 3. Negotiation. 4. Restitution.

SECT. I.
Of Obedience to our Superiours.

Our Superiours are set over us in affairs of the World, or the affairs of the Soul, and things pertaining to Religion, and are called accordingly, *Ecclesiastical* or *Civil.* Towards whom our duty is thus generally described in the new Testament. For *Temporall* or *Civill Governours* the Commands are these. *Render to Cæsar the things that are Cæsars* and [c] *Let every soul be subject to the higher powers: For there is no power but of God: The powers that be are ordained of God: whosoever therefore resisteth the power, resisteth the ordinance of God; and they that resist shall receive to themselves damnation* and [d] *Put them in minde to be subject to principalities and powers and to obey Magistrates* and [e] *Submit your selves to every ordinance of man, for the Lords sake; whether it be to the King as supreme, or unto Governours, as unto them that are sent by him for the punishment of evil doers, and the praise of them that do well.*

For *Spiritual* or *Ecclesiastical governours* thus we are commanded. [f] *Obey them that have the rule over you, and submit your selves, for they watch for your souls, as they that must give an account* and [g] *Hold such in reputation* and [h] *to this end did I write that I might know the proof of you, whether ye be obedient in all things* said S. *Paul* to the Church of Corinth. Our duty is reducible to practise by the following rules.

Acts and duties of Obedience to all our Superiours.

1. We must obey all humane laws appointed and constituted by lawful Authority, that is, of the supreme power, according to the constitu-

[c] Rom. 13: 1.
[d] Titus 3: 1.
[e] 1 Pet. 2: 13.
[f] Heb. 13: 17.
[g] Philip. 2: 29.
[h] 2 Cor. 2: 9.

tion of the place in which we live: all laws I mean, which are not against the law of God.

2. In obedience to humane laws we must observe the letter of the Law where we can without doing violence to the reason of the Law, and the intention of the Law-giver: but where they crosse each other, the charity of the Law is to be preferred before its discipline, and the reason of it before the letter.

3. If the general reason of the Law ceases in our particular, and a contrary reason rises upon us, we are to procure dispensation, or leave to omit the observation of it in such circumstances; if there be any persons or office appointed for granting it: but if there be none, or if it is not easily to be had, or not without an inconvenience greater than the good of the observation of the *Law* in our particular, we are dispensed withall in the nature of the thing, without further processe or trouble.

4. As long as the Law is obligatory, so long our obedience is due; and he that begins a contrary custom without reason, sins: [i]but he that breaks the law when the custom is entered and fixed, is excused, because it is supposed, the legislative power consents, when by not punishing, it suffers disobedience to grow up to a custome.

5. Obedience to humane laws must be *for conscience sake*: that is, because in such obedience publick order, and charity, and benefit is concerned: and because the Law of God commands us, [j]therefore we must make a conscience in keeping the just Laws of Superiors: and although the matter before the making of the Law was indifferent, yet now the obedience is not indifferent, but next to the Laws of God, we are to obey the Laws of all our Superiours, who the more publick they are, the first they are to be in the order of obedience.

6. Submit to the punishment and censure of the Laws, and seek not to reverse their judgement by opposing, but by submitting, or flying, or silence to passe thorow it, or by it as we can: and although from inferiour Judges we may appeal where the Law permits us, yet we must sit down and rest in the judgement of the Supreme: and if we be wronged, let us complain to God of the injury, not of the persons, and he will deliver thy soul from unrighteous Judges.

[i] Mores leges perduxerunt jam in potestatem suam;

. . . .

—leges mori serviunt. Trinum.

[j] Ἐξ ἀρχῆς μὲν οὐθὲν διαφέρει· ὅταν δὲ θῶνται, διαφέρει. Arist. Eth. 5. cap. 7.

17 [i]] *4+, om 1 2 3*

7. Do not believe thou hast kept the Law, when thou hast suffered the punishment. For although patiently to submit to the power of the sword, be a part of obedience, yet this is such a part as supposes another left undone: and the Law punishes, not because she is as well pleased in taking vengeance, as in being obeyed, but because she is displeased, she uses punishment as a means to secure obedience for the future, or in others. Therefore although in such cases the Law is satisfied, and the injury, and the injustice is paid for, yet the sins of irreligion, and scandal, and disobedience to God must still be so accounted for, as to crave pardon, and be washed off by repentence.

8. Humane Laws are not to be broken with scandal, nor at all without reason; for he that does it causelessly is a despiser of the Law, and undervalues the Authority. For humane Laws differ from divine Laws principally in this: 1. That the *positive commands of a man* may be broken upon smaller, and more reasons than *the positive commands of God*: we may upon a smaller reason omit to keep any of the fasting dayes of the Church, than omit to give alms to the poor: onely this, the reason must bear weight according to the gravity and concernment of the Law; a Law in a small matter may be omitted for a small reason, in a great matter not without a greater reason. And 2. *The negative precepts* of men may cease by many instruments, by contrary customs, by publick disrelish, by long omission: but *the negative precepts* of God never can cease, but when they are expressely abrogated by the same Authority. But what those reasons are that can dispence with the command of a man, a man may be his own Judge, and sometimes take his proportions from his own reason and necessity, sometimes from publick fame, and the practise of pious and severe persons, and from popular customs, in which a man shall walk most safely, when he does not walk alone, but a spiritual man takes him by the hand.

9. We must not be too forward in procuring dispensations: nor use them any longer than the reason continues for which we first procured them: for to be dispensed withall is an argument of natural infirmity, if it be necessary; but if it be not, it signifies an indisciplined and unmortified spirit.

10. We must not be too busie in examining the prudence and unreasonablenesse of humane Laws: for although we are not bound to believe them all to be the wisest, yet if by enquiring into the lawfulnesse of them, or by any other instrument we finde them to fail of that

6 displeased] pleased *6+* 33 if it be not] *2+*, if be not *1*

wisdom with which some others are ordained, yet we must never make use of it to disparage the person of the Law-giver, or to countenance any mans disobedience, much lesse our own.

11. Pay that reverence to the person of thy Prince, of his Ministers, of thy Parents and spiritual Guides, which by the customs of the place thou livest in are usually paid to such persons in their several degrees: that is, that the highest reverence be paid to the highest person, and so still in proportion: and that this reverence be expressed in all the circumstances and manners of the city and nation.

12. Lift not up thy hand against thy Prince or Parent upon what pretence soever: but bear all personal affronts and inconveniences at their hands, and seek no remedy but by patience, and piety, yielding and praying, or absenting thy self.

13. *Speak not evil of the Ruler of thy people*, neither *Curse thy Father or Mother*, nor revile thy spiritual Guides, nor discover and lay naked their infirmities: but treat them with reverence and religion, and preserve their Authority sacred by esteeming their persons venerable.

14. Pay tribute and customes to Princes according to the Laws: and maintenance to thy Parents according to their necessity: and honourable support to the Clergy according to the dignity of the work, and the customs of the place.

15. Remember alwayes that duty to our Superiors is not an act of commutative justice, but of distributive: That is, although Kings and Parents and spiritual Guides are to pay a great duty to their Inferiours, the duty of their several charges and government: yet the good government of a King and of Parents are actions of *Religion*, as they relate to God, and of *Piety* as they relate to their people and families. And although we usually call them *just Princes* who administer their Laws exactly to the people, because the actions are in the matter of *justice*, yet in propriety of speech, they are rather to be called *Pious*, and *Religious*. For as he is not called a *just Father* that educates his children well, but *pious*; so that Prince who defends and well rules his people, is *Religious*, and does that duty for which alone he is answerable to God. The consequence of which is this, so far as concerns our duty: If the Prince or Parent fail of their duty, we must not fail of ours: for we are answerable to them and to God too; as being accountable to all our Superiours, and so are they to theirs: they are above us, and God is above them.

29 matter] manner *7 8*

Remedies against disobedience: and means to endear our obedience, by way of consideration.

1. Consider that all authority descends from God, and our Superiours bear the image of the Divine Power, which God imprints on them as on an image of clay, or a coin upon a lesse perfect mettal, which who so defaces, shall not be answerable for the losse or spoil of the materials, but the effacing the Kings Image, and in the same measure will God require it at our hands, if we despise his authority upon whomsoever he hath imprinted it. *He that despiseth you, despiseth me.* And *Dathan* and *Abiram* were said to be *gathered together against the Lord.* And that was S. *Pauls* argument for our obedience. *The powers that be, are ordained of God.*

2. There is very great peace and immunity from sin in resigning our wils up to the command of others: for provided that our duty to God be secured, their commands are warrants to us in all things else; and the case of conscience is determined, if the command be evident and pressing: and it is certain, the action that is but indifferent, and without reward, if done onely upon our own choice, is an act of duty and of religion, and rewardable by the grace and favour of God, if done in obedience to the command of our Superiours. For since naturally we desire what is forbidden us, and (sometimes there is no other evil in the thing, but that it is forbidden us) God hath in grace enjoyned and proportionably accepts obedience as being directly opposed to the former irregularity, and it is acceptable, although there be no other good in the thing that is commanded us, but that it is commanded.

3. By obedience we are made a society and a republick, and distinguished from herds of Beasts, and heaps of Flyes, who do what they list, and are incapable of Laws, and obey none, and therefore are killed and destroyed, though never punished, and they never can have a reward.

4. By obedience we are rendered capable of all the blessings of government, signified by Saint *Paul* in these words, [k] *He is the Minister of God to thee for good*, and by Saint *Peter* in these, [l] *Governours are sent by him for the punishment of evill doers, and for the praise of them that do well.* And he that ever felt, or saw, or can understand the miseries of confusion in publick affaires, or amazement in a heap of sad, tumultuous, and indefinite thoughts, may from thence judge of the admirable effects o

[k] Rom. 13: 4. [l] 1 Pet. 2: 14.

order and the beauty of Government. What health is to the body, and peace is to the Spirit, that is Government to the societies of Men, the greatest blessing which they can receive in the temporal capacity.

5. No Man shall ever be fit to govern others that knows not first how to obey. For if the spirit of a Subject be rebellious, in a Prince it will be tyrannical and intolerable, and of so ill example, that as it will encourage the disobedience of others, so it will render it unreasonable for him to exact of others, what in the like case he refused to pay.

6. There is no sin in the World which God hath punisht with so great severity and high detestation as this of disobedience. For the crime of Idolatory God sent the Sword amongst his people, but it was never heard that the Earth opened and swallowed up any but Rebels against their Prince.

7. Obedience is better than the particular actions of Religion, and he serves GOD better than followes his Prince in lawful services, than he that refuses his command upon pretence hee must goe say his prayers. But Rebellion is compared to that sin which of all sins seems the most unnatural and damned impiety. *Rebellion is as the sin of Witchcraft.*

8. Obedience is a complicated act of vertue, and many graces are exercised in one act of obedience. It is an act of Humility, of mortification and self-denial, of charity to God, of care of the publick, of order and charity to our selves and all our society, and a great instance of a victory over the most refractory and unruly passions.

9. To be a Subject is a greater temporal felicity than to be a King: [m]for all eminent Governments according to their height have a great burden, huge care, infinite businesse, little rest, innumerable fears, and all that he enjoyes above another is, that hee does enjoy the things of the World with other circumstances, and a bigger noise; and if others go at his single command, it is also certain he must suffer inconvenience at the needs and disturbances of all his people: and the evils of one man, and of one family are not enough for him to bear, unlesse also he be almost crushed with the evils of mankinde. He therefore is an ingrateful person that will presse the scales down with a voluntary load, and by disobedience put more thorns into the Crown or Mitre of his Superiour. Much better is the advice of S. *Paul*, *Obey them that have the rule over you, as they that must give an account for your souls, that they may do it with joy and not with grief: for* (besides that it is unpleasant to them) *it is unprofitable for you.*

[m] *Οὐ χρὴ παννύχιον εὕδειν βουληφόρον ἄνδρα,*
Ὧι λαοί τ᾽ ἐπιτετράφαται, καὶ τόσσα μέμηλε. Homer. Il. 2.

10. The Angels are ministering spirits and perpetually execute the will and commandment of God: and all the wise men and all the good men of the world are obedient to their Governours, and the eternal Son of God esteemed it his *Meat and drink to do the will of his Father*, and for his obedience alone obtained the greatest glory: and no man ever came to perfection but by obedience: and thousands of Saints have chosen such institutions and maners of living, in which they might not choose their own work, nor follow their own will, nor please themselves, but be accountable to others, and subject to discipline, and obedient to command, as knowing this to bee the highway of the Crosse, the way that the *King of sufferings* and humility did choose, and so became the *King of Glory*.

11. No man ever perished who followed first the will of God, and then the will of his Superiours: but thousands have been damned meerly for following their own will, and relying upon their own judgements, and choosing their own work, and doing their own fancies: For if we begin with our selves, whatsoever seems good in our eyes, is mos commonly displeasing in the eyes of God.

12. The sin of Rebellion, though it be a spiritual sin and imitable b Devils, yet it is of that disorder, unreasonablenesse and impossibilit amongst intelligent spirits, that they never murmured or mutined i their lower stations against their Superiours. Nay, the good Angels o an inferiour Order durst not revile a Devil of a higher Order. Thi consideration which I reckon to be most pressing in the discourses c reason and obliging next to the necessity of a Divine precept, we lear from S. *Jude*: [n] *Likewise also these filthy dreamers despise dominion and spea evil of dignities: And yet Michael the Archangel, when contending with the Dev he disputed about the body of Moses, durst not bring against him a railir accusation.*

But because our Superiours rule by their example, by their word c law, and by the rod, therefore in proportion there are several degree and parts of obedience, of several excellencies and degrees towarc perfection.

Degrees of Obedience.

1. The first is *the obedience of the outward works* and this is all th Humane Lawes of themselves regard; for because Man cannot jud the heart, therefore it prescribes nothing to it: the publick end

[n] Jude 8, 9.

served not by good wishes, but by real and actual performances; and if a Man obeyes against his will he is not punishable by the Laws.

2. *The obedience of the will*, and this is also necessary in our obedience to Humane Lawes, not because man requires it for himself, but because God commands it towards Man; and of it (although Man cannot, yet) God will demand account. For we are to do it *as to the Lord and not to men*; and therefore we must do it willingly. But by this means our obedience in private is secured against secret arts and subterfuges; and when we can avoid the punishment, yet we shall not decline our duty, but serve Man for Gods sake, that is, *cheerfully, promptly, vigorously*, for these are the proper parts of willingnesse and choice.

3. The *understanding must yeeld obedience in general*, though not in the particular instance; that is, we must be firmly perswaded of the excellency of the obedience, though we be not bound in all cases to think the particular Law to be most prudent. But in this, our rule is plain enough. Our understanding ought to be inquisitive whether the civil constitution agree with our duty to God; but we are bound to inquire no further; And therefore beyond this, although he, who having no obligation to it (as Counsellours have) inquires not at all into the wisdome or reasonablenesse of the Law, be not alwayes the wisest Man, yet he is ever the best Subject. For when he hath given up his understanding to his Prince and Prelate, provided that his duty to God be secured by a precedent search, hath also with the best, and with all the instruments in the World secured his obedience to Man.

SECT. II.

Of Provision, or that part of Justice which is due from Superiours to Inferiours.

As God hath imprinted his authority in several parts upon several estates of Men, as Princes, Parents, Spiritual Guides, so he hath also delegated and committed parts of his care and providence unto them, that they may be instrumental in the conveying such blessings which God knowes we need, and which hee intends should be the effects of Government. For since GOD governes all the World as a King, provides for us as a Father, and is the great Guide and Conductor of our spirits as the Head of the Church, and the great Shepherd and Bishop of our souls, they who have portions of these dignities, have also their share of the administration: the sum of all which is usually signified in these two words *Governing* and *Feeding* and is particularly recited in the following rules.

Duties of Kings and all the Supreme power, as Lawgivers.

1. Princes of the people and all that have Legislative power must provide useful and good Lawes for the defence of propriety, for the encouragement of labour, for the safeguard of their persons, for determining controversies, for reward of noble actions, and excellent arts and rare inventions, for promoting trade, and enriching their people.

2. [o]In the making Lawes Princes must have regard to the publick dispositions, to the affections and disaffections of the people; and must not introduce a Law with publick scandal and displeasure: but consider the publick benefit, and the present capacity of affairs and general inclinations of mens mindes. For he that enforces a Law upon a people against their first and publick apprehensions tempts them to disobedience, and makes Lawes to become snares and hooks to catch the people, and to enrich the treasury with the spoil and tears and curses of the Communalty, and to multiply their mutiny and their sin.

3. Princes must provide that the Lawes be duely executed: for a good Law without execution is like an unperformed promise: and therefore they must be severe exactors of accounts from their Delegates and Ministers of Justice.

4. [p]The severity of Lawes must be tempered with dispensations, pardons, and remissions according as the case shall alter, and new necessities be introduced, or some singular accident shall happen, in which the Law would be unreasonable or intolerable as to that particular. And thus the people with their importunity prevailed against *Saul* in the case of *Jonathan*, and obtained his pardon for breaking the Law which his Father made, because his necessity forced him to taste honey, and his breaking the Law in that case did promote that service whose promotion was intended by the Law.

5. Princes must be Fathers of the people, and provide such instances of gentlenesse, ease, wealth, and advantages, as may make mutuall confidence betweene them; and must fix their security under GOD in the love of the people, which therefore they must with all arts of

[o] Omittenda potius prævalida et adulta vitia, quam hoc adsequi, ut palam fiat quibus flagitiis impares simus. Tacit.

[p] Ἐπιείκειά ἐστιν ἐπανόρθωμα νόμου, ᾗ ἐλλείπει διὰ τὸ καθόλου. Eth. 5. cap. 10

sweetnesse, remission, popularity, noblenesse and sincerity endeavour to secure to themselves.

6. Princes must not multiply publick Oathes without great, eminent, and violent necessity, lest the security of the King become a snare to the people, and they become false when they see themselves suspected, or impatient when they are violently held fast: but the greater and more useful caution is upon things than upon persons; and if security of Kings can be obtained otherwise, it is better that Oathes should be the last refuge, and when nothing else can be sufficient.

7. [q]Let not the people be tempted with arguments to disobey, by the imposition of great and unnecessary taxes: for that lost to the son of *Solomon* the dominion of the ten Tribes of Israel.

8. Princes must in a special manner bee Guardians of Pupils and Widows, not suffering their persons to be oppressed, or their states imbecilled, or in any sense be exposed to the rapine of covetous persons, but be provided for by just lawes, and provident Judges, and good Guardians, ever having an ear ready open to their just complaints, and a heart full of pity, and one hand to support them, and the other to avenge them.

9. Princes must provide that the Laws may be so administered, that they be truly and really an ease to the people, not an instrument of vexation: and therefore must be careful that the shortest and most equal wayes of trials be appointed, fees moderated, and intricacies and windings as much cut off as may bee, lest injured persons be forced to perish under the oppression, or under the Law, in the injury or in the suit. Laws are like Princes, those best and most beloved, who are most easie of accesse.

10. Places of judicature ought at no hand to be sold by pious Princes, who remember themselves to be Fathers of the people. [r]For they that *buy the Office* will *sell the act*, and they that at any rate will be Judges, will not at an easie rate do justice; and their bribery is lesse punishable, when bribery opened the door by which they entered.

11. Ancient priviledges, favours, customes, and Acts of grace indulged by former Kings to their people, must not without high reason and great necessities be revoked by their successours; nor forfeitures be exacted violently, nor penal Laws urged rigorously, nor in light cases, nor Lawes be multiplied without great need, nor vitious

[q] L'avaritia de' Re, peste è de' regni.

[r] Chi compra il magistrato, forza è che vendra la giustitia.

15 imbecilled] imbezilled *4 5 6*   26 those] *7 8*, the *1 2 3 4 5 6*

persons which are publickly and deservedly hated, be kept in defiance of popular desires, nor any thing that may unnecessarily make the yoke heavie, and the affection light, that may increase murmures, and lessen charity; alwayes remembering, that the interest of the Prince and the People is so infolded in a mutual imbrace, that they cannot be untwisted without pulling a limb off, or dissolving the bands and conjunction of the whole body.

12. [s]All Princes must esteem themselves as *much bound* by their word, by their grants, and by their promises, as the meanest of their Subjects are by the restraint and penalty of Laws: and although they are superiour to the people, yet they are not superiour to their own voluntary concessions and ingagements, their promises and Oathes, when once they are passed from them.

The Duty of Superiours as they are Judges.

1. Princes in judgement, and their Delegate Judges must judge the causes of all persons uprightly and impartially, without any persona consideration of the power of the mighty, or the bribe of the rich, o the needs of the poor. For although the poor must fare no worse for hi poverty, yet in justice he must fare no better for it: And although th rich must be no more regarded, yet he must not be lesse. And to thi purpose the Tutor of *Cyrus* instructed him, when in a controversi where a great Boy would have taken a large coat from a little Bo because his own was too little for him, and the others was too big, he adjudged the great coat to the great Boy: his Tutor answered, Sir, I you were made a Judge of decency or fitnesse, you had judged well i giving the biggest to the biggest: but when you were appointed Judg not whom the coat did fit, but whose it was, you should have con sidered the title, and the possession, who did the violence, and wh made it, or who bought it? And so it must be in judgements betwee the rich and the poor: it is not to be considered what the poor Ma needs, but what is his own.

2. A Prince may not, much lesse may inferiour Judges deny justic when it is legally and competently demanded: and if the Prince wi use his Prerogative in pardoning an offender against whom justice required, he must be carefull to give satisfaction to the injured perso

[s] Nulla lex [civilis] sibi soli conscientiam justitiæ suæ debet, sed eis a quibus obs quium expectat. Tertull. Apologet.

8 [s]] *4+*, *om 1 2 3*

or his Relatives by some other instrument; and be watchful to take away the scandal, that is, lest such indulgence might make persons more bold to do injury: and if hee spares the life, let him change the punishment into that which may make the offender (if not suffer justice, yet) doe justice, and more real advantage to the injured person.

These rules concern Princes and their Delegates in the making or administering Laws, in the appointing rules of justice and doing acts of judgement. The duty of Parents to their Children and Nephews is briefly described by S. *Paul.*

The Duty of Parents to their Children.

1. [t]*Fathers provoke not your Children to wrath*, that is, be tender boweld, pitiful and gentle, complying with all the infirmities of the Children; and in their several ages proportioning to them several usages according to their needs and their capacities.

2. *Bring them up in the nurture and admonition of the Lord*, that is, secure their religion, season their younger years with prudent and pious principles, make them in love with vertue, and make them habitually so, before they come to choose or to discern good from evil, that their choice may be with lesse difficulty and danger. For while they are under discipline, they suck in all that they are first taught, and believe it infinitely. [u]Provide for them, wise, learned and vertuous Tutors, and good company and discipline, seasonable baptism, catechism and confirmation. For it is a great folly to heap up much wealth for our Children, and not to take care concerning the Children for whom we get it. It is as if a man should take more care about his shooe than about his foot.

3. [v]*Parents must shew piety at home*, that is, they must give good example and reverent deportment, in the face of their children; and all those instances of charity, which usualy endear each other; sweetnesse of conversation, affability, frequent admonition, all significations of love and tendernesse, care and watchfulnesse must be expressed towards Children, that they may look upon their Parents as their friends and patrons, their defence and sanctuary, their treasure and their Guide. Hither is to be reduced the nursing of Children, which is

[t] Ephes. 6: 4.

[u] Potior mihi ratio vivendi honeste, quam vel optime dicendi videretur. Quintil. lib. 1. c. 2.

[v] Heb. 12: 9. Crates apud Plut. de liber. educand. 1 Tim. 5: 4.

21 infinitely. Provide] *4*+, infinitely, provide *1 2 3* note *u* vel] *cor, om 1*+

the first and most natural and necessary instance of piety, which Mothers can shew to their Babes; a dutie from which nothing will excuse, but a disability, sicknesse, danger, or publick necessitie.

4. [w]Parents must *provide for their own* according to their condition, education, and implyoyment; called by S. *Paul*, *a laying up for the Children*, that is, an enabling them by competent portions, or good trades, arts or learning to defend themselves against the chances of the world, that they may not be exposed to temptation, to beggery, or unworthy arts: and although this must be done without covetousnesse, without impatient and greedy desires of making them rich, yet it must be done with much care, and great affection, with all reasonable provision, and according to our power: and if we can without sin improve our estates for them, that also is part of the duty we owe to God for them: and this rule is to extend to all that descend from us, although we have been overtaken in a fault, and have unlawfull issue; they also become part of our care, yet so as not to injure the production of the lawful bed.

5. This duty is to extend to a provision of conditions and an estate of life. [x]Parents must according to their power and reason provide

[w] 1 Tim. 5: 8.

[x] Liberi sine consensu parentum contrahere non debent. Andromacha apud Euripedem cum petita fuit ad nuptias, respondit, patris sui esse sponsalium suorum curam habere:

> *Νυμφευμάτων μὲν τῶν ἐμῶν πατὴρ ἐμός*
> *μέριμναν ἕξει, κοὐκ ἐμὸν κρίνειν τάδε.* Eurip. Electra.

> Me tibi Tyndareos vita gravis auctor et annis
> Tradidit: arbitrium neptis habebat avus. Ovid. in Epist. Hermione.

Et Achilles apud Homerum regis filiam sine patris sui consensu noluit ducere.

> *Ἢν γὰρ δή με σόωσι θεοὶ, καὶ οἴκαδ' ἵκωμαι,*
> *Πηλεὺς θήν μοι ἔπειτα γυναῖκα γαμέσσεται αὐτός.* Il. 9.

Et Justinianus Imp. ait, naturali simul et civili rationi congruere, ne filii ducant uxores citra parentum auctoritatem. Simo Terentianus parat abdicationem, quia Pamphilus clam ipso duxisset uxorem. Istiusmodi sponsalia fiunt irrita, nisi velint parentes: at si subsequuta est copula, ne temere rescindantur connubia, multæ suadent cautiones et pericula. Liberi autem, quamdiu secundum leges patrias sui juris non sunt, clandestinas nuptias si ineant, peccant contra quintum præceptum, et jus naturale Secundarium. Proprie enim loquendo parentes non habent *ἐξουσίαν*, sive potestatem sed auctoritatem: habent jus jubendi aut prohibendi, sed non irritum faciendi. Atque etiam ista auctoritas exercenda est secundum æquum et bonum; scil. ut ne morosus et difficilis sit Pater. Mater enim vix habet aliquod Juris præter suasionis et amoris et gratitudinis. Si autem Pater filiam non collocasset ante 25 annos, filia nubere poterat cui voluerat, ex jure Romanorum. Patrum enim auctoritas major aut minor est ex legibus Patriis, et solet extendi ad certam ætatem, et tum exspirat quoad matrimonium; et est major in filias quam filios.—Num. 30.

note *x*] *Νυμφευμάτων* . . . Hermione.] *4+*, *om 1 2 3* Secundarium. . . . Num. 30.] *4+*, *om 1 2 3*

Husbands or Wives for their children. [y]In which they must secure piety and Religion, and the affection and love of the interested persons; and after these, let them make what provisions they can for other conveniences or advantages: Ever remembering that they can do no injury more afflictive to the children than to joyn them with cords of a disagreeing affection: It is like tying a Wolf and a Lamb, or planting the Vine in a Garden of Coleworts. Let them be perswaded with reasonable inducements to make them willing and to choose according to the parents wish, but at no hand let them be forced. Better to sit up all night, than to go to bed with a Dragon.

The Duty of Husbands, etc.
See Chapt. 2. Sect. 3. Rules for married persons.

1. [z]Husbands must give to their wives, love, maintenance, duty, and the sweetnesses of conversation (and [a]wives must pay to them all they have, or can with the interest of obedience and reverence) and they must be complicated in affections and interest, that there be no distinction between them of *Mine* and *Thine*: And if the title be the mans, or the womans, yet the use must be common, onely the wisdom of the man is to regulate all extravagancies and indiscretions: in other things, no question is to be made; and their goods should be as their children not to be divided, but of one possession and provision: whatsoever is otherwise is not marriage but merchandise. And upon this ground I suppose it was, that [b]S. *Basil* commended that woman, who took part of her Husbands goods to do good works withall: for supposing him to

[y] Eosdem quos maritus nosse Deos et colere solos uxor debet: supervacaneis autem religionibus, et alienis superstitionibus fores occludere. Nulli enim deum grata sunt sacra quæ mulier clanculum et furtim facit. Plutarch. conjug. præcept. Gen. 24. Vocemus puellam, et quæramus os ejus.

[z] *Σοὶ δὲ θεοὶ τόσα δοῖεν . . .*
Ἄνδρα τε καὶ οἶκον, καὶ ὁμοφροσύνην ὀπάσειαν
Ἐσθλήν· οὐ μὲν γὰρ τοῦ γε κρεῖσσον καὶ ἄρειον,
Ἢ ὅθ᾽ ὁμοφρονέοντε νοήμασιν οἶκον ἔχητον
Ἀνὴρ ἠδὲ γυνή· πόλλ᾽ ἄλγεα δυσμενέεσσι,
Χάρματα δ᾽ εὐμενέτῃσι· μάλιστα δέ τ᾽ ἔκλυον αὐτοί. Odyss. 6.

[a] *Ἔνεστ᾽ ἀληθὲς φίλτρον εὐγνώμων τρόπος·*
Τούτῳ κατακρατεῖν ἀνδρὸς εἴωθεν γυνή. Menand.

Ἦ μοῦνοι φιλέουσ᾽ ἀλόχους μερόπων ἀνθρώπων
Ἀτρεῖδαι; ἐπεὶ ὅστις ἀνὴρ ἀγαθὸς καὶ ἐχέφρων,
Τὴν αὐτοῦ φιλέει καὶ κήδεται· ὡς καὶ ἐγὼ τήν
Ἐκ θυμοῦ φιλέον δουρικτητήν περ ἐοῦσαν. Homer.

[b] *Κλέψασα καλὰ κλέμματα ἄνευ ἀνδρὸς τὰς εὐποιίας ἐποίησε.*

---

13 [z]] *4+, om 1 2 3*

be unwilling, and that the work was his duty, or hers alone, or both theirs in conjunction, or of great advantage to either of their souls, and no violence to the support of their families, she hath right to all that: And *Abigail* of her own right made a costly present to *David*, when her husband *Nabal* had refused it. [c]The Husband must rule over his wife, as the soul does over the body, obnoxious to the same sufferings, and bound by the same affections, and doing or suffering by the permissions and interest of each other: (as [d]the old philosopher said) as the humours of the body are mingled with each other in their whole substances: so marriage may be a mixture of interests, of bodies, of mindes, of friends, a conjunction of the whole life, and the noblest of friendships. But if after all the fair deportments, and innocent chast complyances the Husband be morose and ungentle, [e]let the Wife discourse thus: If while I do my duty my Husband neglects me, what will he do if I neglect him? And if she thinks to be separated by reason of her husbands unchast life, let her consider, that then the man will be uncurably ruined, and her Rivals could wish nothing more than that they might possesse him alone.

The Duty of Masters of Families.

1. The same care is to extend to all of our family in their proportions as to our Children: for as by S. *Pauls* oeconomie the Heir differs nothing from a servant while he is in minority: so a servant should differ nothing from a childe in the substantial part of the care; and the difference is onely in degrees: Servants and Masters are of the same kindred, of the same nature, and heirs of the same promises, and therefore 1. must be provided of necessaries for their support and maintenance. 2. They must be used with mercy. 3. Their work must be tolerable and merciful. 4. Their restraints must be reasonable. 5. Their recreations fitting and healthful. 6. Their religion and the

[c] Lætum esse debet et officiosum mariti imperium. Plut.

Namque es ei Pater, et Frater, venerandaque Mater: nec minus facit ad dignitatem viri, si mulier eum suum Præceptorum, Philosophum, Magistrumque appellet. Plutarch.

[d] Convictio est quasi quædam intensio benevolentiæ.

[e] *Οὐ χρυσὸς, οὐ τθραννὶς, οὐ πλούτου χλιδὴ*
τοσοῦτον εἶχε διαφόρους τὰς ἡδονάς,
ὡς ἀνδρὸς ἐσθλοῦ καὶ γυναικὸς εὐσεβοῦς
γνώμη δικαία, καὶ φρονοῦσα τ' ἀνδρικά.

Inferior Matrona suo sit, Sexte, Marito
Non aliter fiunt fœmina virque pares. Mart.

---

note *e* *Mart.*] *om 7 8*

interest of souls taken care of. 7. And Masters must correct their servants with gentlenesse, prudence and mercy, not for every slight fault, not alwayes, not with upbraiding and disgraceful language, but with such onely as may expresse and reprove the fault, and amend the person. But in all these things measures are to be taken by the contract made, by the Laws and Customs of the place, by the sentence of prudent and merciful men, and by the cautions and remembrances given us by God, such as is that written by S. *Paul*, *as knowing that we also have a Master in Heaven.* The Master must not be a lyon in his house, lest his power be obeyed, and his person hated; his eye be wayted on, and his businesse be neglected in secret. No servant will do his duty unlesse he make a conscience, or love his Master: if he does it not for Gods sake or his masters, he will not need to do it alwayes for his own.

The Duty of Guardians, or Tutors.

Tutors and Guardians are in the place of Parents, and what they are in fiction of Law, they must remember as an argument to engage them to do in reality of duty. They must do all the duty of Parents, excepting those obligations which are merely natural.

The duty of Ministers and Spiritual Guides to the people is of so great burden, so various rules, so intricate and busie caution, that it requires a distinct tractate by it self.

SECT. III.
Of Negotiation, or Civil Contracts.

This part of Justice is such as depends upon the Laws of Man directly, and upon the Laws of God onely by consequence and indirect reason: and from civil Laws or private agreements it is to take its estimate and measures: and although our duty is plain and easy, requiring of us honesty in contracts, sincerity in affirming, simplicity in bargaining, and faithfulnesse in performing, yet it may be helped by the addition of these following rules and considerations.

Rules and measures of justice in bargaining.

1. In making contracts use not many words; for all the businesse of a

31 *in*] *and 2 3*

bargain is summed up in few sentences: and he that speaks least, means fairest, as having fewer opportunities to deceive.

2. Lye not at all, neither in a little thing nor in a great, neither in the substance nor in the circumstance, neither in word nor deed: that is, pretend not what is false, cover not what is true, and let the measure of your affirmation or denyal be the understanding of your contractor: for he that deceives the buyer or the seller by speaking what is true in a sense not intended or understood by the other, is a lyar and a thief. For in bargains you are to avoid not onely what is *false*, but that also *which deceives.*

3. In prices of bargaining concerning uncertain Merchandizes you may buy as cheap ordinarily as you can, and sell as dear as you can, so it be 1. without violence, and 2. when you contract on equal terms, with persons in all senses (as to the matter and skill of bargaining) equal to your self, that is, Merchants with Merchants, wise men with wise men, rich with rich: and 3. when there is no deceit, and no necessity, and no Monopoly: For in these cases, *viz.* when the Contractors are equal, and no advantage on either side, both parties are voluntary, and therefore there can be no injustice or wrong to either. But then adde also this consideration, that the publick bee not oppressed by unreasonable and unjust rates: for which the following rules are the best measure.

4. Let your prices be according to that measure of good and evil which is established in the fame and common accounts of the wisest and most merciful Men skilled in that manufacture or commodity; and the gain such which without scandal is allowed to persons in all the same circumstances.

5. Let no prices be heightened by the necessity or unskilfulnesse of the contractor; for the first is direct uncharitablenesse to the person, and injustice in the thing (because the Mans necessity could not naturally enter into the consideration of the value of the commodity) and the other is deceit and oppression: much lesse must any Man make necessities; as by ingrossing a commodity, by monopoly, by detaining corn, or the like indirect arts: for such persons are unjust to all single persons with whom in such cases they contract, and oppressors of the publick.

6. In entercourse with others do not do all which you may lawfully do; but keep something within thy power: and because there is a latitude of gain in buying and selling, take not thou the utmost peny that is lawfull, or which thou thinkest so; for although it be lawful, yet it is not

safe; and he that gains all that he can gain lawfully this year, possibly next year will be tempted to gain something unlawfully.

7. He that sels dearer by reason he sels not for ready money, must increase his price no higher than to make himself recompence for the losse which according to the Rules of trade he sustained by his forbearance, according to common computation, reckoning in also the hazard, which he is prudently, warily, and charitably to estimate: But although this be the measure of his justice, yet because it happens either to their friends, or to necessitous and poor persons, they are in these cases to consider the rules of friendship and neighbourhood, and the obligations of charity, lest justice turn into unmercifulnesse.

8. [f]No man is to be raised in his price or rents in regard of any accident, advantage or disadvantage of his person. A Prince must be used conscionably as well as a common person, and a Beggar be treated justly as well as a Prince; with this onely difference, that to poor persons the utmost measure and extent of justice is unmerciful, which to a rich person is innocent, because it is just, and he needs not thy mercy and remission.

9. Let no Man for his own poverty become more oppressing and cruel in his bargain, but quietly, modestly, diligently, and patiently recommend his estate to God, and follow its interest and leave the success to him: for such courses will more probably advance his trade, they will certainly procure him a blessing, and a recompence, and if they cure not his poverty, they will take away the evil of it: and there is nothing else in it that can trouble him.

10. Detain not the wages of the hireling: for every degree of detention of it beyond the time is injustice, and uncharitablenesse, and grindes his face till tears and blood come out: but pay him exactly according to Covenant, or according to his needs.

11. Religiously keep all promises and Covenants, though made to your disadvantage, though afterwards you perceive you might have been better: and let not any precedent act of yours be altered by any after-accident. [g]Let nothing make you break your promise, unlesse it be unlawful or impossible, that is, either out of your natural, or out of

[f] Mercanzia non vuol ne amici ne parenti.

[g] Surgam ad sponsalia quia promisi, quamvis non concoxerim: sed non si febricitavero: subest, inquam, tacita exceptio, si potero, si debebo. Effice ut idem status sit cum exigitur, qui fuit cum promiterrem. Destituere levitas erit si aliquid intervenit novi. Eadem mihi omnia præsta, et idem sum. Senec. l. 4. c. 39. de Benefic.

---

note *g* levitas erit] *cor*, levitas non erit *1*+ intervenit] *cor*, intervenerit *1*+

your civil power, your self being under the power of another; or that it be intolerably inconvenient to your self, and of no advantage to another; or that you have leave expressed, or reasonably presumed.

12. Let no Man take wages or fees for a work that he cannot do, or cannot with probability undertake, or in some sense profitably, and with ease, or with advantage manage: Physicians must not meddle with desperate diseases, and known to be incurable, without declaring their sense before hand; that if the patient please he may entertain him at adventure, or to do him some little ease. Advocates must deal plainly with their Clients, and tell them the true state and danger of their case; and must not pretend confidence in an evil cause: but when he hath so cleared his own innocence; if the Client will have collateral and legal advantages obtained by his industry, he may engage his endeavour, provided he do no injury to the right cause, or any Mans person.

13. Let no Man appropriate to his own use what God by a special mercy, or the Republick hath made common; for that is both against Justice and Charity too: and by miraculous accidents God hath declared his displeasure against such inclosures. [h]When the Kings of *Naples* enclosed the Gardens of *Oenotria*, where the best Manna of *Calabria* descends, that no man might gather it without paying tribute the Manna ceased, till the tribute was taken off; and then it came again, and so till after the third trial, the Princes found they could not have that in proper which GOD made to be common, they left it as free as GOD gave it. [i]The like happened in *Epire* when *Lysimachus* laid an impost upon the *Tragasæan* Salt, it vanished, till *Lysimachus* left it publick. And when the procurators of King *Antigonus* imposed a rate upon the sick people that came to *Edepsum* to drink the waters which were lately sprung and were very healthful, instantly the waters dried up, and the hope of gain perished.

The summe of all is in these words of Saint *Paul*, [j]*Let no man go beyond and defraud his brother in any matter; because the Lord is the avenger of all such* and our blessed Saviour in the enumerating the duties of justice, besides the Commandement of *Do not steal* addes [k]*Defraud not* forbidding (as a distinct explication of the old Law) the tacite and secret theft of abusing our Brother in Civil Contracts. And it needs no

[h] Brassavol. in exam. simpl.

[i] Cælius Rhodig. l. 9. c. 12. Athenæ. Deipnos. l. 3.

[j] 1 Thes. 4: 6.

[k] Levit. 19: 13. 1 Cor. 6: 8. Mark 10: 19.

other arguments to enforce this caution, but only, that the Lord hath undertaken to avenge all such persons: And as he alwayes does it in the great day of recompences: so very often he does it here, by making the unclean portion of injustice to be as a Cankerworm eating up all the other increase: it procures beggery, and a declining estate, or a caytive, cursed spirit, an ill name, the curse of the injured and oppressed person, and a Fool or a Prodigal to be his Heir.

SECT. IV.
Of Restitution.

Restitution is that part of Justice to which a man is obliged by a precedent contract or a foregoing fault, by his own act, or another mans, either with, or without his will. [l]He that borrows is bound to pay, and much more he that steals or cheats. For if he that borrows and payes not when he is able be an unjust person, and a robber, because he possesses another mans goods to the right owners prejudice: then, he that took them at first without leave is the same thing in every instant of his possession, which the Debter is after the time in which he should and could have made payment. For in all sins we are to distinguish the transient or passing act from the remaining effect or evil. The act of stealing was soon over, and cannot be undone, and for it the sinner is onely answerable to God, or his Vicegerent, and he is in a particular manner appointed to expiate it, by suffering punishment, and repenting, and asking pardon, and judging and condemning himself, doing acts of justice and charity in opposition and contradiction to that evil action. [m]But because in the case of stealing there is an injury done to our neighbour, and the evil still remains after the action is past, therefore for this we are accountable to our neighbour, and we are to take the evil off from him which we brought upon him, or else he is an injured person, a sufferer all the while: and that any man should be the worse for me and my direct act, and by my intention, is against the rule of equity, of justice and of charity; I do not that to others which I would have done to my self, for I grow richer upon the ruines of his fortune. Upon this ground, it is a determined rule in Divinity, *Our sin can never be pardoned till we have restored what we unjustly took, or wrongfully detain*: restored it (I mean) actually, or in purpose and desire, which

[l] Chi non vuol rendre, fa mal a prendre.
[m] Si tua culpa datum est damnum, jure super his satisfacere te oportet.

we must really perform when we can: and this doctrine, besides its evident and apparent reasonableness, is derived from the expresse words of Scripture, reckoning *Restitution* to be a part of *Repentance*, necessary in order to the remission of our sins. [n] *If the wicked restore the pledge, give again that he had robbed, etc. he shall surely live, he shall not dye.* The practise of this part of justice is to be directed by the following Rules.

Rules of making Restitution.

1. Whosoever is an effective, real cause of doing his Neighbour wrong, by what instrument soever he does it, ([o]whether by commanding or incouraging it, by counselling or commending it, [p]by acting it, or not hindering it when he might and ought, by concealing it, or receiving it) is bound to make restitution to his Neighbour; if without him the injury had not been done, but by him, or his assistance it was. For by the same reason that every one of these is guilty of the sin, and is cause of the injury, by the same they are bound to make reparation; because by him his Neighbour is made worse, and therefore is to be put into that state from whence he was forced. And suppose that thou hast perswaded an injury to be done to thy Neighbour, which others would have perswaded if thou hadst not, yet thou art still obliged, because thou really didst cause the injury; just as they had been obliged if they had done it; and thou art not at all the lesse bound by having persons as ill inclined as thou wert.

2. He that commanded the injury to be done, is first bound: then, he that did it; and after these they also are obliged who did so assist, as without them the thing would not have been done. If satisfaction be made by any of the former, the latter is tyed to repentance, but no restitution: But if the injured person be not righted, every one of them is wholly guilty of the injustice, and therefore bound to restitution singly and intirely.

3. Whosoever intends a little injury to his Neighbour, and acts it

[n] Ezek. 33: 15.

[o] *Ὁ γὰρ ἐπαινέσας τὸν δεδρακότα, οὐδέν τι ἧσσον τῶν πεπραγμένων αὐτοῦργο γίνεται.* Totilas apud Procop. Goth. 3.

Qui laudat servum fugitivum, tenetur. Non enim oportet laudando augeri malitiam Ulpian. in lib. 1. cap. de servo corrupto.

[p] *Ὁ ἐμπρησμὸς τοῦ ἀνάψαντος ἀλλὰ καὶ τοῦ κατασβέσαι δυναμένου, δράσαι δ τι τοιοῦτον ὅλως μὴ βουληθέντος.* —Nicet. Choniat. in Manuel. Comnen.

Sic Scyrii ab Amphyctionibus judicio damnati, quia piraticam non prohibuerunt cum poterant.

---

note *p* Manuel] *cor*, Michael *1*+ Scyrii] *cor*, Syri *1*+

and by it a greater evil accidentally comes, he is obliged to make an intire reparation of all the injurie, of that which he intended, and of that which he intended not, but yet acted by his own instrument, going further than he at first purposed it. [q]He that set fire on a plane Tree to spite his Neighbour, and the plane Tree set fire upon his Neighbours House, is bound to pay for all the losse, because it did all arise from his own ill intention. It is like murder committed by a drunken person, *involuntary in some of the effect*, but *voluntary in the other parts of it*, and *in all the cause*, and therefore the guilty person is answerable for all of it. [r]And when *Ariarathes* the Cappadocian King had but in wantonesse stopped the mouth of the river *Melanus*, although he intended no evil, yet *Euphrates* being swelled by that means, and bearing away some of the strand of Cappadocia did great spoil to the Phrygians and Galatians, he therefore by the Roman Senate was condemned in three hundred talents towards reparation of the damage. Much rather therefore when the lesser part of the evil was directly intended.

4. [s]He that hinders a charitable person from giving alms to a poor man is tyed to restitution, if he hindered him by fraud or violence. Because it was a right which the poor man had when the good man had designed and resolved it; and the fraud or violence hinders the effect, but not the purpose, and therefore he who used the deceit or the force is injurious, and did damage to the poor man. But if the alms were hindered onely by intreaty, the hinderer is not tyed to restitution, because intreaty took not liberty away from the giver, but left him still Master of his own act, and he had power to alter his purpose, and so long there was no injustice done. The same is the case of a Testator giving a legacy either by kindenesse, or by promise and common right. He that hinders the charitable Legacy by fraud or violence, or the due Legacy by intreaty is equally obliged to restitution. The reason of the latter part of this case is, because he that intreats or perswades to a sin is as guilty as he that acts it: and if without his perswasion the sin and the injury would not be acted, he is in his kinde the intire cause, and therefore obliged to repair the injury as much as the person that does the wrong immediately.

[q] Etiamsi partem damni dare noluisti, in totum quasi prudens dederis, tenendus es. Ex toto enim noluisse debet, qui imprudentia defenditur. Senec. Controv. Involuntarium ortum ex voluntario censetur pro voluntario.

[r] Strabo.

[s] *Πλεονεκτεῖ οὐδὲν ὁ οὐ βονθήσας χρήμασι δι' ἀνελευθερίαν.* Eth. l. 5. c. 2.

---

5 upon] on *7 8*   14 he] *7 8*+, and *1 2 3 4 5 6*   note *s* Eth. l. 5. c. 2.] *om 2 3*

5. He that refuses to do any part of his duty (to which he is otherwis obliged) without a bribe, is bound to restore that money, because he took it in his Neighbours wrong, and not as a salary for his labour, or a reward of his wisdom (for his stipend hath paid all that, or) he hath obliged himself to do it by his voluntary undertaking.

6. He that takes any thing from his Neighbour which was justly for feited, but yet takes it not as a Minister of justice, but to satisfie hi own revenge or avarice, is tyed to repentance but not to restitution For my Neighbour is not the worse for my act, for thither the Law an his own demerits bore him, but because I took the forfeiture indirectl I am answerable to God, for my unhandsome, unjust, or uncharitabl circumstances. Thus *Philip* of Macedon was reproved by *Aristides* fo destroying the *Phocenses*; because although they deserved it, yet he di it not in prosecution of the law of Nations, but to enlarge his ow dominions.

7. The heir of an obliged person is not bound to make restitution, the obligation passed onely by a personal act: but if it passed from hi person to his estate, then the estate passes with all its burden. If th Father by perswading his neighbour to do injustice be bound t restore, the action is extinguished by the death of the Father; becaus it was onely the Fathers sin that bound him, which cannot directl binde the son; therefore the son is free. And this is so in all person actions, unlesse where the civil Law interposes and alters the case.

These rules concern the persons that are obliged to make restitution: the oth circumstances of it are thus described.

8. He that by fact, or word, or signe, either fraudulently, or violent does hurt to his Neighbours body, life, goods, good name, friends, soul is bound to make restitution in the several instances, according they are capable to be made. In all these instances we must separa intreaty and inticements from deceit or violence. If I perswade m Neighbour to commit adultery, I still leave him or her in their ow power: and though I am answerable to God for my sin, yet not to m Neighbour. [t]For I made her to be willing; yet she was willing, that the same at last as I was at first: [u]but if I have used fraud, and made h to believe a lie, upon which confidence she did the act, and without she would not (as if I tell a woman her Husband is dead, or intended

[t] *Δι' ἀλλότριαν ἔργον πταίει οὐδείς.* Epict.
[u] *Πᾶσα ψυχὴ ἄκουσα στερεῖται τῆς ἀληθείας.* Plato.
Non licet suffurari mentem vel Samaritani. R. Maimon. Can. Eth.

29 made. In] made, in *2 3*

kill her, or is himself an adulterous man) or if I use violence, that is, either force her or threaten her with death, or a grievous wound, or any thing that takes her from the liberty of her choice, I am bound to restitution, that is, to restore her to a right understanding of things, and to a full liberty, by taking from her the deceit or the violence.

9. An Adulterous person is tyed to restitution of the injury, so far as it is reparable, and can be made to the wronged person; that is, to make provision for the children begotten in unlawful embraces, that they may do no injury to the legitimate by receiving a common portion: and if the injured person do account of it, he must satisfie him with money for the wrong done to his bed. He is not tyed to offer this, because it is no proper exchange, but he is bound to pay it, if it be reasonably demanded: for every man hath justice done him, when himself is satisfyed, though by a word, or an action, or a peny.

10. He that hath kild a man is bound to restitution by allowing such a maintenance to the children and neer relatives of the deceased as they have lost by his death, considering and allowing for all circumstances of the mans age, and health, and probability of living. And thus *Hercules* is said to have made expiation for the death of *Iphitus* whom he slew, [v]by paying a mulct to his children.

11. [w]He that hath really lessened the fame of his neighbour by fraud or violence is bound to restore it by its proper instruments: such as are confession of his fault, giving testimony of his innocence or worth, doing him honour, or (if that will do it, and both parties agree) by money which answers all things.

12. He that hath wounded his neighbour is tyed to the expences of the Surgeon and other incidences, and to repair whatever loss he sustains by his disability to work or trade: and the same is in the case of false imprisonment; in which cases onely the real effect and remaining detriment are to be mended and repaired: for the action it self is to be punished or repented of, and enters not into the question of restitution. But in these and all other cases the injured person is to be restored to that perfect and good condition from which he was removed by my fraud or violence, so far as is possible. Thus a ravisher must repair the temporal detriment or injury done to the maid, and give her a dowry, or marry her if she desire it. For this restores her into that capacity of being a good wife, which by the injury was lost, as far as it can be done.

[v] *Ἃ γὰρ ἡ γυνή, ἢ οἱ συγγενεῖς, τοῦ φονευθέντος ἔλαβον, τρόπον τινὰ ἐκείνῳ δέδοται.* Mich. Ephes. ad 5. Eth.

[w] Sic Vivianus resipuit de injusta accusatione: apud Cassiodor. 4. 41.

13. He that robbeth his Neighbour of his goods, or detains any thing violently or fraudulently, is bound not onely to restore the principall, but all its fruits and emoluments which would have accrued to the right owner during the time of their being detained. By proportion to these rules, we may judge of the obligation that lyes upon all sorts of injurious persons: the sacrilegious, the detainers of tithes, cheaters of mens inheritances, unjust Judges, false witnesses and accusers, those that do fraudulently or violently bring men to sin, that force men to drink, that laugh at and disgrace vertue, that perswade servants to run away, or commend such purposes, violent persecutors of religion in any instance; and all of the same nature.

14. He that hath wronged so many, or in that manner (as in the way of daily trade) that he knows not in what measure he hath done it, or who they are; must redeem his fault by alms, and largesses to the poor, according to the value of his wrongful dealing, as neer as he can proportion it. Better it is to go begging to Heaven, than to go to Hell laden with the spoils of rapine and injustice.

15. The order of paying the debts of contract, or restitution, are in some instances set down by the civil laws of a kingdom, in which cases their rule is to be observed: In destitution or want of such rules, we are 1. to observe the necessity of the Creditor. 2. Then the time of the delay: and 3. The special obligations, of friendship or kindenesse: and according to these in their several degrees, make our restitution, if we be not able to do all that we should: but if we be, the best rule is to do it as soon as we can, taking our accounts in this as in our humane actions, according to prudence, and civil or natural conveniences or possibilities; onely securing these two things. 1. That the duty be not wholly omitted: and 2. That it be not deferred at all out of covetousnesse, or any other principle that is vitious. [x]Remember, that the same day in which *Zacheus* made restitution to all whom he had injured, the same day Christ himself pronounced that salvation was come to his house.

16. [y]But besides the obligation arising from contract or default there is one of another sort which comes from kindenesse, and the acts of charity and friendship. He that does me a favour hath bound me to make him a return of thankfulnesse. The obligation comes not by covenant, not by his own expresse intention, but by the nature of th

[x] Luke 19: 9. [y] Gratitude.

25 as soon] so ~ *4+*

thing; and is a duty springing up within the spirit of the obliged person, to whom it is more natural to love his friend, and to do good for good, than to return evil for evil: because a man may forgive an injury, but he must never forget a good turne. For every thing that is excellent, and every thing that is profitable, whatsoever is good in it self or good to me, cannot but be beloved; and what we love, we naturally cherish and do good to. He therefore that refuses to do good to them whom he is bound to love, or to love that which did him good, is unnatural and monstrous in his affections, and thinks all the world borne to minister to him, with a greedinesse worse than that of the sea, which although it receives all rivers into it self, yet it furnishes the clouds and springs with a return of all they need.

Our duty to benefactors is to esteem and love their persons: to make them proportionable returns of service or duty, or profit, according as we can, or as they need, or as opportunity presents it self, and according to the greatnesses of their kindenesses: and to pray to God to make them recompence for all the good they have done to us; which last office is also requisite to be done for our *Creditors*, who in charity have relieved our wants.

Ad Chap. III.

Prayers to be said in relation to the several Obligations and Offices of Justice.

A Prayer for the Grace of Obedience: to be said by all persons under Command.

O Eternal God, Great Ruler of Men and Angels, who hast constituted all things in a wonderful order, making all the creatures subject to man, and one man to another, and all to thee, the last link of this admirable chain being fastened to the foot of thy throne: teach me to obey all those whom thou hast set over me, reverencing their persons, submitting indifferently to all their lawful commands, cheerfully undergoing those burdens which the publick wisdom and necessity shall impose upon me; at no hand murmuring against government, lest the Spirit of pride and mutiny, of murmur and disorder enter into me, and consigne me to the portion of the disobedient and rebellious,

12 they] *6+*, thy *1 2 3 4 5* 20 *Ad* Chap. III.] *ed, om 1+*

of the Despisers of dominion, and revilers of dignity. Grant this O Holy God for his sake, who for his obedience to the Father hath obtained the glorification of eternal ages, our Lord and Saviour Jesus Christ. *Amen.*

Prayers for Kings and all Magistrates, for our Parents spiritual and natural, are in the following Letanies at the end of the fourth Chapter.

A Prayer to be said by Subjects, when their Land is invaded and overrun by barbarous or wicked people, enemies of the Religion, or the Government.

I.

O Eternal God, thou alone rulest in the Kingdoms of men, thou art the great God of battels and recompences, and by thy glorious wisdom, by thy Almighty power, and by thy secret providence, doest determine the events of war and the issues of humane counsels and the returns of peace and victory, now at last be pleased to let the light of thy countenance, and the effects of a glorious mercy, and a gracious pardon return to this Land. Thou seest how great evils we suffer under the power and tyranny of war, and although we submit to, and adore thy justice in our sufferings, yet be pleased to pity our misery, to hear our complaints, and to provide us of remedy against our present calamities: let not the defenders of a righteous cause go away ashamed, nor our counsels be for ever confounded, nor our parties defeated, nor religion suppressed, nor learning discountenanced, nor us be spoiled of all the exteriour ornaments, instruments and advantages of piety, which thou hast been pleased formerly to minister to our infirmities, for the interests of learning and religion. *Amen.*

II.

We confesse dear God, that we have deserved to be totally extinct and separate from the Communion of Saints, and the comforts of Religion, to be made servants to ignorant, unjust and inferiour persons, or to suffer any other calamitie which thou shalt allot us as the instrument of thy anger, whom we have so often provoked to wrath and jealousie. Lord we humbly lye down under the burden of thy rod, begging of thee to remember our infirmities, and no more to remember our sins,

5 *Kings and all*] *om 2 3* 15 last] *5*+, least *1 2 3 4* 23 nor us] *KC*, and we *1*+

to support us with thy staff, to lift us up with thy hand, to refresh us with thy gracious eye; and if a sad cloud of temporal infelicities must still encircle us, open unto us the window of Heaven, that with an eye of faith and hope we may see beyond the cloud, looking upon those mercies which in thy secret providence and admirable wisdom thou designest to all thy servants, from such unlikely and sad beginnings. Teach us diligently to do all our duty, and cheerfully to submit to all thy will; and at last be gracious to thy people that call upon thee, that put their trust in thee, that have laid up all their hopes in the bosome of God, that besides thee have no helper. *Amen.*

III.

Place a guard of Angels about the person of the King, and immure him with the defence of thy right hand, that no unhallowed arm may do violence to him. Support him with aids from Heaven in all his battels, trials, and dangers, that he may in every instant of his temptation become dearer to thee, and do thou return to him with mercy and deliverance. Give unto him the hearts of all his people, and put into his hand a prevailing rod of iron, a scepter of power, and a sword of justice; and enable him to defend and comfort the Churches under his protection.

IV.

Blesse all his Friends, Relatives, Confederates and Leiges; direct their counsels, unite their hearts, strengthen their hands, blesse their actions: Give unto them holinesse of intention, that they may with much candour and ingenuity pursue the cause of God and the King: Sanctifie all the means and instruments of their purposes, that they may not with cruelty, injustice, or oppression proceed towards the end of their just desires; and do thou crown all their endeavours with a prosperous event, that all may cooperate to, and actually produce those great mercies which we beg of thee; honour and safety to our Soveraign, defence of his just rights, peace to his people, establishment and promotion to Religion, advantages and encouragement to Learning and holy living, deliverance to all the oppressed, comfort to all thy faithful people; and from all these, glory to thy holy Name.

12–170.24 Place a guard . . . *Amen.*] *2+, the three prayers in appendix at end of chap. 4 1*
12 King] Ruler *2 3*   25 the King] his Vicegerent *2 3*   30–1 our Soveraign] the Ruler *2 3*

Grant this *O King* of Kings, for his sake by whom thou hast consigned us to all thy mercies and promises, and to whom thou hast given all power in Heaven and Earth, our Lord and Saviour Jesus Christ. *Amen.*

A Prayer to be said by Kings or Magistrates, for themselves and their people.

O my God and King, thou rulest in the Kingdoms of Men; by thee Kings reign, and Princes decree justice; thou hast appointed me under thy self [[z] *and under my Prince*] to govern this portion of thy Church according to the Laws of Religion and the Common-wealth. O Lord, I am but an infirm man, and know not how to decree certain sentences without erring in judgement: but do thou give to thy servant an understanding heart to judge this people, that I may discern between good and evil. Cause me to walk before thee and all the people in truth and righteousness, and in sincerity of heart, that I may not regard the person of the mighty, nor be afraid of his terrour, nor despise the person of the poor, and reject his petition; but that doing justice to all men, I and my people may receive mercy of thee, peace and plenty in our dayes, and mutual love, duty and correspondence, that there be no leading into captivity, no complaining in our streets; but we may see the Church in prosperity all our dayes, and Religion established and increasing. Do thou establish the house of thy servant, and bring me to a participation of the glories of thy kingdom, for his sake who is my Lord and King, the holy and ever blessed Saviour of the world, our Redeemer Jesus. *Amen.*

A Prayer to be said by Parents for their Children.

O Almighty and most merciful Father, who hast promised children as a reward to the Righteous, and hast given them to me as a testimony of thy mercy, and an engagement of my duty; be pleased to be a Father unto them, and give them healthful bodies, understanding souls, and sanctified spirits, that they may be thy servants, and thy children all their dayes. Let a great mercy and providence lead them through the dangers and temptations and ignorances of their youth, that they may never run into folly, and the evils of unbridled appetite. So order the accidents of their lives, that by good education, careful Tutors, holy example, innocent company, prudent counsel, and thy restraining

[z] These words to be added by a delegate or inferiour.

4 *Kings or*] *om 2 3*   8 *Prince*] *Ruler 2 3*

grace, their duty to thee may be secured in the midst of a crooked and untoward generation: and if it seem good in thy eyes, let me be enabled to provide conveniently for the support of their persons, that they may not be destitute and miserable in my death; or if thou shalt call me off from this World by a more timely summons, let their portion be, thy care, mercy, and providence over their bodies and souls: and may they never live vitious lives, nor dye violent or untimely deaths; but let them glorifie thee here with a free obedience, and the duties of a whole life, that when they have served thee in their generations, and have profited the Christian Common-wealth, they may be coheirs with Jesus in the glories of thy eternal Kingdom, through the same, our Lord Jesus Christ. *Amen.*

A Prayer to be said by Masters of Families, Curats, Tutors, or other obliged persons for their charges.

O Almighty God, merciful and gracious, have mercy upon my Family [or Pupils, or Parishioners, etc.] and all committed to my charge: sanctifie them with thy grace, preserve them with thy providence, guard them from all evil by the custody of Angels, direct them in the wayes of peace and holy Religion by my Ministery and the conduct of thy most holy Spirit, and consigne them all with the participation of thy blessings and graces in this World, with healthful bodies, with good understandings, and sanctified spirits to a full fruition of thy glories hereafter, through Jesus Christ our Lord. *Amen.*

A Prayer to be said by Merchants, Tradesmen, and Handicrafts men.

O Eternal God, thou Fountain of justice, mercy and benediction, who by my education and other effects of thy providence hast called me to this profession, that by my industry I may in my small proportion work together for the good of my self and others: I humbly beg thy grace to guide me in my intention, and in the transaction of my affairs, that I may be diligent, just, and faithful: and give me thy favour, that this my labour may be accepted by thee as a part of my necessary duty, and give me thy blessing to assist and prosper me in my Calling, to such measures as thou shalt in mercy choose for me: and be pleased to let thy holy Spirit be for ever present with me, that I may never be given to covetousnesse and sordid appetites, to lying and falsehood, or any other base, indirect and beggerly arts, but give me prudence, honesty and Christian sincerity, that my trade may be sanctified by my religion, my labour by my intention and thy blessing, that when I have done my portion of work thou hast allotted me, and improved the talent thou hast intrusted to me, and served the Common-wealth in my capacity, I may receive the mighty price of my high calling, which I expect and beg, in the portion and inheritance of the ever blessed Saviour and Redeemer Jesus. *Amen.*

A Prayer to be said by Debtors and all persons obliged whether by crime or contract.

O Almighty God who art rich unto all, the treasure and Fountain of all good, of all justice, and all mercy, and all bounty, to whom we owe all that we are, and all that we have, being thy Debtors by reason of our sins, and by thy own gracious contract made with us in Jesus Christ: teach me in the first place to perform all my Obligations to thee, both of duty and thankfulnesse; and next enable me to pay my duty to all my friends, and my debts to all my Creditors, that none bee made miserable, or lessened in his estate by his kindenesse to me, or traffick with me. Forgive me all those sins and irregular actions by which I entered into debt further than my necessity required, or by which such necessity was brought upon me: but let not them suffer by occasion of my sin. Lord reward all their kindnesse into their bosomes, and make them recompence where I cannot, and make me very willing in all that I can, and able for all that I am obliged to, or if it seem good in thine eyes to afflict me by the continuance of this condition, yet make it up by some means to them, that the prayer of thy servant may obtain of thee, at least to pay my debt in blessings. *Amen.*

II.

Lord sanctifie and forgive all that I have tempted to evil by my discourse or my example: instruct them in the right way whom I have lead to errour, and let me never run further on the score of sinne; but do thou blot out all the evils I have done, by the spunge of thy passion, and the blood of thy Crosse; and give me a deep and an excellent repentance, and a free and a gracious pardon, that thou mayest answer for me, O Lord, and enable me to stand upright in judgement; for in thee, O Lord, have I trusted, let me never be confounded. Pity me, and instruct me; guide me and support me, pardon and save me, for my sweet Saviour Jesus Christ his sake. *Amen.*

A Prayer for Patron and Benefactours.

O Almighty GOD thou Fountain of all good, of all excellency both to Men and Angels, extend thine abundant favour and loving kindnesse to my Patron, to all my friends and Benefactors: Reward them, and make them plentiful recompence for all the good which from thy merciful providence they have conveyed unto me: Let the light of thy countenance shine upon them, and let them never come into affliction or sadnesse, but such as may be an instrument of thy glory and their eternal comfort. Forgive them all their sins; let thy Divinest Spirit preserve them from all deeds of Darknesse. Let thy ministering Angels guard their persons from the violence of the spirits of Darknesse: And thou who knowest every degree of their necessity by thy infinite wisdom, give supply to all their needs by thy glorious mercy, preserving their persons, sanctifying their hearts, and leading them in the wayes of righteousnesse, by the waters of comfort, to the land of eternal rest and glory, through Jesus Christ our Lord. *Amen.*

Chap. IV.

Of Christian Religion.

RELIGION in a large sense does signifie the whole duty of Man, comprehending in it Justice, Charity, and Sobriety: because all these being commanded by God they become a part of that honour and worship which we are bound to pay to him. And thus the word is used in S. *James*, [a] *Pure Religion and undefiled before God and the Father is this, To visit the fatherlesse and Widows in their affliction, and to keep himself unspotted from the world.* But in a more restrained sense it is taken for that part of duty which particularly relates to God in our worshippings and adoration of him, in confessing his excellencies, loving his person, admiring his goodnesse, believing his Word, and doing all that which may in a proper and direct manner do him honour. It containes the duties of the first Table onely, and so it is called [b] *Godlinesse*, and is by Saint *Paul*, distinguished from *Justice* and *Sobriety.* In this sense I am now to explicate the parts of it.

Of the internal actions of Religion.

Those I call the internal actions of Religion, in which the soul onely is imployed, and ministers to God in the special actions of *Faith, Hope, and Charity. Faith* believes the revelations of God: *Hope* expects his promises: and *Charity* loves his excellencies and mercies. *Faith* gives our understanding to God: *Hope* gives up all the passions and affections to Heaven and heavenly things: and *Charity* gives the will to the service of God. *Faith* is opposed to Infidelity: *Hope* to Despair: *Charity* to Enmity and Hostility; and these three sanctifie the whole Man, and make our duty to God and obedience to his commandments to be *chosen*, *reasonable*, and *delightful*, and therefore to be *intire*, *persevering*, and *universal.*

[a] James 1: 27.
[b] Tit. 2: 12.

3 does] doth *4+*

SECT. I.
Of Faith.

The Acts and Offices of Faith, are

1. [c]To believe every thing which God hath revealed to us; and when once we are convinced that God hath spoken it, to make no further enquiry; but humbly to submit, ever remembering that there are some things which our understanding cannot fathom nor search out their depth.

2. To believe nothing concerning God but what is honourable and excellent, as knowing that belief to be no honouring of God which entertains of him any dishonourable thoughts. Faith is the parent of Charity, and whatsoever Faith entertains must be apt to produce love to God: but he that believes God to be cruel or unmerciful, or a rejoycer in the unavoidable damnation of the greatest part of mankinde, or that he speaks one thing and privately means another, thinks evil thoughts concerning God, and such, as for which we should hate a man, and therefore are great enemies of Faith, being apt to destroy charity. Our Faith concerning God must be as himself hath revealed and described his own excellencies: and in our discourses we must remove from him all imperfection, and attribute to him all excellency.

3. To give our selves wholly up to Christ in heart and desire to become Disciples of his doctrine with choice (besides conviction) being in the presence of God, but as Ideots, that is, without any principles of our own to hinder the truth of God; but sucking in greedily all that God hath taught us, believing it infinitely, and loving to believe it. For this is an act of Love reflected upon Faith, or an act of Faith leaning upon Love.

4. To believe all Gods promises, and that whatsoever is promised in Scripture shall on Gods part be as surely performed as if we had it in possession. This act makes us to rely upon God with the same confidence as we did on our Parents when we were children, when we made no doubt, but whatsoever we needed we should have it if it were in their power.

5. To believe also the conditions of the promise, or that part of the revelation which concerns our duty. Many are apt to believe the Article of remission of sins, but they believe it without the condition of

[c] Demus, Deum aliquid posse, quod nos fateamur investigare non posse. S. August. 21. cap. 7. de Civitat.

repentance, or the fruits of holy life: and that is to believe the Article otherwise than God intended it. For the Covenant of the Gospel is the great object of Faith, and that supposes our duty to answer his grace; that God will be our God, so long, as we are his people; The other is not Faith but Flattery.

6. To professe publickly the doctrine of Jesus Christ, openly owning whatsoever he hath revealed and commanded, not being ashamed of the word of God, or of any practises enjoyned by it; and this, without complying with any mans interest, not regarding favor, nor being moved with good words, not fearing disgrace, or losse, or inconvenience, or death it self.

7. To pray without doubting, without wearinesse, without faintnesse, entertaining no jealousies, or suspitions of God, but being confident of Gods hearing us, and of his returns to us, whatsoever the manner or the instance be, that if we do our duty, it will be gracious and merciful.

These acts of Faith are in several degrees in the servants of Jesus: some have it but as a grain of mustard-seed, some grow up to a plant, some have the fulnesse of faith: but the least faith that is must be a perswasion so strong as to make us undertake the doing of all that duty which Christ built upon the foundation of believing: but we shall best discern the truth of our faith by these following signes. [d]S. *Hierom* reckons three.

Signes of true Faith.

1. An earnest and vehement prayer: for it is impossible we should heartily believe the things of God and the glories of the Gospel, and not most importunately desire them. For every thing is desired according to our belief of its excellency and possibility.

2. To do nothing for vain glory, but wholly for the interests of religion, and these Articles we believe; valuing not at all the rumours of men, but the praise of God, to whom by faith, we have given up all our intellectual faculties.

3. To be content with God for our Judge, for our Patron, for our Lord, for our friend, desiring God to be all in all to us, as we are in our understanding and affections wholly his.

Adde to these.

4. To be a stranger upon earth in our affections, and to have all our

[d] Dial. adver. Lucif.

thoughts and principal desires fixed upon the matters of Faith, the things of Heaven. For if a man were adopted heir to *Cæsar*, he would (if he believed it real and effective) despise the present, and wholly be at court in his Fathers eye; and his desires would outrun his swiftest speed, and all his thoughts would spend themselves in creating Ideas, and little phantastick images of his future condition. Now God hath made us Heirs of his Kingdom, and Coheirs with Jesus: if we believed this, we would think and affect, and study accordingly. But he that rejoyces in gain, and his heart dwells in the world, and is espoused to a fair estate, and transported with a light momentany joy, and is afflicted with losses, and amazed with temporal persecutions, and esteems disgrace, or poverty in a good cause to be intolerable, this man either hath no inheritance in Heaven, or believes none; and believes not that he is adopted to be the Son of God, the Heir of eternal Glory.

5. S. *James's* signe is the best: *Shew me thy faith by thy works.* Faith makes the Merchant diligent and venturous, and that makes him rich. *Ferdinando* of Arragon believed the story told him by *Columbus*, and therefore he furnished him with ships, and got the west Indies by his Faith in the undertaker. But *Henry* the seventh of *England* believed him not, and therefore trusted him not with shipping, and lost all the purchase of that Faith. It is told us by Christ: *He that forgives shall be forgiven.* If we believe this, it is certain we shall forgive our enemies; for none of us all but need and desire to be forgiven. No man can possibly despise or refuse to desire such excellent glories as are revealed to them that are servants of Christ: and yet we do nothing that is commanded us as a condition to obtain them. No man could work a dayes labor without faith: but because he believes he shall have his wages at the dayes or weeks end, he does his duty. But he onely believes who does that thing which other men in the like cases do, when they do believe. He that believes, money gotten with danger is better than poverty with safety, will venture for it in unknown lands or seas: and so will he that believes it better to get Heaven with labour, than to go to Hell with pleasure.

6. *He that believes does not make haste*, but waits patiently till the times of refreshment come, and dares trust God for the morrow, and is no more sollicitous for next year, than he is for that which is past: and it is certain, that man wants faith who dares be more confident of being supplied when he hath money in his purse, than when he hath it onely

15 S. *James's* signe] S. *James's* his signe *8* 36 for next] for the next *7 8*

in bills of exchange from God: or that relyes more upon his own industry than upon Gods providence, when his own industry fails him. If you dare trust to God when the case to humane reason seems impossible, and trust to God then also out of choice, not because you have nothing else to trust to, but because he is the onely support of a just confidence, then you give a good testimony of your faith.

7. True Faith is confident, and will venture all the world upon the strength of its persuasion. Will you lay your life on it, your estate, your reputation, that the doctrine of JESUS CHRIST is true in every Article? Then you have true Faith. But he that fears men more than God, believes men more than he believes in God.

8. Faith, if it be true, living, and justifying cannot be separated from a good life: it works miracles, makes a Drunkard become sober, a lascivious person become chast, a covetous man become liberal: [e] *it overcomes the world, it works righteousnesse*, and makes us diligently to do, and cheerfully to suffer whatsoever God hath placed in our way to Heaven.

The Means and Instruments to obtain Faith, are

1. An humble, willing, and docible minde, or desire to be instructed in the way of God: For persuasion enters like a sun-beam, gently, and without violence: and open but the window, and draw the curtain and the Sun of righteousnesse will enlighten your darknesse.

2. Remove all prejudice and love to every thing which may be contradicted by Faith: [f] *How can ye believe* (said Christ) *that receive praise one of another*? An unchast man cannot easily be brought to believe that without purity he shall never see God. He that loves riches can hardly believe the doctrine of poverty and renunciation of the world: and alms and Martyrdom, and the doctrine of the crosse is folly to him that loves his ease and pleasures. He that hath within him any principle contrary to the doctrines of Faith, cannot easily become a Disciple.

3. Prayer which is instrumental to every thing hath a particular promise in this thing. [g] *He that lacks wisdom let him ask it of God*: and, [h] *if you give good things to your children, how much more shall your Heavenly Father give his Spirit to them that ask him.*

4. [i] The consideration of the Divine Omnipotence, and infinite

[e] 2 Cor. 13: 5. Rom. 8: 10. [f] John 5: 44.
[g] James 1: 5. [h] Luke 11: 13.
[i] In rebus miris summa credendi ratio est omnipotentia Creatoris. S. Aug.

24 [f]] *GH, om 1+* 32 [g]] *GH, om 1+* [h]] *GH, om 1+*

wisdom, and our own ignorance, are great instruments of curing all doubting, and silencing the murmures of infidelity.

5. Avoid all curiosity of inquiry into particulars, and circumstances and mysteries: for true faith is full of ingenuity, and hearty simplicity, free from suspicion, wise and confident, trusting upon generals without watching and prying into unnecessary or undiscernable particulars. No Man carries his bed into his field to watch how his corn grows; but believes upon the general order of Providence and Nature; and at Harvest findes himself not deceived.

6. In time of temptation be not busie to dispute, but relye upon the conclusion; and throw your self upon God, and contend not with him, but in prayer, and in the presence, and with the help of a prudent untempted guide: and be sure to esteem all changes of belief which offer themselves in the time of your greatest weaknesse (contrary to the perswasions of your best understanding) to bee temptations, and reject them accordingly.

7. It is a prudent course that in our health and best advantages we lay up particular arguments and instruments of perswasion and confidence, to be brought forth and used in the great day of expence; and that especially in such things in which we use to be most tempted, and in which we are least confident, and which are most necessary, and which commonly the Devil uses to assault us withal in the days of our visitation.

8. The wisdom of the Church of God is very remarkable in appointing Festivals or Holidayes, whose solemnity and Offices have no other special businesse but to record the Article of the day; such as, *Trinity Sunday*, *Ascension*, *Easter*, *Christmas-day*: and to those persons who can onely believe, not prove or dispute, there is no better instrument to cause the remembrance, and plain notion, and to endear the affection and hearty assent to the Article, than the proclaiming and recommending it by the festivity and joy of a Holy day.

SECT. II.
Of the Hope of a Christian.

Faith differs from Hope in the extension of its object, and in the intention of degree. [j]Saint *Austin* thus accounts their differences. Faith is of

[j] Enchirid. c. 8.

all things revealed, good and bad, rewards and punishments, of things past, present, and to come, of things that concern us, and of things that concern us not: But Hope hath for its Object things onely that are good and fit to be hoped for, future, and concerning our selves: and because these things are offered to us upon conditions of which we may so fail as we may change our will; therefore our certainty is lesse than the adherences of faith; which (because Faith relyes onely upon one proposition, that is, the truth of the Word of God) cannot be made uncertain in themselves, though the object of our Hope may become uncertain to us, and to our possession: for it is infallibly certain, that there is Heaven for all the godly, and for me amongst them all, if I do my duty. But that I shall enter into Heaven is the object of my Hope not of my Faith, and is so sure, as it is certain I shall persevere in the wayes of God.

The Acts of Hope, are

1. To relye upon God with a confident expectation of his promises ever esteeming that every promise of God is a magazine of all tha grace and relief which we can need in that instance for which th promise is made. *Every degree of hope is a degree of confidence.*

2. To esteem all the danger of an action and the possibilities of mis carriage, and every crosse accident that can intervene, to be no defec on Gods part, but either a mercy on his part, or a fault on ours: for the we shall be sure to trust in God when we see him to be our confidence and our selves the cause of all mischances. *The hope of a Christian prudent and religious.*

3. To rejoyce in the midst of a misfortune or seeming sadness knowing that this may work for good, and will, if we be not wanting t our souls. This is a direct act of Hope to look through the cloud, an look for a beam of light from God, and this is called in Scriptur *Rejoycing in tribulation*, when *the God of hope fils us with all joy in believin Every degree of hope brings a degree of joy.*

4. To desire, to pray, and to long for the great object of our hope, th mighty price of our high calling; and to desire the other things of th life, as they are promised, that is, so far as they are made necessary an useful to us in order to Gods glory, and the great end of souls. *Ho* and *Fasting* are said to be the two wings of *Prayer.* Fasting is but as th wing of a Bird, but Hope is like the wing of an Angel soaring up

29 of light] of the light *4+*

Heaven, and bears our prayers to the throne of Grace. Without Hope it is impossible to pray; but Hope makes our prayers reasonable, passionate, and religious; for it relyes upon Gods promise, or experience, or providence, and story. *Prayer is always in proportion to our Hope, zealous and affectionate.*

5. Perseverance is the perfection of the duty of hope, and its last act: and so long as our hope continues, so long we go on in duty and diligence: but he that is to raise a Castle in an hour, sits down and does nothing towards it: and *Herod* the Sophister left off to teach his son, when he saw that 24 Pages appointed to wait on him, and called by the several Letters of the Alphabet could never make him to understand his letters perfectly.

Rules to govern our Hope.

1. *Let your Hope be moderate*, proportioned to your state, person and condition, whether it be for gifts or graces, or temporal favours. It is an ambitious hope for persons whose diligence is like them that are least in the Kingdom of Heaven, to believe themselves endeared to God as the greatest Saints, or that they shall have a throne equal to S. *Paul* or the blessed Virgin *Mary.* A Stammerer cannot with moderation hope for the gift of Tongues, or a Peasant to become learned as *Origen*: or if a Beggar desires or hopes to become a King, or asks for a thousand pound a year, we call him impudent, not passionate, much lesse reasonable. Hope that God will crown your endeavours with equal measures of that reward which he indeed freely gives, but yet gives according to our proportions. Hope for good successe according to, or not much beyond the efficacy of the causes and the instrument, and let the Husbandman hope for a good Harvest, not for a rich Kingdom, or a victorious Army.

2. *Let your hope be well founded*, relying upon just confidences, that is, upon God according to his revelations and promises. For it is possible for a Man to have a vain hope upon God: and in matters of Religion it is presumption to hope that Gods mercies will be powred forth upon lazy persons that do nothing towards holy and strict walking, nothing (I say) but trust, and long for an event besides and against all disposition of the means. Every false principle in Religion is a Reed of *Egypt*, false and dangerous. Relye not in temporal things upon uncertain prophecies, and Astrology, not upon our own wit or industry, not upon

16 for persons] *7 8*, for a person *1 2 3 4 5 6*

gold or friends, not upon Armies and Princes, expect not health from Physicians that cannot cure their own breath, much lesse their mortality: use all lawful instruments, but expect nothing from them above their natural or ordinary efficacy, and in the use of them from God expect a blessing. [k]A hope that is easie and credulous is an arm of flesh, an ill supporter without a bone.

3. *Let your hope be without vanity*, or garishnesse of spirit, but sober, grave and silent, fixed in the heart, not born upon the lip, apt to support our spirits within, but not to provoke envy abroad.

4. [l]Let your hope be of things possible, safe and useful. He that hopes for an opportunity of acting his revenge, or lust, or rapine, watches to do himself a mischief. All evils of our selves or Brethren are objects of our fear, not hope: and when it is truly understood, things uselesse and unsafe can no more be wished for, than things impossible can be obtained.

5. *Let your hope be patient*, without tediousnesse of spirit, or hastinesse of prefixing time. Make no limits or prescriptions to God, but let your prayers and endeavours go on still with a constant attendance on the periods of Gods providence. The men of *Bethulia* resolved to wait upon God but five dayes longer. But deliverance stayed seven dayes, and yet came at last: and take not every accident for an argument of despair: but go on still in hoping, and begin again to work if any ill accident have interrupted you.

Means of Hope, and remedies against Despair.

The means to cure Despair, and to continue or increase Hope, are partly by consideration, partly by exercise.

1. Apply your minde to the cure of all the proper causes of Despair and they are weaknesse of spirit, or violence of passion. He that greedily covets, is impatient of delay, and desperate in contrary accidents; [m]and he that is little of heart, is also little of hope, and apt to sorrow and suspition.

2. Despise the things of the World, and be indifferent to all changes and events of providence; and for the things of God the promises are

[k] Jer. 17: 5.
[l] Di cose fuori di credenza,
Non fare isperienza.
[m] *Μικρόψυχοι μακρόλυποι.*

---

note *l* Non fare isperienza] *cor*, far speranza *1*+

certain to be performed in kinde; [n]and where there is lesse variety of chance, there is lesse possibility of being mocked: but he that creates to himself thousands of little hopes, uncertain in the promise, fallible in the event, and depending upon ten thousand circumstances (as are all the things of this World) shall often fail in his expectations, and be used to arguments of distrust in such hopes.

3. So long as your hopes are regular and reasonable, though in temporal affairs, such as are deliverance from enemies, escaping a storm or shipwrack, recovery from a sicknesse, ability to pay your debts, etc. remember that there are some things ordinary, and some things extraordinary to prevent despair. *In ordinary*, Remember that the very hoping in God is an endearment of him, and a means to obtain the blessing: *I will deliver him because he hath put his trust in me.* 2. There are in God all those glorious Attributes and excellencies which in the nature of things can possibly create or confirm Hope. God is 1. Strong. 2. Wise. 3. True. 4. Loving. There cannot be added another capacity to create a confidence; for upon these premises we cannot fail of receiving what is fit for us. 3. God hath obliged himself by promise that we shall have the good of every thing we desire: for even losses and denials shall *work for the good of them that fear God.* And if we will trust the truth of God for performance of the general, we may well trust his wisdome to choose for us the particular. But *the extraordinaries* of God are apt to supply the defect of all natural and humane possibilities. 1. God hath in many instances given extraordinary vertue to the active causes and instruments: to a jawbone to kill a multitude: to 300 Men to destroy a great Army, to *Jonathan* and his Armour-bearer to rout a whole Garrison. 2. He hath given excellent sufferance and vigorousnesse to the sufferers, arming them with strange courage, heroical fortitude, invincible resolution, and glorious patience: and thus, he layes no more upon us than we are able to bear: for when he increases our sufferings, he lessens them by increasing our patience. 3. His providence is extraregular and produces strange things beyond common rules: and he that lead Israel through a Sea, and made a Rock

[n] *Ἐλπὶς, καὶ σὺ Τύχη, μέγα χαίρετε· τὴν ὁδὸν εὗρον·*
οὐκέτι γὰρ σφετέροις ἐπιτέρπομαι· ἔῤῥετε ἄμφω.
οὕνεκεν ἐν μερόπεσσι πολυπλανέες μάλα ἐστέ·
ὅσσα γὰρ ἀτρεκέως οὐκ ἔσσεται, ὔμμες ἐν ἡμῖν
φάσματα, ὡς ἐν ὕπνῳ, ἐμβάλλετε, οἷα τ᾽ ἐόντα·
παίζοιτε, στροφέοιτε, ὅσους ἐμεῦ ὕστερον ὄντας
εὗροιτ᾽ οὐ νοέοντας ὅπερ θέμις ἐστὶ νοῆσαι. Homer.

1 [n]] *4+, om 1 2 3*

powre forth waters, and the Heavens to give them bread and flesh, and whole Armies to be destroyed with phantastick noises, and the fortune of all *France* to be recovered and intirely revolved by the arms and conduct of a Girle against the torrent of the *English* fortune and Chivalry; can do what he please, and still retains the same affections to his people, and the same providence over mankinde as ever: [o]and it is impossible for that Man to despair, who remembers that *his Helper is Omnipotent*, and can do what he please: let us rest there awhile; he can if he please: And he is *infinitely loving*: willing enough; and he is *infinitely wise*, choosing better for us than we can do for our selves. This in all ages and chances hath supported the afflicted people of God and carried them on dry ground through a red Sea. God invites and cherishes the hopes of Men by all the variety of his providence.

4. If your case be brought to the last extremity, and that you are at the pits brink, even the very Margent of the Grave, yet then despair not; at least put it off a little longer: and remember that whatsoever final accident takes away all hope from you, if you stay a little longer and in the mean while bear it sweetly, it will also take away all despair too. For when you enter into the Regions of death, you rest from all your labours and your fears.

5. Let them who are tempted to despair of their salvation, consider how much Christ suffered to redeem us from sin and its eternal punishment: and he that considers this, must needs believe, that the desires which God had to save us were not lesse than infinite, and therefore not easily to be satisfied without it.

6. Let no Man despair of Gods mercies to forgive him, unlesse he be sure that his sinnes are greater than Gods mercies. If they be not, we have much reason to hope that the stronger ingredient will prevail so long as we are in the time and state of repentance, and within the possibilities and latitude of the Covenant; and as long as any promise can but reflect upon him with an oblique beam of comfort. Possibly the Man may erre in his judgement of circumstances, and therefore let him fear: but because it is not certain he is mistaken, let him not despair.

7. Consider that God who knows all the events of Men, and what their final condition shall be, who shall be saved, and who will perish yet he treateth them as his own, calls them to be his own, offers fai

[o] Heb. 2: 18.

8 there] these *4*

conditions as to his own, gives them blessings, arguments of mercy, and instances of fear to call them off from death, and to call them home to life, and in all this shews no despair of happinesse to them, and therefore much lesse should any Man despair for himself, since he never was able to reade the Scrols of the eternal predestination.

8. Remember that despair belongs onely to passionate Fools or Villains, (such as were *Achitophel* and *Judas*) or else to Devils and damned persons: and as the hope of salvation is a good disposition towards it; so is despair a certain consignation to eternal ruine. A Man may be damned for despairing to be saved. Despair is the proper passion of damnation. [p] *God hath placed truth and felicity in Heaven: Curiosity and repentance upon Earth: but misery and despair are the portions of Hell.*

9. Gather together into your spirit, and its treasure-house (the Memory) not onely all the promises of GOD, but also the remembrances of experience, and the former senses of the Divine favours, that from thence you may argue from times past to the present, and enlarge to the future, and to greater blessings. For although the conjectures and expectations of Hope are not like the conclusions of Faith, yet they are a Helmet against the scorchings of Despair in temporal things, and an anchor of the soul sure and stedfast against the fluctuations of the Spirit in matters of the soul. Saint *Bernard* reckons divers principles of Hope by enumerating the instances of the Divine Mercy; and wee may by them reduce this rule to practise in the following manner. 1. GOD hath preserved mee from many sinnes; his mercies are infinite, I hope he will still preserve me from more, and for ever. 2. I have sinned and GOD smote me not: his mercies are still over the penitent, I hope he will deliver me from all the evils I have deserved. He hath forgiven me many sins of malice, and therefore surely he will pity my infirmities. 3. God visited my heart, and changed it: he loves the work of his own hands, and so my heart is now become: I hope he will love this too. 4. When I repented he received me graciously; and therefore I hope if I do my endeavour he will totally forgive me. 5. He helped my slow and beginning endeavours, and therefore I hope he will lead me to perfection. 6. When he had given me something first, then he gave me more. I hope therefore he will keep me from falling, and give me the grace of perseverance. 7. He hath chosen me to be a Disciple of Christs institution; he hath elected me to his Kingdom of grace, and therefore I hope also, to the Kingdom of his glory. 8. He

[p] V. Bede.

died for me when I was his enemy, and therefore I hope he will save me when he hath reconciled me to him, and is become my friend. 9. *God hath given us his Son, how should not he with him give us all things else?* All these S. *Bernard* reduces to these three Heads, as the instruments of all our hopes. 1. The charity of God adopting us. 2. The truth of his promises. 3. The power of his performance: which if any truly weighs, no infirmity or accident can break his hopes into undiscernable fragments, but some good planks will remain after the greatest storm and shipwrack. This was S. *Pauls* instrument: *Experience begets hope, and hope maketh not ashamed.*

10. Do thou take care onely of thy duty, of the means and proper instruments of thy purpose, and leave the end to God: lay that up with him, and he will take care of all that is intrusted to him: and this being an act of confidence in God, is also a means of security to thee.

11. By special arts of spiritual prudence and arguments secure the confident belief of the Resurrection, and thou canst not but hope for every thing else which you may reasonably expect, or lawfully desire upon the stock of the Divine mercies and promises.

12. If a despair seizes you in a particular temporal instance, let it not defile thy spirit with impure mixture, or mingle in spiritual considerations; but rather let it make thee fortifie thy soul in matters of Religion, that by being thrown out of your Earthly dwelling and confidence, you may retire into the strengths of grace, and hope the more strongly in that, by how much you are the more defeated in this, that despair of a fortune or a successe, may become the necessity of all vertue.

SECT. III.

Of Charity, or the love of God.

Love is the greatest thing that God can give us, for himself is love, and it is the greatest thing we can give to God, for it will also give our selves, and carry with it all that is ours. The Apostle cals it the band of perfection; it is *the Old*, and it is *the New*, and it is *the great Commandement*, and it is all the Commandements, for it *is the fulfilling of the Law*. It does the work of all other graces without any instrument but its own immediate vertue. For as the love to sinne makes a Man sinne against all his own reason, and all the discourses of wisdom, and all the advices of his friends, and without temptation, and without opportunity: so does the love of God, it makes a man chast without the laborious arts of fasting and exteriour disciplines, temperate in the midst of feasts, and is active enough to choose it without any intermedial appetites, and reaches at Glory thorough the very heart of Grace, without any other arms but those of Love. It is a grace that loves God for himself, and our Neighbours for God. The consideration of Gods goodnesse and bounty, the experience of those profitable and excellent emanations from him, may be, and most commonly are the first motive of our love: but when we are once entered, and have tasted the goodnesse of God, we love the spring for its own excellency, passing from passion to reason, from thanking to adoring, from sence to spirit, from considering our selves, to an union with God: and this is the image and little representation of Heaven; it is beatitude in picture, or rather the infancy and beginnings of glory.

We need no incentives by way of special enumeration to move us to the love of God, for we cannot love any thing for any reason real or imaginary, but that excellency is infinitely more eminent in God. There can but two things create love, *Perfection* and *Usefulnesse*: to which answer on our part, first *admiration*, and 2. *Desire*: and both these are centred in love. *For the entertainment of the first*, there is in God an infinite nature, immensity or vastnesse without extension or limit, Immutability, Eternity, Omnipotence, Omniscience, Holinesse, Dominion, Providence, Bounty, Mercy, Justice, Perfection in himself, and the end to which all things and all actions must be directed, and will at last arrive. The consideration of which may be heightened, if we consider our distance from all these glories: Our smallnesse and limited nature, our nothing, our inconstancy, our age like a span, our weaknesse and ignorance, our poverty, our inadvertency, and inconsideration, our disabilities and disaffections to do good, our harsh natures and unmerciful inclinations, our universal iniquitie, and our necessities and dependencies, not onely on God originally, and essentially, but even our need of the meanest of Gods creatures, and our being obnoxious to the weakest and the most contemptible. But *for the entertainment of the second* we may consider that in him is a torrent of pleasure for the voluptuous, he is the fountain of honour for the ambitious, an inexhaustible treasure for the covetous: [q] our vices are in love with phantastick pleasures and images of perfection, which are truely and really to be found no where but in God. And therefore our vertues have such proper objects, that it is but reasonable they should all turn into love:

[q] S. Aug. lib. 2. confes. cap. 6.

for certain it is that this love will turn all into vertue. For in the scrutinies for righteousnesse and judgement, *when it is inquired whether such a person be a good man or no, the meaning is not, what does he believe, or what does he hope, but what he loves?*

The acts of Love to God, are

1. Love does all things which may please the beloved person, it performs all his commandments: and this is one of the greatest instances and arguments of our love that God requires of us. This is love that we keep his commandments. *Love is obedient.*

2. It does all the intimations and secret significations of his pleasure whom we love: and this is an argument of a great degree of it. The first instance is it that makes the love accepted: but this gives a greatnesse and singularity to it. The first is the least, and lesse than it cannot do our duty; but without this second, we cannot come to perfection. *Great love is also plyant and inquisitive* in the instances of its expression.

3. Love gives away all things that so he may advance the interest of the beloved person: it relieves all that he would have relieved, and spends it self in such real significations as it is enabled withall. He never loved God that will quit any thing of his Religion, to save his money. *Love is alwayes liberal and communicative.*

4. It suffers all things that are imposed by its beloved, or that can happen for his sake, or that intervene in his service, cheerfully, sweetly, willingly, expecting that God should turn them into good, and instruments of felicity. [r] *Charity hopeth all things, endureth all things. Love is patient* and content with any thing so it be together with its beloved.

5. Love is also impatient of any thing that may displease the beloved person, hating all sin as the enemy of its friend; for love contracts all the same relations and marries the same friendships, and the same hatreds; and all affection to a sin is perfectly inconsistent with the love of God, love is not divided between God and Gods enemy: we must love God with all our heart, that is, give him a whole and undivided affection, having love for nothing els but such things which he allows, and which he commands, or loves himself.

6. *Love endeavours for ever to be present*, to converse with, to enjoy, to be united with its object, loves to be talking of him, reciting his praises, telling his stories, repeating his words, imitating his gestures, tran-

[r] 1 Cor. 13: 7.

22 intervene] *7 8*, intervenes *1 2 3 4 5 6*

scribing his copy in every thing; and every degree of union and every degree of likenesse is a degree of love; and it can endure any thing but the displeasure and the absence of its beloved. For we are not to use God and Religion, as men use perfumes, with which they are delighted when they have them, but can very well be without them. [s]True charity is restlesse till it enjoyes God in such instances in which it wants him: it is like hunger and thirst, it must be fed or it cannot be answered, and nothing can supply the presence, or make recompence for the absence of God, or of the effects of his favour, and the light of his countenance.

7. *True love in all accidents looks upon the beloved person*, and observes his countenance, and how he approves or disproves it, and accordingly looks sad or cheerful. He that loves God is not displeased at those accidents which God chooses, nor murmurs at those changes which he makes in his family, nor envies at those gifts he bestowes, but chooses as he likes, and is ruled by his judgement, and is perfectly of his persuasion, loving to learn where God is the Teacher, and being content to be ignorant or silent where he is not pleased to open himself.

8. *Love is curious of little things*: of circumstances and measures, and little accidents, not allowing to it self any infirmity, which it strives not to master: aiming at what it cannot yet reach at, desiring to be of an Angelical purity and of a perfect innocence, and a Seraphical fervour, and fears every image of offence, [t]is as much afflicted at an idle word, as some at an act of adultery, and will not allow to it self so much anger as will disturb a childe; nor endure the impurity of a dream, and this is the curiosity and nicenesse of divine Love; this is *the fear of God*, and is the daughter and production of Love.

The Measures and Rules of Divine Love.

But because this passion is pure as the brightest and smoothest mirrour, and therefore is apt to be sullyed with every impurer breath, we must be careful that our love to God be governed by these measures.

1. That our love be sweet, even and full of tranquility, having in it no violences or transportations, but going on in a course of holy actions and duties which are proportionable to our condition, and present

[s] Amoris et morsum qui vere senserit.

[t] Plutarchus citans carmen de suo Apolline, adjecit ex Herodoto quasi de suo, De eo s meum continens esto.

12 disproves] disapproves *6+* 22 at[2]] *om 6+*

state; not to satisfie all the desire, but all the probabilities and measures of our strength. A new beginner in religion hath passionate and violent desires, but they must not be the measure of his actions: But he must consider his strength, his late sicknesse and state of death, the proper temptations of his condition, and stand at first upon his defence, not go to storm a strong Fort, or attaque a potent enemy, or do heroical actions and fitter for gyants in Religion. Indiscreet violences, and untimely forwardnesse are the rocks of religion against which tender spirits often suffer shipwrack.

2. Let our love be prudent and without illusion: that is, that it expresse it self in such instances which God hath chosen, or which we choose our selves by proportion to his rules and measures. Love turns into doting when religion turns into Superstition. No degree of love can be imprudent, but the expressions may: we cannot love God too much, but we may proclaim it in undecent manners.

3. Let our love be firm, constant and inseparable, not coming and returning like the tide, but descending like a never failing river, ever running into the Ocean of Divine excellency, passing on in the chanels of duty and a constant obedience, and never ceasing to be what it is, till it comes to be what it desires to be; still being a river till it be turned into sea and vastnesse, even the immensitie of a blessed Eternity.

Although the consideration of the Divine excellencies and mercies be infinitely sufficient to produce in us love to God (who is invisible and yet not distant from us, but we feel him in his blessings, he dwells in our hearts by faith, we feed on him in the Sacrament, and are made all one with him in the incarnation and glorifications of Jesus) yet that we may the better enkindle and encrease our love to God, the following advices are not uselesse.

Helps to encrease our love to God; by way of exercise.

1. Cut off all earthly and sensual loves, for they pollute and unhallow the pure and Spiritual love. Every degree of inordinate affection to the things of this world, and every act of love to a sin is a perfec enemy to the love of God: and it is a great shame to take any part of ou affection from the eternal God to bestow it upon his creature in defiance of the Creator, or to give it to the Devil, our open enemy, in disparagement of him who is the fountain of all excellencies an Coelestial amities.

2. Lay fetters and restraints upon the imaginative and phantastick part: because our fancie being an imperfect and higher facultie is usually pleased with the entertainment of shadowes and gauds; and because the things of the world fill it with such beauties and phantastick imagery, the fancy presents such objects as amiable to the affections, and elective powers. Persons of fancy, such as are women and children have alwayes the most violent loves; but therefore if we be careful with what representments we fill our fancy, we may the sooner rectifie our loves. To this purpose, it is good that we transplant the instruments of fancy into religion: and for this reason musick was brought into Churches, and ornaments, and perfumes, and comely garments, and solemnities, and decent ceremonies, that the busie and lesse discerning fancy being bribed with its proper objects may be instrumental to a more coelestial and spiritual love.

3. Remove solicitude or worldly cares, and multitudes of secular businesses; for if these take up the intention and actual application of our thoughts and our imployments, they will also possesse our passions; which if they be filled with one object though ignoble, cannot attend another though more excellent. We alwayes contract a friendship and relation with those with whom we converse: our very Countrey is dear to us for our being in it: and the Neighbours of the same Village, and those that buy and sell with us have seized upon some portions of our love, and therefore if we dwell in the affairs of the World, we shall also grow in love with them; and all our love, or all our hatred, all our hopes, or all our fears, which the eternal God would willingly secure to himself, and esteem amongst his treasures and precious things, shall be spent upon trifles and vanities.

4. Do not onely choose the things of God, but secure your inclinations and aptnesses for God and for Religion. For it will be a hard thing for a Man to do such a personal violence to his first desires, as to choose whatsoever he hath no minde to. A Man will many times satisfie the importunity and daily solicitations of his first longings: and therefore there is nothing can secure our loves to God, but stopping the natural Fountains, and making Religion to grow neer the first desires of the soul.

5. Converse with God by frequent prayer. In particular, desire that your desires may be right, and love to have your affections regular and holy: To which purpose make very frequent addresses to God by ejaculations and communions, and an assiduous daily devotion: Discover to him all your wants, complain to him of all your affronts, do as

Hezekiah did, lay your misfortunes and your ill news before him, *spread them before the Lord*, call to him for health, run to him for counsel, beg of him for pardon; and it is as natural to love him to whom we make such addresses, and of whom we have such dependancies, as it is for children to love their parents.

6. Consider the immensity and vastnesse of the Divine love to us, expressed in all the emanations of his providence. 1. *In his Creation.* 2. *In his conservation of us.* For it is not my Prince or my Patron, or my Friend that supports me, or relieves my needs, but God, who made the Corn that my friend sends me, who created the Grapes and supported him, who hath as many dependances, and as many natural necessities, and as perfect disabilities as my self. God indeed made him the instrument of his providence to me, as he hath made his own Land or his own Cattel to him: with this onely difference, that God by his ministration to me intends to do him a favour and a reward, which to natural instruments he does not. 3. *In giving his Son.* 4. *In forgiving our sins.* 5. *In adopting us to glory*: and ten thousand times ten thousand little accidents and instances happening in the doing every of these; and it is not possible but for so great love we should give love again, for *God* we should give *Man*, for felicity we should part with our misery. [u] Nay, so great is the love of the holy Jesus, God incarnate, that he would leave all his triumphant glories, and dye once more for Man, if it were necessary for procuring felicity to him.

In the use of these instruments love will grow in several knots and steps like the Sugar-canes of *India* according to a thousand varieties in the person loving, and it will be great or lesse in several persons, and in the same, according to his growth in Christianity: but in general discoursing there are but two states of love, and those are *Labour of love*, and the *zeal of love*: the first is duty, the second is perfection.

The two states of love to God.

1. The least love that is must be *obedient, pure, simple, and communicative*: that is, it must exclude all affection to sin, and all inordinate affection to the World; and must be expressive according to our power, in the instance of duty, and must be love for loves sake; and of this love Martyrdom is the highest instance; that is, a readinesse of minde rather to *suffer* any evil than *to do* any. Of this our blessed Saviour affirmed, *That no man had greater love than this*: that is, this is the highest

[u] Sic Jesus dixit S. Carpo apud Dionysium epist. ad. Demophilum.

oint of duty, the greatest love that God requires of Man. And yet he hat is the most imperfect must have this love also in preparation of ninde, and must differ from another in nothing, except in the degrees f promptnesse and alacrity. And in this sense, he that loves God truly though but with a beginning and tender love) yet he loves God with ll his heart, that is, with that degree of love which is the highest point f duty, and of Gods charge upon us; and he that loves God with all his eart, may yet increase *with the increase of God*, just as there are degrees f love to God among the Saints, and yet each of them love him with ll their powers and capacities.

2. But the greater state of love is the *zeal of love*, which runs out into xcrescencies, and suckers like a fruitful and pleasant tree, or bursting nto gums, and producing fruits, not of a monstrous, but of an xtraordinary and heroical greatnesse. Concerning which, these autions are to be observed.

Cautions and rules concerning zeal.

1. If zeal be in the beginnings of our spiritual birth, or be short, sudden and transient, or be a consequent of a mans natural temper, r come upon any cause, but after a long growth of a temperate and ell regulated love, it is to be suspected for passion, and forwardnesse, ather than the vertical point of love.

2. That zeal onely is good which in a fervent love hath temperate xpressions. For let the affection boyl as high as it can, yet if it boyl ver into irregular and strange actions, it will *have but few*, but *will need any excuses. Elijah* was zealous for the Lord of Hosts, and yet he was transported with it, that he could not receive answer from God, till y Musick he was recomposed and tamed: and *Moses* broke both the ables of the Law by being passionately zealous against them that rake the first.

3. Zeal must spend its greatest heat principally in those things that ncern our selves; but with great care and restraint in those that concern others.

4. Remember that zeal being an excrescence of Divine love, must in sense contradict any action of love: Love to God includes love to r Neighbour, and [w]therefore no pretence of zeal for Gods glory

[v] *Καλὸν δὲ τὸ ζηλοῦσθαι ἐν τῷ καλῷ πάντοτε.* Gal. 4: 18.
[w] Phil. 3: 6.

12 excrescencies] excrescences *6 7*

must make us uncharitable to our brother, for that is just so pleasing to God, as hatred is an act of love.

5. That zeal that concernes others, can spend it self in nothing but arts, and actions and charitable instruments for their good: and when it concernes the good of many that one should suffer, it must bee done by persons of a competent authority, and in great necessity, in seldom instances, according to the Law of God or Man; but never by private right, or for trifling accidents, or in mistaken propositions. The Zealots in the Old Law had authority to transfix and stab some certain persons; but GOD gave them warrant; it was in the case of Idolatry, or such notorious huge crimes; the danger of which was insuportable and the cognizance of which was infallible: And yet that warrant expired with the Synagogue.

6. Zeal in the instances of our own duty, and personal deportment is more safe than in matters of counsel, and actions besides our just duty and tending towards perfection. Though in these instances there is not a direct sin, even where the zeal is lesse wary, yet there is much trouble and some danger: (as, if it be spent in the too forward vowes of Chastity, and restraints of natural and innocent liberties.)

7. Zeal may be let loose in the instances of internal, personal, and spiritual actions, that are matters of direct duty: as in prayers, and acts of adoration, and thanksgiving, and frequent addresses: provided that no indirect act passe upon them to defile them; such as complacency and opinions of sanctity, censuring others, scruples and opinions of necessity, unnecessary fears, superstitious numberings of times and houres; but let the zeal be as forward as it will, as devout as it will, as Seraphicall as it will, in the direct addresse and entercourse with God there is no danger, no transgression. [x]Do all the parts of your duty as earnestly as if the salvation of all the world, and the whole glory of God, and the confusion of all Devils, and all that you hope or desire did depend upon every one action.

8. [y]Let zeal be seated in the will and choice, and regulated with prudence and a sober understanding, not in the fancies and affections: for *these* will make it full of noise and empty of profit, but *that* will make it deep and smooth, material and devout.

The summe is this: That, zeal is not a direct duty, no where

[x] Lavora, come tu avessi a campar ognora:
Adora, come tu avessi a morir allora.

[y] Rom. 10: 2.

note *x* ognora] *cor*, ogni hora *1+*

commanded for it self, and is nothing but a forwardnesse and circumstance of another duty, [z]and therfore is then onely acceptable when it advances the love of God and our Neighbours, whose circumstance it is: That zeal is onely safe, onely acceptable which increases charity directly; and because love to our Neighbour, and obedience to God are the two great portions of charity, we must never account our zeal to be good, but as it advances both these, if it be in a matter that relates to both; or severally, if it relates severally. S. *Pauls* zeal was expressed in preaching without any offerings or stipend, in travelling, in spending and being spent for his flock, in suffering, in being willing to be accursed for love of the people of God, and his Countreymen: Let our zeal be as great as his was, so it be in affections to others, but not at all in angers against them: In the first then is no danger; in the second there is no safety. In brief; let your zeal (if it must be expressed in anger) [a]be alwayes more severe against thy self, than against others.

The other part of Love to God is Love to our Neighbour, for which I have reserved the Paragraph of Alms.

Of the external actions of Religion.

Religion teaches us to present to God our bodies as well as our souls; for God is the Lord of both; and if the body serves the soul in actions natural and civil, and intellectual, it must not be eased in the onely offices of Religion, unlesse the body shall expect no portion of the rewards of Religion, such as are resurrection, reunion, and glorification. [b] *Our bodies* are to God *a living sacrifice*, and to *present them to God is holy and acceptable.*

The actions of the body as it serves to religion, and as it is distinguished from Sobriety and Justice; either relate to the word of God, or to prayer, or to repentance, and make these kindes of external actions of religion. 1. Reading and hearing the word of God. 2. Fasting and corporal austerities, called by S. *Paul*, *bodily exercise.* 3. Feasting or keeping dayes of publick joy and thanksgiving.

[z] Titus 2: 14. Revel. 3: 19. [a] 2 Cor. 7: 11. [b] Rom. 12:1.

note *z* Revel. 3: 19] Rev. 3: 16 *4+*

Sect. IV.

Of Reading, or Hearing the Word of God.

Reading and Hearing the word of God are but the several circumstances of the same duty; instrumental especially to faith, but consequently to all other graces of the Spirit. It is all one to us whether by th eye or by the eare the Spirit conveyes his precepts to us. If we hear S *Paul* saying to us, that *Whoremongers and Adulterers God will judge*: or rea it in one of his Epistles; in either of them we are equally and sufficientl instructed. The Scriptures read are the same thing to us, which th same doctrine was, when it was preached by the Disciples of ou blessed Lord; and we are to learn of either with the same disposition There are many that cannot reade the word, and they must take it in b the ear; and they that can reade, finde the same word of God by th eye. It is necessary that all men learn it some way or other, and it is sufficient in order to their practise that they learn it any way. *The word God* is all those Commandments and Revelations, those promises an threatenings, the stories and sermons recorded in the Bible: nothin else is *the word of God*, that we know of, by any certain instrument. Th good books and spiritual discourses, the sermons or homilies writte or spoken by men are but *the word of men*, or rather explications of, an exhortations according to the *Word of God*: but of themselves they a not the *Word of God.* In a Sermon, the Text onely is in a proper sence be called *Gods Word*: and yet good Sermons are of great use and convenience for the advantages of Religion. He that preaches an ho together against drunkennesse with the tongue of men or Angels, ha spoke no other word of God but this, *Be not drunk with wine wherein the is excesse*: and he that writes that Sermon in a book, and publishes th book, hath preached to all that reade it, a louder Sermon than could l spoken in a Church. This I say to this purpose that we may separa truth from error, popular opinions from substantial Truths. For Go preaches to us in the Scripture, and by his secret assistances and spiritual thoughts and holy motions: Good men preach to us when they l popular arguments, and humane arts and complyances expound a presse any of those doctrines which God hath preached unto us in h holy Word. But

1. The Holy Ghost is certainly the best Preacher in the world, a the words of Scripture the best sermons.

2. All the doctrine of salvation is plainly set down there, that t

most unlearned person by hearing it read, may understand all his duty. What can be plainer spoken than this, *Thou shalt not kill. Be not drunk with wine: Husbands love your wives: whatsoever ye would that men should do to you, do ye so to them.* The wit of man cannot more plainly tell us our duty, or more fully, than the Holy Ghost hath done already.

3. Good sermons, and good books are of excellent use: but yet they can serve no other end but that we practise the plain doctrines of Scripture.

4. What *Abraham* in the parable said concerning the brethren of the rich man, is here very proper: [c] *They have Moses and the Prophets, let them hear them: But if they refuse to hear these, neither will they believe though one should arise from the dead* to preach unto them.

5. [d] Reading the holy Scriptures is a duty expressely commanded us, and is called in Scripture *Preaching*: all other preaching is the effect of humane skill and industry, and although of great benefit, yet it is but an Ecclesiastical ordinance; the Law of God concerning preaching, being expressed in the matter of reading the Scriptures, and hearing that word of God, *which is*, and *as it is* there described.

But this duty is reduced to practise in the following Rules.

Rules for hearing or reading the word of God.

1. Set apart some portion of thy time according to the opportunities of thy calling and necessary imployment, for the reading of holy Scripture; and if it be possible, every day reade or hear some of it read: you are sure that book teaches all truth, commands all holinesse, and promises all happinesse.

2. When it is in your power to choose, accustome your self to such portions which are most plain and certain duty, and which contain the story of the Life and Death of our blessed Saviour. Read the Gospels, the Psalms of *David*; and especially those portions of Scripture which by the wisdom of the Church are appointed to be publikely read upon Sundayes and holy-dayes, *viz.* the Epistles and Gospels. In the choice of any other portions, you may advise with a Spiritual Guide, that you may spend your time with most profit.

3. Fail not, diligently to attend to the reading of holy Scriptures upon those dayes wherein it is most publickly and solemnly read in

[c] Luke 16: 29, 31.
[d] Deut. 31: 11. Luke 24: 45. Matth. 22: 29. Acts 15: 21. Revel. 1: 3. 2 Tim. 3: 16.

note *d* Deut. 31: 11] *cor*, Deut. 31: 13 *1*+

Churches: for at such times, besides the learning our duty, we obtain a blessing along with it, it becoming to us upon those dayes a part of the solemn Divine worship.

4. When the word of God is read or preached to you, be sure you be of a ready heart and minde, free from worldly cares and thoughts, diligent to hear, careful to mark, studious to remember, and desirous to practise all that is commanded, and to live according to it. Do not hear for any other end but to become better in your life, and to be instructed in every good work, and to increase in the love and service of God.

5. Beg of God by prayer that he would give you the spirit of obedience and profit, and that he would by his Spirit write the word in your heart, and that you describe it in your life. To which purpose serve your self of some affectionate ejaculations to that purpose, before and after this duty.

Concerning spiritual books and ordinary Sermons take in these advices also.

6. Let not a prejudice to any mans person hinder thee from receiving good by his doctrine, if it be according to godlinesse: but (if occasion offer it, or especially if duty present it to thee; that is, if it be preached in that assembly where thou art bound to be present) accept the word preached as a message from God, and the Minister as his Angel in that ministration.

7. Consider and remark the doctrine that is represented to thee in any discourse; and if the Preacher addes any accidental advantages, any thing to comply with thy weaknesse, or to put thy spirit into action, or holy resolution, remember it, and make use of it; but if the Preacher be a weak person, yet the text is the doctrine thou art to remember; that contains all thy duty, it is worth thy attendance to hear that spoken often, and renewed upon thy thoughts, and though thou beest a learned man, yet the same thing which thou knowest already, if spoken by another, may be made active by that application. I can better be comforted by my own considerations, if another hand applyes them than if I do it my self; because the word of God does not work as a natural agent, but as a divine instrument: it does not prevail by the force of deduction, and artificial discoursings onely, but chiefly by way of blessing in the ordinance, and in the ministery of an appointed person. At least obey the publick order, and reverence the constitution, and give good example of humility, charity and obedience.

2 a part] *3*+, apart *1 2*

8. When Scriptures are read, you are onely to enquire with diligence and modesty into the meaning of the Spirit: but if homilies or sermons be made upon the words of Scripture, you are to consider, whether all that be spoken be conformable to the Scriptures. For although you may practise for humane reasons, and humane arguments, ministered from the Preachers art, yet you must practise nothing but the command of God, nothing but the Doctrine of Scripture, that is, the text.

9. Use the advice of some spirituall or other prudent man for the choice of such spiritual books which may be of use and benefit for the edification of thy spirit in the wayes of holy living; and esteem that time well accounted for, that is prudently and affectionately imployed, in hearing or reading good books and pious discourses: ever remembering that God by hearing us speak to him in prayer, obliges us to hear him speak to us in his word, by what instrument soever it be conveyed.

SECT. V.
Of Fasting.

Fasting, if it be considered in it self without relation to Spiritual ends, is a duty no where enjoyned, or counselled. But Christianity hath to do with it, as it may be made an instrument of the Spirit by subduing the lusts of the flesh, or removing any hindrances of religion; And it hath been practised by all ages of the Church, and advised in order to three ministeries. 1. To Prayer. 2. To Mortification of bodily lusts. 3. To Repentance: and is to be practised according to the following measures.

Rules for Christian Fasting.

1. Fasting in order to prayer is to be measured by the proportions of the times of prayer: that is, it ought to be a total fast from all things during the solemnity (unlesse a probable necessity intervene.) Thus the Jews eate nothing upon the Sabbath-dayes till their great offices were performed, that is, about the sixth hour: and S. *Peter* used it as an argument, that the Apostles in Pentecost were not drunk, because it was but the third hour of the day, of such a day, in which it was not lawful to eat or drink til the sixth hour: and the Jews were offended at

24 is] it is *7 8* 30 eate] ate *7*, are *8*

the Disciples for plucking the ears of corn upon the Sabbath early in the morning, because it was before the time in which by their customs they esteemed it lawful to break their fast. In imitation of this custom, and in prosecution of the reason of it, the Christian Church hath religiously observed fasting before the Holy Communion: and the more devout persons (though without any obligation at all) refused to eat or drink till they had finished their morning devotions: and further yet upon dayes of publick humiliation, which are designed to be spent wholly in Devotion, and for the averting Gods judgements (if they were imminent) fasting is commanded together with prayer, commanded (I say) by the Church to this end, that the Spirit might be clearer and more Angelical when it is quitted in some proportions from the loads of flesh.

2. Fasting, when it is *in order to Prayer*, must be a total abstinence from all meat, or else an abatement of the quantity: for the help which fasting does to prayer cannot be served by changing flesh into fish, or milk-meats into dry diet, but by turning much into little, or little into none at all during the time of solemn and extraordinary prayer.

3. Fasting *as it is instrumental to Prayer*, must be attended with other aids of the like vertue and efficacy, such as are, removing for the time all worldly cares and secular businesses; and therefore our blessed Saviour enfolds these parts within the same caution. *Take heed lest your hearts be overcharged with surfetting and drunkennesse and the cares of this world, and that day overtake you unawares.* To which adde *alms*; [e]for upon the wings of fasting and alms, holy prayer infallibly mounts up to Heaven.

4. When *Fasting is intended to serve the duty of Repentance*, it is then best chosen when it is short, sharp and afflictive; that is, *either a total abstinence* from all nourishment (according as we shall appoint, or be appointed) during such a time as is separate for the solemnity and attendance upon the imployment: or if we shall extend our severity beyond the solemn dayes, and keep our anger against our sin, as we are to keep our sorrow, that is, alwayes in a readinesse, and often to be called upon; *then, to refuse a pleasant morsel*, to abstaine from the bread of our desires, and onely to take wholsome and lesse pleasing nourishment, vexing our appetite by the refusing a lawful satisfaction, since in its petulancie and luxurie it preyed upon an unlawfull.

5. *Fasting designed for repentance* must be ever joyned with an extream

[e] Jejunium sine eleemosyna lampas sine aleo. S. August.

care that we fast from sin: for there is no greater folly or undecency in the world, than to commit that for which I am now judging and condemning my self. This is the best fast: and the other may serve to promote the interest of this, by increasing the disaffection to it, and multiplying arguments against it.

6. He that *fasts for repentance*, must, during that solemnity, abstain from all bodily delghts, and the sensuality of all his senses, and his appetites; for a man must not when he mourns in his fast be merry in his sport; weep at dinner, and laugh all day after; have a silence in his kitchen, and musick in his chamber; judge the stomack, and feast the other senses. I deny not but a man may in a single instance punish a particular sin with a proper instrument: If a man have offended in his palate, he may choose to fast onely; if he have sinned in softnesse and in his touch, he may choose to lye hard, or work hard, and use sharp inflictions: but although this Discipline be proper and particular, yet because the sorrow is of the whole man, no sense must rejoyce, or be with any study or purpose feasted and entertained softly. This rule is intended to relate to the solemn dayes appointed for repentance publickly or privately: besides which in the whole course of our life, even in the midst of our most festival and freer joyes we may sprinkle some single instances, and acts of self condemning, or punishing: as to refuse a pleasant morsel, or a delicious draught with a tacit remembrance of the sin that now returns to displease my spirit: and though these actions be single, there is no undecency in them, because a man may abate of his ordinary liberty and bold freedom with great prudence, so he does it without singularity in himself, or trouble to others: but he may not abate of his solemn sorrow: *that* may be *caution*; but *this* would be softnesse, effoeminacy and undecency.

7. When *fasting is an act of mortification*, that is, is intended to subdue a bodily lust; as the spirit of fornication, or the fondness of strong and impatient appetites, it must not be a sudden, sharp, and violent fast, but *a state of fasting*, a dyet of fasting, a daily lessening our portion of meat and drink, [f]and a choosing such a course dyet which may make the least preparation for the lusts of the body. He that fasts 3 dayes without food, will weaken other parts more than the ministers of fornication: and when the meals return as usually, they also will be served assoon as any. In the mean time they will be supplyed and made active by the accidental heat that comes with such violent fastings: for this is

[f] Digiuna assai chi mal mangia.

a kinde of aerial Devil; the Prince that rules in the air is the Devil of fornication; [g]and he will be as tempting with the windinesse of a violent fast, as with the flesh of an ordinary meal. But a daily substraction of the nourishment will introduce a lesse busy habit of body, and that will prove the more effectual remedy.

8. Fasting alone will not cure this Devil, though it helps much towards it; but it must not therefore be neglected, but assisted by all the proper instruments of remedy against this unclean spirit; and what it is unable to do alone, in company with other instruments, and Gods blessing upon them it may effect.

9. All fasting for whatsoever end it be undertaken, must be done without any opinion of the necessity of the thing it self, without censuring others, with all humility, in order to the proper end; and just as a man takes physick of which no man hath reason to be proud, and no man thinks it necessary, but because he is in sicknesse, or in danger and disposition to it.

10. All fasts ordained by lawful authority are to be observed in order to the same purposes to which they are enjoyned; and to be accompanied with actions of the same nature, just as it is in private fasts; for there is no other difference, but that in publick our Superiours choose for us, what in private we do for our selves.

11. Fasts ordained by lawful authority are not to be neglected because alone they cannot do the thing in order to which they were enjoyned. It may be one day of Humiliation will not obtain the blessing, or alone kill the lust, yet it must not be despised, if it can do any thing towards it. An act of Fasting is an act of self-denial, and though it do not produce the habit, yet it is a good act.

12. When the principal end why a Fast is publickly prescribed, is obtained by some other instrument in a particular person; as if the spirit of Fornication be cured by the rite of Marriage, or by a gift of chastity, yet that person so eased, is not freed from the Fasts of the Church by that alone, if those fasts can prudently serve any other end of Religion, as that of prayer, or repentance, or mortification of some other appetite: for when it is instrumental to any end of the Spirit, it is freed from superstition, and then we must have some other reason to quit us from the Obligation, or that alone will not do it.

13. When the Fast publickly commanded by reason of some indis-

[g] Chi digiuna, et altro ben non fa,
Sparagna il pan, et al inferno va.
See Chap. 2. Sect. 2 and 3.

position in the particular person cannot operate to the end of the Commandment, yet the avoiding offence, and the complying with publick order is reason enough to make the obedience to be necessary. For he that is otherwise disobliged (as when the reason of the Law ceases, as to his particular, yet) remains still obliged if he cannot do otherwise without scandal: but this is an obligation of charity, not of justice.

14. All fasting is to be used with prudence and charity: for there is no end to which fasting serves, but may be obtained by other instruments, and therefore it must at no hand be made an instrument of scruple, or become an enemy to our health, or be imposed upon persons that are sick or aged, or to whom it is in any sense uncharitable; such as are wearied Travellers; or to whom in the whole kinde of it, it is uselesse, such as are Women with childe, poor people, and little children. But in these cases the Church hath made provision, and inserted caution into her Laws, and they are to be reduced to practise according to custome, and the sentence of prudent persons, with great latitude, and without nicenesse and curiosity: [h]having this in our first care, that we secure our vertue, and next that we secure our health, that we may the better exercise the labours of vertue, lest out of too much austerity we bring our selves to that condition, that it be necessary to be indulgent to softnesse, ease and extream tendernesse.

15. Let not intemperance be the Prologue or the Epilogue to your fast, lest the fast be so far from taking off any thing of the sin, that it bee an occasion to increase it; and therefore when the fast is done, [i]be careful that no supervening act of gluttony, or excessive drinking unhallow the religion of the passed day; but eat temperately according to the proportion of other meals, lest gluttony keep either of the gates to abstinence.

The benefits of Fasting.

He that undertakes to enumerate the benefits of fasting, may in the next page also reckon all the benefits of physick: for fasting is not to be commended as a duty, but as an instrument; and in that sense, no Man can reprove it, or undervalue it; but he that knows neither spiritual arts, nor spiritual necessities: but by the Doctors of the Church it is

[h] S. Basil. Monast. Constit. cap. 4. Cassiani coll. 21. c. 22. Ne per causam necessitatis eo impingamus, ut voluptatibus serviamus.

[i] Ἀμυνόμενοι τὴν ἡμέραν. Naz.

note *h* cap. 4] *cor*, cap. 5 *1*+

called, the nourishment of prayer, the restraint of lust, the wings of the soul, the diet of Angels, the instrument of humility, and self-denial, the purification of the Spirit: and that palenesse and maigrenesse of visage which is consequent to the daily fast of great mortifiers, is by Saint *Basil* said to be the mark in the Forehead which the Angel observed, when he signed the Saints in the forehead to escape the wrath of God. [j] *The soul that is greatly vexed, which goeth stooping and feeble, and the eyes that fail, and the hungry soul shall give thee praise and righteousnesse, O Lord.*

SECT. VI.

Of Keeping Festivals and dayes holy to the Lord: particularly, the Lords day.

True naturall Religion, that which was common to all Nations and Ages did principally relye upon four great propositions. 1. That there is one God. 2. That God is nothing of those things which wee see. 3. That God takes care of all things below and governs all the World. 4. That hee is the Great Creator of all things without himself: and according to these were framed the four first precepts of the Decalogue. In the first, the Unity of the Godhead is expresly affirmed. In the second, his invisibility and immateriality. In the third is affirmed Gods government and providence, by avenging them that swear falsly by his Name, by which also his Omniscience is declared. In the fourth Commandement, hee proclaims himself the Maker of Heaven and Earth: for in memory of Gods rest from the work of six dayes the seventh was hallowed into a Sabbath: and the keeping it was a confessing GOD to bee the great Maker of Heaven and Earth; and consequently to this, it also was a confession of his goodnesse, his Omnipotence and his Wisdom, all which were written with a Sun beam in the great book of the Creature.

So long as the Law of the Sabbath was bound upon Gods people, so long GOD would have that to be the solemn manner of confessing these attributes; but when *the Priesthood being changed there was a change also of the Law*, the great duty remained unalterable in changed circumstances. We are eternally bound to confesse God Almighty to be the

[j] Baruch 2: 18.

---

3 that] the *4+*

Maker of Heaven and Earth; but the manner of confessing it, is changed from a rest or a doing nothing, to a speaking something, from a day to a symbol, from a ceremony to a substance, from a Jewish rite to a Christian duty: we professe it in our Creed, we confesse it in our lives, we describe it by every line of our life, by every action of duty, by faith, and trust, and obedience: and we do also upon great reason comply with the Jewish manner of confessing the Creation, so far as it is instrumental to a real duty. We keepe one day in seven, and so confesse the manner and circumstance of the Creation: and we rest also that we may tend holy duties: so imitating Gods rest better than the Jew in *Synesius* who lay upon his face from evening to evening, and could not by stripes or wounds be raised up to steer the ship in a great storm: Gods rest was not a natural cessation: hee who could not labour could not be said to rest; but Gods rest is to be understood to be a beholding and a rejoycing in his work finished: and therefore we truly represent Gods rest, when we confesse and rejoyce in Gods works and Gods glory.

This the Christian Church does upon every day, but especially upon the Lords day, which she hath set apart for this and all other Offices of Religion, being determined to this day, by the Resurrection of her dearest Lord, it being the first day of joy the Church ever had. And now, upon the Lords day we are not tyed to the rest of the Sabbath, but to all the work of the Sabbath: and we are to abstain from bodily labour, not because it is a direct duty to us as it was to the Jews, but because it is necessary in order to our duty, that we attend to the Offices of Religion.

The observation of the Lords day differs nothing from the observation of the Sabbath *in the matter of Religion*, but *in the manner.* They differ *in the ceremony and external rite.* Rest with them was the principal: with us it is the accessory. They differ *in the office or forms of worship*: For they were then to worship God as a Creator and a gentle Father: we are to adde to that, *Our Redeemer*, and all his other excellencies and mercies: and though we have more natural and proper reason to keep the Lords day than the Sabbath, yet the Jews had a Divine Commandement for their day, which we have not for ours: but we have many Commandements to do all that honour to GOD which was intended in the fourth Commandement: and the Apostles appointed the first day of the week, for doing it in solemne Assemblies; and the manner of worshipping God and doing him solemn honour and service upon this day we may best observe in the following measures.

Rules for keeping the Lords day and other Christian Festivals.

1. When you go about to distinguish Festival dayes from common, do it not by lessening the devotions of ordinary dayes, that the common devotion may seem bigger upon Festivals, but on every day keep your ordinary devotions intire, and enlarge upon the Holy day.

2. Upon *the Lords day* wee must abstaine from all servile and laborious workes, except such which are *matters of necessity, of common life, or of great charity*: for these are permitted by that authority which hath separated the day for holy uses. The Sabbath of the Jewes though consisting principally in rest, and established by God, did yeeld to these. The *labour of Love* and labours of Religion were not against the reason and the spirit of the Commandement, for which the Letter was decreed, and to which it ought to minister: And therefore much more is it so on the Lords day, where the Letter is wholly turned into Spirit, and there is no Commandement of God, but of spiritual and holy actions. The Priests might kill their beasts and dresse them for sacrifice; and Christ though born under the law, might heal a sick man, and the sick man might carry his bed to witnesse his recovery, and confesse the mercy, and leap and dance to God for joy: and an Ox might be led to water, and an Asse be haled out of a ditch, and a man may take physick, and he may eat meat, and therefore there were of necessity some to prepare and minister it: and the performing these labours did not consist in minutes, and just determined stages, but they had, even then, a reasonable latitude: so onely as to exclude unnecessary labour, or such as did not minister to charity or religion. And therefore this is to be enlarged in the Gospel, whose Sabbath or rest is but a circumstance, and accessory to the principal and spiritual duties: Upon the Christian Sabbath, necessity is to be served first, then charity, and then religion; for this is to give place to charity *in great instances*; and the second to the first *in all*; and in all cases *God is to be worshipped in spirit and in truth.*

3. The Lords day being the remembrance of a great blessing, must be a day of joy, festivity, spiritual rejoycing and thanksgiving, and therefore it is a proper work of the day to let your devotions spend themselves in singing or reading Psalms, in recounting the great works of God, in remembering his mercies, in worshipping his excellencies, in celebrating his attributes, in admiring his person, in sending

23 determined] determining *6+*   34 day] duty *2 3*

portions of pleasant meat to them for whom nothing is provided, and in all the arts and instruments of advancing Gods glory, and the reputation of religion: in which it were a great decency that a memorial of the resurrection should be inserted, that the particular religion of the day be not swallowed up in the general: And of this we may the more easily serve our selves by rising seasonably in the morning to private devotion, and by retiring at the leisures and spaces of the day not imployed in publick offices.

4. Fail not to be present at the publick hours and places of prayer, entering early and cheerfully, attending reverently and devoutly, abiding patiently during the whole office, piously assisting at the prayers, and gladly also hearing the Sermon, and at no hand omitting to receive the Holy Communion when it is offered (unlesse some great reason excuse it) this being the great solemnity of thanksgiving, and a proper work of the day.

5. After the solemnities are past, and in the intervalls between the morning and evening devotion (as you shall finde opportunity) visit sick persons, reconcile differences, do offices of Neighbourhood, inquire into the needs of the poor, especially house-keepers, relieve them as they shall need, and as you are able: for then we truely rejoyce in God, when we make our neighbours, the poor members of Christ, rejoyce together with us.

6. Whatsoever you are to do your self as necessary, you are to take care that others also, who are under your charge, do in their station and manner. Let your servants be called to Church, and all your family that can be spared from necessary and great houshold ministeries: those that cannot, let them go by turns, and be supplyed otherwise as well as they may: and provide on these days especially that they be instructed in the articles of faith, and necessary parts of their duty.

7. Those who labour hard in the week, must be eased upon the Lords day; such ease being a great charity and alms: but at no hand must they be permitted to use any unlawful games, any thing forbidden by the laws, any thing that is scandalous, or any thing that is dangerous, and apt to mingle sin with it; no games prompting to wantonnesse, to drunkennesse, to quarrelling, to ridiculous and superstitious customs, but let their refreshments be innocent, and charitable, and of good report, and not exclusive of the duties of religion.

8. Beyond these bounds because neither God nor man hath passed any obligation upon us, we must preserve our *Christian liberty and not suffer our selves to be intangled with a yoke of bondage*: for even a good action

may become a snare to us, if we make it an occasion of scruple by a pretence of necessity, binding loads upon the conscience not with the bands of God, but of men, and of fancy, or of opinion, or of tyranny. Whatsoever is laid upon us by the hands of man, must be acted and accounted of by the measures of a man; but our best measure is this: He keeps the Lords day best that keeps it with most religion, and with most charity.

9. What the Church hath done in the article of the resurrection, she hath in some measure done in the other articles of the Nativity, of the Ascension, and of the Descent of the Holy Ghost at Pentecost: And so great blessings deserve an anniversary solemnity, since he is a very unthankful person that does not often record them in the whole year, and esteem them the ground of his hopes, the object of his faith, the comfort of his troubles, and the great effluxes of the divine mercy. greater than all the victories over our temporal enemies, for which all glad persons usually give thanks. And if with great reason the memory of the resurrection does return solemnly every week, it is but reason the other should return once a year. To which I adde, that the commemoration of the articles of our Creed in solemn dayes and offices is a very excellent instrument to convey and imprint the sense and memory of it upon the spirits of the most ignorant person. For as a picture may with more fancy convey a story to a man, than a plain narrative either in word or writing: so a real representment, and an office of remembrance, and a day to declare it, is far more impressive than a picture, or any other art of making and fixing imagery.

10. The memories of the Saints are precious to God, and therefore they ought also to be so to us; and such persons who served God by holy living, industrious preaching, and religious dying, ought to have their names preserved in honour, and God be glorified in them, and their holy doctrines and lives published and imitated; and we by so doing give testimony to the article of *the communion of Saints.* But in these cases as every Church is to be sparing in the number of dayes, so also should she be temperate in her injunctions, not imposing them but upon voluntary and unbusied persons, without snare or burden. But the Holy day is best kept by giving God thanks for the excellent persons, Apostles or Martyrs we then remember, and by imitating their lives: this all may do: and they that can also keep the solemnity, must do that too, when it is publickly enjoyned.

The mixt actions of religion are, 1. Prayer. 2. Alms. 3. Repentance. 4. Receiving the blessed Sacrament.

SECT. VII.
Of Prayer.

There is no greater argument in the world of our spiritual danger and unwillingness to religion than the backwardnesse which most men have alwayes, and all men have sometimes to say their prayers: so weary of their length, so glad when they are done, so witty to excuse and frustrate an opportunity: and yet all is nothing but a desiring of God to give us the greatest and the best things we can need, and which can make us happy: it is a work so easy, so honourable, and to so great purpose, that in all the instances of religion and providence (except onely the incarnation of his Son) God hath not given us a greater argument of his willingnesse to have us saved, and of our unwillingnesse to accept it, his goodnesse and our gracelessenesse, his infinite condescension, and our carelesseness and folly, than by rewarding so easy a duty with so great blessings.

Motives to prayer.

I cannot say any thing beyond this very consideration and its appendages to invite Christian people to pray often. But we may consider: That first it is a duty commanded by God and his holy Son: 2. It is an act of grace and highest honour that we dust and ashes are admitted to speak to the Eternal God, to run to him as to a Father, to lay open our wants, to complain of our burdens, to explicate our scruples, to beg remedy and ease, support and counsel, health and safety, deliverance and salvation: and 3. God hath invited us to it by many gracious promises of hearing us. 4. He hath appointed his most glorious Son to be the president of prayer, and to make continual intercession for us to the throne of grace. 5. He hath appointed an Angel to present the prayers of his servants: and 6. Christ unites them to his own, and sanctifies them, and makes them effective and prevalent: and 7. Hath put it into the hands of men to rescind or alter all the decrees of God which are of one kinde, (that is, conditional, and concerning our selves and our final estate, and many instances of our intermedial or temporal) by the power of prayers. 8. And the prayers of men have saved cities and kingdoms from ruine; prayer hath raised dead men to life, hath stopped the violence of fire, shut the mouths of wilde beasts, hath

26 president] Precedent *7 8* 29 effective] affective *6+*

altered the course of nature, caused rain in Egypt, and drowth in the sea, it made the Sun to go from West to East, and the Moon to stand still, and rocks and mountains to walk, and it cures diseases without physick, and makes physick to do the work of nature, and nature to do the work of grace, and grace to do the work of God; and it does miracles of accident and event: and yet prayer that does all this, is of it self nothing but an ascent of the minde to God, a desiring things fit to be desired, and an expression of this desire to God as we can, and as becomes us: And our unwillingnesse to pray, is nothing else but a not desiring what we ought passionately to long for; or if we do desire it, it is a choosing rather to misse our satisfaction and felicity, than to ask for it.

There is no more to be said in this affair, but that we reduce it to practise according to the following Rules.

[k] *Rules for the practise of Prayer.*

1. We must be careful that we never ask any thing of God that is sinful, or that directly ministers to sin: for that is to ask of God to dishonour himself, and to undoe us: we had need consider what we pray; for before it returns in blessing it must be joyned with Christs intercession, and presented to God: Let us principally ask of God power and assistances to do our duty, to glorifie God, to do good works; to live a good life, to dye in the fear and favour of God, and eternal life: these things God delights to give, and commands that we shall ask, and we may with confidence expect to be answered graciously; for these things are promised without any reservation of a secret condition: if we ask them, and do our duty towards the obtaining them, we are sure never to misse them.

2. We may lawfully pray to God for the gifts of the Spirit that minister to holy ends, such as are the gift of preaching, the spirit of prayer, good expression, a ready and unloosed tongue, good understanding, learning, opportunities to publish them, etc. with these onely restraints 1. That we cannot be so confident of the event of those prayers, as of the former. 2. That we must be curious to secure our intention in these desires, that we may not ask them to serve our own ends, but only for Gods glory, and then we shall have them, or a blessing for desiring

[k] When thou beginnest thy office, for the time lay aside all worldly cares, all thought of civill imployment, and for that time be as a man unconcerned in the world.

---

15 [k]] *GH, om 1+*

Chap. 4. *Of Prayer.* Sect. 7. 283

God, a deſiring things fit to be deſired, and an expreſſion of this deſire to God as we can, and as becomes us: And our unwillingneſſe to pray, is nothing elſe but a not deſiring what we ought paſſionately to long for; or if we do deſire it, it is a chooſing rather to miſſe our ſatisfaction and felicity, then to aſk for it.

There is no more to be ſaid in this affair, but that we reduce it to practiſe according to the following Rules.

Rules for the practiſe of Prayer.

1. We muſt be careful that we never aſk any thing of God that is ſinful, or that directly miniſters to ſin: for that is to aſk of God to diſhonour himſelf, and to undoe us: we had need conſider what we pray; for before it returns in bleſſing it muſt be joyn'd with Chriſts interceſſion, and preſented to God: Let us principally aſk of God power and aſſiſtances to do our duty, to glorifie God, to do good works, to live a good life, to dye in the fear and favour of God, and eternal life: theſe things God delights to give, and commands that we ſhall aſk, and we may with confidence expect to be anſwered graciouſly; for theſe things are promiſed without any reſervation of a ſecret condition: if we aſk them, and do our duty towards the obtaining them, we are ſure never to miſſe them.

When thou beginnest thy offices, for the time lay aside all worldly cares, all thoughts of civil imployment and for that time be as a man unconcerned in the world.

2. We may lawfully pray to God for the gifts of the Spirit that miniſter to holy ends, ſuch as are the gift of preaching, the ſpirit of prayer, good expreſſion, a ready and unlooſed tongue, good underſtanding, learning, opportunities to publiſh them, &c. with theſe onely reſtraints. 1. That we cannot be ſo confident

of

9. Taylor's autograph additions in the Wyat presentation copy of the first edition, 1650, p. 283.

them: In order to such purposes our intentions in the first desires cannot be amisse; because they are able to sanctifie other things, and therefore cannot be unhallowed themselves. 3. We must submit to Gods will, desiring him to choose our employment, and to furnish out our persons as he shall see expedient.

3. Whatsoever we may lawfully desire of temporall things, wee may lawfully ask of God in prayer, and we may expect them as they are promised. 1. Whatsoever is necessary to our life and being is promised to us; and therefore we may with certainty expect food and raiment; food to keep us alive; clothing to keepe us from nakednesse and shame; so long as our life is permitted to us, so long all things necessary to our life shall be ministered: we may be secure of maintenance, but not secure of our life, for that is promised, not this: onely concerning food and raiment we are not to make accounts by the measure of our desires, but by the measure of our needs. 2. Whatsoever is convenient for us, pleasant, and modestly delectable, we may pray for; so we do it 1. with submission to Gods will. 2. Without impatient desires. 3. That it be not a trifle and inconsiderable, but a matter so grave and concerning, as to be a fit matter to be treated on between God and our souls. 4. That we ask it not to spend upon our lusts, but for ends of justice, or charity, or religion, and that they be imployed with sobriety.

4. [l]He that would pray with effect must live with care and piety. For although God gives to sinners and evil persons the common blessings of life and chance, yet either they want the comfort and blessing of those blessings, or they become occasions of sadder accidents to them, or serve to upbraid them in their ingratitude or irreligion: and in all cases, they are not the effects of prayer, or the fruits of promise, or instances of a fathers love; for they cannot be expected with confidence, or received without danger, or used without a curse and mischief in their company. But as all sin is an impediment to prayer, so some have a special indisposition towards acceptation; such are uncharitablenesse and wrath, Hypocrisie in the present action, Pride and Lust: because these by defiling the body or the spirit, or by contradicting some necessary ingredient in prayer (such as are Mercy, Humility, Purity, and Sincerity) do defile the prayer and make it a direct sin in the circumstances or formality of the action.

5. All prayer must be made with Faith and Hope: that is, [m]we mu

[l] 1 John 3: 21. John 9: 31. Isa. 1: 15 and 48: 7. Mal. 3: 10. 1 Tim. 2: 8. Psal. 34: 16 and 66:
[m] Mark 11: 24. James 1: 5, 6, 7.

4 out] *om 4+*   note *m* James 1: 5, 6, 7] *7 8*, James 5, 6, 7 *1 2 3 4 5*, James 1. 6, 7

certainly believe wee shall receive the grace which GOD *hath commanded us to ask*: and wee must *hope* for such things which hee hath *permitted us to ask*; and our Hope shall not bee vain, though wee misse what is not absolutely promised, because we shall at least have an equal blessing in the denial, as in the grant. And therefore the former conditions must first be secured, that is, that we ask things necessary, or at least good and innocent and profitable; and that our persons be gracious in the eyes of God; or else what God hath promised to our natural needs, he may in many degrees deny to our personal incapacity; but the thing being secured, and the person disposed, there can be no fault at all: for whatsoever else remains is on Gods part, and that cannot possibly fail. But because the things which are not commanded cannot possibly be secured (for we are not sure they are good in all circumstances) we can but hope for such things, even after we have secured our good intentions. Wee are sure of a blessing, but in what instance we are not yet assured.

6. Our prayers must be fervent, intense, earnest and importunate when we pray for things of high concernment and necessity. [n] *Continuing instant in prayer: striving in prayer: labouring fervently in prayer: night and day praying exceedingly: praying alwayes with all prayer*, so S. *Paul* calls it: [o] *watching unto prayer*, so Saint *Peter*: [p] *praying earnestly*, so S. *James*: and this is not at all to be abated in matters spiritual and of duty: for according as our desires are, so are our prayers; and as our prayers are, so shall be the grace; and as that is, so shall be the measure of glory. But this admits of degrees according to the perfection or imperfection of our state of life: but it hath no other measures, but ought to be as great as it can; the bigger the better; we must make no positive restraints upon it our selves. In other things we are to use a bridle: and as we must limit our desires with submission to Gods will: so also we must limit the importunity of our prayers by the moderation and term of our desires. Pray for it as earnestly as you may desire it.

7. Our desires must be lasting, and our prayers frequent, assiduous, and continual: not asking for a blessing once and then leaving it; but daily renewing our suits, and exercising our hope, and faith and patience, and long-suffering, and Religion, and resignation, and self-denyal in all the degrees we shall be put to. This circumstance of duty

[n] Rom. 12: 12 and 15: 30. Col. 4: 12; 1 Thes. 3: 10. Ephes. 6: 18.
[o] 1 Pet. 4: 7.
[p] James 5: 16.

28 it] *om 7 8*

our blessed Saviour taught, saying, [q] *That men ought alwayes to pray and not to faint. Alwayes to pray* signifies the frequent doing of the duty in general: but because we cannot alwayes ask several things, and we also have frequent need of the same things, and those are such as concern our great interest, the precept comes home to this very circumstance; and S. *Paul* cals it, [r] *praying without ceasing* and himself in his own case gave a precedent: *For this cause I besought the Lord thrice*, and so did our blessed Lord, *he went thrice* to God on the same errand, with the same words in a short space, about half a night; for his time to sollicite his suit was but short: and the *Philippians* were remembered by the Apostle, their spiritual Father [s] *alwayes in every prayer of his.* And thus we must alwayes pray for the pardon of our sins, for the assistance of Gods grace, for charity, for life eternal, never giving over till we dye: and thus also we pray for supply of great temporal needs in their several proportions: in all cases being curious we do not give over out of wearinesse, or impatience: For God oftentimes defers to grant our suit, because he loves to hear us beg it, and hath a design to give us more than we ask, even a satisfaction of our desires, and a blessing for the very importunity.

8. Let the words of our prayers be pertinent, grave, material, not studiously many, but according to our need, sufficient to expresse our wants, and to signifie our importunity. God hears us not the sooner for our many words, but much the sooner for an earnest desire, to which, let apt and sufficient words minister, be they few, or many, according as it happens. A long prayer and a short, differ not in their capacities of being accepted; for both of them take their value according to the fervency of spirit, and the charity of the prayer. That prayer which is short by reason of an impatient spirit, or dulnesse, or despite of holy things, or indifferency of desires, is very often criminall, alwayes imperfect: and that prayer which is long out of ostentation, or superstition, or a trifling spirit, is as criminal and imperfect as the other in their several instances. This rule relates to private prayer. In publick our devotion is to be measured by the appointed office, and we are to support our spirit with spiritual arts, that our private spirit may be a part of the publick spirit, and be adopted into the society and blessings of the communion of Saints.

9. In all formes of prayer mingle petition with thanksgiving, that you may endear the present prayer, and the future blessing by returning

[q] Luke 18: 1; 21: 36. [r] 1 Thes. 5: 17. [s] Phil. 1: 4.

praise and thanks for what we have already received. This is Saint *Pauls* advice, [t] *Be careful for nothing, but in every thing by prayer and supplication with thanksgiving let your requests be made known unto God.*

10. Whatever we beg of God, let us also work for it; if the thing be matter of duty, or a consequent to industry. For God loves to blesse labour and to reward it, [u] but not to support idlenesse. And therefore our blessed Saviour in his Sermons joyns watchfulness with prayer: for Gods graces are but assistances, not new creations of the whole habit in every instant, or period of our life. Reade Scriptures, and then pray to GOD for understanding: Pray against temptation, but you must also *resist the Devil*, and then *hee will flee from you.* Ask of GOD competency of living, but you must also *work with your hands, the things that are honest, that ye may have to supply in time of need*: We can but do our endeavour, and pray for blessing, and then leave the successe with GOD: and beyond this we cannot deliberate, we cannot take care; but so far we must.

11. To this purpose let every man studie his praiers, and read his dutie in his petitions. For the bodie of our prayers is the summe of our dutie; and as wee must ask of God whatsoever we need; so we must labour for all that we ask. Because it is our dutie, therefore wee must pray for Gods grace: but because Gods grace is necessarie, and without it we can do nothing, we are sufficiently taught, that in the proper matter of our religious praiers, is the just matter of our duty: and if wee shall turn our praiers into precepts, we shall the easier turn our hearty desires into effective practices.

12. [v] In all our prayers we must be carefull to attend our present work, having a present minde, not wandering upon impertinent things, not distant from our words, much lesse contrary to them: and if our thoughts do at any time wander, and divert upon other objects, bring them back again with prudent and severe arts; by all means striving to obtain a diligent, a sober, an untroubled and a composed spirit.

13. Let your posture and gesture of body in prayers bee reverent,

[t] Phil. 4: 6.

[u] *Εἶτα λέγομεν, κύριε ὁ θεός, πῶς μὴ ἀγωνιῶ; μωρέ, χεῖρας οὐκ ἔχεις; οὐκ ἐποίησέ σοι αὐτὰς ὁ θεός; εὔχου νῦν καθήμενος, ὅπως αἱ μυξαί σου μὴ ῥέωσιν· ἀπόμυξαι μᾶλλον.* Arrian. lib. 2. c. 16.

[v] Inter sacra et vota verbis etiam profanis abstinere mos. Tacit.

7–25 11. To this purpose . . . effective practices.] *4*+, *om 1 2 3*   note *t* Phil. 4: 6] +, Phil. 9: 6 *1 2 3 4 5*   note *u* 16] *cor*, 36 *1*+

grave, and humble; according to publike order, or the best examples, if it be in publick; if it be in private, either stand, or kneel, or lye flat upon the ground on your face, in your ordinary and more solemn prayers; but in extraordinary, casual, and ejaculatory prayers, the reverence and devotion of the soul, and the lifting up the eyes and hands to God with any other posture not undecent, is usual and commendable; for we may pray in bed, on horseback, [w] *every where, and at al times*, and in all circumstances: and it is well if we do so; and some servants have not opportunity to pray so often as they would, unlesse they supply the appetites of Religion by such accidental devotions.

14. [x] *Let prayers and supplications, and giving of thanks be made for all men for Kings and all that are in authority: for this is good and acceptable in the sigh of God our Saviour.* We who must love our Neighbours as our selves must also pray for them as for our selves: with this onely difference: that we may enlarge in our temporal desires for Kings, and pray for secular prosperity to them with more importunity than for our selves because they need more to enable their duty and government, and for the interests of Religion and Justice. This part of prayer is by the Apostle called *intercession* in which with special care we are to remember our Relatives, our Family, our Charge, our Benefactours, ou Creditours; not forgetting to beg pardon and charity for our Enemies and protection against them.

15. Relye not on a single prayer in matters of great concernment: bu make it as publick as you can by obtaining of others to pray for you this being the great blessing of the communion of Saints, that a praye united is strong like a well ordered Army; and God loves to be tyed fas with such cords of love, and constrained by a holy violence.

16. Every time that is not seized upon by some other duty, is seasonable enough for prayer; but let it be performed as a solemn duty morning and evening, that God may begin and end all our businesse, an *the out goings of the morning and evening may praise him*; for so we bless God, and God blesses us. And yet fail not to finde or make opportunities to worship God at some other times of the day; at least by ejaculations and short addresses: more or lesse, longer or shorter, solemnl or without solemnity, privately or publickly, as you can, or are permitted: alwayes remembering, that as every sin is a degree of danger an unsafety: so every pious prayer and well imployed opportunity is degree of return to hope and pardon.

[w] 1 Tim. 2: 8. [x] 1 Tim. 2: 1–3.

31 *out goings*] *outgoing 7 8* note *x* 1 Tim. 2: 1–3] *cor*, 1 Tim. 2. 2 *1*+

Cautions for making vowes.

A vow to God is an act of prayer, and a great degree and instance of opportunity, and an increase of duty by some new uncommanded instance, or some more eminent degree of duty, or frequency of action, or earnestnesse of spirit in the same. And because it hath pleased God in all Ages of the World to admit of entercourse with his servants in the matter of vows, it is not ill advice, that we make vows to God in such cases in which we have great need, or great danger. But let it be done according to these rules, and by these cautions.

1. That the matter of the vow be lawful. 2. That it be useful in order to Religion or charity. 3. That it be grave, not trifling and impertinent, but great in our proportion of duty towards the blessing. 4. That it be in an uncommanded instance, that is, that it be *of something*, or *in some manner*, or *in some degree* to which formerly wee were not obliged, or which wee might have omitted without sinne. 5. That it bee done with prudence, that is, that it be safe in all the circumstances of person, lest we beg a blessing and fall into a snare. 6. That every vow of a new action bee also accompanied with a new degree and enforcement of our essential and unalterable duty: such as was *Jacobs* vow; that (besides the payment of a tithe) *God should be his God*: that so hee might strengthen his duty to him first in essentials and precepts; and then in additionals and accidentals. For it is but an ill Tree that spends more in leaves and suckers and gummes, than in fruit: and that thankfulnesse and Religion is best, that first secures duty, and then enlarges in counsels. Therefore let every great prayer and great need, and great danger draw us nearer to GOD by the approach of a pious purpose to live more strictly, and let every mercy of GOD answering that prayer produce a real performance of it. 7. [y]Let not young beginners in Religion enlarge their hearts and streighten their liberty by vowes of long continuance: nor (indeed) any one else without a great experience of himself, and of all accidental dangers. Vowes of single actions are safest, and proportionable to those single blessings ever begged in such cases of sudden and transient importunities. 8. Let no action

[y] Angustum annulum non gesta, Dixit Pythagoras: id est, vitæ genus liberum sectare, nec vinculo temetipsum obstringe. Plutarch.

Sic Novatus novitios suos compulit ad jurandum, ne unquam ad catholicos episcopos redirent. Euseb. l. 6. Eccl. hist.

---

7 matter] matters *6+* 14 were not obliged] were not formerly obliged *4 5*
26 draw us nearer to GOD] *6+*, draw us to GOD, nearer *1 2 3 4 5* note *y* 6] *cor*, *2 1+*

which is matter of question and dispute in Religion, ever become the matter of a vow. He vowes foolishly that promises to God to live and dye in such an opinion, in an article not necessary, not certain; or that upon confidence of his present guide, bindes himself for ever to the profession of what he may afterwards more reasonably contradict, or may finde not to be useful, or not profitable; but of some danger, or of no necessity.

If we observe the former rules we shall pray piously and effectually; but because even this duty hath in it some especial temptations, it is necessary that we be armed by special remedies against them. The dangers are, 1. Wandering thoughts. 2. Tediousnesse of spirit. Against the first these advices are profitable.

Remedies against wandering thoughts in Prayer.

If we feel our spirits apt to wander in our prayers, and to retire into the World, or to things unprofitable, or vain and impertinent.

1. Use prayer to bee assisted in prayer: pray for the spirit of supplication, for a sober, fixed, and recollected spirit: and when to this you adde a moral industry to be steady in your thoughts, whatsoever wanderings after this do return irremediably, are a misery of Nature, and an imperfection, but no sinne while it is not cherished and indulged too.

2. In private it is not amisse to attempt the cure by reducing your prayers into Collects, and short forms of prayer, making voluntary interruptions and beginning again, that the want of spirit and breath may be supplied by the short stages and periods.

3. When you have observed any considerable wandering of your thoughts, binde your self to repeat that prayer again with actual attention, or else revolve the full sense of it in your spirit, and repeat it in all the effect and desires of it: and possibly the tempter may be driven away with his own art, and may cease to interpose his trifles, when hee perceives they doe but vex the person into carefulnesse, and piety: and yet hee loses nothing of his devotion, but doubles the earnestnesse of his care.

4. If this bee not seasonable, or opportune, or apt to any Mans circumstances, yet be sure with actual attention to say a hearty Amen to the whole prayer, with one united desire, earnestly begging the graces mentioned in the prayer: for that desire does the great work of the prayer

3 not certain; or] nor *4+*   21 too] to *4+*

6. It helps much to attention and actual advertisement in our prayers, if we say our prayers silently, without the voice, onely by the spirit. For in mental prayer, if our thoughts wander, we onely stand still; when our minde returns, we go on again, there is none of the prayer lost, as it is, if our mouths speak and our hearts wander.

actuall desires & the

7. To incite you to the use of these or any other counsels you shall meet with, remember that it is a great undecency to desire of God to hear those prayers, a great part whereof we do not hear our selves. If they be not worthy of our attention, they are far more unworthy of Gods.

Signes of tediousnesse of spirit in our prayers and all actions of religion.

The second temptation in our prayer is a tediousnesse of spirit, or a wearinesse of the imployment: like that of the Jews, who complained that they were weary of the new moons, and their souls loathed the frequent return of their Sabbaths: so do very many Christians, who first pray without fervour and earnestnesse of spirit: and secondly meditate but seldom, and that without fruit, or sence or affection: or thirdly who seldom examine their consciences, and when they do it, they do it but sleepily, slightly, without compunction, or hearty purpose, or fruits of amendment. 4. They enlarge themselves in the thoughts and fruition of temporal things, running for comfort to them onely in any sadnesse and misfortune. 5. They love not to frequent the Sacraments, nor any the instruments of religion, as sermons, confessions, prayers in publick, fastings,

10. Taylor's autograph corrections in the Wyat presentation copy of the first edition, 1650, p. 295.

and secures the blessing, if the wandering thoughts were against our will, and disclaimed by contending against them.

5. Avoid multiplicity of businesses of the World; and in those that are unavoidable, labour for an evennesse and tranquillity of spirit, that you may be untroubled and smooth in all tempests of fortune: for so we shall better tend Religion, when we are not torn in pieces with the cares of the World, and seized upon with low affections, passions and interest.

6. It helps much to attention and actual advertisement in our prayers, if we say our prayers silently, without the voice, onely by actuall desires and the spirit. For in mental prayer, if our thoughts wander, we onely stand still; when our minde returns, we go on again, there is none of the prayer lost, as it is, if our mouths speak and our hearts wander.

7. To incite you to the use of these or any other counsels you shall meet with, remember that it is a great undecency to desire of God to hear those prayers, a great part whereof we do not hear our selves. If they be not worthy of our attention, they are far more unworthy of Gods.

Signes of tediousnesse of spirit in our prayers and all actions of religion.

The second temptation in our prayer is a tediousnesse of spirit, or a wearinesse of the imployment: like that of the Jews, who complained that they were weary of the new moons, and their souls loathed the frequent return of their Sabbaths: so do very many Christians, who 1. first pray without fervour and earnestnesse of spirit: and 2. secondly meditate but seldom, and that without fruit, or sence or affection: or 3. thirdly who seldom examine their consciences, and when they do it, they do it but sleepily, slightly, without compunction, or hearty purpose, or fruits of amendment. 4. They enlarge themselves in the thoughts and fruition of temporal things, running for comfort to them onely in any sadnesse and misfortune. 5. They love not to frequent the Sacraments, nor any the instruments of religion, as sermons, confessions, prayers in publick, fastings, but love ease, and a loose undisciplined life. 6. They obey not their superiours, but follow their own judgement, when their judgement follows their affections, and their affections follow sence and worldly pleasures. 7. They neglect, or dissemble, or defer, or do not attend to the motions and inclinations to

10–11 by actuall desires and] *GH, om 1+*

vertue which the spirit of God puts into their soul. 8. They repent them of their vows and holy purposes, not because they discover any indiscretion in them, or intolerable inconvenience, but because they have within them labour, and (as the case now stands to them) displeasure. 9. They content themselves with the first degrees, and necessary parts of vertue, and when they are arrived thither, they sit down, as if they were come to the mountain of the Lord, and care not to proceed on toward perfection. 10. They enquire into all cases in which it may be lawful to omit a duty, and though they will not do lesse then they are bound to, yet they will do no more than needs must; for they do out of fear, and self love, not out of the love of God, or the spirit of holinesse and zeal. The event of which will be this. He that will do no more than needs must, will soon be brought to omit something of his duty, and will be apt to believe lesse to be necessary than is.

Remedies against tediousnesse of spirit.

The Remedies against this temptation are these.

1. Order your private devotions so, that they become not arguments and causes of tediousnesse by their indiscreet length; but reduce your words into a narrower compasse, still keeping all the matter, and what is cut off in the length of your prayers, supply in the earnestnesse of your spirit; for so nothing is lost while the words are changed into matter, and length of time into fervency of devotion. The forms are made not the lesse perfect, and the spirit is more, and the scruple is removed.

2. It is not imprudent if we provide variety of forms of Prayer to the same purposes; that the change by consulting with the appetites of fancy, may better entertain the Spirit: and possibly we may be pleased to recite a hymn, when a collect seems flat to us and unpleasant, and we are willing to sing rather than to say, or to sing this rather than that: we are certain that variety is delightful, and whether that be natural to us, or an imperfection, yet if it be complyed with, it may remove some part of the temptation.

3. Break your office and devotion into fragments, and make frequent returnings by ejaculations and abrupt entercourses with God; for so, no length can oppresse your tenderness and sicklinesse of spirit; and by often praying in such manner and in all circumstances, we shall habituate our souls to prayer, by making it the businesse of many lesser portions of our time: and by thrusting in between all our

4 and] *om* 4+

other imployments, it will make every thing relish of religion, and by degrees turn all into its nature.

4. Learn to abstract your thoughts and desires from pleasures and things of the world. For nothing is a direct cure to this evill, but cutting off all other loves and adherences. Order your affairs so, that religion may be propounded to you as a reward, and prayer as your defence, and holy actions as your security, and charity and good works as your treasure: Consider that all things else are satisfactions but to the brutish part of a man, and that these are the refreshments and relishes of that noble part of us by which we are better than beasts: and whatsoever other instrument, exercise or consideration is of use to take our loves from the world, the same is apt to place them upon God.

5. Do not seek for deliciousnesse and sensible consolations in the actions of religion, but onely regard the duty and the conscience of it. For although in the beginning of religion most frequently, and at some other times irregularly, God complyes with our infirmity, and encourages our duty with little overflowings of spiritual joy, and sensible pleasure, and delicacies in prayer, so as we seem to feel some little beam of Heaven and great refreshments from the spirit of consolation; yet this is not alwayes safe for us to have, neither safe for us to expect and look for: and when we do, it is apt to make us cool in our enquiries and waitings upon Christ when we want them: It is a running after him, not for the miracles, but for the loaves; not for the wonderful things of God, and the desires of pleasing him, but for the pleasures of pleasing our selves. And as we must not judge our devotion to be barren or unfruitful when we want the overflowings of joy running over: so neither must we cease for want of them; If our spirits can serve God choosingly and greedily out of pure conscience of our duty, it is better in it self, and more safe to us.

6. Let him use to soften his spirit with frequent meditation upon sad and dolorous objects, as of death, the terrours of the day of judgement; fearful judgements upon sinners, strange horrid accidents, fear of Gods wrath, the pains of Hell, the unspeakable amazements of the damned, the intolerable load of a sad Eternity. For whatsoever creates fear, or makes the spirit to dwell in a religious sadnesse, is apt to entender the spirit, and make it devout and plyant to any part of duty. For a great fear, when it is ill managed, is the parent of superstition; but a discreet and well guided fear produces religion.

38 well] will *2*

7. Pray often and you shall pray oftner, and when you are accustomed to a frequent devotion, it will so insensibly unite to your nature and affections, that it will become trouble to omit your usual or appointed prayers: and what you obtain at first by doing violence to your inclinations, at last will not be left without as great unwillingnesse as that by which at first it entered. This rule relyes not onely upon reason derived from the nature of habits, which turn into a second nature, and make their actions easy, frequent and delightful: but it relyes upon a reason depending upon the nature and constitution of grace, whose productions are of the same nature with the parent, and increases it self, naturally growing from granes to huge trees, from minutes to vast proportions, and from moments to Eternity. But be sure not to omit your usual prayers without great reason, though without sin it may be done; because after you have omitted something, in a little while you will be passed the scruple of that, and begin to be tempted to leave out more: keep your self up to your usual forms; you may enlarge when you will; but do not contract or lessen them without a very probable reason.

8. Let a man frequently and seriously by imagination place himself upon his death-bed, and consider what great joyes he shall have for the remembrance of every day well spent; and what then he would give that he had so spent all his dayes: He may guesse at it by proportions: for it is certain he shall have a joyful and prosperous night, who hath spent his day holily; and he resignes his soul with peace into the hands of God, who hath lived in the peace of God, and the works of religion in his life time. This consideration is of a real event, it is of a thing that will certainly come to passe. *It is appointed for all men once to die, and after death comes judgement*; the apprehension of which is dreadful, and the presence of it is intolerable, unlesse by religion and sanctity we are disposed for so venerable an appearance.

9. To this may be useful that we consider the [z]easinesse of Christs yoke, the excellences and sweetnesses that are in religion, the peace of conscience, the joy of the Holy Ghost, the rejoycing in God, the simplicity and pleasure of vertue, the intricacy, trouble and businesse of sin; the blessings and health and reward *of that*, the curses, the sicknesses and sad consequences *of this*; and that, if we are weary of the labours of religion, we must eternally sit still and do nothing: for

[z] See the Great Exemplar, Part 3. Disc. 14. of the easinesse of Christian Religion.

8 and] *2+*, & an *1*

whatsoever we do, contrary to it, is infinitely more full of labour, care, difficulty, and vexation.

10. Consider this also, that tediousnesse of spirit, is the beginning of the most dangerous condition and estate in the whole World. For it is a great disposition to the sinne against the Holy Ghost; it is apt to bring a Man to backsliding, and the state of unregeneration, to make him return to his vomit and his sink, and either to make the Man impatient, or his condition scrupulous, unsatisfied, irksome and desperate: and *it is better that he had never known the way of godlinesse, than after the knowledge of it, that he should fall away.* There is not in the World a greater signe that the spirit of Reprobation is beginning upon a Man, than when hee is habitually and constantly, or very frequently, weary, and slights, or loaths holy Offices.

11. The last remedy that preserves the hope of such a Man, and can reduce him to the state of zeal and the love of God, is a pungent, sad, and a heavy affliction; not desperate, but recreated with some intervals of kindenesse, and little comforts, or entertained with hopes of deliverance: which condition, if a Man shall fall into, by the grace of God he is likely to recover: but if this help him not, it is infinite oddes but he will *quench the Spirit.*

SECT. VIII.
Of Almes.

Love is as communicative as fire, as busie, and as active, and it hath four twin Daughters, extreme like each other; and but that the Doctors of the School have done as *Thamars* Midwife did, who bound a Scarlet threed, something to distinguish them, it would be very hard to call them asunder. Their names are: 1. *Mercy.* 2. *Beneficence*, or well-doing. 3. *Liberality.* And 4. *Almes*; which by a special priviledge hath obtained to be called after the Mothers name, and is commonly called, *Charity.* The first or eldest is seated in the affection, and it is that, which all the other must attend. For Mercy without Almes is acceptable, when the person is disabled to expresse outwardly, what he heartily desires. But Almes without Mercy, are like prayers without devotion, or Religion without Humility. 2. *Beneficence*, or well doing, is a promptnesse and noblenesse of minde, making us to do offices of

17 and] or *4+*

curtesie, and humanity to all sorts of persons in their need, or out of their need. 3. *Liberality* is a disposition of minde opposite to covetousnesse, and consists in the despite and neglect of money upon just occasions, and relates to our friends, children, kindred, servants and other relatives. 4. But *Almes* is a relieving the poor and needy. The first and the last onely are duties of Christianity. The second and third are circumstances and adjuncts of these duties: for *Liberality* increases the degree of Almes, making our gift greater; and *Beneficence* extends it to more persons and orders of Men, spreading it wider. The former makes us sometimes to give more than we are able; and the latter gives to more than need by the necessity of Beggars, and serves the needs and conveniencies of persons, and supplies circumstances: whereas properly, *Almes* are doles and largesses to the necessitous and calamitous people; supplying the necessities of Nature, and giving remedies to their miseries.

Mercy and Almes are the body and soul of that charity which we must pay to our Neighbours need: and it is a precept which God therefore enjoyned to the World, that the great inequality which he was pleased to suffer in the possessions and accidents of Men, might be reduced to some temper and evennesse; and the most miserable person might be reconciled to some sense and participation of felicity.

Works of mercy, or the several kindes of corporal Almes.

The workes of Mercy are so many as the affections of Mercy have objects, or as the World hath kindes of misery. Men want meat or drink, or clothes, or a house, or liberty, or attendance, or a grave. In proportion to these, seven works are usually assigned to Mercy; and there are seven kindes of corporal almes reckoned. 1. [a]To feed the hungry. 2. To give drink to the thirsty. 3. Or clothes to the naked. 4. To redeem Captives. 5. To visit the sick. 6. To entertain strangers. 7. [b]To bury the dead. But many more may be added. Such as are. 8. To give physick to sick persons. 9. To bring cold and starved people to warmth and to the fire: for sometimes clothing will not do it; or this may be done when we cannot do the other. 10. To lead the blinde in right wayes. 11. To lend money. 12. To forgive debts. 13. To remit forfeitures. 14. To mend high wayes and bridges. 15. To reduce or guide wandering travellers. 16. To ease their labours by accomodating their work with apt instruments; or their journey with beasts of

[a] Mat. 25: 35. [b] Matt. 26: 12. 2 Sam. 2: 5.

carriage. 17. To deliver the poor from their oppressors. 18. [c]To dye for my brother. 19. To pay maydens dowries, and to procure for them honest and chast marriages.

Works of spiritual Almes and mercy, are

1. To teach the ignorant. 2. To counsell doubting persons. 3. To admonish sinners *diligently, prudently, seasonably and charitably*: [d]To which also may be reduced, provoking and encouraging to good works. 4. To comfort the afflicted. 5. To pardon offenders. 6. [e]To suffer and support the weak. 7. To pray for all estates of men, and for relief to all their necessities. To which may be added. 8. To punish or correct refractorinesse. 9. To be gentle and charitable in censuring the actions of others. 10. To establish the scrupulous, wavering, and inconstant spirits. 11. To confirm the strong. 12. Not to give scandal. 13. To quit a man of his fear. 14. [f]To redeem maydens from prostitution and publication of their bodies.

To both these kindes, a third also may be added of a mixt nature, partly corporall, and partly spiritual: such are, 1. [g]Reconciling enemies. 2. Erecting publick Schools of Learning. 3. Maintaining Lectures of Divinity. 4. Erecting Colledges for Religion, and retirement from the noises and more frequent temptations of the World. 5. Finding imployment for unbusied persons, and putting children to honest Trades. For the particulars of Mercy or Almes cannot be narrower than Mens needs are: and the old method of Almes is too narrow to comprize them all; and yet the kindes are too many to be discoursed of particularly: onely our blessed Saviour in the precept of *Almes*, uses the instances of *relieving the poor*, and *forgivenesse of injuries*; and by proportion to these, the rest, whose duty is plain, simple, easie and necessary, may be determined. But Almes in general are to be disposed of according to the following Rules.

[c] Nobilis hæc esset pietatis rixa duobus;
Quod pro fratre mori vellet uterque prior. Mart.

[d] Hebr. 10: 24.

[e] 1 Thess. 5: 14.

[f] Puella, prosternes se ad pedes: Miserere virginitatis meæ, ne prostituas hoc corpus sub tam turpi titulo. Hist. Apoll. Tyr.

[g] Laudi ductum apud Vett.
Αἶψά τε καὶ μέγα νεῖκος ἐπισταμένως κατέπαυσε.

Rules for giving Almes.

1. [h]Let no Man do Almes of that which is none of his own; for of that he is to make restitution; that is due to the owners, not to the poor: for every Man hath need of his own, and that is first to be provided for; and then you must think of the needs of the poor. He that gives the poor what is not his own, makes himself a thief, and the poor to be the receivers. This is not to be understood, as if it were unlawful for a Man that is not able to pay his debts, to give smaller Almes to the poor. [i]He may not give such portions as can in any sence more disable him to do justice: but such, which if they were saved could not advance the other duty, may retire to this, and do here what they may, since in the other duty they cannot do what they should. But generally [j]Cheaters and Robbers cannot give almes of what they have cheated and robbed, unlesse they cannot tell the persons whom they have injured, or the proportions; and in such cases they are to give those unknown portions to the poor by way of restitution, for it is no almes: onely God is the supreme Lord to whom those escheats devolve, and the poor are his Receivers.

2. Of money unjustly taken and yet voluntarily parted with, we may and are bound to give almes: such as is money given and taken for false witnesse, bribes, simoniacal contracts, because the Receiver hath no right to keep it, nor the Giver any right to recall it, it is unjust money, and yet payable to none but to the supreme Lord (who is the person injured) and to his Delegates, that is, the poor. To which I insert these cautions. 1. If the person injured by the unjust sentence of a bribed Judge, or by false witnesse, be poor, he is the proper object and bosome to whom the restitution is to be made. 2. [k]In case of Simony, the Church, to whom the Simony was injurious, is the lap into which the restitution is to be powred, and if it be poor and out of repair, the almes or restitution (shall I call it) are to be paid to it.

3. There is some sort of gain that hath in it no injustice properly so called; but it is unlawful and *filthy lucre*: such as is money taken for worke done unlawfully upon the *Lords day*, hire taken for disfiguring ones self, and for being professed jesters, the wages of such as make

[h] S. Greg. 7. l. 106. Epist.
[i] Præbeant misericordia ut conservetur justitia. S. Aug.
[j] Prov. 3: 9.
[k] Decret. ep. tit. de Simonia.

note *h* 106 Epist.] *cor*, 110 Epist. *1*+

unjust bargains, and of harlots: of this money there is some preparation to be made before it be given in Almes. The money is infected with the plague, and must passe thorough the fire or the water befor it be fit for almes: the person must repent and leave the crime, an then minister to the poor.

4. He that gives almes must do it in mercy, that is, [l]out of a tru sence of the calamity of his brother, first feeling it in himself in som proportion, and then endeavouring to ease himself and the other o their common calamity. Against this rule they offend who give alme out of custome, or to upbraid the poverty of the other, or to make hin mercenary and obliged, or with any unhandsome circumstances.

5. He that gives almes must do it with a single eye and heart; that is without designes to get the praise of men: and if he secures that, h may either give them publickly, or privately: for Christ intended onl to provide against pride and hypocrisie, when he bade almes to b given in secret; it being otherwise one of his Commandments, *that ou light should shine before men*: this is more excellent, that is more safe.

6. To this also appertains, [m]that he who hath done a good turn should so forget it as not to speak of it: but he that boasts it or upbraid it, hath paid himself, and lost the noblenesse of the charity.

7. Give alms with a cheerful heart and countenance, [n]*not grudgin or of necessity, for God loveth a cheerful giver*; and therefore give quickl when the power is in thy hand, and the need is in thy Neighbor, an thy Neighbor at the door. He gives twice that relieves speedily.

8. [o]According to thy ability give to all men that need; and in equa needs give first to good men, rather than to bad men; and if the need be unequal, do so too; provided that the need of the poorest be n violent or extream: but if an evil man be in extream necessity, he is t be relieved rather than a good man who can tarry longer, and may subsist without it; and if he be a good man, he will desire it should be s because himself is bound to save the life of his brother with doin some inconvenience to himself: and no difference of vertue or vic can make the ease of one begger equal with the life of another.

9. Give no almes to vitious persons, if such almes will support the sin: as if they will continue in idlenes, [p]*if they will not work, neither l*

[l] Donum nudum est, nisi consensu vestiatur. l. 2. C. de Pactis.
[m] Qui dedit beneficium taceat: narret, qui accepit. Senec.
[n] 2 Cor. 9: 7.
[o] Luke 6: 30. Gal. 6: 10.
[p] 2 Thes. 3: 10. A cavallo che non porta sella, biada non si crivella.

24 the door] thy ~ *4*+ 32 to] of *2*, or *3* note *l* l. 2] *cor*, l. 3 *1*+

them eat, [q]or if they will spend it in drunkenness, or wantonness: such persons when they are reduced to very great want, must be relieved in such proportions, as may not relieve their dying lust, but may refresh their faint or dying bodies.

10. The best objects of charity are poor house keepers that labour hard, and are burdened with many children; or Gentlemen fallen into sad poverty, especially if by innocent misfortune (and if their crimes brought them into it, yet they are to be relieved according to the former rule) persecuted persons, widows, and fatherlesse children, putting them to honest trades or schools of learning: [r]and search into the needs of numerous and meaner families; for there are many persons that have nothing left them but misery and modesty: and towards such we must adde two circumstances of charity. 1. To enquire them out. 2. To convey our relief to them so as we do not make them ashamed.

11. Give, looking for nothing again, that is, without consideration of future advantages: give to children, to old men, to the unthankful, and the dying, and to those you shall never see again: for else your alms or curtesy is not charity, but traffick and merchandise: and be sure that you omit not to relieve the needs of your enemy and the injurious; for so possibly you may win him to your self; but do you intend the winning him to God.

12. Trust not your almes to intermedial, uncertain and under dispensers: by which rule is not onely intended the securing your almes in the right chanel; but the humility of your person, and that which the Apostle calls *the labour of love*: and if you converse in Hospitals, and Alms-houses, and minister with your own hands what your heart hath first decreed, you will finde your heart endeared and made familiar with the needs and with the persons of the poor, those excellent images of Christ.

13. [s]Whatsoever is superfluous in thy estate is to be dispensed in alms. *He that hath two coats must give to him that hath none*; that is, he that hath beyond his need must give that which is beyond it: Only among

[q] De Mendico male meretur qui ei dat quod edat aut quod bibat: Nam et illud quod dat perdit, et illi producit vitam ad miseriam. Trinum.

[r] Beatus qui intelligit super egenum et pauperem. Psal.
A donare e tenere ingegno bisogna havere.

[s] —Præmonstro tibi
Ut ita te aliorum miserescat, ne tui alios misereat. Trinum.

---

1 [q]] *4+*, *om 1 2 3* 14 to them] unto ~ *4+* 28 heart] *3 6+*, hearts *1 2 4 5*
31 [s]] *4+*, *om 1 2 3* note *s* tui] *cor*, tis *4+*

needs we are to reckon not onely what will support our life, but also what will maintain the decency of our estate and person; not onely in present needs, but in all future necessities, and very probable contingencies, but no further: we are not obliged beyond this, unlesse we see very great, publick and calamitous necessities: but yet, if we do extend beyond our measures, and give more than we are able, we have the *Philippians* and many holy persons for our precedent, we have S. *Paul* for our encouragement, we have Christ for our Counseller, we have God for our rewarder, and a great treasure in Heaven for our recompence and restitution. But I propound it to the consideration of all Christian people, that they be not nice and curious, fond and indulgent to themselves in taking accounts of their personal conveniences, and that they make their proportions moderate and easy, according to the order and manner of Christianity; and the consequent will be this, that the poor will more plentifully be relieved, themselves will be more able to do it, and the duty will be lesse chargeable, and the owners of estates charged with fewer accounts in the spending them. It cannot be denied, but in the expences of all liberal and great personages many things might be spared: some superfluous servants, some idle meetings, some unnecessary and imprudent feasts, some garments too costly, some unnecessary Law-suits, some vain journeyes: and when we are tempted to such needlesse expences, if we shall descend to moderation, and lay aside the surplusage, we shall finde it with more profit to be laid out upon the poor members of Christ, than upon our own with vanity. But this is onely intended to be an advice in the manner of doing almes: for I am not ignorant that great variety of clothes alwayes have been permitted to Princes and Nobility, and others in their proportion; and they usually give those clothes as rewards to servants, and other persons needful enough, and then they may serve their own fancy and their duty too: but it is but reason and religion to be careful, that they be given to such onely where duty, or prudent liberality, or almes determine them: but in no sence let them do it so as to minister to vanity, to luxury, to prodigality. The like also is to be observed in other instances. And if we once give our mindes to the study and arts of almes, we shall finde wayes enough to make this duty easy, profitable and useful.

1. He that playes at any game must resolve before hand to be indifferent to win or lose: but if he gives to the poor all that he wins, it is better than to keep it to himself: but it were better yet, that he lay by so

much as he is willing to lose, and let the game alone, and by giving so much almes, traffick for eternity. That is one way.

2. Another is, keeping the fasting dayes of the Church; which if our condition be such as to be able to cast our accounts, and make abatements for our wanting so many meals in the whole year, (which by the old appointment did amount to 153, and since most of them are fallen into desuetude, we may make up as many of them as we please by voluntary fasts) we may from hence finde a considerable reliefe for the poor. But if we be not willing sometimes to fast that our brother may eat, we should ill dye for him. S. *Martin* had given all that he had in the world to the poor, save one coat, and that also he divided between two beggers. A Father in the mount of *Nitria* was reduced at last to the Inventary of one Testament, and that book also was tempted from him by the needs of one whom he thought was poorer than himself. Greater yet. S. *Paulinus* sold himself to slavery to redeem a young man, for whose captivity his Mother wept sadly; and it is said that S. *Katherine* suckt the envenomed wounds of a villain who had injured her most impudently: And I shall tell you of a greater charity than all these put together: Christ gave himself to shame and death to redeem his enemies from bondage, and death, and Hell.

3. Learn of the frugal man, and onely avoid sordid actions and turn good husband and change your arts of getting into providence for the poor, and we shall soon become rich in good works; and why should we not do as much for charity, as for covetousnesse, for Heaven, as for the fading world, for God and the Holy Jesus, as for the needlesse superfluities of back and belly?

14. In giving almes to beggers and persons of that low ranck, it is better to give little to each that we may give to the more, so extending our alms to many persons: but in charities of religion, as building Hospitals, Colledges, and houses for devotion, and in supplying the accidental wants of decayed persons, fallen from great plenty to great necessity, it is better to unite our almes than to disperse them, to make a noble relief or maintenance to one, and to restore him to comfort, than to support only his natural needs, and keep him alive only, unrescued from sad discomforts.

15. The Precept of almes or charity bindes not indefinitely to all the instances and kindes of charity: for he that delights to feed the poor,

30 in] *om 7 8*

and spends all his proportion that way is not bound to enter into prisons and redeem captives: but we are obliged by the presence of circumstances, and the special disposition of providence, and the pityablenesse of an object, to this or that particular act of charity. The eye is the sence of mercy, and the bowels are its organ, and that enkindles pity, and pity produces almes: *when the eye sees what it never saw, the heart will think what it never thought*: but when we have an object present to our eye, then we must pity, for there the providence of God hath fitted our charity with circumstances. He that is in thy sight or in thy Neighbourhood is fallen into the lot of thy charity.

16. [t]If thou hast no money, yet thou must have mercy, and art bound to pity the poor, and pray for them, and throw thy holy desires and devotions into the treasure of the Church: and if thou doest what thou art able, be it little or great, corporal or spiritual, the charity of almes, or the charity of prayers, a cup of wine, or a cup of water, if it be but [u]*love to the brethren*, or a desire to help all, or any of Christs poor, it shall be [v]*accepted according to what a man hath, not according to what he hath not.* For *Love* is all this, and all the other Commandments: and it will expresse it self where it can, and where it cannot, yet it is *love* still, and it is also *sorrow* that it cannot.

Motives to Charity.

The motives to this duty are such as holy Scripture hath propounded to us by way of consideration and proposition of its excellencies, and consequent reward. 1. [w]There is no one duty which our blessed Saviour did recommend to his Disciples with so repeated an injunction as this of Charity and Almes. To which adde the words spoken by our Lord, [x]*It is better to give than to receive*; and when we consider how great a blessing it is that we beg not from door to door, it is a ready instance of our thankfulness to God, for his sake to relieve them that do. 2. This duty is that alone wherby the future day of judgment shall be transacted. For nothing but charity and almes is that whereby Christ shall declare the justice and mercy of the eternal sentence. Martyrdom it self is not there expressed, and no otherwise involved

[t] Luke 21: 2; Act. 3: 6. Chi ti da un' ossa, non ti verebbe morto.

[u] 1 Pet. 1: 22.

[v] 2 Cor. 8: 12.

[w] Matth. 6: 4. et Matth. 13: 12, 33 et 25: 45. Luke 11: 41.

[x] 1 Tim. 4: 4.

---

27 [x]] *om 6+*   note *w* 25: 45] *cor*, 25: 30 *1+*

but as it is the greatest charity. 3. Christ made himself the greatest and daily example of almes or charity. He went up and down doing good, preaching the Gospel, and healing all diseases: and God the Father is imitable by us in nothing but in purity and mercy. 4. [y]Almes given to the poor redound to the emolument of the Giver both temporal and eternal. 5. [z]They are instrumental to the remission of sins, our forgivenesse and mercy to others being made the very rule and proportion of our confidence and hope and our prayer to be forgiven our selves. 6. It is a treasure in Heaven, it procures friends when we dye. It is reckoned as done to Christ whatsoever we do to our poor brother; and therefore when a poor man begs for Christ his sake, if he have reason to ask for Christ his sake, give it him if thou canst. Now every man hath title to ask for Christs sake, whose need is great, and himself unable to cure it, and if the man be a Christian. Whatsoever charity Christ will reward, all that is given for Christs sake, and therefore it may be asked in his name: but every man that uses that sacred name for an endearment, hath not a title to it, neither he nor his need. 7. It is one of the wings of prayer, by which it flyes to the throne of grace. 8. [a]It crowns all the works of piety. 9. It causes thanksgiving to God on our behalf. 10. And the bowels of the poor blesse us, and they pray for us. 11. And that portion of our estate, out of which a tenth, or a fifth, or a twentieth, or some offering to God for religion and the poor goes forth, certainly returns with a greater blessing upon all the rest. It is like the effusion of oyl by the *Sidonian* woman; [b]as long as she poures into empty vessels, it could never cease running: or like the Widows barrel of meal, it consumes not as long as she fed the Prophet. 12. The summe of all is contained in the words of our blessed Saviour: *Give almes of such things as you have, and behold all things are clean unto you.* 13. To which may be added, that charity or mercy is the peculiar character of Gods Elect, and a signe of predestination; which advantage we are taught by S. *Paul*: [c]*Put on therefore as the elect of God, holy and beloved, bowels of mercy, kindnesse, etc. forbearing one another, and forgiving one another; if any man have a quarrel against any.* The result of all which we may reade in the words of S. *Chrysostome*: *To know the art of almes, is greater than to be*

[y] Philip. 4: 17.

[z] Acts 10: 4. Hebr. 13: 16. Eccles. 3: 1. Dan. 4: 27.

[a] Nunquam memini me legisse mala morte mortuum qui libenter opera charitatis exercuit. S. Hieron. Epist. ad Nepot.

[b] 2 Ki. 4: 1 and 1 Ki. 17: 14.

[c] Coloss. 3: 12.

23 greater] great *6+* 24 [b]] *GH, om 1+*

crowned with the Diadem of kings. And yet to convert one soul is greater than to poure out ten thousand talents into the baskets of the poor.

But because giving Almes is an act of the vertue of mercifulnesse, our endeavour must be by proper arts to mortifie the parents of unmercifulnesse, which are 1. Envy. 2. Anger. 3. Covetousnesse, in which we may be helped by the following rules or instruments.

Remedies against unmercifulnesse, and uncharitablenesse.

I.
Against Envy: by way of consideration.

Against Envy I shall use the same argument I would use to perswade a man from the Fever or the dropsie. 1. Because it is a disease, it is so far from having pleasure in it, or a temptation to it, that it is full of pain, a great instrument of vexation; it eats the flesh, and dries up the marrow, and makes hollow eyes, and lean cheeks, and a pale face. 2. It is nothing but a direct resolution never to enter into Heaven by the way of noble pleasure taken in the good of others. 3. It is most contrary to God. 4. And a just contrary state to the felicities and actions of Heaven, where every star encreases the light of the other, and the multitude of guests at the supper of the Lamb makes the eternal meal more festival. 5. [d]It is perfectly the state of Hell, and the passion of Devils: for they do nothing but despair in themselves, and envy others quiet or safety, and yet cannot rejoyce either in their good, or in their evil, although they endeavour to hinder that, and procure this, with all the devices and arts of malice and of a great understanding. 6. Envy can serve no end in the world; it cannot please any thing, nor do any thing, nor hinder any thing, but the content and felicity of him that hath it. 7. Envy can never pretend to justice, as hatred and uncharitableness sometimes may: for there may be causes of hatred, and I may have wrong done me, and then hatred hath some pretence, though no just argument: But no man is unjust or injurious for being prosperous or wise. 8. And therefore many men *professe* to hate another, but *no man owns envy*, as being an enmity and displeasure for no cause but goodnesse or felicity: [e]Envious men being like Cantharides and Caterpillars, that delight most to devour ripe and most excellent fruits. 9. It

[d] Nemo alienæ virtuti invidet qui satis confidet suæ. Cic. contr. M. Anth.

[e] Homerus, Thersites malos mores describens, malitiæ summam apposuit, Pelidæ imprimis erat atque inimicus Ulyssi.

is of all crimes the basest: for malice and anger are appeased with benefits, but envy is exasperated, as envying to fortunate persons both their power and their will to do good: and never leaves murmuring till the envied person be levelled, and then only the Vultur leaves to eat the liver: for if his Neighbour be made miserable the envious man is apt to be troubled: like him that is so long unbuilding the turrets till all the roof is low or flat, or that the stones fall upon the lower buildings, and do a mischief that the man repents of.

2.
Remedies against anger by way of exercise.

The next enemy to mercifulnes and the grace of Almes is Anger, against which there are proper instruments both in prudence and religion.

1. Prayer is the great remedy against anger: for it must suppose it in some degree removed before we pray, and then it is the more likely it will be finished when the prayer is done: We must lay aside the act of anger, as a preparatory to prayer, and the curing the habit will be the effect and blessing of prayer: so that if a man to cure his anger, resolves to addresse himself to God by prayer, it is first necessary that by his own observation and diligence he lay the anger aside, before his prayer can be fit to be presented; and when we so pray, and so endeavour, we have all the blessings of prayer which God hath promised to it, to be our security for successe.

2. [f]If Anger arises in thy breast, instantly seal up thy lips, and let it not go forth: for like fire when it wants vent, it will suppresse it self. It is good *in a fever* to have a tender and a smooth tongue; but it is better that it be so *in anger*; for if it be rough and distempered, *there* it is an ill signe, but *here* it is an ill cause. Angry passion is a fire, and angry words are like breath to fan them; together they are like steel and flint sending out fire by mutual collision: some men will discourse themselves into passion, and if their neighbour be enkindled too, together they flame with rage and violence.

3. Humility is the most excellent natural cure for anger in the world: for he that by daily considering his own infirmities and failings makes the errour of his neighbour or servant to be his own case, and

[f] Ira cum pectus rapida occupavit,
Futiles linguæ jubeo cavere
Vana latratus jaculantis. Sappho.

Turbatus sum, et non sum locutus. Psal. 76.

remembers that he daily needs Gods pardon, and his brothers charity, will not be apt to rage at the levities or misfortunes, or indiscretions of another; greater than which he considers that he is very frequently, and more inexcusably guilty of.

4. Consider the example of the ever blessed Jesus, who suffered all the contradictions of sinners, and received all affronts and reproaches of malicious, rash and foolish persons, and yet in all them was as dispassionate and gentle as the morning sun in Autumn: and in this also he propounded himself imitable by us. For if innocence it self did suffer so great injuries and disgraces, it is no great matter for us quietly to receive al the calamities of fortune and indiscretion of servants, and mistakes of friends, and unkindnesses of kindred, and rudenesses of enemies, since we have deserved these and worse, even Hell it self.

5. If we be tempted to anger in the actions of Government and Discipline to our inferiours (in which case anger is permitted so far as it is prudently instrumental to Government, and onely is a sin when it is excessive and unreasonable, and apt to disturbe our own discourse, or to expresse it self in imprudent words or violent actions) let us propound to our selves the example of God the Father, who at the same time, and with the same tranquillity decreed Heaven and Hell, the joyes of blessed Angels and souls, and the torments of Devils and accursed spirits: and at the day of judgement when all the World shall burn under his feet, God shall not be at all inflamed, or shaken in his essential seat and centre of tranquillity and joy. And if at first the cause seems reasonable, yet defer to execute thy anger till thou mayest better judge. For as *Phocion* told the *Athenians*, who upon the first news of the death of *Alexander* were ready to revolt, *stay awhile, for if the King be not dead, your haste will ruine you. But if he be dead, your stay cannot prejudice your affairs, for he will be dead to morrow as well as today*: so if thy servant or inferiour deserve punishment, staying till to morrow will not make him innocent, but it may possibly preserve thee so, by preventing thy striking a guiltlesse person, or being furious for a trifle.

6. Remove from thy self all provocations and incentives to anger; especially 1. Games of chance, and great wagers. [g] *Patroclus* killed his friend, the son of *Amphidamus*, in his rage and sudden fury, rising upon a crosse game at tables. Such also are petty curiosities and worldly businesse and carefulnesse about it; but manage thy self with

[g] *Ἤματι τῷ ὅτε παῖδα κατέκτανον Ἀμφιδάμαντος,*
Νήπιος, οὐκ ἐθέλων, ἀμφ᾽ ἀστραγάλοισι χολωθείς. Homer. Il.

34 wagers.] *4*+, ~, *1 2 3*   [g]] *4*+, *om 1 2 3*   34–6 *Patroclus* killed . . . Such also are] *4*+, *om 1 2 3*

indifferency, or contempt of those external things, and do not spend a passion upon them, for it is more then they are worth. [h]But they that desire but few things can be crossed but in a few. 2. In not heaping up with an ambitious or curious prodigality, any very curious or choice Utensils, Seals, Jewels, Glasses, precious stones, because those very many accidents which happen in the spoiling or losse of these rarities, is in event, an irresistable cause of violent anger. 3. Do not entertain nor suffer talebearers: for they abuse our ears first, and then our credulity, and then steal our patience, and it may be for a lye; and if it be true, the matter is not considerable; or if it be, yet it is pardonable: and we may alwayes escape with patience at one of these out-lets: either [1] By not hearing slanders, or [2] By not believing them, or [3] By not regarding the thing, or [4] By forgiving the person. 4. To this purpose also it may serve well if we choose (as much as we can) to live with peaceable persons, for that prevents the occasions of confusion: and if we live with prudent persons they will not easily occasion our disturbance. But because these things are not in many Mens power, therefore I propound this rather as a felicity than a remedy or a duty; and an art of prevention rather than of cure.

7. Be not inquisitive into the affairs of other Men, nor the faults of thy servants, nor the mistakes of thy friends; but what is offered to you, use according to the former rules but do not thou go out to gather sticks to kindle a fire to burn thy own house. And adde this; if my friend said or did well in that for which I am angry, I am in the fault, not he: But if he did amisse, he is in the misery, not I: for either he was deceived, or he was malitious, and either of them both is all one with a miserable person; and that is an object of pity, not of anger.

8. Use all reasonable discourses to excuse the faults of others, considering that there are many circumstances of time, of person, of accident, of inadvertency, of infrequency, of aptnesse to amend, of sorrow for doing it; and it is well that we take any good in exchange for the evil is done or suffered.

9. Upon the arising of anger instantly enter into a deep consideration of the joyes of Heaven, or the pains of Hell: for [i]*fear and joy are naturally apt to appease this violence.*

10. In contentions be alwayes passive, never active; upon the defensive, not the assulting part, and then also give a gentle answer,

[h] Qui pauca requirunt, non multis excidunt. Plut.
[i] Homer.

7 is] are *7 8* 23 thy] thine *6+*

receiving the furies and indiscretions of the other like a stone into a bed of Mosse and soft compliance; and you shall finde it sit down quietly; whereas anger and violence makes the contention loud, and long and injurious to both the parties.

11. In the actions of Religion be careful to temper all thy instances with meeknesse, and the proper instruments of it: and if thou beest apt to be angry, neither fast violently, nor entertain the too forward heats of zeal: but *secure thy duty* with constant and regular actions, and *a good temper of body* with convenient refreshments and recreations.

12. If anger rises suddenly and violently, first restrain it with consideration, and then let it end in a hearty prayer for him that did the real or seeming injury: The former of the two stops its growth, and the latter quite kils it, and makes amends for its monstrous and involuntary birth.

Remedies against Anger by way of consideration.

1. Consider that Anger is a professed enemy to counsel, it is a direct storm, in which no Man can be heard to speak, or call from without: for if you counsel gently, you are despised, if you urge it and be vehement, you provoke it more: [j]bee careful therefore to lay up beforehand a great stock of reason and prudent consideration, that like a besieged Town you may be provided for, and be defensible from within, since you are not likely to be relieved from without. Anger is not to be suppressed but by something that is as inward as it self, and more habitual: To which purpose adde, that 2. of all passions it endeavours most to make reason useless. 3. That it is an universal poyson, of an infinite object; for no Man was ever so amorous as to love a Toad, none so envious as to repine at the condition of the miserable, no Man so timorous as to fear a dead Bee; but anger is troubled at every thing, and every Man, and every accident, and therefore unlesse it be suppressed it will make a Mans condition restlesse. 4. If it proceeds from a great cause it turns to fury; if from a small cause, it is peevishnesse, [k]and so is alwayes either terrible or ridiculous. 5. It makes a Mans body monstrous, deformed, and contemptible, the voice horrid, the eyes cruel, the face pale or fiery, the gate fierce, the speech clamorous

[j] *Καὶ μανθάνω μέν, οἷα δρᾶν μέλλω κακά·*
θυμὸς δὲ κρείσσων τῶν ἐμῶν βουλευμάτων. Medea.

[k] *Ὁ θυμὸς φόνων αἴτιον, συμφορᾶς σύμμαχον, βλάβης σύνεργον καὶ ἀτιμίας χρημάτων ἀπώλεια, ἔτι δὲ καὶ φθορᾶς ἀρχηγόν.* Aristot.

32 [k]] *4+*, *om 1 2 3* note *j* Medea] Meded *3*, *om 5*, Medica *8*

and loud. 6. It is neither manly nor ingenuous. 7. It proceeds from softnesse of spirit and pusillanimity; which makes that Women are more angry than Men, sick persons more than the healthful, old Men more than yong, unprosperous and calamitous people than the blessed and fortunate. 8. It is a passion fitter for Flies and Insects than for persons professing noblenesse and bounty. 9. It is troublesome not onely to those that suffer it, but to them that behold it; [l]there being no greater incivility of entertainment than for the Cooks fault, or the negligence of the servants, to be cruel, or outragious, or unpleasant in the presence of the guests. 10. It makes marriage to be a necessary and unavoidable trouble, friendships, and societies, and familiarities to be intolerable. 11. It multiplies the evils of drunkennesse, and makes the levities of Wine to run into madnesse. 12. It makes innocent jesting to bee the beginning of Tragedies. 13. It turns friendship into hatred, it makes a Man lose himself, and his reason and his argument in disputation. It turnes the desires of knowledge into an itch of wrangling. It addes insolency to power. It turnes justice into cruelty, and judgement into oppression. It changes discipline into tediousnesse and hatred of liberal institution. It makes a prosperous Man to be envyed and the unfortunate to be unpittied. It is a confluence of all the irregular passions: there is in it envy and sorrow, fear and scorn, pride and prejudice, rashnesse and inconsideration, rejoycing in evil and a desire to inflict it, self love, impatience and curiosity. And lastly, though it be very troublesome to others, yet it is most troublesome to him that hath it.

In the use of these arguments and the former exercises be diligent to observe, lest in your desires to suppresse anger you be passionate and angry at your self for being angry; [m]like Physicians who give a bitter potion when they intend to eject the bitternesse of choler; for this will provoke the person and increase the passion: But placidly and quietly set upon the mortification of it; and attempt it first for a day; resolving that day not at all to be angry; and to be watchful and observant, for a day is no great trouble: but then, after one dayes watchfulnesse it will be as easie to watch two dayes, as at first it was to watch one day; and so you may increase till it becomes easie and habitual.

Onely observe that such an anger alone is criminal which is against charity to my self or my neighbour; but anger against sin is a holy zeal, and an effect of love to God and my brother, for whose interest I am

[l] Dicere quid cœna possis ingratius ista?

[m] Amaram amaro bilem pharmaco qui eluunt.

passionate, like a concerned person: and if I take care that my anger makes no reflexion of scorn or cruelty upon the offender, or of pride and violence, or transportation to my self, anger becomes charity and duty: [n]And when one commended *Charilaus* the King of *Sparta*, for a gentle, a good and a meek Prince, his collegue said well, *How can he be good who is not an enemy even to vitious persons.*

3.
Remedies against Covetousnesse, the third enemy of mercy.

Covetousnesse is also an enemy to Almes, though not to all the effects of mercifulnesse: but this is to be cured by the proper motives to charity before mentioned, and by the proper rules of justice; which being secured, the arts of getting money are not easily made criminal. To which also we may adde.

1. [o]Covetousnesse makes a man miserable; because riches are not means to make a man happy: and unless felicity were to be bought with money he is a vain person who admires heaps of gold and rich possessions; for what *Hippomachus* said to some persons, who commended a tall man as fit to be a Champion in the Olympick games: *it is true* (said he) *if the crown hang so high that the longest arm could reach it*: The same we may say concerning riches, they were excellent things, if the richest man were certainly the wisest and the best: but as they are, they are nothing to be wondered at, because they contribute nothing towards felicity: which appears because some men choose to be miserable that they may be rich, rather than be happy with the expence of money and doing noble things.

2. Riches are uselesse and unprofitable; for beyond our needs and conveniences nature knowes no use of riches; and they say, that the Princes of *Italy* when they sup alone, eate out of a single dish, and drink in a plain glasse, and the wife eats without purple: *for nothing is more frugal than the back and belly*, if they be used as they should, [p]but when they would entertain the eyes of strangers, when they are vain and would make a noyse, then riches come forth to set forth the spectacle, and furnish out the *Comedie of wealth, of vanity.* No man can with

[n] Plut. de odio et invidia.

[o] Quid refert igitur quantis jumenta fatiget
Porticibus, quanta nemorum vectetur in umbra,
Jugera quot vicina foro, quas emerit ædes?
Nemo malus fœlix. Juv. Sat. 4.

[p] Plut.

all the wealth in the world buy so much skill as to be a good Lutenist; he must go the same way that poor people do, he must learn and take pains; much lesse can he buy constancy, or chastity, or courage: nay not so much as the contempt of riches: and by possessing more than we need, we cannot obtain so much power over our souls, as not to require more: And certainly riches must deliver me from no evil, if the possession of them cannot take away the longing for them. If any man be thirsty, drink cools him. If he be hungry, eating meat satisfies him; and when a man is cold and calls for a warme cloak, he is pleased if you give it him; but you trouble him, if you load him with six or eight cloaks. Nature rests and sits still when she hath her portion; but that which exceeds it, is a trouble and a burden: and therefore in true Philosophy, No man is rich but he that is poor according to the common account: for when God hath satisfied those needs which he made; that is, all that is natural, whatsoever is beyond it, is thirst and a disease, and unlesse it be sent back again in charity or religion, can serve no end but vice or vanity, it can encrease the appetite to represent the man poorer, and full of a new and artificial, unnatural need; but it never satisfies the need it makes, or makes the man richer. *No wealth can satisfie the covetous desire of wealth.*

3. Riches are troublesome: but the satisfaction of those appetites which God and nature hath made are cheap and easy: for who ever paid use-money for bread and onions and water to keep him alive? but when we covet after houses of the frame and design of *Italy*, or long for jewels, or for my next neighbours field, or horses from *Barbary*, or the richest perfumes of *Arabia*, or *Galatian* mules, or fat Eunuchs for our slaves from *Tunis*, or rich coaches from *Naples*,[q] then we can never be satisfied till we have the best thing that is fancied, and all that can be had, and all that can be desired, and that we can lust no more: but before we come to the one half of our first wilde desires, we are the bondmen of Usurers, and of our worse tyrant appetites, and the tortures of envy and impatience. But I consider that those who drink on still when their thirst is quenched, or eat even after they well dined are forced to vomit, not onely their superfluity, but even that which at first was necessary: so those that covet more than they can temperately use, are oftentimes forced to part even with that patrimony which would have supported their

[q] Ergo solicitæ tu causa, pecunia, vitæ es:
Per te immaturum mortis adimus iter. Propert.

28 [q]] *4+, om 1 2 3* 34 even] *om 4+* they] they have *7 8*

persons in freedom and honour, and have satisfied all their reasonable desires.

4. Contentednesse is therefore health because covetousnesse is a direct sicknesse: and it was well said of *Aristippus* (as *Plutarch* reports him) if any man after much eating and drinking be still unsatisfied, he hath no need of more meat or more drink, but of a Physician; he more needs to be purged than to be filled; and therefore since covetousnesse cannot be satisfied, it must be cured by emptinesse, and evacuation; The man is without remedy, unlesse he be reduced to the scantling of nature, and the measures of his personal necessity. Give to a poor man a house, and a few cowes, pay his little debt, and set him on work, and he is provided for and quiet; but when a man enlarges beyond a fair possession and desires another Lordship, you spite him if you let him have it; for by that he is one degree the further off from rest in his desires and satisfaction: and now he sees himself in a bigger capacity to a larger fortune; and he shall never finde his period, till you begin to take away something of what he hath: for then he will begin to be glad to keep that which is left; but reduce him to natures measures, and there he shall be sure to finde rest: for there no man can desire beyond his belly full, and when he wants that, any one friend or charitable man can cure his poverty; but all the world cannot satisfie his covetousnes.

5. Covetousnesse is the most phantastical and contradictory disease in the whole world, and it must therefore be incurable, because it strives against its own cure. No man therefore abstains from meat because he is hungry, nor from wine because he loves it and needs it: but the covetous man does so: for he desires it passionately because he sayes he needs it, and when he hath it, he will need it still, because he dares not use it. He gets cloaths because he cannot be without them; but when he hath them, then he can: as if he needed corn for his granary, and cloaths for his wardrope, more than for his back and belly. For covetousness pretends to heap much together for fear of want, and yet after all his pains and purchase, he suffers that really which at first he feared vainly; and by not using what he gets, he makes that suffering to be actual, present, and necessary, which in his lowest condition was but future, contingent and possible. It stirs up the desire, and takes away the pleasure of being satisfied. It increases the appetite and will not content it, it swells the *principal* to no purpose and lessens the *use* to all purposes; disturbing the order of nature, and

2 desires] desire *4+* 23 and] *om 7 8*

the designes of God; making *money* not to be the instrument of exchange or charity, nor corn to feed himself or the poor, nor wool to cloath himself or his brother, nor wine to refresh the sadnesse of the afflicted, nor his oyl to make his own countenance cheerful: but all these to look upon, and to tell over, and to take accounts by and make himself considerable, and wondered at by fools, that while he lives he may be called Rich, and when he dyes may be accounted Miserable, and like the Dishmakers of *China*, may leave a greater heap of dirt for his Nephews, while he himself hath a new lot fallen to him in the portion of *Dives*: But thus the Asse carried wood and sweet herbs to the Baths, but was never washed or perfumed himself: he heaped up sweets for others, while himself was filthy with smoak and ashes. And yet it is considerable; If the man can be content to feed hardly, and labour extreamly, and watch carefully, and suffer affronts and disgrace that he may get money more than he uses in his temperate and just needs, with how much ease might this man be happy? And with how great uneasinesse and trouble does he make himself miserable? For he takes pains to get content, and when he might have it, he lets it go. He might better be content with a vertuous and quiet poverty, than with an artificial troublesom and vitious: The same diet and a less labor would at first make him happy, and for ever after rewardable.

6. The sum of all is that which the Apostle sayes; *Covetousnesse is Idolatry*; that is, it is an admiring money for it self, not for its use; it relyes upon money, and loves it more than it loves God and religion: and *it is the root of all evil*: ⌜it teaches men to be cruel and crafty, industrious in evil, full of care and malice: it devours young heirs, and grindes the face of the poor, and undoes those who specially belong to Gods protection, helpless, craftlesse and innocent people; it inquires into our parents age, and longs for the death of our friends: it makes friendship an art of rapine, and changes a partner into a Vultur, and a companion into a thief; and after all this it is for no good to it self, for it dare not spend those heaps of treasure which it snatched: and men hate Serpents and Basilisks worse then Lyons and Bears; for these kill because they need the pray, but they sting to death and eat not. And if

⌜ *Ἡ φιλοχρημοσύνη μήτηρ κακότητος ἁπάσης.*
Χρυσὸς ἀεὶ δόλος ἐστὶ καὶ ἄργυρος ἀνθρώποισιν.
Χρυσέ, κακῶν ἀρχηγέ, βιοφθόρε, πάντα χαλέπτων,
Εἴθέ σε μὴ θνητοῖσι γενέσθαι πῆμα ποθεινόν·
Σοῦ γὰρ ἕκητι μάχαι τε, λεηλασίαι τε, φόνοι τε,
Ἐχθρὰ δὲ τέκνα γονεῦσιν, ἀδέλφειοί τε συναίμοις. Phocylid.

25 ⌜] *4*+, *om 1 2 3*   30 an] *2*+, and *1*

they pretend all this care and heap for their Heirs, (like the Mice of *Africa* hiding the golden oare in their bowels, and refusing to give back the indigested gold till their guts be out) they may remember, that what was unnecessary for themselves, is as unnecessary for their sons and why cannot they be without it as well as their Fathers who did no use it? and it often happens, that to the sons it becomes an instrumen to serve some lust or other; that as the gold was uselesse to thei Fathers, so may the sons be to the publick; fools or prodigals, loads to their Countrey, and the curse and punishment of their Father avarice; and yet all that wealth is short of one blessing; but it is a loa coming with a curse, and descending from the family of a long derive sin. However the Father transmits it to the son, and it may be the so to one more, till a Tyrant, or an Oppressour, or a War, or a change o government, or the Usurer, or folly, or an expensive vice makes hole in the bottom of the bag, and the wealth runs out like water, and flie away like a Bird from the hand of a childe.

7. [s]Adde to these, the consideration of the advantages of poverty that it is a state freer from temptation, secure in dangers: but of on trouble; safe under the Divine Providence: cared for in Heaven by daily ministration, and for whose support God makes every day a ne decree: a state of which Christ was pleased to make open profession and many wise Men daily make vows: that a rich Man is but like a poo to whom the poor run, and first trouble it and then draw it dry: that h enjoyes no more of it than according to the few and limited needs of Man; he cannot eat like a Wolf or an Elephant: [t]that variety of daint fare ministers but to sin and sicknesses: [u]that the poor Man feast oftner than the rich; because every little enlargement is a feast to th poor; but he that feasts every day feasts no day, there being nothing le to which he may beyond his Ordinary extend his appetite: that the ric Man sleeps not so soundly as the poor labourer; that his fears ar more, and his needs are greater (for who is poorer, he that needs 5 l. o

[s] Provocet ut segnes animos, rerumque remotas
Ingeniosa vias paulatim exploret egestas. Claudian.

[t] —sed olim
Prodigio par est in nobilitate Senectus.

[u] Hortulus hic, puteusque brevis, nec reste movendus,
In tenues plantas facili diffunditur haustu.
Vive bidentis amans, et culti villicus horti,
Unde epulum possis centum dare Pythagoreis.
Est aliquid, quocunque loco, quocunque recessu,
Unius sese Dominum fecisse lacertæ. Juven. Sat. 3.

---

17 [s]] *4+*, *om 1 2 3* note *u* sese Dominum] *cor*, Dominum sese *1+*

he that needs 5000?) the poor Man hath enough to fill his belly, and the rich hath not enough to fill his eye: that the poor Mans wants are easie to be relieved by a common charity, but the needs of rich Men cannot be supplyed but by Princes; and they are left to the temptation of great vices to make reparation of their needs: and the ambitious labours of Men to get great estates is but like the selling of a Fountain to buy a Fever, a parting with content to buy necessity, a purchase of an unhandsome condition at the price of infelicity: that Princes and they that enjoy most of the world, have most of it but in title and supreme rights, and reserved priviledges, pepper-corns, homages, trifling services and acknowledgements, the real use descending to others to more substantial purposes: These considerations may be useful to the curing of covetousnesse, that the grace of mercifulnesse enlarging the heart of a Man, his hand may not be contracted, but reached out to the poor in almes.

SECT. IX.
Of Repentance.

Repentance, of all things in the World makes the greatest change: it changes things in Heaven and Earth; for it changes the whole Man from sin to grace, from vitious habits to holy customes, from unchaste bodies to Angelical soules, from Swine to Philosophers, from drunkennesse to sober counsels; and GOD himself, *with whom is no variablenesse or shadow of change*, is pleased by descending to our weak understandings, to say, that he changes also upon Mans repentance, that he alters his decrees, revokes his sentence, cancels the Bils of accusation, throws the Records of shame and sorrow from the Court of Heaven, and lifts up the sinner from the grave to life, from his prison to a throne, from Hell and the guilt of eternal torture, to Heaven and to a title to never ceasing felicities. If we be *bound on earth*, we shall be *bound in heaven*; if we be absolved here, we shall be loosed there; if we repent, God will repent, and not send the evil upon us which we had deserved.

But repentance is a conjugation and society of many duties; and it containes in it all the parts of a holy life, from the time of our return to the day of our death inclusively; and it hath in it some things specially relating to the sins of our former dayes which are now to be abolished

33 of our return] *4+*, of return *1 2 3*

by special arts, and have obliged us to special labours, and brought in many new necessities, and put us into a very great deal of danger; and because it is a duty consisting of so many parts and so much imployment, it also requires much time, and leaves a Man in the same degree of hope of pardon, as is his restitution to the state of righteousness and holy living, for which we covenanted in Baptism.

For wee must know that there is but one repentance in a Mans whole life, if repentance be taken in the proper, and strict Evangelicall Covenant-sense, and not after the ordinary understanding of the word: That is, wee are but once to change our whole state of life, from the power of the Devil and his intire possession, from the state of sin and death, from the body of corruption, to the life of grace, to the possession of Jesus, to the kingdom of the Gospel; and this is done in the baptism of water, or in the baptism of the Spirit, when the first rite comes to be verified by Gods grace coming upon us, and by our obedience to the heavenly calling, we working together with God. After this change, if ever we fall into the contrary state, and be wholly estranged from God and Religion, and professe our selves servants of unrighteousnesse, God hath made no more covenant of restitution to us, there is no place left for any more repentance, or intire change of condition, or new birth: a Man can be regenerated but once: and such are voluntary, malicious Apostates, Witches, obstinate impenitent persons, and the like: But if we be overtaken by infirmity, or enter into the marches or borders of this estate, and commit a grievous sin, or ten, or twenty, so we be not in the intire possession of the Devil, we are for the present in a damnable condition if we dye; but if we live we are in a recoverable condition; for so we may repent often: we repent or rise from death but once, but from sicknesse many times; and by the grace of God we shall be pardoned if so we repent. But our hopes of pardon are just as is the repentance, which if it be timely, hearty, industrious and effective, God accepts: not by weighing granes or scruples, but by estimating the great proportions of our life; a hearty endeavour and an effectual general change shall get the pardon; the unavoidable infirmities, and past evils, and present imperfections, and short interruptions, against which we watch, and pray, and strive, being put upon the accounts of the crosse, and payed for by the Holy Jesus. This is the state and condition of repentance; its parts and actions must be valued according to the following rules.

Acts and parts of Repentance.

1. He that repents truely is greatly sorrowful for his past sins; not with a superficial sigh or tear, but a pungent afflictive sorrow; such a sorrow as hates the sin so much, that the man would choose to dye rather than act it any more: This sorrow is called in Scripture [v] *a weeping sorely, a weeping with bitternesse of heart, a weeping day and night, a sorrow of heart, a breaking of the spirit, mourning like a dove, and chattering like a swallow*: and we may read the degree and manner of it by the lamentations and sad accents of the Prophet *Jeremy*, when he wept for the sins of the nation; by the heart breaking of *David*, when he mourned for his murder and adultery: and the bitter weeping of S. *Peter*, after the shameful denying of his Master. The expression of this sorrow differs according to the temper of the body, the sex, the age, and circumstance of action, and the motive of sorrow, and by many accidental tendernesses, or Masculine hardnesses; and the repentance is not to be estimated by the tears, but by the grief; and the grief is to be valued not by the sensitive trouble, but by the cordial hatred of the sin, and ready actual dereliction of it, and a resolution and reall resisting its consequent temptations. Some people can shed tears for nothing, some for any thing; but the proper and true effects of a godly sorrow are; fear of the divine judgements, apprehension of Gods displeasure, watchings and strivings against sin, patiently enduring the crosse of sorrow (which God sends as their punishment) in accusation of our selves, in perpetually begging pardon, in mean and base opinion of our selves, and in all the natural productions from these according to our temper and constitution: for if we be apt to weep in other accidents, it is ill if we weep not also in the sorrows of repentance: not, that weeping is of it self a duty, but that the sorrow, if it be as great, will be still expressed in as great a manner.

2. Our sorrow for sins must retain the *proportion* of our sins, though *not the equality*; we have no particular measures of sins: we know not which is greater of Sacriledge or Superstition, Idolatry or Covetousnesse, Rebellion or Witchcraft; and therefore God ties us not to nice measures of sorrow, but onely that we keep the general Rules of proportion; that is, that a great sin have a great grief; a smaller crime being to be washed off with a lesser shower.

3. [w] Our sorrow for sins is then best accounted of for its degree,

[v] Jer. 13: 17. Joel 2: 13. Ezek. 27: 31. James 4: 9.

[w] Hugo de S. Victor.

when it together with all the penal and afflictive duties of repentance, shall have equalled or exceeded the pleasure we had in commission of the sin.

4. True repentance is a punishing duty, and acts its sorrow, and judges and condemns the sin by voluntary submitting to such sadnesses as God sends on us, or (to prevent the judgement of God) by judging our selves, and punishing our bodies and our spirits by such instruments of piety as are troublesome to the body: such as are, fasting, watching, long prayers, troublesome postures in our prayers, expensive alms, and all outward acts of humiliation. For he that must judge himself, must condemn himself if he be guilty; and if he be condemned he must be punished; and if he be so judged, it will help to prevent the judgement of the Lord, [x]S. *Paul* instructing us in this particular. But I before intimated that the *punishing actions* of repentance are onely actions of sorrow, and therefore are to make up the proportions of it. For our grief may be so full of trouble as to outweigh all the burdens of fasts and bodily afflictions, and then the other are the lesse necessary; and when they are used, the benefit of them is to obtain of God a remission or a lessening of such temporal judgements which God hath decreed against the sins, as it was in the case of *Ahab*: but the sinner is not by any thing of this reconciled to the eternal favour of God; for as yet, this is but the Introduction to Repentance.

5. Every true penitent is obliged to confesse his sins, and to humble himself before God for ever: Confession of sins hath a special promise [y]*If we confesse our sins he is faithful and just to forgive us our sins*: meaning that God hath bound himself to forgive us if we duly confesse our sins, and do all that for which confession was appointed; that is, be ashamed of them, and own them no more. For, confession of our sins to God can signifie nothing of it self in its direct nature: He sees us when we act them, and keeps a record of them; and we forget them unlesse he reminds us of them by his grace; so *that to confess them to God does not punish us, or make us ashamed*, but *confession to him, if it proceeds from shame and sorrow, and is an act of humility and self condemnation*, and is a laying open our wounds for cure, then it is a duty God delights in: in all which circumstances, because we may very much be helped if we take in the assistance of a spiritual Guide; [z]therefore the Church of God in

[x] 1 Cor. 11: 31. [y] 1 John 1: 9.

[z] Ἀναγκαῖον τοῖς πεπιστευμένοις τὴν οἰκονομίαν τῶν μυστηρίων τοῦ θεοῦ ἐξομολογεῖσθαι τὰ ἁμαρτήματα. S. Basil. reg. brev. 288.
Concil. Laod. c. 2; Concil. Quinisext. c. 102.
Tertull. de pœnit.

all ages hath commended, and in most ages enjoyned that we confesse our sins, and discover the state and condition of our souls to such a person whom we or our superiours judge fit to help us in such needs. For so *if we confesse our sins one to another* as S. *James* advises, wee shall obtaine the prayers of the holy Man whom God and the Church hath appointed solemnly to pray for us: and when he knowes our needs he can best minister comfort, or reproof, oyl or Causticks, he can more opportunely recommend your particular state to GOD, he can determine your cases of conscience, and judge better for you than you do for your self; and the shame of opening such Ulcers, may restrain your forwardnesse to contract them; and all these circumstances of advantage will do very much towards the forgivenesse. And this course was taken by the new Converts in the dayes of the Apostles, [a] *For many that believed, came and confessed and shewed their deeds.* And it were well if this duty were practised prudently and innocently in order to publick Discipline, or private comfort and instruction: but that it be done to God, is a duty, not directly for it self, but for its adjuncts, and the duties that go with it, or before it, or after it: which duties because they are all to be helped and guided by our Pastors and Curates of souls, he is careful of his eternal interest that will not lose the advantage of using a private guide and judge. [b] *He that hideth his sins shall not prosper* (*Non dirigetur*, saith the Vulgar Latin, *he shall want a guide*) *but who confesseth and forsaketh them shall have mercy.* And to this purpose *Climacus* reports that divers holy persons in that age did use to carry Table-books with them, and in them described an account of all their determinate thoughts, purposes, words and actions, in which they had suffered infirmity, that by communicating the estate of their souls they might be instructed and guided, and corrected, or incouraged.

6. [c] True repentance must reduce to act all its holy purposes, and enter into and run through *the state of holy living*, which is contrary to that state of darknesse in which in times past we walked. [d] For to resolve to do it, and yet not to do it, is to break our resolution and our faith, to mock God, to falsifie and evacuate all the preceding acts of repentance, and to make our pardon hopelesse, and our hope fruitlesse. He that resolves to live well when a danger is upon him, or a

[a] Acts 19: 18. [b] Prov. 28: 13.

[c] Rom. 6: 3, 4, 7; 8: 10; 13: 13, 14; 11: 22, 27. Gal. 5: 6, 24; 6: 15. 1 Cor. 7: 19. 2 Cor. 13: 5. Colos. 1: 21–3. Heb. 12: 1, 14, 16; 10: 16, 22. 1 Pet. 1: 15; 2 Pet. 1: 4, 9, 10; 3: 11. 1 John 1: 6; 3: 8, 9; 5: 16.

[d] Nequam illud verbum'st, Bene volt, nisi qui bene facit. Trinum.

31 [d]] *4+*, *om 1 2 3*

violent fear, or when the appetites of Lust are newly satisfied, or newly served, and yet when the temptation comes again, sins again, and then is sorrowful, and resolves once more against it, and yet fals when the temptation returns, is a vain Man, but no true penitent, nor in the state of grace; and if he chance to dye in one of these good moods is very far from salvation: for if it be necessary that we resolve to live well, it is necessary we should do so. For resolution is an imperfect act, a term of relation, and signifies nothing but in order to the action: it is as a faculty is to the act, as Spring is to the Harvest, as Egges are to Birds, as a Relative to its Correspondent, nothing without it. No Man therefore can be in the state of grace and actual favour by resolutions and holy purposes; these are but the gate and portal towards pardon: a holy life is the onely perfection of Repentance, and the firme ground upon which we can cast the anchor of hope in the mercies of God through Jesus Christ.

7. No Man is to reckon his pardon immediately upon his returnes from sin to the beginnings of good life, but is to begin his hopes and degrees of confidence according as sin dyes in him, and grace lives; as the habits of sin lessen, and righteousnesse growes, according as sin returnes but seldom in smaller instances and without choice, and by surprize without deliberation, and is highly disrelished and presently dashed against the Rock Christ Jesus by a holy sorrow and renewed care, and more strict watchfulnesse. For a holy life being the condition of the Covenant on our part, as we return to God, so God returns to us, and our state returns to the probabilities of pardon.

8. Every Man is to work out his salvation with fear and trembling; and after the commission of sinnes his feares must multiply, because every new sin, and every great declining from the wayes of God is still a degree of new danger, and hath increased Gods anger, and hath made him more uneasie to grant pardon: and when he does grant it, it is upon harder terms both for doing and suffering; that is, we must do more for pardon, and it may be, suffer much more. For we must know that God pardons our sins by parts: as our duty increases, and our care is more prudent and active, so Gods anger decreases: and yet it may be the last sin you committed, made God unalterably resolved to send upon you some sad judgement. Of the particulars in all cases wee are uncertain; and therefore wee have reason alwayes to mourn for our sinnes that have so provoked GOD, and made our condition so full of danger, that it may be, no prayers, or tears or duty can alter his sentence concerning some sad judgement upon us. Thus GOD irrevocably

decreed to punish the Israelites for Idolatry, although *Moses* prayed for them, and God forgave them in some degree; that is, so that he would not cut them off from being a people; yet he would not forgive them so, but he would visit that their sin upon them: and he did so.

9. [e]A true penitent must all the dayes of his life pray for pardon, and never think the work completed till he dyes; not by any act of his own, by no act of the Church, by no forgivenesse by the party injured, by no restitution: these are all instruments of great use and efficacy, and the means by which it is to be done at length: but still the sin lyes at the door ready to return upon us in judgement, and damnation, if we return to it in choice or action: [f]and whether God hath forgiven us or no, we know not, and how far we know not; and all that we have done is not of sufficient worth to obtain pardon: therefore still pray, and still be sorrowful for ever having done it, and for ever watch against it; and then those beginnings of pardon which are working all the way, will at last be perfected in the day of the Lord.

10. Defer not at all to repent; much lesse mayest thou put it off to thy death-bed: [g]It is not an easie thing to root out the habits of sin, which a Mans whole life hath gathered and confirmed. We finde worke enough to mortifie one beloved lust, in our very best advantage of strength and time, and before it is so deeply rooted as it must needs be supposed to be at the end of a wicked life: and therefore it will prove impossible when the work is so great, and the strength is so little, when sinne is so strong and grace so weak: for they alwayes keep the same proportion of increase and decrease, and as sin growes, grace decayes: so that the more need wee have of grace, the lesse at that time wee shall have: because the greatnesse of our sinnes which makes the need, hath lessened the grace of GOD (which should help us) into nothing. To which adde this consideration; that on a Mans death-bed, the day of repentance is past: for repentance being the renewing of a holy life, a living the life of Grace, it is a contradiction to say, that a Man can live a holy life upon his death-bed: [h]especially, if we consider, that for a sinner to live a holy life must first suppose him to have overcome all his evil habits, and then to have made a purchase of the contrary graces, by the labours of

[e] Dandum interstitium penitentiae. Tacit.

[f] I peccati et i debbiti son sempre più di quel che si crede.

[g] *Τί οὖν πρὸς ἔθος ἐστὶν εὑρίσκειν βοήθημα; τὸ ἐναντίον ἔθος.* Arria.

[h] Mortem venientem nemo hilaris excipit, nisi qui se ad illam diu composuerat.

23 strength is] *2 3*, strength's *1 4 5 6*, strengths *7 8*

great prudence, watchfulnesse, self denyal and severity. [i] *Nothing that is excellent can be wrought suddenly.*

11. After the beginnings of thy recovery, be infinitely fearful of a relapse, and therefore upon the stock of thy sad experience, observe where thy failings were, and by especial arts fortifie that faculty, and arm against that temptation. For if all those arguments which God uses to us to preserve our innocence, and thy late danger, and thy fears, and the goodnesse of God making thee once to escape, and the shame of thy fall, and the sence of thy own weaknesses will not make thee watchful against a fall, especially knowing how much it costs a man to be restored, it will be infinitely more dangerous if ever thou fallest again, not onely for fear God should no more accept thee to pardon; but even thy own hopes will be made more desperate and thy impatience greater; and thy shame turn to impudence, and thy own will be more estranged, violent, and refractory, and *thy latter end will be worse than thy beginning.* To which adde this consideration: That thy sin which was formerly in a good way of being pardoned, will not onely return upon thee with all its own loads, but with the basenesse of unthankfulnesse, and thou wilt be set as far back from Heaven as ever; and all thy former labours and fears, and watchings and agonies will be reckoned for nothing, but as arguments to upbraid thy folly, who when thou hadst set one foot in Heaven, didst pull that back and carry both to Hell.

Motives to Repentance.

I shall use no other arguments to move a sinner to repentance, but to tell him unlesse he does he shall certainly perish; and if he does repent timely and intirely, that is, live a holy life, he shall be forgiven and be saved: But yet I desire that this consideration be enlarged with some great circumstances; and let us remember.

1. That to admit mankinde to repentance and pardon was a favour greater than ever God gave to the angels and devils: for they were never admitted to the condition of second thoughts: Christ never groaned one groan for them; he never suffered one stripe, nor one affront, nor shed one drop of blood to restore them to hopes of blessednesse after their first failings. But this he did for us, he paid the score of our sins, only that we might be admitted to repent, and that this repentance might be effectual to the great purposes of felicity and salvation.

[i] *Οὐδὲν τῶν μεγάλων ἄφνω γίνεται.* Arrian.

2. Consider that as it cost Christ many millions of prayers and groans, and sighs, so he is now at this instant and hath been for these 1600 years night and day incessantly praying for grace to us that we may repent, and for pardon when we do, and for degrees of pardon beyond the capacities of our infirmities, and the merit of our sorrows and amendment: and this prayer he will continue till his second coming; [j] *for he ever liveth to make intercession for us*, and that we may know what it is in behalf of which he intercedes, S. *Paul* tells us his designe, [k] *we are Embassadours for Christ, as though he did beseech you by us, we pray you in Christs stead to be reconciled to God*; and what Christ prayes us to do, he prayes to God that we may do; that which he desires of us as his servants, he desires of God who is the fountain of the grace and powers unto us, and without whose assistance we can do nothing.

3. That ever we should repent, was so costly a purchase, and so great a concernment, and so high a favour, and the event is esteemed by God himself so great an excellency, that our blessed Saviour tells us, [l] *there shall be joy in Heaven over one sinner that repenteth*: meaning that when Christ shall be glorified and at the right hand of his Father make intercession for us, praying for our repentance, the conversion and repentance of every sinner is part of Christs glorification; it is the answering of his prayers, it is a portion of his reward, in which he does essentially glory by the joyes of his glorified humanity. This is the joy of our Lord himself directly, not of the Angels, save onely by reflexion: The joy (said our blessed Saviour) shall be *in the presence* of the Angels; they shall see the glory of the Lord, the answering of his prayers, the satisfaction of his desires, and the reward of his sufferings, in the repentance and consequent pardon of a sinner. For therefore he once suffered, and for that reason he rejoyces for ever: and therefore when a penitent sinner comes to receive the effect and full consummation of his pardon, it is called an *entering into the joy of our Lord*, that is, a partaking of that joy which Christ received at our conversion and enjoyed ever since.

4. Adde to this, that the rewards of Heaven are so great and glorious, and Christs burden is so light, his yoke is so easy, that it is a shameless impudence to expect so great gloryes at a lesse rate than so little a service; at a lower rate than a holy life. It cost the heart blood of the Son of God to obtain Heaven for us upon that condition; and who shall dye again to get Heaven for us upon easier terms? What would

[j] Hebr. 7: 25. [k] 2 Cor. 5: 20. [l] Luke 15: 7.

you do, if God should command you to kill your eldest son, or to work in the mines for a thousand years together, or to fast all thy life time with bread and water? Were not Heaven a very great bargain even after all this? And when God requires nothing of us, but to live soberly, justly and godly (which things of themselves are to a man a very great felicity, and necessary to our present well being) shall we think this to be an intolerable burden, and that Heaven is too little a purchase at that price? and that God in meer justice will take a death-bed sigh or groan, and a few unprofitable tears and promises in exchange for all our duty?

If these motives joyned together with our own interest, even as much as felicity and the sight of God, and the avoyding the intolerable pains of Hell and many intermedial judgements comes to, will not move us to leave, 1. The filthinesse, and 2. The trouble, and 3. The uneasinesse, and 4. The unreasonablenesse of sinne, and turn to God there is no more to be said, we must perish in our folly.

SECT. X.

Of preparation to, and the manner how to receive the holy Sacrament of the Lords Supper.

The celebration of the holy Sacrament is the great mysteriousnesse o the Christian religion, and succeeds to the most solemn rite of natura and Judaical religion, the Law of sacrificing. For God spared man kinde, and took the sacrifice of beasts together with our solem prayers for an instrument of expiation. But these could not purifie th soul from sin, but were typical of the sacrifice of something that could But nothing could do this, but either the offering of all that sinned that every man should be the *anathema* or *devoted thing*, or else by som one of the same capacity, who by some superadded excellency migh in his own personal sufferings have a value great enough to satisfie fo all the whole kinde of sinning persons. This the Son of God JESU CHRIST, God and Man undertook, and finished by a Sacrifice of him self upon the Altar of the Crosse.

2. This Sacrifice, because it was perfect, could be but one, an that once; but because the needs of the world should last as long a the world it self, it was necessary that there should be a perpetu

35 world it self] *3*+, world self *1 2*

ministery established, whereby this one sufficient sacrifice should be made eternally effectual to the several new arising needs of all the world who should desire it, or in any sence be capable of it.

3. To this end Christ was *made a Priest for ever*: he was initiated or consecrated on the crosse, and there began his Priesthood, which was to last till his coming to judgement. It began on earth, but was to last and be officiated in Heaven, where he sits perpetually, representing and exhibiting to the Father that great effective sacrifice (which he offered on the crosse) to eternal and never failing purposes.

4. As Christ is pleased to represent to his Father that great Sacrifice as a means of atonement and expiation for all mankinde, and with special purposes and intendment for all the elect, all that serve him in holinesse: so he hath appointed that the same ministery shall be done upon earth too, in our manner, and according to our proportion; and therefore hath constituted and separated an order of men, who by *shewing forth the Lords death* by Sacramental representation may pray unto God after the same manner that our Lord and high Priest does, that is, offer to God and represent in this solemn prayer and Sacrament, Christ as already offered, so sending up a gracious instrument whereby our prayers may for his sake and in the same manner of intercession be offered up to God in our behalf, and for all them for whom we pray to all those purposes for which Christ dyed.

5. As the Ministers of the Sacrament do in a Sacramental manner present to God the sacrifice of the crosse, by being imitators of Christs intercession; so the people are sacrificers too in their manner; for besides that, by saying *Amen*, they joyn in the act of him that ministers, and make it also to be their own: so when they eat and drink the consecrated and blessed Elements worthily, they receive Christ within them, and therefore may also offer him to God, while in their sacrifice of obedience and thanksgiving they present themselves to God with Christ whom they have spiritually received, that is, themselves with that which will make them gracious and acceptable. [m]The offering their bodies and souls and services to God *in him*, and *by him*, and *with him*, who is his Fathers *well-beloved, and in whom he is well pleased*, cannot but be accepted to all the purposes of blessing, grace, and glory.

6. This is the sum of the greatest mystery of our Religion: it is the

[m] Nosti tempora tu Jovis sereni,
Cum fulget placidus, suoque vultu,
Quo nil supplicibus solet negare. Mart. Ep. l. 5. 6.

32 [m]] *4+*, *om 1 2 3*

copy of the passion, and the ministration of the great mystery of our Redemption; and therefore whatsoever intitles us to the general priviledges of Christs passion, all that is necessary by way of disposition to the celebration of the Sacrament of his passion: because this celebration is our manner of applying or using it. The particulars of which preparation are represented in the following rules.

1. [n]No Man must dare to approach to the holy Sacrament of the Lords Supper if he be in a state of any one sin, that is, unlesse he have entered into the state of repentance, that is, of sorrow and amendment; lest it be said concerning him, as it was concerning *Judas*, the hand of him that betraieth me is with me on the Table: and he that receiveth Christ into an impure soul or body, first turns his most excellent nourishment into poyson, and then feeds upon it.

2. Every communicant must first have examined himself, that is, tried the condition and state of his soul, searched out the secret Ulcers, enquired out its weaknesses and indiscretions, and all those aptnesses where it is exposed to temptation, that by finding out its diseases he may finde a cure, and by discovering its aptnesses he may secure his present purposes of future amendment, and may be armed against dangers and temptations.

3. This examination must be a Mans own act, and inquisition into his life; but then also it should leade a Man on to run to those whom the Great physician of our souls Christ Jesus hath appointed to minister physick to our diseases, that in all dangers and great accidents we may be assisted for comfort and remedy, for medicine and caution.

4. In this affair let no Man deceive himself, and against such a time which publick Authority hath appointed for us to receive the Sacrament, weep for his sins by way of solemnity and ceremony, and stil retain the affection: but he that comes to this feast must have on the Wedding garment, that is, he must have *put on Jesus Christ*, and he must have *put off the old man with his affections and lusts*, and he must be *wholly conformed to Christ in the image of his minde*: For then we have put on Christ, when our souls are clothed with his righteousnesse, when every faculty of our soul is proportioned and vested according to the patern of Christs life. And therefore a Man must not leape from his last nights Surfet, and Bath, and then communicate: but when he hath begun the work of God effectually, and made some progresse in

[n] Vasa pura ad rem divinam. Plaut. in cap. Act 2. sc. 1.

---

note *n* Act 2] *cor*, Act 4 *1*+

repentance, and hath walked some stages and periods in the wayes of godlinesse, then let him come to him that is to minister it, and having made known the state of his soul, he is to be admitted: but to receive it into an unhallowed soul and body, is to receive the dust of the Tabernacle in the waters of jealousie; it will make the belly to swell, and the thigh to rot: it will not convey Christ to us, but the Devil will enter and dwell there, till with it he returns to his dwelling of torment. Remember alwayes that after a great sin or after a habit of sins, a Man is not soon made clean; and no unclean thing must come to this Feast. It is not the preparation of two or three dayes that can render a person capable of this banquet: For in this feast, all Christ, and Christs passion, and all his graces, the blessings and effects of his sufferings are conveyed: nothing can fit us for this, but what can unite us to Christ, and obtain of him to present our needs to his heavenly Father: this Sacrament can no otherwise be celebrated upon the same terms on which we may hope for pardon and Heaven it self.

5. When we have this general and indispensably necessary preparation, we are to make our souls more adorned and trimmed up with circumstances of pious actions, and special devotions, setting apart some portion of our time immediately before the day of solemnity according as our great occasions will permit; and this time is specially to be spent in actions of repentance, confession of our sins, renewing our purposes of holy living, praying for pardon of our failings, and for those graces which may prevent the like sadnesses for the time to come; meditation upon the passion, upon the infinite love of God expressed in so great mysterious manners of redemption; and indefinitely in all acts of vertue which may build our soules up into a Temple fit for the reception of Christ himself and the inhabitation of the holy Spirit.

6. The celebration of the holy Sacrament being the most solemne prayer, joyned with the most effectual instrument of its acceptance, must suppose us in the love of God, and in charity with all the World: and therefore we must before every Communion especially, remember what differences or jealousies are between us and any one else; and recompose all disunions, and cause right understandings betweene each other; offering to satisfie whom we have injured, and to forgive them who have injured us, without thoughts of resuming the quarrel when the solemnity is over; for that is but to rake the embers in light and phantastick ashes: it must be quenched, and a holy flame enkindled: no fires must be at all, but the fires of love and zeal; and the altar of incense will send up a sweet perfume, and make atonement for us.

7. When the day of the feast is come, lay aside all cares and impertinencies of the World, and remember that this is thy *Souls day*; a day of traffique and entercourse with Heaven. Arise early in the morning 1. Give God thanks for the approach of so great a blessing. 2. Confesse thy own unworthinesse to admit so Divine a Guest. 3. Then remember and deplore thy sinnes which have made thee so unworthy. 4. Then confesse Gods goodnesse and take sanctuary there, and upon him place thy hopes. 5. And invite him to thee with renewed acts of love, of holy desire, of hatred of his enemy, sin. 6. Make oblation of thy self wholly to be disposed by him, to the obedience of him, to his providence and possession, and pray him to enter, and dwell there for ever. And after this, with joy and holy fear, and the forwardness of love addresse thy self to the receiving of *him*, to whom and by whom, and for whom, all faith, and all hope, and all love in the whole Catholick Church, both in Heaven and Earth is designed; *him*, whom Kings and Queens, and whole Kingdoms are in love with, and count it the greatest honour in the World, that their Crowns and Scepters are laid at his holy feet.

8. When the holy Man stands at *the Table of blessing* and ministers the rite of consecration, then do as the Angels do, who behold, and love and wonder, that the Son of *God* should become food to the souls of his servants; that he who cannot suffer any change or *lessening* should be broken into pieces and enter into the body to support and nourish the spirit, and yet at the same time remain in Heaven while he descends to thee upon Earth; that he who hath essential felicity should become miserable and dye for thee, and then give himself to thee for ever to redeem thee from sin and misery; that by his wounds he should procure health to thee, by his affronts he should intitle thee to glory by his death he should bring thee to life, and by becoming a Man he should make thee *partaker of the Divine nature.* These are such glories that although they are made so obvious that each eye may behold them, yet they are also so deep, that no thought can fathome them: But so it hath pleased him to make these mysteries to be *sensible*, because the excellency and depth of the mercy is *not intelligible*; that while we are ravished and comprehended within the infinitenesse of so vast and mysterious a mercy, yet we may be as sure of it, as of that thing we see and feel, and smell and taste; but yet is so great, that we cannot understand it.

14 faith] faiths *4 5 6*

9. These holy mysteries are offered to our senses, but not to bee placed under our feet; they are sensible, but not common: and therefore as the weaknesse of the Elements addes wonder to the excellency of the Sacrament: so let our reverence and venerable usages of them adde honour to the Elements, and acknowledge the glory of the mystery, and the Divinity of the mercy. Let us receive the consecrated Elements with all devotion, and humility of body and spirit; and do this honour to it, that it be the first food we eat, and the first beverage we drink that day, unlesse it be in case of sicknesse, or other great necessity: and that your body and soul both be prepared to its reception with abstinence from secular pleasures, that you may better have attended fastings and preparatory prayers. [o]For if ever it be seasonable to observe the counsel of Saint *Paul*, that married persons by consent should abstain for a time that they may attend to solemne Religion, it is now. It was not by Saint *Paul* nor the after ages of the Church called a duty so to do, but it is most reasonable, that the more solemne actions of Religion should be attended to without the mixture of any thing that may discompose the minde, and make it more secular, or lesse religious.

10. In the act of receiving, exercise acts of Faith, with much confidence and resignation, believing it not to be common bread and wine, but holy in their use, holy in their signification, holy in their change, and holy in their effect, [p]and believe if thou art a worthy Communicant thou doest as verily receive Christs body and blood to all effects and purposes of the spirit, as thou doest receive the blessed Elements into thy mouth; that thou puttest thy finger to his hand, and thy hand into his side, and thy lips to his fontinel of blood, sucking life from his heart: and yet if thou doest communicate unworthily, thou eatest and drinkest Christ to thy danger, and death, and destruction. Dispute not concerning the secret of the mystery, and the nicety of the manner of Christs presence: it is sufficient to thee that Christ shall be present to thy soul, as an instrument of grace, as a pledge of the resurrection, as the earnest of glory and immortality, and a means of many intermedial blessings, even all such as are necessary for thee, and are in order to thy salvation: and to make all this good to thee, there is nothing necessary on thy part but a holy life, and a true belief of all the

[o] —Discedite ab aris
Cui tulit hesterna gaudia nocte Venus. Tibull.

[p] Cruci hæramus, sanguinem sugimus, et inter ipsa Redemptoris nostri vulnera figimus linguam. Cyprian. de Cœna Dom.

sayings of Christ; amongst which, indefinitely assent to the words of institution, and believe that Christ in the holy Sacrament gives thee his bodie and his blood. He that believes not this, is not a Christian: He that believes so much, needs not to enquire further, nor to intangle his faith by disbelieving his sence.

11. Fail not this solemnity according to the custom of pious and devout people to make an offering to God for the uses of religion and the poor, according to thy ability. For when Christ feasts his body, let us also feast our fellow members who have right to the same promises and are partakers of the same Sacrament, and partners of the same hope, and cared for under the same providence, and descended from the same common parents, and whose Father God is, and Christ is their Elder Brother. If thou chancest to communicate where this holy custom is not observed publickly, supply that want by thy private charity, but offer it to God at his holy Table, at least by thy private designing it there.

12. When you have received, pray and give thanks. Pray for all estates of men: for they also have an interest in the body of Christ whereof they are members: and you in conjunction with Christ (whom then you have received) are more fit to pray for them in that advantage and in the celebration of that holy sacrifice which then is Sacramentally represented to GOD. Give thanks for the passion of our Deares Lord: remember all its parts, and all the instruments of your Redemption: and beg of GOD that by a holy perseverance in well doing you ma from shadowes passe on to substances, from eating his body to seein his face, from the Typicall, Sacramentall, and Transient, to the Reall and Eternall Supper of the Lambe.

13. After the solemnity is done, let Christ dwell in your hearts b faith, and love, and obedience, and conformity to his life and death; a you have taken CHRIST *into you*, so *put* CHRIST *on you*, and conform every faculty of your soul and body to his holy image and perfection. Remember that now Christ is all one with you; and therefore when yo are to do an action, consider how Christ did, or would do the like, an do you imitate his example, and transcribe his copy, and understan all his Commandments, and choose all that he propounded, an desire his promises and fear his threatenings, and marry his loves an hatreds, and contract all his friendships; for then you do every da communicate; especially when Christ thus dwells in you, and you i Christ, growing up towards *a perfect man in Christ Jesus.*

15 by] let *2 3*   37 all] *om 6+*

14. Do not instantly upon your return from Church, return also to the world, and secular thoughts and imployments; but let the remaining parts of that day be like a *post-Communion* or an *after-office*, entertaining your blessed Lord with all the caresses and sweetnesse of love and colloquies, and entercourses of duty and affection, acquainting him with all your needs, and revealing to him all your secrets, and opening all your infirmities; and as the affairs of your person or imployment call you off, so retire again with often ejaculations and acts of entertainment to your beloved Guest.

The effects and benefits of worthy communicating.

When I said that the sacrifice of the crosse which Christ offered for all the sins and all the needs of the world is represented to God by the Minister in the Sacrament, and offered up in prayer and Sacramental memory, after the manner that Christ himself intercedes for us in Heaven (so far as his glorious Priesthood is imitable by his Ministers on earth) I must of necessity also mean, that all the benefits of that sacrifice are then conveyed to all that communicate worthily: But if we descend to particulars; Then and there the Church is nourished in her faith, strengthened in her hope, enlarged in her bowels with an increasing charity: there all the members of Christ are joyned with each other, and all to Christ their head; and we again renew the Covenant with God in Jesus Christ, and God seals his part, and we promise for ours, and Christ unites both, and the holy Ghost signes both in the collation of those graces which we then pray for, and exercise and receive all at once: there our bodies are nourished with the signes, and our souls with the mystery: our bodies receive into them the seed of an immortal nature, and our souls are joyned with him, who is the first fruits of the resurrection and never can dye: and if we desire any thing else and need it, here it is to be prayed for, here to be hoped for, here to be received. Long life and health, and recovery from sicknesse, and competent support and maintenance, and peace, and deliverance from our enemies, and content, and patience, and joy, and sanctified riches, or a cheerful poverty and liberty, and whatsoever else is a blessing, was purchased for us by Christ in his death and resurrection, and in his intercession in Heaven: and this Sacrament being that to our particulars, which the great mysteries are in themselves, and by designe to all the world, if we receive worthily we shall receive any of these blessings, according as God shall choose for us;

and he will not onely choose with more wisdom, but also with more affection than we can for our selves.

After all this, it is advised by the Guides of souls, wise men and pious, that all persons should communicate very often, even as often as they can without excuses or delayes: Every thing that puts us from so holy an imployment when we are moved to it, being either a sin or an imperfection, an Infirmity or indevotion, and an unactivenesse of Spirit. All Christian people must come: They indeed that are in the state of sin must not come *so*, but yet they must come: First they must quit their state of death, and then partake of the bread of life. They that are at enmity with their neighbours must come, that is no excuse for their not coming; onely they must not bring their enmity along with them, but leave it, and then come. [q]They that have variety of secular imployments must come; onely they must leave their secular thoughts and affections behinde them, and then come and converse with God. If any man be well grown in grace he must needs come, because he is excellently disposed to so holy a feast: but he that is but in the infancy of piety had need to come that so he may grow in grace. The strong must come lest they become weak, and the weak that they may become strong. The sick must come to be cured; the healthful to be preserved. They that have leisure must come because they have no excuse: They that have no leisure must come hither, that by so excellent religion they may sanctifie their businesse. The penitent sinners must come, that they may be justified: and *they that are justified, that they may be justified still.* They that have fears and great reverence to these mysteries, and think no preparation to be sufficient must receive, that they may learn how to receive the more worthily: and they that have a lesse degree of reverence, must come often to have it heightened: 'that as those Creatures that live amongst the snowes of the Mountains turne white with their food and conversation with such perpetual whitenesses': so our souls may be transformed into the similitude and union with Christ by our perpetual feeding on him, and conversation, not onely in his Courts, but in his very heart, and most secret affections, and incomparable purities.

[q] L'Eveque de Genève, introd. à la vie dévote.

Ad Sect. I, II, III.

Prayers for all sorts of Men, and all necessities; relating to the several parts of the vertue of Religion.

A Prayer for the Graces of Faith, Hope, Charity.

O Lord God of infinite mercy, of infinite excellency, who hast sent thy holy Son into the world to redeem us from an intolerable misery, and to teach us a holy religion, and to forgive us an infinite debt: give me thy holy Spirit, that my understanding and all my faculties may be so resigned to the discipline and doctrine of my Lord, that I may be prepared in minde and will to dye for the testimony of Jesus, and to suffer any affliction or calamity that shall offer to hinder my duty, or tempt me to shame or sin, or apostacy: and let my faith be the parent of a good life, a strong shield to repell the fiery darts of the Devil, and the Author of a holy hope, of modest desires, of confidence in God, and of a never failing charity to thee my God, and to all the world, that I may never have my portion with the unbelievers, or uncharitable, and desperate persons; but may be supported by the strengths of faith in all temptations, and may be refreshed with the comforts of a holy hope in all my sorrows, and may bear the burden of the Lord, and the infirmities of my neighbour by the support of charity, that the yoak of Jesus may become easy to me, and my love may do all the miracles of grace, till from grace it swell to glory, from earth to heaven, from duty to reward, from the imperfections of a beginning, and little growing love it may arrive to the consummation of an eternal and never ceasing charity, through Jesus Christ the Son of thy love, the Anchor of our hope, and the Author and finisher of our faith, to whom with thee, O Lord God, Father of Heaven and Earth, and with thy holy Spirit be all glory, and love, and obedience, and dominion now and forever. *Amen.*

Acts of love by way of prayer and ejaculation: to be used in private.

1. [r]O God thou art my God, early will I seek thee: my soul thirsteth for thee, my flesh longeth for thee in a dry and thirsty land where no water is, to see thy power and thy glory so as I have seen thee in the

[r] Psal. 63: 1–3.

---

1 *Ad* Sect. I, II, III.] *ed, om 1+* note *r* Psal. 63: 1–3] *cor*, Psal. 63. *1 2 3 4 5 6*, Psal. 63. 1 etc. *7 8*.

sanctuary: because thy loving kindnes is better than life, my lips shall praise thee.

2. [s]I am ready not only to be bound, but to dye for the name of the Lord Jesus.

3. [t]How amiable are thy Tabernacles thou Lord of Hosts: my soul longeth, yea even fainteth for the courts of the Lord: My heart and my flesh crieth out for the living God: Blessed are they that dwell in thy house, they will still be praising thee.

4. O Blessed Jesu thou art worthy of all adoration, and all honour, and all love: Thou art the Wonderful, the Counsellor, the mighty God, the Everlasting Father, the Prince of peace, of thy government and peace there shall be no end: thou art the brightnesse of thy Fathers glory, the expresse image of his person, the appointed Heir of all things: Thou upholdest all things by the word of thy power: Thou didst by thy self purge our sins: Thou art set on the right hand of the Majesty on high: Thou art made better than the Angels, thou hast by inheritance obtained a more excellent name than they. Thou, O dearest Jesus, art the head of the Church, the beginning and the first born from the dead: in all things thou hast the preheminence, and it pleased the Father that in thee should all fulnesse dwell. Kingdoms are in love with thee: Kings lay their crowns and scepters at thy feet, and Queens are thy handmaids, and wash the feet of thy servants.

A Prayer to be said in any affliction, as death of children, of husband or wife, in great poverty, in imprisonment, in a sad and disconsolate spirit, and in temptations to despair.

O Eternal God, Father of Mercyes and God of all comfort with much mercy look upon the sadnesses and sorrowes of thy servant. My sins lye heavy upon me, and presse me sore, and there is no health in my bones by reason of thy displeasure and my sin. The waters are gone over me, and I stick fast in the deep mire, and my miseries are without comfort, because they are punishments of my sin: and I am so evil and unworthy a person, that though I have great desires, yet I have no dispositions or worthiness towards receiving comfort. My sins have caused my sorrow, and my sorrow does not cure my sins: and unless for thy own sake, and merely because thou art good, thou shalt pity me

[s] Acts 21: 13. [t] Psal. 84: 1, 2, 4.

note *s* Acts 21: 13] *78*, Psal. 23 *123456* note *t* Psal. 84: 1, 2, 4] *78*, Psal. 84 *123456*

and relieve me, I am as much without remedy, as now I am without comfort. Lord pity me; Lord let thy grace refresh my Spirit. Let thy comforts support me, thy mercy pardon me, and never let my portion be amongst hopelesse and accursed spirits; for thou art good and gracious; and I throw my self upon thy mercy. Let me never let my hold go, and do thou with me what seems good in thy own eyes: I cannot suffer more than I have deserved: and yet I can need no relief so great as thy mercy is: for thou art infinitely more merciful than I can be miserable: and thy mercy which is above all thy own works, must needs be far above all my sin and all my misery. Dearest Jesus, let me trust in thee for ever, and let me never be confounded. *Amen.*

Ejaculations and short meditations to be used in time of sickness and sorrow, or danger of Death.

1. [u]Hear my Prayer, O Lord, and let my crying come unto thee. Hide not thy face from me in the time of my trouble, incline thine ear unto me when I call: O hear me and that right soon. For my dayes are consumed like smoak, and my bones are burnt up as it were a firebrand. My heart is smitten down and withered like grass; so that I forget to eat my bread: and that because of thine indignation and wrath: for thou hast taken me up and cast me down. [v]Thine arrows stick fast in me and thy hand presseth me sore. There is no health in my flesh because of thy displeasure: neither is there any rest in my bones by reason of my sin. My wickednesses are gone over my head and are a sore burden too heavy for me to bear. But I will confesse my wickednesse, and be sorry for my sin. [w]O Lord rebuke me not in thy indignation, neither chasten me in thy displeasure. [x]Lord be merciful unto me, heal my soul for I have sinned against thee.

2. [y]Have mercy upon me, O God, after thy great goodnesse, according to the multitude of thy mercies do away mine offences. [z]O remember not the sins and offences of my youth: but according to thy mercy think thou upon me, O Lord for thy goodnesse. [a]Wash me thoroughly from my wickednesse: and cleanse me from my sin. Make me a clean heart, O God, and renew a right spirit within me. Cast me not away from thy presence, from thy all-hallowing and life-giving presence:

[u] Psal. 102: 1–4, 10. [v] Psal. 38: 2–4, 18. [w] Psal. 6:1. [x] Psal. 41:4. [y] Psal. 51: 1. [z] Psal. 25:7. [a] Psal. 51:2, 10, 11.

14 crying] cry *7 8* 25 thy] thine ~ *7 8* notes *u* to *h* *These notes all appear for the first time in* 7 *and are reprinted in subsequent editions.*

and take not thy holy Spirit, thy sanctifying, thy guiding, thy comforting, thy supporting, and confirming Spirit from me.

3. [b]O God, thou art my God for ever and ever: thou shalt be my guide unto death. [c]Lord comfort me now that I lye sick upon my bed: make thou my bed in all my sicknesse. [d]O deliver my soul from the place of Hell: and do thou receive me. [e]My heart is disquieted within me, and the fear of death is fallen upon me. [f]Behold thou hast made my dayes as it were a span long, and mine age is even as nothing in respect of thee, and verily every man living is altogether vanity. When thou with rebukes doest chasten man for sin, thou makest his beauty to consume away like a moth fretting a garment: every man therefore is but vanity. And now Lord what is my hope? truly my hope is even in thee. Hear my prayer, O Lord, and with thine ears consider my calling, hold not thy peace at my tears. Take this plague away from me: I am consumed by the means of thy heavy hand. I am a stranger with thee and a sojourner, as all my Fathers were. O spare me a little that I may recover my strength before I go hence and be no more seen. [g]My soul cleaveth unto the dust: O quicken me according to thy word. [h]And when the snares of death compasse me round about: let not the pains of hell take hold upon me.

An Act of Faith concerning resurrection and the day of judgment, to be said by sick persons or meditated.

[i]I know that my Redeemer liveth, and that he shall stand at the latter day upon the earth: and though after my skin worms destroy this body, yet in my flesh shall I see God: whom I shall see for my self, and mine eyes shal behold, though my reins be consumed within me.

[j]God shall come and shall not keep silence: there shall go before him a consuming fire, and a mighty tempest shall be stirred up round about him: he shall call the heaven from above, and the earth that he may judge his people. [k]O blessed Jesu, thou art my judge and thou art my Advocate: have mercy upon me in the hour of my death, and in the day of judgment.

[b] Psal. 48: 14. [c] Psal. 41: 3. [d] Psal. 49: 15.
[e] Psal. 55: 4. [f] Psal. 39: 6, 12, 13, 11, 14, 15.
[g] Psal. 119: 25. [h] Psal. 116: 3. [i] Job 19: 25.
[j] Psal. 50: 3–4. [k] See John 5: 28 and 1 Thessal. 4: 15.

8 mine] my *7 8*   27 [i]] *7 8, om 1 2 3 4 5 6*   note *d* Psal. 49: 15.] *cor, om 1 2 3 4 5 6*, Psal. 49. 5. *7 8*   note *e* Psal. 55: 4.] *cor, om 1 2 3 4 5 6*, Psal. 55. 14. *7 8*   note *f* Psal. 39: 6, 12, 13, 11, 14, 15] *cor, om 1 2 3 4 5 6*, Psal. 39: 5, 11, 7, 12, 10, 12, 13 *7 8*   note *i* Job 19: 25] *7 8*, Job 19. *1 2 3 4 5 6*

Short Prayers to be said by sick persons.

1. O Holy Jesus, thou art a merciful High Priest and touched with the sense of our infirmities; thou knowest the sharpnesse of my sicknesse, and the weaknesse of my person. The clouds are gathered about me, and thou hast covered me with thy storm: My understanding hath not such apprehension of things as formerly: Lord let thy mercy support me, thy spirit guide me, and lead me through the valley of this death safely; that I may passe it patiently, holily, with perfect resignation, and let me rejoyce in the Lord, in the hopes of pardon, in the expectation of glory, in the sence of thy mercies, in the refreshments of thy spirit, in a victory over all temptations.

2. Thou hast promised to be with us in tribulation. Lord, my soul is troubled, and my body is weak, and my hope is in thee, and my enemies are busy and mighty, now make good thy holy promise. Now O holy Jesus, now let thy hand of grace be upon me: restrain my ghostly enemies, and give me all sorts of spiritual assistances: Lord remember thy servant in the day when thou bindest up thy Jewels.

3. O take from me all tediousnesse of Spirit, all impatience and unquietnesse: Let me possesse my soul in patience, and resigne my soul and body into thy hands, as into the hands of a faithful Creator, and a blessed Redeemer.

4. O holy Jesu, thou didst dye for us; by thy sad, pungent, and intolerable pains which thou enduredst for me, have pity on me, and ease my pain, or increase my patience. Lay on me no more than thou shalt enable me to bear. I have deserved it all and more, and infinitely more. Lord I am weak and ignorant, timerous and inconstant, and I fear lest something should happen that may discompose the state of my soul, that may displease thee: Do what thou wilt with me, so thou doest but preserve me in thy fear and favour. Thou knowest that it is my great fear, but let thy Spirit secure, that nothing may be able to separate me from the love of God in Jesus Christ; and then smite me here, that thou mayest spare me for ever; and yet O Lord smite me friendly: for thou knowest my infirmities. Into thy hands I commend my spirit, for thou hast redeemed me, O Lord, thou God of truth. Come holy Spirit, help me in this conflict. Come Lord Jesus, come quickly.

2 1.] *om 6+* 12 2.] *om 6+* 31 and then smite] and smite *4+*

Let the sick person often meditate upon these following promises and gracious words of God.

My help cometh of the Lord who preserveth them that are true of heart, *Psal. 7: 11.*

And all they that know thy Name will put their trust in thee: for thou Lord hast never failed them that seek thee, *Psal. 9: 10.*

O how plentiful is thy goodnesse which thou hast laid up for them that fear thee, and that thou hast prepared for them that put their trust in thee, even before the sons of men, *Psal. 31: 20.*

Behold the eye of the Lord is upon them that fear him, and upon them that put their trust in his mercy, to deliver their souls from death, *Psal. 33: 17.*

The Lord is nigh unto them that are of a contrite heart: and will save such as are of an humble spirit, *Psal. 34: 18.*

Thou Lord shalt save both man and beast: how excellent is thy mercy, O God: and the children of men shall put their trust under the shadow of thy wings, *Psal. 36: 7.*

They shall be satisfied with the plenteousness of thy house: and thou shalt give them to drink of thy pleasures as out of the rivers, *v. 8.*

For with thee is the well of life: and in thy light we shall see light, *v. 9.*

Commit thy way unto the Lord, and put thy trust in him, and he shall bring it to passe, *Ps. 37: 5.*

But the salvation of the righteous cometh of the Lord: who is also their strength in the time of trouble, *v. 40.*

So that a Man shall say, verily there is a reward for the righteous: doubtlesse there is a God that judgeth the earth, *Psal. 58: 10.*

Blessed is the man whom thou choosest and receivest unto thee: he shall dwell in thy court, and shall be satisfied with the pleasures of thy house, even of thy holy temple, *Psal. 65: 4.*

They that sow in tears shall reap in joy, *Psal. 126: 6.*

It is written, I will never leave thee nor forsake thee, *Heb. 13: 5.*

The prayer of faith shall save the sick: and the Lord shall raise him up: and if he have committed sins they shalbe forgiven, *Jam. 5: 15.*

Come and let us return unto the Lord: for he hath torn and he will heal us, he hath smitten, and he will binde us up, *Hos. 6: 1.*

1 *person*] *man 4+* 12 *Psal. 33: 17*] *7 8, Psal. 33 1 2 3 4 5 6* 34 *Jam. 5: 15*] *Jam. 5. 5 7*

If we sin we have an Advocate with the Father, Jesus Christ the righteous, and he is the propitiation for our sins, *1 John 2: 1, 2.*

If we confesse our sins he is faithful and righteous to forgive us our sins, and to cleanse us from all unrighteousnesse, *1 John 1: 9.* He that forgives shall be forgiven, *Luke 6: 37.*

And this is the confidence that we have in him, that if we ask any thing according to his will he heareth us, *1 John 5: 14.* And ye know that he was manifested to take away our sins, *1 John 3: 5.*

If ye being evil know to give good things to your children, how much more shall your Father which is in Heaven give good things to them that ask him? *Matth. 7: 11.*

This is a faithful saying and worthy of all acceptation, that Jesus Christ came into the World to save sinners. *1 Tim. 1: 15.* He that hath given us his Son, how should not he with him give us all things else? *Rom. 8: 32.*

Acts of hope to be used by sick persons, after a pious life.

1. I am perswaded that neither death nor life, nor Angels, nor principalities, nor powers, nor things present, nor things to come, nor height, nor depth, nor any other creature shall be able to separate me from the love of God which is in Christ Jesus our Lord, *Rom. 8: 38, 39.*

2. I have fought a good fight, I have finished my course, I have kept the faith. Henceforth there is laid up for me a crown of righteousnesse, which the Lord the righteous Judge shall give me at that day, and not to me onely, but unto all them also that love his appearing, *2 Tim. 4: 7, 8.*

3. Blessed be the God, even the Father of our Lord Jesus Christ, the Father of mercies and the God of all comforts who comforts us in all our tribulation, *2 Cor. 1: 3, 4.*

A prayer to be said in behalf of a sick or dying person.

1. O Lord God, there is no number of thy dayes, nor of thy mercies; and the sins and sorrowes of thy servant also are multiplied. Lord look upon him with much mercy and pity, forgive him all his sinnes, comfort his sorrowes, ease his pain, satisfie his doubts, relieve his feares, instruct his ignorances, strengthen his understanding, take from him

2 *1 John 2: 1, 2*] 7 8, *1 John 2. 2* 1 2 3 4 5 6 13 *1 Tim. 1: 15.*] 7 8, *om* 1 2 3 4 5 6
15 *Rom. 8: 32.*] 7 8, *om* 1 2 3 4 5 6 20 *Rom. 8: 38, 39*] 7 8, *Rom. 8. 38* 1 2 3 4 5 6
28 *2 Cor. 1: 3, 4*] 7 8, *2 Cor. 1. 3* 1 2 3 4 5 6

all disorders of spirit, weaknesse and abuse of fancy: Restraine the malice and power of the spirits of darknesse; and suffer him to be injured neither by his ghostly enemies, nor his own infirmities, and let a holy and a just peace, the peace of God be within his conscience.

2. Lord preserve his senses till the last of his time, strengthen his faith, confirm his hope, and give him a never ceasing charity to thee our God, and to all the world: stir up in him a great and proportionable contrition for all the evils he hath done, and give him a just measure of patience for all he suffers: give him prudence, memory, and consideration, rightly to state the accounts of his soul, and do thou remind him of all his duty, that when it shall please thee that his soul goes out from the prison of his body, it may be received by Angels, and preserved from the surprize of evil spirits, and from the horrors and amazements of new and stranger Regions; and be laid up in the bosom of our Lord, till at the day of thy second coming it shall be reunited to the body, which is now to be laid down in weaknes and dishonour, but we humbly beg may then be raised up with glory and power for ever to live and to behold the face of God in the glories of the Lord Jesus, who is our hope, our resurrection, and our life, the light of our eyes and the joy of our soules, our blessed and ever glorious Redeemer. Amen.

Hither the sick person may draw in, and use the acts of several vertues respersed in the several parts of this book, the several Letanies, viz. *of repentance, of the passion, and the single prayers, according to his present needs.*

A prayer to be said in a storm at Sea.

O my God, thou didst create the earth and the Sea for thy glory and the use of Man, and doest daily shew wonders in the deep: look upon the danger and fear of thy servant: my sins have taken hold upon me, and without the supporting arm of thy mercy I cannot look up; but my trust is in thee. Do thou, O Lord, rebuke the Sea, and make it calm; for to thee the windes and the sea obey: let not the waters swallow me up, but let thy Spirit, the Spirit of gentlenesse and mercy move upon the waters: Be thou reconciled unto thy servants, and then the face of the waters will be smooth. I fear that my sinnes make me, like *Jonas*, the cause of the tempest. Cast out all my sins, and throw not thy servants away from thy presence, and from the land of the living into the depths where all things are forgotten: But if it be thy wil that we shall go down

21 *person*] *persons* 4 5 7 8

into the waters, Lord receive my soul into thy holy hands, and preserve it in mercy and safety till the day of restitution of all things: and be pleased to unite my death to the death of thy Son, and to accept of it so united as a punishment for all my sinnes, that thou mayest forget all thine anger, and blot my sinnes out of thy book, and write my soul there for Jesus Christ his sake, our dearest Lord and most mighty Redeemer. Amen.

Then make an act of resignation, thus,

To God pertain the issues of life and death. It is the Lord, let him do what seemeth good in his own eyes. Thy will be done in earth as it is in Heaven.

Recite Psalm 107. and 130.

A form of a vow to be made in this or the like danger.

If the Lord will be gracious and hear the prayer of his servant, and bring me safe to shore, then I will praise him secretly and publickly, and pay unto the uses of charity [or Religion] [then name the sum you designe for holy uses.] O my God my goods are nothing unto thee: I will also be thy servant all the dayes of my life, and remember this mercy and my present purposes, and live more to Gods glory, and with a stricter duty: And do thou please to accept this vow as an instance of my importunity, and the greatnesse of my needs, and be thou graciously moved to pity and deliver me. *Amen.*

This form also may be used in praying for a blessing on an enterprize; and may be instanced in actions of devotion as well as of charity.

A prayer before a journey.

O Almighty God who fillest all things with thy presence, and art a God afar off as well as neer at hand: thou didst send thy Angel to blesse *Jacob* in his journey, and didst leade the children of *Israel* through the Red Sea, making it a wall on the right hand and on the left: be pleased to let thy Angel go out before me and guide me in my journey, preserving me from dangers of robbers, from violence of enemies, and sudden and sad accidents, from falls and errours: and prosper my journey to thy glory, and to all my innocent purposes: and preserve me from all sin, that I may return in peace and holinesse, with thy favour and thy blessing, and may serve thee in thankfulnesse and obedience all the dayes of my pilgrimage, and at last bring me to thy countrey, to the coelestial Jerusalem, there to dwell in thy house and to sing praises to thee for ever. *Amen.*

Ad Sect. IV.

A prayer to be said before hearing or reading the word of God.

O holy and eternal Jesus who hast begotten us by thy word, renewed us by thy Spirit, fed us by thy Sacraments, and by the dayly ministery of thy word: still go on to build us up to life eternal. Let thy most holy Spirit be present with me and rest upon me in the reading [or hearing] thy sacred word; that I may do it humbly, reverently, without prejudice, with a minde ready and desirous to learn and to obey; that I may be readily furnished and instructed to every good work, and may practise all thy holy laws and commandments, to the glory of thy holy name, O holy and eternal Jesus. *Amen.*

Ad Sect. V, IX, X.

A form of confession of sins, and repentance to be used upon fasting dayes, or dayes of humiliation; especially in Lent, and before the Holy Sacrament.

Have mercy upon me, O God, after thy great goodnesse, according to the multitude of thy mercies do away mine offences. For I will confesse my wickednesse and be sorry for my sin. O my Dearest Lord, I am not worthy to be accounted amongst the meanest of thy servants: not worthy to be sustained by the least fragments of thy mercy, but to be shut out of thy presence for ever with dogs and unbelievers. *But for thy names sake, O Lord, be merciful unto my sin, for it is great.*

I am the vilest of sinners, and the worst of men: proud and vain glorious, impatient of scorn or of just reproof: not enduring to be slighted, and yet extreamly deserving it: I have been cosened by the colours of humility, and when I have truly called my self vitious, I could not endure any man else should say so or think so. I have been disobedient to my Superiours, churlish and ungentle in my behaviour, unchristian and unmanly. *But for thy names sake, etc.*

O Just and Dear God, how can I expect pitty or pardon who am so angry and peevish, with and without cause, envious at good, rejoycing in the evil of my neighbours, negligent of my charge, idle and uselesse, timerous and base, jealous and impudent, ambitious and hard hearted, soft, unmortified and effeminate in my life, indevout in my prayers, without fancie or affection, without attendance to them or perseverance in them; but passionate and curious in pleasing my appetite of meat and drink and pleasures, making matter both for sin and sicknesse; and I have reaped the cursed fruits of such improvidence, entertaining undecent and impure thoughts; and I have brought them forth in undecent and impure actions, and the spirit of uncleanness hath entered in, and unhallowed the temple which thou didst consecrate for the habitation of thy Spirit of love and holinesse. *But for thy names sake, O Lord, be merciful unto my sin, for it is great.*

Thou hast given me a whole life to serve thee in, and to advance my hopes of heaven: and this pretious time I have thrown away upon my sins and vanities, being improvident of my time and of my talent, and of thy grace and my own advantages; resisting thy Spirit, and quenching him. I have been a great lover of my self, and yet used many wayes to destroy my self: I have pursued my temporal ends with greedinesse and indirect means: I am revengeful and unthankful, forgetting benefits, but not so soon forgetting injuries: curious and murmuring: a great breaker of promises: I have not loved my neighbours good, nor advanced it in all things where I could: I have bin unlike thee in all things, I am unmerciful and unjust; a sottish admirer of things below, and careless of heaven and the wayes that lead thither.

But for thy names sake, O Lord, be merciful unto my sin, for it is great.

All my senses have been windows to let sin in, and death by sin; Mine eyes have been adulterous and covetous; mine ears open to slander and detraction: my tongue and palate loose and wanton, intemperate, and of foul language, talkative and lying, rash and malicious, false and flattering, irreligious and irreverent, detracting and censorious: My hands have bin injurious and unclean: my passions violent and rebellious: my desires impatient and unreasonable: all my members and all my faculties have been servants of sin: and my very best actions have more matter of pity, than of confidence; being imperfect in my best, and intolerable in most. *But for thy names sake, O Lord, etc.*

Unto this and a far bigger heap of sin, I have added also the faults of others to my own score, by neglecting to hinder them to sin in all hat I could and ought: but I also have encouraged them in sin, have aken off their fears and hardened their consciences and tempted hem directly, and prevailed in it to my own ruine and theirs, unlesse thy glorious and unspeakable mercy hath prevented so intolerable a calamity.

Lord I have abused thy mercy, despised thy judgements, turned thy grace into wantonnesse; I have been unthankful for thy infinite loving kindnesse: I have sinned and repented, and then sinned again, and resolved against it, and presently broke it; and then I tyed my self up with vows, and then was tempted, and then I yielded by little and little till I was willingly lost again, and my vows fell off like cords of vanity.

Miserable man that I am, who shall deliver me from this body of sin?

And yet O Lord, I have another heap of sins to be unloaded. My secret sins O Lord, are innumerable; sins I noted not, sins that I willingly neglected, sins that I acted upon willfull ignorance and voluntary mispersuasion; sins that I have forgot; and sins which a diligent and a watchful spirit might have prevented, but I would not. Lord I am confounded with the multitude of them, and the horrour of their remembrance though I consider them nakedly in their direct appearances, without the deformity of their unhandsome and aggravating circumstances: but so dressed they are a sight too ugly: an instance of amazement, infinite in degrees, and insufferable in their load.

And yet thou hast spared me all this while, and hast not thrown me into Hell, where I have deserved to have been long since, and even now to have been shut up to an eternity of torments with insupportable amazement, fearing the revelation of thy day.

Miserable man that I am, who shall deliver me from this body of sin?

Thou shalt answer for me, O Lord my God; Thou that Prayest for me shalt be my Judge.

The Prayer.

Thou hast prepared for me a more healthful sorrow. O deny not thy servant when he begs sorrow of thee: Give me a deep contrition for my sins, a hearty detestation and loathing of them, hating them worse than death with torments. Give me grace intirely, presently, and for ever to forsake them; to walk with care and prudence, with fear and watchfulnesse all my dayes; to doe all my duty with diligence and charity, with zeal and a never fainting spirit: to redeem the time, to trust upon thy mercies, to make use of all the instruments of grace, to work out my salvation with fear and trembling, that thou mayest have the glory of

11 secret] *2 3 7 8*, secrets *1 4 5 6* 17 appearances] appearance *4*+

pardoning all my sins, and I may reap the fruit of all thy mercies, and al thy graces, of thy patience and long-suffering, even to live a holy life here, and to reign with thee for ever, through Jesus Christ our Lord. *Amen.*

Ad Sect. VI.

Special devotions to be used upon the Lords-day, and the great Festivalls of Christians.

In the Morning recite the following forme of Thanksgiving: upon the special Festivalls adding the commemoration of the special blessing according to the following prayers: adding such prayers as you shall choose out of the foregoing Devotions.

Besides the ordinary and publick duties of the day, if you retire into your closet to read and meditate; after you have performed that duty, say the song of S. Ambrose *commonly called the* Te Deum *or 'We praise thee, etc.' then add the prayers for particular graces which are at the end of the former Chapters, such and as many of them as shall fit your present needs and affections: ending with the Lords prayer. This form of devotion, may for variety, be indifferently used at other times.*

A forme of thanksgiving with a recital of publick and private blessings: To be used upon Easter-day, Whit-sunday, Ascension-day, and all Sundayes of the year: but the middle part of it may be reserved for the more solemn Festivals; and the other used upon the ordinary; as every mans affections or leisure shall determine.

Ex Liturgia S. Basilii magna ex parte.

O Eternal Essence, Lord God, Father Almighty, Maker of all things in Heaven and Earth, it is a good thing to give thanks to thee, O Lord, and to pay to thee all reverence, worship and devotion from a clean and prepared heart; and with an humble spirit to present a living and reasonable sacrifice to thy holinesse and Majesty: for thou hast given unto us the knowledge of thy truth: and who is able to declare thy greatnesse, and to recount all thy marvellous works which thou hast done in all the generations of the world?

O Great Lord and Governour of all things, Lord and Creator of all things visible and invisible, who sittest upon the throne of thy glory, and beholdest the secrets of the lowest abysse and darknesse, thou art without beginning, uncircumscribed, incomprehensible, unalterable, and seated for ever unmoveable in thy own essential happinesse and tranquillity: Thou art the Father of our Lord JESUS CHRIST: who is,

Our Dearest and most Gracious Saviour, our hope, the wisdom of the Father, the image of thy goodnesse, the Word eternal and the brightnesse of thy person, the power of God from eternal ages, the true light that lightneth every Man that cometh into the World, the Redemption of Man, and the Sanctification of our Spirits.

By whom the holy Ghost descended upon the Church; the holy Spirit of truth, the seal of adoption, the earnest of the inheritance of the Saints, the first fruits of everlasting felicity, the life-giving power, the fountain of sanctification, the comfort of the Church, the ease of the afflicted, the support of the weak, the wealth of the poor, the teacher of the doubtful, scrupulous and ignorant, the anchor of the fearful, the infinite reward of all faithful souls, by whom all reasonable and understanding creatures serve thee, and send up a never-ceasing, and a never-rejected sacrifice of prayer, and praises, and adoration.

All Angels and Archangels, all Thrones and Dominions, all Principalities and Powers, the Cherubins with many eyes, and the Seraphins covered with wings from the terror and amazement of thy brightest glory: These and all the powers of Heaven do perpetually sing praises and never-ceasing Hymns, and eternal Anthems to the glory of the eternal God, the Almighty Father of Men and Angels.

Holy is our God: Holy is the Almighty: Holy is the Immortal: Holy, Holy, Holy, Lord God of Sabaoth, Heaven and Earth are full of the Majesty of thy glory. Amen. With these holy and blessed Spirits I also thy servant, O thou great lover of souls, though I be unworthy to offer praise to such a Majesty, yet out of my bounden duty humbly offer up my heart and voice to joyn in this blessed quire, and confesse the glories of the Lord. For thou art holy, and of thy greatnesse there is no end; and in thy justice and goodnesse thou hast measured out to us all thy works.

Thou madest man out of the earth and didst form him after thine own image: thou didst place him in a garden of pleasure, and gavest him laws of righteousnesse to be to him a seed of immortality.

O that men would therefore praise the Lord for his goodnesse: and declare the wonders that he hath done for the children of men.

For when man sinned and listened to the whispers of a tempting spirit, and refused to hear the voice of God, thou didst throw him out from Paradise, and sentest him to till the Earth; but yet left not hi

39 left] leftest *2 3 6+*

condition without remedy, but didst provide for him the salvation of a new birth, and by the blood of thy Son didst redeem and pay the price to thine own justice for thine own creature, lest the work of thine own hands should perish.

O that men would therefore praise the Lord, etc.

For thou, O Lord, in every age didst send testimonies from Heaven, blessings and Prophets, and fruitful seasons, and preachers of righteousness, and miracles of power, and mercy: thou spakest by thy Prophets and saidst, *I will help by one that is mighty*: and in the fulnesse of time spakest to us by thy Son, by whom thou didst make both the Worlds: who by the word of his power, sustains all things in Heaven and Earth: who thought it no robbery to be equal to the Father: who being before all time was pleased to be born in time, to converse with men, to be incarnate of a holy Virgin: he emptied himself of all his glories, took on him the form of a servant, in all things being made like unto us, in a soul of passions and discourse, in a body of humility and sorrow, but in all things innocent, and in all things afflicted: and suffered death for us, that we by him might live and be partakers of his nature and his glories, of his body and of his Spirit, of the blessings of earth, and of immortal felicities in Heaven.

O that men would therefore praise the Lord, etc.

For thou O holy and immortal God, O sweetest Saviour Jesus, wert made under the Law to condemn sin in the flesh: thou who knewest no sin wert made sin for us: thou gavest to us righteous Commandements, and madest known to us all thy Fathers will: thou didst redeem us from our vain conversation, and from the vanity of Idols, false principles, and foolish confidences, and broughtest us to the knowledge of the true and onely God and our Father, and hast made us to thy self a peculiar people, of thy own purchase, a royal Priesthood, a holy Nation: Thou hast washed our soules in the Laver of Regeneration, the Sacrament of Baptisme: Thou hast reconciled us by thy death, justified us by thy Resurrection, sanctified us by thy Spirit, sending him upon thy Church in visible formes, and giving him in powers, and miracles, and mighty signes, and continuing this incomparable favour in gifts and sanctifying graces, and promising that hee shall abide with us for ever; thou hast fed us with thine own broken body, and given drink to our soules out of thine own heart: and hast ascended up on high, and hast overcome all the powers of Death and Hell, and redeemed us from the miseries of a sad eternity: and sittest at the right hand of God, making intercession for us with a never ceasing charity.

O that men would therefore praise the Lord, etc.

The grave could not hold thee long, O holy and eternal Jesus, thy body could not see corruption, neither could thy soul be left in Hell; thou wert free among the dead, and thou brakest the iron gates of Death, and the bars and chains of the lower prisons: Thou broughtest comfort to the souls of the Patriarchs who waited for thy coming, who longed for the redemption of Man, and the revelation of thy day. *Abraham*, *Isaac*, and *Jacob* saw thy day, and rejoyced: and when thou didst arise from thy bed of darknesse, and leftest the grave-clothes behinde thee, and didst put on a robe of glory (over which for 40 dayes thou didst wear a vail) and then entered up into a cloud, and then into glory, then the powers of Hell were confounded, then Death lost its power and was swallowed up into victory; and though death is not quite destroyed, yet it is made harmlesse and without a sting, and the condition of Humane Nature is made an entrance to eternal glory; and Thou art the Prince of life, the first fruits of the resurrection, the first-born from the dead, having made the way plain before our faces, that we may also rise again in the Resurrection of the last day, when thou shalt come again unto us to render to every Man according to his works.

O that men would therefore praise the Lord, etc.

O give thanks unto the Lord, for he is gracious: and his mercy endureth for ever.

O all ye angels of the Lord, praise ye the Lord: praise him and magnifie him for ever.

O ye spirits and souls of the Righteous, praise ye the Lord: praise him and magnifie him for ever.

And now, O Lord God, what shall I render to thy Divine Majesty for all the benefits thou hast done unto thy servant in my personal capacity?

Thou art my Creator and my Father, my Protector and my Guardian, thou hast brought me from my Mothers wombe, thou hast told all my joynts, and in thy book were all my members written: Thou hast given me a comely body, Christian and careful parents, holy education; Thou hast been my guide and my teacher all my dayes: Thou hast given me ready faculties, an unloosed tongue, a cheerful spirit, strait limbs, a good reputation, and liberty of person, a quiet life, and a tender conscience [*a loving wife or husband, and hopeful children*]; thou

10 and didst put] *KC 6+*, and put *1 2 3 4 5*   11 entered] entredst *2 3 6+*   up] *KC*, *om 1+*   16 Thou art] *KC*, art become *1+*

wert my hope from my youth, through thee have I been holden up ever since I was born: Thou hast clothed me and fed me, given me friends and blessed them; given me many dayes of comfort and health, free from those sad infirmities, with which many of thy Saints and dearest servants are afflicted: Thou hast sent thy Angel to snatch me from the violence of fire and water, to prevent praecipices, fracture of bones, to rescue me from thunder and lightning, plague and pestilential diseases, murder and robbery, violence of chance and enemies, and all the spirits of darknesse: and in the dayes of sorrow thou hast refreshed me: in the destitution of provisions thou hast taken care of me, and thou hast said unto me, [1] *I will never leave thee nor forsake thee.*

I will give thanks unto the Lord with my whole heart, secretly among the faithful and in the congregation.

Thou O my dearest Lord and Father hast taken care of my soul, hast pitied my miseries, sustained my infirmities, relieved and instructed my ignorances; and though I have broken thy righteous Lawes and Commandements, run passionately after vanities and was in love with Death, and was dead in sin, and was exposed to thousands of temptations, and fell foully, and continued in it, and loved to have it so, and hated to be reformed; yet thou didst call me with the checks of conscience, with daily Sermons and precepts of holinesse, with fear and shame, with benefits and the admonitions of thy most holy Spirit, by the counsel of my friends, by the example of good persons, with holy books and thousands of excellent arts, and wouldest not suffer me to perish in my folly, but didst force me to attend to thy gracious calling, and hast put me into a state of repentance, and possibilities of pardon, being infinitely desirous I should live, and recover, and make use of thy grace, and partake of thy glories.

I will give thanks unto the Lord with my whole heart, secretly among the faithful, and in the congregation. For salvation belongeth unto the Lord, and thy blessing is upon thy servant. But as for me, I will come into thy house in the multitude of thy mercies, and in thy fear will I worship toward thy holy temple. For of thee, and in thee, and through thee, and for thee are all things. Blessed be the name of God from generation to generation. Amen.

[1] Joshua 1: 5; Deut. 31: 8; Hebr. 13: 5; Ps. 37: 33.

11 [1]] *KC, om 1+* 33 *through thee, and*] *through and 4+*

A short Form of thanksgiving to be said upon any special deliverance, as from Child-birth, from Sickness, from battel, or imminent danger at sea, or Land, etc.

O most merciful and gracious God, thou fountain of all mercy and blessing, thou hast opened the hand of thy mercy to fill me with blessings, and the sweet effects of thy loving kindnesse: thou feedest us like a Shepherd, thou governest us as a king, thou bearest us in thy arms like a nurse, thou doest cover us under the shadow of thy wings, and shelter us like a hen; thou (O Dearest Lord) wakest for us as a Watchman, thou providest for us like a Husband, thou lovest us as a friend, and thinkest on us perpetually, as a careful mother on her helplesse babe, and art exceeding merciful to all that fear thee; and now, O Lord, thou hast added this great blessing of deliverance from my late danger, [*here name the blessing*] it was thy hand and the help of thy mercy that relieved me, the waters of affliction had drowned me, and the stream had gone over my soul, if the spirit of the Lord had not moved upon these waters: Thou O Lord, didst revoke thy angry sentence which I had deserved, and which was gone out against me: Unto thee, O Lord, I ascribe the praise and honour of my redemption: I will be glad and rejoyce in thy mercy, for thou hast considered my trouble, and hast known my soul in adversity: As thou hast spread thy hand upon me for a covering, so also enlarge my heart with thankfulnesse, and fill my mouth with praises, that my duty and returns to thee may be great as my needs of mercie are; and let thy gracious favours, and loving kindnesse endure for ever and ever upon thy servant: and grant that what thou hast sown in mercy may spring up in duty: and let thy grace so strengthen my purposes that I may sin no more, lest thy threatning return upon me in anger, and thy anger break me into pieces: but let me walk in the light of thy favour, and in the paths of thy Commandments; that I living here to the glory of thy name, may at last enter into the glory of my Lord, to spend a whole eternity in giving praise to thy exalted and ever glorious name. *Amen.*

We praise thee O God: we knowledge thee to be the Lord, All the earth doth worship thee the Father Everlasting. To thee All Angels cry aloud, the Heavens and all the powers therein. To thee Cherubim and Seraphim continually do cry. Holy, Holy, Holy, Lord God of Sabaoth Heaven and Earth are full of the Majesty of thy glory. The glorious

7 thy] thine *2 3*

company of the Apostles praise thee. The goodly fellowship of the Prophets praise thee. The noble army of Martyrs praise thee. The holy Church throughout all the world doth knowledge thee. The Father of an infinite Majesty, Thy honourable, true and only Son. Also the Holy Ghost the Comforter. Thou art the King of glory O Christ. Thou art the everlasting Son of the Father. When thou tookest upon thee to deliver man, thou didst not abhor the Virgins womb. When thou hadst overcome the sharpnesse of death, thou didst open the Kingdom of Heaven to all Believers. Thou sittest at the right hand of God in the glory of the Father. We believe that thou shalt come to be our Judge. We therefore pray thee help thy servants whom thou hast redeemed with thy precious blood. Make them to be numbered with thy Saints in glory everlasting. O Lord save thy people, and blesse thine heritage. Govern them and lift them up for ever. Day by day we magnifie thee. And we worship thy name ever world without end. Vouchsafe O Lord, to keep us this day without sin. O Lord have mercy upon us: have mercy upon us. O Lord let thy mercy lighten upon us as our trust is in thee. O Lord in thee have I trusted: let me never be confounded. *Amen.*

A Prayer of thanksgiving after the receiving some great blessing, as the birth of an Heir, the successe of an honest designe, a victory, a good harvest, etc.

O Lord God, Father of mercies, the fountain of comfort and blessing, of life and peace, of plenty and pardon, who fillest Heaven with thy glory, and earth with thy goodnes; I give thee the most earnest, most humble, and most enlarged returnes of my glad and thankful heart, for thou hast refreshed me with thy comforts, and enlarged me with thy blessing, thou hast made my flesh and my bones to rejoyce: for besides the blessings of all mankinde, the blessings of nature, and the blessings of grace, the support of every minute, and the comforts of every day, thou hast opened thy bosom, and at this time hast powred out an excellent expression of thy loving kindnesse [*here name the blessing*]. What am I O Lord, and what is my Fathers house, what is the life, and what are the capacities of thy servant that thou shouldst do this unto me, that the great God of men and Angels should make a special decree in Heaven for me, and send out an Angel of blessing, and instead of condemning and ruining me as I miserably have deserved, to distinguish me from many my equals and my betters, by this and many other special acts of grace and favour.

Praised be the Lord daily, even the Lord that helpeth us and powreth his benefits upon us. He is our God, even the God of whom cometh salvation: God is the Lord by whom we escape death. Thou hast brought me to great honour, and comforted me on every side.

Thou Lord hast made me glad through thy works, I will rejoyce in giving praise for the operation of thy hands.

O give thanks unto the Lord, and call upon his name: tell the people what things he hath done.

As for me, I will give great thanks unto the Lord: and praise him among the multitude.

Blessed be the Lord God, even the Lord God of Israel: which only doth wondrous and gracious things.

And blessed be the name of his Majesty for ever: and all the earth shall be filled with his Majesty. *Amen. Amen.*

Glory be to the Father, etc.

As it was in the beginning, etc.

A Prayer to be said on the Feast of Christmas, or the birth of our blessed Saviour Jesus; the same also may be said upon the Feast of the Annunciation, and the Purification of the Blessed Virgin Mary.

1. O Holy and Almighty God, Father of mercies, Father of our Lord Jesus Christ, the Son of thy love and Eternal mercies, I adore and praise, and glorifie thy infinite and unspeakable love, and wisdom, who hast sent thy Son from the bosom of felicities to take upon him our nature and our misery, and our guilt, and hast made the Son of God to become the Son of Man, that we might become the Sons of God, and partakers of the divine nature: since thou hast so exalted humane nature, be pleased also to sanctify my person, that by a conformity to the humility and laws, and sufferings of my dearest Saviour I may be united to his spirit, and be made all one with the most Holy Jesus. *Amen.*

2. O Holy and Eternal Jesus who didst pity mankinde lying in his blood, and sin and misery, and didst choose our sadnesses and sorrows that thou mightest make us to pertake of thy felicities: let thine eyes pity me, thy hands support me, thy holy feet tread down all the difficulties in my way to Heaven, let me dwell in thy heart, be instructed with thy wisdom, moved by thy affections, choose with thy will, and be clothed with thy righteousness, that in the day of judge-

33 pertake] partake *4*+

ment I may be found having on thy garments, sealed with thy impression; and that bearing upon every faculty and member the character of my elder brother, I may not be cast out with strangers and unbelievers. *Amen.*

3. O Holy and ever blessed spirit, who didst overshadow the holy Virgin-Mother of our Lord, and causedst her to conceive by a miraculous and mysterious manner: be pleased to overshadow my soul, and enlighten my spirit, that I may conceive the holy Jesus in my heart, and may bear him in my minde, and may grow up to the fulnesse of the stature of Christ, to be a perfect man in Christ Jesus. *Amen.*

To God the Father of our Lord Jesus Christ. To the eternal Son that was incarnate and born of a virgin. To the spirit of the Father and the Son be all honour and glory, worship and adoration, now and for ever. Amen.

The same Form of Prayer may be used upon our own Birth-day, or day of our Baptisme: adding the following prayer.

A Prayer to be said upon our Birth-day, or day of Baptisme.

O Blessed and Eternal God, I give thee praise and glory for thy great mercy to me in causing me to be born of Christian parents, and didst not allot to me a portion with Misbelievers and Heathen that have not known thee; thou didst not suffer me to be strangled at the gate of the womb, but thy hand sustained and brought me to the light of the world, and the illumination of baptisme, with thy grace preventing my election, and by an artificial necessity, and holy prevention engaging me to the profession and practises of Christianity: Lord since that, I have broken the promises made in my behalf, and which I confirmed by my after act; I went back from them by an evil life; and yet thou hast still continued to me life and time of repentance; and didst not cut me off in the beginning of my dayes, and the progresse of my sins: O Dearest God, pardon the errours and ignorances, the vices and vanities of my youth, and the faults of my more forward years, and let me never more stain the whiteness of my baptismal robe: and now that by thy grace, I still persist in the purposes of obedience, and do give up my name to Christ, and glory to be a Disciple of thy institution, and a servant of Jesus, let me never fail of thy grace; let no root of bitterness spring up and disorder my purposes, and defile my spirit. O let my years be so many degrees of neerer approach to thee; and forsake me

5–10 O Holy and ever blessed . . . Christ Jesus. *Amen.*] 2+, *in appendix at end of chapter 4 1*

not O God, in my old age, when I am gray-headed; and when my strength faileth me be thou my strength and my guide unto death, that I may reckon my years and apply my heart unto wisdom, and at last after the spending a holy and a blessed life, I may be brought unto a glorious eternity, through Jesus Christ our Lord. *Amen.*

Then adde the form of thanksgiving formerly described.

A prayer to be said upon the dayes of the memory of Apostles, Martyrs, etc.

O Eternal God to whom do live the spirits of them that depart hence in the Lord, and in whom the souls of them that be elected after they be delivered from the burden of the flesh be in peace and rest from their labours, and their works follow them, and their memory is blessed: I blesse and magnifie thy holy and ever glorious name, for the great grace and blessing manifested to thy Apostles and Martyrs, and other holy persons who have glorified thy name in the dayes of their flesh, and have served the interest of religion, and of thy service, and this day we have thy servant [*name the Apostle or Martyr, etc.*] in remembrance, whom thou hast lead thorough the troubles and temptations of this World, and now hast lodged in the bosome of a certain hope and great beatitude until the day of restitution of all things. Blessed be the mercy and eternal goodnesse of God; and the memory of all thy Saints is blessed: Teach me to practise their doctrine, to imitate their lives following their example, and being united as a part of the same mystica body, by the band of the same faith, and a holy hope, and a neve ceasing charity: and may it please thee of thy gracious goodness shortly to accomplish the number of thine elect, and to hasten th Kingdom, that we with thy servant [*] and all others departed in th true faith and fear of thy holy Name, may have our perfect consumma tion and blisse in body and soul in thy eternal and everlasting king dom. *Amen.*

A form of prayer recording all the parts and mysteries of Christs passion; being a short history of it: to be used especially in the week of the passion; and before the receiving the blessed Sacrament.

All praise, honour, and glory be to the holy and eternal Jesus. I ador thee O blessed Redeemer, eternal God, the light of the Gentiles an

31 *of prayer*] *of a prayer 2 3*

the glory of Israel; for thou hast done and suffered for me more than I could wish, more than I could think of, even all that a lost and a miserable perishing sinner could possibly need.

Thou wert afflicted with thirst and hunger, with heat and cold, with labours and sorrowes, with hard journeys and restlesse nights; and when thou wert contriving all the mysterious and admirable wayes of paying our scores, thou didst suffer thy self to be designed to slaughter by those for whom in love thou wert ready to dye.

What is man that thou art mindful of him, and the Son of man that thou thus visitest him?

Blessed be thy Name, O holy Jesus; for thou wentest about doing good, working miracles of mercy, healing the sick, comforting the distressed, instructing the ignorant, raising the dead, inlightening the blinde, strengthening the lame, straitening the crooked, relieving the poor, preaching the Gospel, and reconciling sinners by the mightinesse of thy power, by the wisdom of thy Spirit, by the Word of God, and the merits of thy Passion, thy healthful and bitter passion.

Lord what is man that thou art mindful of him, etc.

Blessed be thy Name O holy Jesus who wert content to be conspired against by the Jews, to be sold by thy servant for a vile price, and to wash the feet of him that took money for thy life, and to give to him and to all thy Apostles thy most holy Body and Blood, to become a Sacrifice for their sins, even for their betraying and denying thee; and for all my sins, even for my crucifying thee afresh, and for such sins which I am ashamed to think, but that the greatnesse of my sins magnifie the infinitenesse of thy mercies who didst so great things for so vile a person.

Lord what is man, etc.

Blessed be thy Name O holy Jesus, who being to depart the World didst comfort thy Apostles, powring out into their ears and hearts treasures of admirable discourses; who didst recommend them to thy Father with a mighty charity, and then didst enter into the Garden set with nothing but Bryers and sorrowes, where thou didst suffer a most unspeakable agony, until the sweat strained through thy pure skin like drops of blood; and there didst sigh and groan, and fall flat upon the earth, and pray and submit to the intolerable burden of thy Fathers wrath which I had deserved and thou sufferedst.

Lord what is man, etc.

Blessed be thy Name O holy Jesus, who hast sanctified to us all our natural infirmities and passions, by vouchsafing to be in fear and trembling, and sore amazement, by being bound and imprisoned, by being harrassed and dragged with cords of violence and rude hands; by being drenched in the brook in the way, by being sought after like a thief, and used like a sinner, who wert the most holy and the most innocent, cleaner than an Angel and brighter than the Morning-Star.

Lord what is man, etc.

Blessed be thy Name O holy Jesus, and blessed be that loving kindnesse and pity, by which thou didst neglect thy own sorrows, and go to comfort the sadnesse of thy Disciples, quickening their dulnesse, incouraging their duty, arming their weaknesse with excellent precepts against the day of trial. Blessed be that humility and sorrow of thine, who being Lord of the Angels, yet wouldest need, and receive comfort from thy servant the Angel; who didst offer thy self to thy persecutors, and madest them able to seiz thee, and didst receive the Traytors kisse, and sufferedst a veil to be thrown over thy holy face, that thy enemies might not presently be confounded by so bright a lustre; and wouldest do a miracle to cure a wound of one of thy spiteful enemies; and didst reprove a zealous servant in behalf of a malicious adversary; and then didst go like a Lamb to the slaughter without noise or violence, or resistance, when thou couldest have commanded millions of Angels for thy guard and rescue.

Lord what is man, etc.

Blessed be thy Name O holy Jesus, and blessed be that holy sorrow thou didst suffer when thy Disciples fled, and thou wert left alone in the hands of cruel men, who like evening Wolves thirsted for a draught of thy best blood: and thou wert led to the house of *Annas*, and there asked insnaring questions, and smitten on the face by him whose ear thou hadst but lately healed: and from thence wert dragged to the house of *Caiaphas*, and there all night didst endure spittings, affronts, scorn, contumelies, blowes, and intolerable insolencies, and all this for man who was thy enemy and the cause of all thy sorrows.

Lord what is man, etc.

Blessed be thy Name, O holy Jesus, and blessed be thy mercy, who when thy servant *Peter* denied thee, and forsook thee, and forswore thee, didst look back upon him, and by that gracious and chiding look didst call him back to himself and thee: who were accused before the High Priest, and railed upon, and examined to evil purposes, and with designes of blood: who wert declared guilty of death for speaking a

7 that] thy *6+*

most necessary and most profitable truth: who wert sent to *Pilate* and found innocent, and sent to *Herod* and still found innocent, and wert arrayed in white both to declare thy innocence and yet to deride thy person, and wert sent back to *Pilate* and examined again, and yet nothing but innocence found in thee and malice round about thee to devour thy life, which yet thou wert more desirous to lay down for them, than they were to take it from thee.

Lord what is man, etc.

Blessed by thy Name, O holy Jesus, and blessed be that patience and charity by which for our sakes thou wert content to be smitten with canes, and have that holy face which Angels with joy and wonder do behold, be spit upon, and be despised when compared with *Barabbas*, and scourged most rudely with unhallowed hands, till the pavement was purpled with that holy blood; and condemned to a sad and shameful, a publick and painful death, and arayed in Scarlet, and crowned with thorns, and stripped naked, and then clothed, and loaden with the crosse, and tormented with a tablet stuck with nails at the fringes of thy garment, and bound hard with cords and dragged most vilely and most piteously till the load was too great, and did sink thy tender and virginal body to the earth; and yet didst comfort the weeping women, and didst more pity thy persecutors than thy self, and wert grieved for the miseries of Jerusalem to come forty years after more than for thy present passion.

Lord what is man, etc.

Blessed be thy Name, O holy Jesus, and blessed be that incomparable sweetnesse and holy sorrow which thou sufferedst, when thy holy hands and feet were nailed upon the crosse, and the crosse being set in a hollownesse of the earth did in the fall rend the wounds wider, and there naked and bleeding, sick and faint, wounded and despised, didst hang upon the weight of thy wounds three long hours, praying for thy persecutors, satisfying thy Fathers wrath, reconciling the penitent thief, providing for thy holy and afflicted mother, tasting vinegar and gall, and when the fulnesse of thy suffering was accomplished, didst give thy soul into the hands of God, and didst descend to the regions of longing souls who waited for the revelation of this thy day in their prisons of hope: and then thy body was transfixed with a spear and issued forth two Sacraments, Water and blood, and thy body was composed to burial, and dwelt in darkness 3 days and 3 nights.

14 was] *om 2 3*

Lord what is man that thou art mindful of him, and the Son of man that thou thus visitest him?

The prayer.

Thus O blessed Jesu thou didst finish thy holy passion with pain and anguish so great, that nothing could be greater than it, except thy self and thy own infinite mercy, and all this for man, even for me, than whom nothing could be more miserable, thy self onely excepted who becamest so by understanding our guilt and our punishment. And now Lord who hast done so much for me, be pleased onely to make it effectual to me, that it may not be uselesse and lost as to my particular, lest I become eternally miserable, and lost to all hopes and possibilities of comfort. All this deserves more love than I have to give: but Lord do thou turn me all into love, and all my love into obedience, and let my obedience be without interruption, and then I hope thou wilt accept such a return as I can make: make me to be something that thou delightest in, and thou shalt have all that I am or have from thee, even whatsoever thou makest fit for thy self. Teach me to live wholly for my Saviour Jesus, and to be ready to dye for Jesus, and to be conformable to his life and sufferings, and to be united to him by inseparable unions, and to own no passions but what may be servants to Jesus, and Disciples of his institution. O sweetest Saviour clothe my soul with thy holy robe: hide my sins in thy wounds, and bury them in thy grave, and let me rise in the life of grace, and abide and grow in it till I arrive at the Kingdom of Glory. *Amen. Our Father, etc.*

Ad Sect. VII, VIII, X.

A form of prayer or intercession for all estates of people in the Christian Church. The parts of which may be added to any other formes: and the whole office intirely as it lyes is proper to be said in our preparation to the holy Sacrament, or on the day of celebration.

I.

For our selves.

O thou gracious Father of mercy, Father of our Lord Jesus Christ, have mercy upon thy servants who bow our heads, and our knees, and our hearts to thee: pardon and forgive us all our sins, give us the grace of holy repentance and a strict obedience to thy holy word; strengthen us in the inner man with the power of the holy Ghost for all the parts and duties of our calling and holy living: preserve us for ever in the unity of the holy Catholick Church, and in the integrity of the Christian faith, and in the love of God, and of our neighbours, and in hope of life Eternal. *Amen.*

2.
For the whole Catholick Church.

O holy Jesus King of the Saints, and Prince of the Catholick Church, preserve thy spouse whom thou hast purchased with thy right hand, and redeemed and cleansed with thy blood; the whole Catholick Church from one end of the Earth to the other; she is founded upon a rock, but planted in the sea. O preserve her safe from schisme, heresy, and sacriledge. Unite all her members with the bands of Faith, Hope and Charity, and an external communion, when it shall seem good in thine eyes: let the daily sacrifice of prayer and Sacramental thanksgiving never cease, but be for ever presented to thee, and for ever united to the intercession of our dearest Lord, and for ever prevail for the obtaining for every of the members of thy Church grace and blessing, pardon and salvation. *Amen.*

3.
For all Christian Kings, Princes and Governours.

O King of Kings, the Prince of all the Rulers of the Earth, give thy grace and Spirit to all Christian Princes, the spirit of wisdom and counsel, the spirit of government and godly fear: Grant unto them to live in peace and honour, that their people may love and feare them, and they may love and fear God: speak good unto their hearts concerning the Church, that they may be nursing Fathers to it, Fathers of the Fatherlesse, Judges and Avengers of the cause of Widowes, that they may be compassionate to the wants of the poor, and the groans of the oppressed, that they may not vex or kill the Lords people with unjust or ambitious wars, but may feed the flock of God, and may inquire after and do all things which may promote peace, publick honesty and holy religion, so administering things present, that they may not fail of the everlasting glories of the world to come, where all thy faithful people shall reign Kings for ever. *Amen.*

18 our] *KC*, her *1*+ 19 the members of thy Church] *KC*, its members *1*+

4.
For al the orders of them that minister about Holy things.

O thou great Shepherd and Bishop of our souls, Holy and Eternal Jesus, give unto thy servants the Ministers of the Mysteries of Christian religion the Spirit of prudence and sanctity, faith and charity, confidence and zeal, diligence and watchfulnesse, that they may declare thy will unto the people faithfully, and dispense the Sacraments rightly, and intercede with thee graciously and acceptably for thy servants. Grant O Lord, that by a holy life and a true beliefe, by well doing and patient suffering (when thou shalt call them to it) they may glorifie thee the great lover of souls, and after a plentiful conversion of sinners from the errour of their wayes they may shine like the stars in glory. *Amen.*

Give unto thy servants the Bishops a discerning Spirit that they may lay hands suddenly on no man, but may depute such persons to the Ministeries of religion, who may adorn the Gospel of God, and whose lips may preserve knowledge, and such who by their good preaching, and holy living may advance the service of the Lord Jesus. *Amen.*

5.
For our neerest relatives, as Husband, Wife, Children, Family, etc.

O God of infinite mercy, let thy loving mercy and compassion descend upon the head of thy servants [*my wife, or husband, children and family*:] be pleased to give them health of body and of spirit, a competent portion of temporals, so as may with comfort support them in their journey to Heaven: preserve them from all evil and sad accidents, defend them in all assaults of their enemies, direct their persons and their actions, sanctify their hearts and words, and purposes, that we all may by the bands of obedience and charity be united to our Lord Jesus, and alwayes feeling thee our merciful and gracious Father, may become a holy family, discharging our whole duty in all our relations, that we in this life being thy children by adoption and grace, may be admitted into thy holy family hereafter for ever to sing praises to thee in the Church of the first born, in the family of thy redeemed ones. *Amen.*

7 the[2]] thy *4*+

6.

For our Parents, our Kindred in the flesh, our Friends and Benefactors.

O God merciful and gracious, who hast made [*my Parents*,] my Friends and my Benefactors ministers of thy mercy and instruments of providence to thy servant, I humbly beg a blessing to descend upon the heads of [*name the persons or the relations.*] Depute thy holy Angels to guard their persons, thy holy spirit to guide their souls, thy providence to minister to their necessities: and let thy grace and mercy preserve them from the bitter pains of eternal death, and bring them to everlasting life through Jesus Christ. *Amen.*

7.

For all that lye under the rod of war, famine, pestilence: to be said in the time of plague, or war, etc..

O Lord God Almighty, thou art our Father, we are thy children, thou art our Redeemer, we thy people purchased with the price of thy most precious blood, be pleased to moderate thy anger towards thy servants, let not thy whole displeasure arise, lest we be consumed and brought to nothing. Let health and peace be within our dwellings, let righteousness and holyness dwell for ever in our hearts, and be expressed in all our actions, and the light of thy countenance be upon us in all our sufferings, that we may delight in the service and the mercies of God for ever. *Amen.*

O gracious Father and merciful God, if it be thy wil, say unto the destroying Angel, it is enough, and though we are not better than our brethren who are smitten with the rod of God, but much worse, yet may it please thee, even because thou art good, and because we are timerous and sinful, not yet fitted for our appearance, to set thy mark upon our foreheads, that thy Angel the Minister of thy justice may passe over us, and hurt us not: let thy hand cover thy servants and hide us *in the clefts of the rock*, in the wounds of the holy Jesus, from the present anger that is gone out against us: that though we walk thorough the valley of the shadow of death we may fear no evil, and suffer none: and those whom thou hast smitten with thy rod, support with thy staff, and visit them with thy mercies and salvation, through Jesus Christ. *Amen.*

29 thy Angel the] *4*+, the Angel thy *1 2 3*

8.

For all women with childe and for unborn children.

O Lord God who art the Father of them that trust in thee, and shewest mercy to a thousand generations of them that fear thee, have mercy upon all women great with childe. [*] Be pleased to give them a joyful and a safe deliverance; and let thy grace preserve the fruit of their wombs, and conduct them to the holy Sacrament of Baptisme, that they being regenerated by thy Spirit, and adopted into thy family and the portion and duty of Sons, may live to the glory of God, to the comfort of their parents and friends, to the edification of the Christian Common-wealth, and the salvation of their own souls thorough Jesus Christ. *Amen.*

9.

For all estates of Men and Women in the Christian Church.

O Holy God, King Eternal, out of the infinite store-houses, of thy grace and mercy give unto all Virgins chastity, and a religious spirit; to all persons dedicated to thee and to religion, continence and meeknesse, an active zeal, and an unwearied spirit: to all married paires faith and holinesse: to widows and fatherless, and all that are oppressed, thy patronage, comfort and defence: to all Christian women simplicity and modesty, humility and chastity, patience and charity: give unto the poor, to all that are robbed and spoiled of their goods, a competent support, and a contented spirit, and a treasure in heaven hereafter: give unto prisoners and captives, to them that toil in the mines, and row in the gallyes strength of body and of spirit, liberty and redemption, comfort and restitution: to all that travel by land about lawful occasions thy Angel for their guide, and a holy and prosperous journey and return: to all that travel by sea about lawful occasions freedom from Pirates and shipwrack, and bring them to the Haven where they would be: to distressed and scrupulous consciences, to melancholy and disconsolate persons, to all that are afflicted with evil and unclean spirits give a light from heaven, great grace and proportionable comforts, and timely deliverance; give them patience and resignation; let their sorrows be changed into grace and comfort, and let the storm waft them certainly to the regions of rest and glory.

26 about lawful occasions] *KC, om 1+* 27 journey and] *KC, om 1+* 28 abou[t] lawful occasions] *KC, om 1+*

Lord God of Mercy give to thy Martyrs, Confessors and all thy persecuted, constancy and prudence, boldness and hope, a full faith and a never failing charity: To all who are condemned to death do thou minister comfort, a strong, a quiet, and a resigned spirit: take from them the fear of death, and all remaining affections to sin, and all imperfections of duty, and cause them to dye full of grace, full of hope: and give to all faithfull, *and particularly to them who have recommended themselves to the prayers of thy unworthy servant*, a supply of all their needs temporal and spiritual, and according to their several states and necessities, rest and peace, pardon and refreshment: and shew us all a mercy in the day of judgment. *Amen.*

Give O Lord, to the Magistrates justice and equity, sinceritie, courage and prudence, that they may protect the good, defend religion, and punish the wrong-doers: Give to the Nobility wisdom, valour, and loyalty: To Merchants justice and faithfulnesse: to all Artificers and Labourers truth and honesty: to our enemies forgivenesse and brotherly kindnesse.

Preserve to us the Heavens and the Ayre in healthful influence and disposition, the Earth in plenty, the kingdom in peace and good government, our marriages in peace, and sweetnesse and innocence of society, thy people from famine and pestilence, our houses from burning and robbery, our persons from being burnt alive, from banishment and prison, from Widowhood and destitution, from violence of pains and passions, from tempests and earth-quakes, from inundation of waters, from rebellion and invasion, from impatience and inordinate cares, from tediousnes of spirit and despair, from murder, and all violent accursed and unusual deaths, from the surprize of sudden and violent accidents, from passionate and unreasonable fears, from all thy wrath, and from all our sins, good Lord deliver and preserve thy servants for ever. *Amen.*

Represse the violence of all implacable warring and tyrant Nations: bring home unto thy fold all that are gone astray: call into the Church all strangers: increase the number and holinesse of thy own people: bring infants to ripenesse of age and reason; confirm all baptized people with thy grace and with thy Spirit: instruct the Novices and new Christians: let a great grace and merciful providence bring youthful persons safely and holily through the indiscretions and passions and temptations of their younger years: and to those whom thou hast

12 justice and] *KC, om 1+* 25 and[1]] or *4+* 33 thy] thine *7 8*
38 and to] *2+*, and *1*

or shalt permit to live to the age of a man, give competent strength and wisdom, take from them covetousnesse and churlishnesse, pride and impatience, fill them full of devotion and charity, repentance and sobriety, holy thoughts and longing desires after Heaven and heavenly things: give them a holy and a blessed death, and to us all a joyful resurrection through Jesus Christ our Lord. *Amen.*

Ad Sect. X.

The manner of using these devotions by way of preparation to the receiving the blessed Sacrament of the Lords Supper.

The just preparation to this holy Feast consisting principally in a holy life, and consequently in the repetition of the acts of all vertues, and especially of Faith, Repentance, Charity and Thanksgiving, to the exercise of these four graces let the person that intends to communicate in the times set apart for his preparation and devotion; for the exercise of his faith recite the prayer or Letany of the passion. For the exercise of Repentance, the form of confession of sins with the prayer annexed: And for the graces of thanksgiving and charity, let him use the special formes of prayer above described: or if a lesse time can be allotted for preparatory devotion, the two first will be the more proper as containing in them all the personal duty of the communicant. To which upon the morning of that holy solemnity, let him adde,

A prayer of preparation or addresse to the holy Sacrament.

An act of Love.

O most gracious and eternal God, the helper of the helplesse, the comforter of the comfortlesse, the hope of the afflicted, the bread of the hungry, the drink of the thirsty, and the Saviour of all them that wait upon thee, I blesse and glorifie thy Name, and adore thy goodnesse, and delight in thy love, that thou hast once more given me the opportunity of receiving the greatest favour which I can receive in this World, even the body and blood of my dearest Saviour. O take from me all affection to sin or vanity: let not my affections dwell below, but soar upwards to the element of love, to the seat of God, to the Regions of Glory, and the inheritance of Jesus, that I may hunger and thirst for the bread of life, and the wine of elect soules, and may know no loves but the love of God, and the most merciful Jesus. *Amen.*

12 *all*] *om 2 3* 17 *And*] *And then 2 3*

An act of Desire.

) blessed Jesus, thou hast used many arts to save mee, thou hast given hy life to redeem me, thy holy Spirit to sanctifie me, thy self for my xample, thy Word for my Rule, thy grace for my guide, the fruit of thy ody hanging on the tree of the crosse, for the sin of my soul: and after ll this thou hast sent thy Apostles and Ministers of salvation to call ne, to importune me, to constraine me to holinesse and peace and elicity. O now come Lord Jesus, come quickly: my heart is desirous of hy presence, and thirsty of thy grace, and would fain entertain thee, ot as a guest, but as an inhabitant, as the Lord of all my faculties. nter in and take possession, and dwell with me for ever, that I also nay dwell in the heart of my dearest Lord which was opened for me vith a spear and love.

An act of contrition.

ord thou shalt finde my heart full of cares and worldly desires, heated with love of riches, and neglect of holy things, proud and nmortified, false and crafty to deceive it self, intricated and intangled ith difficult cases of conscience, with knots which my own wildnesse nd inconsideration and impatience have tied and shuffled together:) my dearest Lord, if thou canst behold such an impure seat, behold ne place to which thou art invited is full of passion and prejudice, evil rinciples and evil habits, peevish and disobedient, lustful and intemerate, and full of sad remembrances that I have often provoked to alousie and to anger thee my God, my dearest Saviour, him that dyed r me, him that suffered torments for me, that is infinitely good *to me*, nd infinitely good and perfect *in himself.* This O dearest Saviour is a d truth, and I am heartily ashamed, and truly sorrowful for it, and do eeply hate all my sins, and am full of indignation against my self for) unworthy, so carelesse, so continued, so great a folly: and humbly eg of thee to increase my sorrow, and my care, and my hatred against n; and make my love to thee swell up to a great grace, and then to ory, and immensity.

An act of Faith.

his indeed is my condition: But I know O blessed Jesus that thou dst take upon thee my nature, that thou mightest suffer for my sins, nd thou didst suffer to deliver me from them and from thy Fathers wrath: and I was delivered from this wrath that I might serve thee ir holinesse and righteousnesse all my dayes: Lord I am as sure thoı didst the great work of Redemption for me and all mankinde, as that am alive: This is my hope, the strength of my spirit, my joy and m confidence: and do thou never let the spirit of unbelief enter into m and take me from this Rock: Here I will dwell for I have a deligh therein: Here I will live, and here I desire to dye.

The Petition.

Therefore O blessed Jesu, who art my Saviour and my God, whos body is my food, and thy righteousnesse is my robe, thou art the Pries and the Sacrifice, the Master of the feast, and the Feast it self, th Physician of my soul, the light of my eyes, the purifier of my stains enter into my heart, and cast out from thence all impurities, all th remains of *the Old man*; and grant I may partake of this holy Sacramer with much reverence and holy relish, and great effect; receiving henc the communication of thy holy body and blood, for the establishmer of an unreproveable faith, of an unfained love, for the fulnesse of wis dom, for the healing my soul, for the blessing and preservation of m body, for the taking out the sting of temporal death, and for the assur ance of a holy resurrection, for the ejection of all evil from within m and the fulfilling all thy righteous Commandements, and to procur for me a mercy and a fair reception at the day of judgement, throug thy mercies O holy and ever blessed Saviour Jesus. *Amen.*

Here also may be added the prayer after receiving the cup.

Ejaculations to be said before or at the receiving the holy Sacrament.

[m]Like as the Hart desireth the water brooks: so longeth my soul aft thee, O God. My soul is athirst for God, yea even for the living Go when shall I come before the presence of God?

[n]O Lord my God great are thy wondrous works which thou ha done: like as be also thy thoughts which are to us-ward, and yet the is no man that ordereth them unto thee.

[o]O send out thy light and thy truth, that they may lead me, and brir

[m] Psal. 42: 1, 2. [n] Psal. 40: 6. [o] Psal. 43: 3, 4.

notes *m* to *x These notes all appear for the first time in* 7 *and are reprinted in subsequent e tions.*

me unto thy holy hill and to thy dwelling: And that I may go unto the Altar of God, even unto the God of my joy and gladnesse: and with my heart will I give thanks to thee O God my God.

[p]I will wash my hands in innocency, O Lord: and so will I go to thine altar: that I may shew the voice of thanksgiving, and tell of all thy wondrous works.

[q]Examine me, O Lord, and prove me, try thou my reins and my heart: For thy loving kindnesse is now and ever before my eyes: and I will walk in thy truth.

[r]Thou shalt prepare a table before me against them that trouble me: thou hast anointed my head with oil, and my cup shall be full. But thy loving kindnesse and mercy shall follow me all the dayes of my life, and I will dwell in the house of the Lord for ever.

[s]This is the bread that cometh down from Heaven, that a man may eat thereof and not dye.

[t]Whoso eateth my flesh and drinketh my blood, dwelleth in me and in him: and hath eternal life abiding in him, and I wil raise him up at the last day.

[u]Lord whither shall we go but to thee? thou hast the words of eternal life.

[v]If any man thirst let him come unto me and drink.

[w]The bread which we break, is it not the communication of the body of Christ? and the cup which we drink, is it not the communication of the blood of Christ? [x]What are those wounds in thy hands? They are those with which I was wounded in the house of my friends.

Immediately before the receiving, say

[y]Lord I am not worthy that thou shouldest enter under my roof. But do thou speak the word onely and thy servant shall be healed.

Lord open thou my lips, and my mouth shall shew thy praise. O God make speed to save me, O Lord make haste to help me.

Come Lord Jesus, come quickly.

After receiving the consecrated and blessed bread, say,

O taste and see how gracious the Lord is: blessed is the man that trusteth in him. The beasts do lack and suffer hunger; but they which

[p] Psal. 26: 6, 7. [q] Psal. 26: 2, 3. [r] Psal. 23: 5–6. [s] John 6: 50.
[t] John: 6: 54, 56. [u] John 6: 68. [v] John 7: 37. [w] 1 Cor. 10: 16.
[x] Zech. 13: 6. [y] Matt. 8: 8.

7 thou] *6+*, out *1 2 3 4 5*

seek the Lord shall want no manner of thing that is good. Lord wha am I, that my Saviour should become my food, that the Son of Goc should be the meat of Wormes, of dust and ashes, of a sinner, of hin that was his enemy? But this thou hast done to me because thou ar infinitely good and wonderfully gracious, and lovest to blesse every one of us, in turning us from the evil of our wayes. Enter into me blessed Jesus, let no root of bitternesse spring up in my heart; but be thou Lord of all my faculties. O let me feed on thee by faith, and grow up by the increase of God to a perfect man in Christ Jesus. *Amen.* Lord I believe, help mine unbelief. *Glory be to God the Father, Son, etc.*

After the receiving the cup of blessing.

It is finished. Blessed be the mercies of God revealed to us in Jesu Christ. O blessed and eternal high Priest, let the sacrifice of the Crosse which thou didst once offer for the sinnes of the whole World and which thou doest now and alwayes represent in Heaven to th Father by thy never ceasing intercession, and which this day hath been exhibited on thy holy Table Sacramentally, obtain mercy and peace faith and charity, safety, and establishment to thy holy Church whicl thou hast founded upon a Rock, the Rock of a holy Faith; and let no the gates of Hell prevail against her, nor the enemy of mankinde tak any soul out of thy hand, whom thou hast purchased with thy blooc and sanctified by thy Spirit. Preserve all thy people from Heresie, and division of spirit, from scandal and the spirit of delusion, from sacri ledge and hurtful persecutions. Thou O blessed Jesus didst dye for us keep me for ever in holy living, from sin and sinful shame, in the com munion of thy Church, and thy Church in safety and grace, in trut and peace unto thy second coming. *Amen.*

Dearest Jesu, since thou art pleased to enter into me, O be jealous c thy house and the place where thine honour dwelleth: suffer n unclean spirit, or unholy thought to come near thy dwelling, lest defile the ground where thy holy feet have trod. O teach me so to walk that I may never disrepute the honour of my Religion, nor stain th holy Robe which thou hast now put upon my soul, nor break my hol Vows, which *I have made* and *thou hast sealed*, nor lose my right of in heritance, my priviledge of being coheir with Jesus, into the hope c which I have now further entered: but be thou pleased to love me wit the love of a Father, and a Brother, and a Husband, and a Lord; an make me to serve thee in the communion of Saints, in receiving th Sacrament, in the practise of all holy vertues, in the imitation thy life, and conformity to thy sufferings; that I having now put on the Lord Jesus, may marry his loves and his enmities, may desire his glory, may obey his laws, and be united to his Spirit; and in the day of the LORD I may be found having on the Wedding Garment, and bearing in my body and soul the marks of the LORD JESUS, that I may enter into the joy of my LORD, and partake of his glories for ever and ever. *Amen.*

Ejaculations to be used any time that day, after the solemnity is ended.

Lord, if I had lived innocently, I could not have deserved to receive the crumbs that fall from thy Table: How great is thy mercy who has feasted me with the Bread of Virgins, with the Wine of Angels, with Manna from Heaven!

O when shall I passe from this dark glasse, from this vail of Sacraments, to the vision of thy eternal clarity, from eating thy Body, to beholding thy face in thy eternal Kingdom!

Let not my sins crucifie the Lord of life again: Let it never be said concerning me, the hand of him that betraieth me is with me on the Table.

O that I might love thee, as well as ever any creature loved thee! Let me think nothing but thee, desire nothing but thee, enjoy nothing but thee!

O Jesus be a Jesus unto me. Thou art all things unto me. Let nothing ever please me but what favours of thee, and thy miraculous sweetnesse.

Blessed be the mercies of our Lord, who of God is made unto me Wisdom, and Righteousnesse, and Sanctification, and Redemption.

He that glorieth, let him glory in the Lord. Amen.

THE END.

TABLE OF THE PRAYERS.[1]

[1] TABLE OF THE PRAYERS.] *GH*, $S4^{v}$ and flyleaf, in Taylor's autograph.

EMENDATION OF ACCIDENTALS

17. 6 *instruments*,] *ed*, ~∧ *1*+
17. 7 *life*] *ed*, *cap 1*+
17. 7 *introduction*] *ed*, *cap 1*+
18. 28 religion.] *4*+, ~, *1*, ~; *2 3*
20. 25 offices,] *4 5*, ~∧ *1 2 3 6*+
24. 7 glut] *2*+, glat *1*
24. 31 be,] *2 4*+, ~∧ *1 3*
25. 25 themselves∧] *4*+, ~, *1 2 3*
33. 18 heart∧] *2 6*+, ~, *1 4 5*, hearts∧ *3*
33. 31 that,] *GH 2 3 5*+, ~∧ *1 4*
33. 31 religion,] *GH 2 3 6*+, ~; *1 4 5*
38. 30 omnipresent,] *7 8*, ~∧ *1 2 3 4 5 6*
40. 18 *brother*;] *6*+, ~, *1 2 3 4 5*
43. 30 Priests,] *2*, ~∧ *1*
44. 3 Lord,] *2*, ~∧ *1*
44. 21 counsel,] *3 7 8*, ~∧ *1 2 4 5 6*
44. 34 *intemperate*,] *ed*, ~∧ *1*+
46. 34 prayers,] *2*, ~∧ *1*
49. 11–14 *To this ... children, etc.*] *4*+, *rom 1 2 3*
49. 17 body,] *2*, ~∧ *1*
49. 18 judgement, holy∧] *2 3 5*+, ~∧ ~, *1*, ~, ~, *4*
49. 32 He ruleth ... ever.] *7 8*, *part of next paragraph 1 2 3 4 5 6*
50. 2–4 He is the God ... scarce-nesse.] *7 8*, *separate paragraph 1 2 3 4 5 6*
50. 15 *note f*] *7 8*, *cited in text 1 2 3 4 5 6*
50. 24 Hosts,] *4*+, ~∧ *1 2 3*
51. 6 which,] *2*, ~∧ *1*
53. 2 Sabbaoth] *2 3 4 5*, Sabaoth *1*
53. 17 mercy,] *2*, ~∧ *1*
56. 2 Sabbaoth] *2 3 4 5*, Sabaoth *1*
56. 8 flesh,] *2*+, ~∧ *1*
56. 11 *note s*] *7 8*, *cited in text 1 2 3 4 5 6*
56. 35 *note u*] *7 8*, *cited in text 1 2 3 4 5 6*
57. 4 hastening] *ed*, hastning *4*+, hasting *1 2 3*
57. 5 God?] *4*+, ~. *1 2 3*
57. 6 Lord,] *6*+, ~∧ *1 2 3 4 5*
58. 18 live,] *ed*, ~∧ *MS*
58. 24 one∧] *ed*, ~, *MS*
62. 33 said the Philosopher] *6*+, *ital 1 2 3 4 5*
63. 3 *You*] *6*+, *lc 1 2 3 4 5*
63. 12 him.] *ed*, ~∧ 1+
63. 12–13 *Hard marches ... next day*] *ed*, *rom and in square brackets 1*+
68. 8 *drunkennesse.*] *2 3 6*+, ~∧ *1 4 5*
68. 9 effects,] *2*+, ~∧ *1*
76. 15 argument:] *ed*, ~∧ *1 4*+, ~, *2 3*
76. 32 actions,] *2 3 5*+, ~∧ *1 4*
77. 20 scorn:] *ed*, ~∧ *1 2 3 4 5 6*, ~, *7 8*
78. 10 *But ... crime*] *6*+, *rom 1 2 3 4 5*
80. 29 remember:] *4 5*, ~. *1 2 3*, ~, *6*+
87. 1 Therefore] *ed*, *with preceding paragraph 4*+, *om 1 2 3*
96. 19 First,] *6*+, I. *1 2 3 4 5*
100. 16 *note j* Eccles.] *cor*, Ecclus. *1*+
101. 28 compares∧] *4*+, ~, *1 2 3*
103. 3 *note m* ep. 34] *cor*, ep. 35 *1*+
104. 28 amorous] *2*+, amarous *1*
109. 28 fear:] *6*+, ~, *1 2 3*, ~; *4 5*
110. 26 cry:] *2 3 4 5*, ~, *1*, ~; *6*+
111. 13 spectacle] *2*+, spectale *1*
112. 14 it] *2*+, *cap 1*
117. 5 Heaven,] *5*+, ~∧ *1 2 3 4*
118. 7 Sacriledge?] *3*+, ~: *1 2*
121. 10 weakest∧] *4*+, ~, *1 2 3*
121. 29 allayes:] *6*+, ~; *1 2 3 4 5*
122. 4 alone:] *2 3*, ~; *1 4 5*, ~. *6*
123. 30 *Theramenes*,] *ed*, ~∧ *1*+
127. 27 arguments!] *6*+, ~. *1 2 3 4 5*
127. 33 *Which*] *4*+, *lc 1 2 3*
128. 3 *seek.*] *ed*, ~; *1 2 3*, ~∧ *4*+

128. 20 words.] *6*+, ~; *1 2 3 4 5*
128. 30 Do] *2*+, *lc 1*
128. 37 We] *6*+, *lc 1 2 3 4 5*
131. 8 *Paulina*,] *7 8*, ~∧ *1 2 3 4 5 6*
133. 32 The] *6*+, *lc 1 2 3 4 5*
134. 13 death.] *2*+, ~∧ *1*
134. 31 *Evil*,] *ed*, ~∧ *1*+
135. 13 You] *ed*, *lc 1*+
139. 24–30 What is . . . a Worm] *ital 7 8*
141. 32 Commandment:] *ed*, ~∧ *1*+
146. 32 words,] *7 8*, ~∧ *1 2 3 4 5 6*
146. 33 these,] *7 8*, ~∧ *1 2 3 4 5 6*
148. 26 *Jude*:] *ed*, ~∧ *1 2 3*, ~, *4*+
148. 27 *Archangel*,] *7 8*, ~∧ *1 2 3 4 5 6*
148. 28 *Moses*,] *4*+, ~∧ *1 2 3*
150. 4 *as*∧] *3 6*+, ~, *1 2 4 5*
175. 15 another,] *6*+, ~; *1 2 3 4 5*
177. 15 *works.*] *6*+, ~∧ *1 2 3 4 5*
177. 21–22 Christ: . . . *forgiven.*] *ed*, ~∧ . . . ~∧ *1 2 3 4 5*, ~∧ . . . ~: *6*+
183. 13 blessing:] *ed*, ~∧ *1*+
192. 16–17 *In giving . . . glory*] *4*+, *rom 1 2 3*
196. 26 this,] *7 8*, ~∧ *1 2 3 4 5 6*
197. 10 *Prophets*,] *4*+, ~∧ *1 2 3*
201. 28 softnesse,] *4*+, ~∧ *1 2 3*
209. 22 wants,] *2*+, ~∧ *1*
213. 20 *prayer*,] *ed*, ~∧ *1*+
213. 21 *Peter*:] *4*+, ~∧ *1 2 3*
213. 21 *earnestly* ,] *ed*, ~∧ *1*+
214. 7 *thrice*,] *ed*, ~∧ *1 2 3*, ~. *4*+
220. 25 1. . . . 2.] *ed*, *om 1*+
220. 27 3.] *ed*, *om 1*+
222. 27 them:] *ed*, ~; *1 2 3 4 5*, ~. *6*+
228. 35 idlenes,] *7 8*, ~∧ *1 2 3 4 5 6*
229. 1 *eat*,] *ed*, ~∧ *1*+
236. 26–9 *stay . . . today*] *ed*, *rom 1*+
240. 18–19 *it is . . . reach it*] *ed*, *rom 1*+
241. 23 alive?] *4*+, ~. *1 2*, ~: *3*
245. 1 5000?] *7 8*, ~∧ *1 2 3 4 5 6*
245. 34 some things] *7 8*, somethings *1*+
248. 13 Lord,] *4*+, ~. *1 2 3*
248. *note z* 288] *cor*, 228 *1*+
248. 13 Lord,] *4*+, ~. *1 2 3*
249. 13 Apostles,] *2 3*, ~∧ *1 4*+
249. 22 Latin, . . . *guide*)] *6*+, ~) . . . ~, *1 2 3 4 5*
253. 8 designe,] *7 8*, ~∧ *1 2 3 4 5 6*
253. 19 repentance,] *7 8*, ~; *1 2 3 4 5 6*
253. 30 *Lord*,] *ed*, ~∧ *1*+
261. 30 received.] *6*+, ~; *1 2 3 4 5*
262. 7 imperfection,] *6*+, ~; *1 2 3 4 5*
266. 12 hope?] *6*+, ~, *1 2 3 4 5*
266. 23 *note i*] *ed*, *cited in text 1*+
266. 30 *note k*] *ed*, *cited in text 1*+
269. 1 Father,] *7 8*, ~∧ *1 2 3 4 5 6*
270. 33 me, like *Jonas*,] *6*+, ~∧ ~ ~∧ *1 2 3 4 5*
274. 9 *am*,] *3 4 5*, ~∧ *1 2*, ~! *6*+
275. 12 *Besides*] *ed*, 2. ~ *1*+
275. 23 *Ex*] *ed*, [I.] ~ *1*+
275. 31 world?] *4*+, ~. *1 2 3*
277. 32 Spirit, sending] *ed*, ~∧ [sending *1*+
277. 36 ever;] *ed*, ever∧ *1*+
278. 30 capacity?] *4 6 7 8*, ~. *1 2 3 5*
278. 38 *children*];] *ed*, ~]∧ *1*+
281. 31 *here . . . blessing*] *4*+, *rom 1 2 3*
288. 9 *Amen*] *4*+, *rom 1 2 3*
292. 5 childe.] *2 3*, ~∧ *1 4 5*, ~, *6*+
292. 5 Be] *ed*, be *1*+
293. 7–8 *and particularly . . . unworthy servant*] *KC*, *rom 1*+
297. 19 thee?] *4*+, ~: *1 2 3*
297. 20 life.] *4*+, ~? *1 2 3*
298. 27 *Amen*] *4*+, *rom 1 2 3*
299. 6 *Amen*] *4*+, *rom 1 2 3*
299. 27 *Amen*] *4*+, *rom 1 2 3*

COMMENTARY

This Commentary provides glosses, documents sources, and gives translations of Taylor's notes. Taylor's quotations of some Greek authors are from Latin versions of their works. For convenience, references are to modern editions of Greek texts and their modern English translations, usually in the Loeb Classical Library. When the source of a translation is not given in a note, the translation is by the editor. Scriptural references are to the Authorized Version unless otherwise indicated. Complete details of works cited by author or title only are provided in the Bibliography that follows.

5. 3 *Richard Lord Vaughan.* Born *c.* 1600, the eldest son of John, first Earl of Carbery. He was knighted at the coronation of Charles I in 1625, was a Member of Parliament for Carmarthen from 1624 to 1629, and succeeded to his earldom in 1634. In 1642 he was appointed Lieutenant-General of the King's forces in Carmarthen, Cardigan, and Pembroke. A year later he was defeated by Rowland Laugharne. Following his defeat and surrender, impeachment proceedings were started against him in Parliament, but he had received a promise of pardon from Laugharne, and also had a powerful friend in the Earl of Essex. As a result of influence exerted on his behalf, he was pardoned in January 1647. He spent the rest of the war in his ancestral home of Golden Grove. He was married three times: first to Bridget Lloyd, then to Frances Altham (for whom Taylor wrote *Holy Dying* and his most famous funeral sermon), and then to Alice Egerton, daughter of the Earl of Bridgewater. After the Restoration, Carbery became President of the Court of Marches and Lord-Lieutenant of Wales, and had his seat at Ludlow. Taylor is not the only literary figure with whom Carbery's name is associated. While Lord-Lieutenant, Carbery appointed Samuel Butler as his secretary, and it was at Ludlow Castle that Butler is said to have written the first part of *Hudibras.* Carbery died in 1686.

5. 9–11 *Tabernacle . . . Curtains.* An echo of Exod. 26, with an obviously ironic contrast. The tabernacle that Moses was ordered to build to house the sanctuary of the Lord had 'ten curtains of fine twined linen, and blue, and purple, and scarlet'. It was covered with 'curtains of goats' hair' and was held together with 'taches of gold'. Taylor is writing with the Civil War in the background; the King himself had been executed within the past year.

5. 10 *ambulatory.* Shifting, moving from place to place.

5. 30 *plot.* Design or purpose.

7. 10 bands. That is, 'bonds'. Cf. Phil. 1: 13: 'My bonds in Christ are manifest.'

7. 40 *quicknesse.* Liveliness.

8. 9 *Hellebore.* A poisonous plant of the genus *Helleborus.* In earlier times, hellebore was used as a drug to treat madness and other mental disorders.

8. 22 *curious.* Ingenious, clever.

8. 36 *nice.* Fastidious, over-scrupulous.

18. 28, note *c* 'Now when someone asked [Epictetus] how it is possible to eat acceptably to the gods, he said, "If it is done justly and graciously and fairly and restrainedly and decently, is it not also done acceptably to the gods?"' See Arrian, *Discourses of Epictetus*, i. 13 (Loeb, i. 99).

19. 6–7 Elisha . . . *childe.* See 1 Kgs. 17: 17–22.

19. 25–6 every idle word. See Matt. 12: 36.

21. 7, note *f* The reference is to a phrase in Seneca's Epistle LXXXII: 'Leisure without study is death; it is a tomb for the living man'.

21. 23 *conveniencies.* Obsolete variant of 'conveniences'.

21. 34 high calling. An echo of Phil. 3: 14. 'A summons, invitation, or impulse of God to salvation or to his service; the inward feeling or conviction of a divine call; also, the state of grace and obedience into which the Christian is called; duty' (*OED*). See also 22. 21–2, 'inward calling'; 23. 5–6, 'being called by God . . . to judge a people'.

22. 11, note *h* See St Bernard, *Sermones de diversis*, 17: 'De triplici custodia, manus, linguæ et cordis', §3 (*PL*, clxxxiii. 584).

22. 17, note *i* 'Augustus Caesar is praised by Lucan: "Always in the midst of battle he had time for the courses of the stars and for the gods above."' See Lucan, *Pharsalia*, x. 185–6 (Loeb, p. 603).

22. 24 *assoon.* As readily, as willingly.

23. 2 Domitian . . . *flyes.* See Suetonius, *Lives of the Caesars*, 8, 'Domitian', 3 (Loeb, ii. 345).

23. 8–9 Nero . . . *trade.* See Suetonius, *Lives of the Caesars*, 6, 'Nero', 22–4 (Loeb, ii. 121–7).

23.9–11 Aeropus . . . *needles.* See Nicolas Caussin's *The Holy Court*, I. ii. 6: '*Hartabus*, King of the *Hyrcans* caught Moles, *Bias* King of the *Lydians* stabbed frogges, *Aeropus* King of the Macedonians made Lanternes' (p. 87).

23. 14 Theophylact. Archbishop of Achrida (i.e. Ochrid), *c.* 1078. See J. Curopalata, *Historiarum compendium* (Venice, 1570), p. 63b. 'C.P.' = Constantinopolitan Patriarchate. As head of the autocephalous Bulgarian church, Theophylact would have assumed the traditional title of 'Patriarch'. But in fact Theophylact exercised authority within the Patriarchate of Constantinople because of the defeat in 1018 of Bulgaria by the Byzantines.

24. 14–16 learn . . . *neighbourhood.* See 1 Tim. 2: 10.

25. 8–10, note *j* *Natural . . . unstrung.* The reference is to John Cassian (*c.* 360–435, never officially canonized) who tells this story of St John the Evangelist. See Collatio xxiv. 21, 'Concerning mortification': 'Non oportet, ne jugi curvamine rigoris fortitudo laxata mollescat atque depereat; et cum oportuerit ut fortiora in aliquam feram spicula dirigantur, rigore per nimietatem

continuæ tensionis amisso, violentior ictus non possit emitti. Nec nostri ... animi te offendat ... tam parva hæc brevisque laxatio; quæ nisi remissione quadam rigorem intentionis suæ interdum relevet ac relaxet, irremisso vigore lentescens, virtuti spiritus, cum necessitas poscit, obsecundare non poterit' (*PL*, xlix. 1314–15).
('One must not [always carry one's bow strung at maximum tension], lest the strength of the tension, weakened by the curve of the bow, relaxes and disappears. And when one must aim more powerful arrows at some wild animal, a stronger blow cannot be given, because the bow's power has been lost through too much unrelieved tension. So do not let this small, brief relaxation of my spirit upset you. Unless it relieves and relaxes the rigor of its application from time to time, the spirit, weakened because of its unbroken tension, will not be able to come to the help of virtue when necessity demands.') Cf. the apocryphal Acts of John, chap. 55, in *The Apocryphal New Testament*, ed. M. R. James (Oxford: Clarendon Press, 1924), p. 241.

25. 14 rule. Daily custom or habit.

25. 26–8 *Patriarch* ... Phorbante. See J. Curopalata, *Historiarum compendium*, p. 63b.

25. 29–32 More ... *Kings.* The incident is not related in Roper's *Life*, though it is entirely typical of More. But see *Selected Letters*, ed. E. F. Rogers (New Haven: Yale Univ. Press, 1961), p. 247: 'My whole study should be upon the passion of Christ and mine own passage out of this world' (2 or 3 May 1535).

25. 32–4 and note *l* Rusticus ... *Lecture.* See Plutarch, *Moralia*, 552E, 'De curiositate', 15 (Loeb, vi. 513).

26. 7, note *m* The passage is from a general's harangue to his troops: '[For] those who win applause in the very matter of their former wrong-doing always gain for themselves a fairer apology': from Procopius, *History of the Wars*, IV. ii. 16 (= *Vandalica*, II) (Loeb, ii. 361).

26. 7 redeem the time. See Eph. 5: 16 and Col. 4: 5.

26. 25, note *o* 'Do not welcome sleep to your weary eyes before you go thrice over each of your deeds of the day [and ask yourself], "In what way did I transgress? Why did I do it? What obligation of mine was left unfulfilled?"': from Pythagoras, *Carmina aurea*, 40–2.

27. 24 *incurious.* Heedless, inattentive, careless.

28. 17–19 Hezekiah ... *God.* See 2 Kgs. 20: 1 and Luke 18: 9.

28. 19, note *q* 'If Atticus dines sumptuously, he is thought a fine gentleman; if Rutilus does the same, people say he has lost his senses.' See Juvenal, *Satires*, xi. 1–2.

28. 21–6 Zecharias ... *incapacity.* See Luke 1: 15–20, 26–35.

28. 27–9 *mourning of* David ... Judas. See 2 Sam. 1: 17–27; 2 Chr. 33: 12–13; Matt. 26: 75 and 27: 3–5.

28. 29–34 and note *r* '*For the praise ... separation.*' Taylor is paraphrasing a

passage in Seneca's 'De beneficiis', i. 6: 'What counts is not what is done or what is given, but the spirit of the action, because a benefit consists, not in what is done or given, but in the intention of the giver or doer.'

29. 5 *poor Farmer*... Artaxerxes. See Plutarch's *Life of Artaxerxes*, 5 (Loeb, xi. 135).

29. 7 a Disciple. See Matt. 10: 42.

30. 9 Nebuchadnezzars *image.* See Dan. 3: 1–6.

30. 9, note *s* 'He who steals so that he can commit adultery is more of an adulterer than a thief.' The passage in Aristotle's *Nicomachean Ethics* closest to Taylor's occurs in v. 2: 'Suppose two men to commit adultery, one for profit, and gaining by the act, the other from desire, and having to pay, and so losing by it: then the latter would be deemed to be a profligate rather than a man who takes more than his due, while the former would be deemed unjust, but not profligate; clearly therefore it is being done for profit that makes the action unjust' (Loeb, xix. 263).

30. 32–6 *S.* Bernard ... end. See Jacobus de Voragine, *The Golden Legend*, 'St Bernard', p. 472.

32. 4 Pharaohs *chariots.* See Exod. 14: 24–5.

32. 20–2 and note *u He*... well gotten. See Seneca, Epistle CXIII. 32, which Taylor loosely adapts for his purpose: 'Qui virtutem suam publicari vult, non virtuti laborat, sed gloriæ. Non vis esse justus sine gloria? At mehercules sæpe justus esse debedis cum infamia. Et tunc, si sapis, mala opinio bene parta delectet.'

32. 23, note *v* See St John Chrysostom, *Ad Stelechium de compunctione*, ii. 6 (*PG*, xlvii. 420).

32. 25, note *w* See St Gregory the Great (*c.* 540–604), *Moralia in Job*, vii. 43 (*PL*, lxxv. 844).

32. 35–6 *S.* James ... Spain. The tradition (now generally discredited) is that St James the Apostle preached in Spain before his martyrdom in AD 44. See Jacobus de Voragine, *The Golden Legend*, 'St James the Greater', p. 369.

33. 8–9 Moses ... prophets. See Num. 11: 29.

34. 12–13 alms ... Ahab. See Luke 18: 10–14; 1 Kgs. 21: 5–14; Isa. 1: 10–17; 1 Kgs. 21: 27–9.

34. 18–20 Saul *the King*... Saul *the Pharisee* [i.e. Paul]. See 1 Sam. 15: 9–15, Phil. 3: 15, and Gal. 1: 14.

34. 22, note *x* See St Bernard, *De præcepto et dispensatione*, 17 (*PL*, clxxxii. 859–94).

34. 30–4 and note *y* Taylor has patched together and loosely translated four 'sayings' from Publilius (not Publius) Syrius the Mime. His selected *Sententiæ* were published separately (for example, at Lyons in 1589), and also in Gruter, *Florilegium* (1610), which is where Taylor probably read him. The four statements (in Taylor's order) are: 'Malus est vocandus, qui sua causa est bonus'; 'Puras Deus, non plenas aspicit manus'; 'Quum vitia prosunt, peccata qui

recte facit' (with an echo also of 'Geminat peccatum, quem delicti non pudet'; and 'Timidus vocat se cautum, parcum sordidus.' See St Augustine, Epistle CLIII. 6: 'Men are not to be called good because they refrain from wrong-doing through their fear of [punishment]—no one is good through dread of punishment, but through love of righteousness' (*PL*, xxxiii. 630; trans. W. Parsons, in *Letters of St. Augustine* (New York: Fathers of the Church, 1953), iii. 293).

35. 13, note *c* See St Augustine, *City of God*, vii. 30 (Loeb, ii. 487).

35. 27–9 *as . . . beams.* 'Someone having reproached [Diogenes] for going into dirty places, his reply was that the sun too visits cesspools without being defiled.' See Diogenes Laertius, *Lives of Eminent Philosophers*, vi. 2 (Loeb, ii. 165).

36. 1, note *d* 'God encompasses by His Will the Universe, . . . [He Who is] greater than the Universe, as in Being, so also in Merit.' See Justin Martyr, *Quæstiones et responsiones ad orthodoxos* (*PG*, vi. 1317).

36. 1 *roules.* Rolls, perhaps suggesting also 'rules'.

36. 8–14 *He . . . Almightinesse.* See Ps. 104, but Taylor has provided some of his own imagery, especially in the pairing of creatures.

36. 24 I desire . . . *said* Paul. See Phil. 1: 23.

36. 33 *ordinarily.* On a regularly occurring basis.

37. 7 *in ordinary . . . degree.* According to a set form (as in the *BCP*) and in a regular pattern.

38. 6, note *h* See St Augustine, Sermon 69, 'De verbis Evangelii Mathei' (also known as Sermon 10, 'De verbis Domini'), 2 (*PL*, xxxviii. 441) 'Multi enim propterea mala faciunt, dum putant quod non videantur a Deo' ('Many therefore do evil so long as they suppose that they are not in the sight of God').

38. 9–10 *For . . . conversation.* 'We can get rid of most sins, if we have a witness who stands near us when we are likely to go wrong.' See Seneca, Epistle XI.

39. 1, note *j* Taylor summarizes in the text the concluding portion of Book 5 of Boethius, *De consolatione.*

39. 26–7 Seven . . . David. See Ps. 119: 164–5.

40. 11 Enoch . . . with God. See Gen. 5: 22–4.

40. 29 and note *l* Taylor translates from the Vulgate: 'Quid est, quod dilectus meus in domo mea fecit scelera multa?' (Clementine ed. 1592).

41. 26 Rejoyce . . . rejoyce. See Phil. 4: 4.

41. 27, note *m* See St Athanasius, *Life of Antony*, 42 (*PG*, xxvi. 906).

42. 5–6 Abraham . . . perfect. See Gen. 17: 1.

42. 9 Eye-service. To serve God as 'one who does his duty only when under the eye of his master' (*OED*) surely is 'displeasing', or at least of limited service; but God 'also sees the heart' and that is compensation for man's poor vision.

42. 15–16 we . . . men. See 1 Cor. 4: 9.

44. 2 An Act of thanksgiving. The following prayer is based primarily on Ps. 30, with some additional phrases from Ps. 28.

47. 20–1 *wrath and indignation.* Cf. the General Confession at Holy Communion in the *BCP.*

47. 29 III [The Third Collect]. There are several phrases from the *BCP*: from the Third Collect at Evening Prayer, the Prayer of Humble Access, and the Absolution at Holy Communion.

48. 22 VI [The Sixth Collect]. See Ps. 141: 3 and Eph. 4: 30.

49. 11 prayer of intercession. See pp. 45–7.

49. 13–14 end of the third or fourth Chapter. See pp. 167–73 and 288–99.

52. 7 *destroying Angel.* See 1 Chr. 21: 12.

52. 8–10 *thy rod . . . changes.* See Ps. 23: 4.

54. 2–3 *Teach . . . wisdom.* See Ps. 90: 13.

55. 25–7 *Blessed . . . day.* See Ps. 91: 5–6.

55. 32–4 *Blessing . . . ever.* See Rev. 5: 13.

56.16 Jacobs *wrastling.* See Gen. 32: 24–32.

56. 19 *Angel . . . Israel.* See Exod. 14: 19–31.

56. 22–5 *Angel . . .* comfort. See 2 Kgs. 19: 35 (perhaps conflated in Taylor's memory with 1 Cor. 10: 8) and Ps. 16: 7.

56. 26 *agonies of Christ.* See Matt. 26: 36–46.

58. 16–59. 25 An additional prayer. This prayer is printed from Taylor's autograph. It appears on a blank leaf (sig. S3[v] of the Wyat presentation copy of the first edition of *Holy Living* (1650, state II, described in Gathorne-Hardy and Williams, *Bibliography*, pp. 34–5, item 11A. See Figs. 6 and 9. I have divided the prayer into paragraphs and also inserted the missing words in 59. 9 and 24. See textual notes.

61. 1, note *b* Philto is speaking to his only son, Lysiteles: 'If you, my boy, have conquered your inclinations rather than they you, you should rejoice: . . . Those who conquer their inclinations, rather than they them, are always known as men of probity indeed.' See Plautus, *Trinummus*, II. ii. 29 and 31.

61. 13, note *c* 'Only consider at what price you sell your freedom of will. If you must sell it, man, at least do not sell it cheap.' See Arrian's *Discourses of Epictetus*, i. 2 (Loeb, i. 23).

61. 16, note *d* 'Do you wish to win an Olympic victory? . . . You have to submit to discipline, follow a strict diet, give up sweet cakes, train under compulsion.' See Epictetus, *Enchiridion*, 29 (Loeb, ii. 507).

62. 26, note *g* 'Hold back your desires a little, for you only have to worry about one thing, namely, that they cease.' Taylor misattributes this passage to Seneca; but I have not been able to locate the real source.

62. 28 *scantlings.* A small or scanty portion or amount, a modicum (*OED*).

62. 31–3 and note *h* See Aristotle, *Nicomachean Ethics*, iii. 12.

62. 34, note *i* 'For it is easier to stop [sensual desires] in the beginning than to control them when they gather force.' The passage occurs in Seneca, Epistle LXXXV.

63. 10–14 and note *j* *For . . . provisions.* See Plutarch, *Life of Alexander*, 22. The Greek phrase appears in this source, and it means 'night marches and a small breakfast'.

63. 18, note *k* Taylor quotes from two different sources; he wrongly attributes the first sentence to Seneca, and does not identify the second. 'Nature has subdued in our hearts the tired pleasures that are going away full of repentance so that they have little desire to return.' 'Venus is in the habit of coming happily and departing sadly.'

63. 34–5 Solomon . . . *all.* See 1 Kgs. 11: 1–25.

64. 21, note *l* 'Self-control: from having passion in one's own control.' The source has not been identified.

65. 26–8 Jonathan . . . *commandment.* See 1 Sam. 14: 27–8, 41–6.

66. 3–13 *sons of Israel* . . . eat. See Num. 11: 18–20, 31–3; 1 Sam. 2: 12–17; and Luke 10: 8.

66. 16, note *m* *Fœlix . . . glande.* 'The first age was happy in the beginning, when men were content with the sweet [returns from their] fields and broke their long fasts with an easily gotten acorn': from Boethius, *De consolatione*, ii, Song 5, 1–2, 4–5. *Arbuteos . . . legebant.* 'They gathered the [arbutus] fruit, strawberries from the mountainside': from Ovid, *Metamorphoses*, i. 104.

66. 25–30 If thou sit . . . upon his bed. See Ecclus. 31: 12–14, 19.

67. 4, note *o* 'Cicero calls temperance an ornament of life in which everything decorous and honest is situated.' See *De officiis*, i. 27.

67. 15–21, note *r* Stratonicus . . . *is gone.* See Plutarch, *Moralia*, 525C, 'De cupiditate divitiarium', 5 (Loeb, vii. 19).

67. 15 *handsomely.* In a fit, appropriate, and apt manner.

68. 12, note *t* κραιπάλη . . . οἰνοποσίας. '"Intoxication from the day before" or "from yesterday's drinking binge". Scholium in Aristophanes [*Acharnians*, i. 278]. It is almost the same in Plutarch. Being drunk on wine signifies a certain slackness and levity of the mind, drunkenness signifies futility.' Plutarch, *Moralia*, 504B, 'De garrulitate', 4 (Loeb, vi. 407).

68. 14–16 *But he that drinks . . . drunkennes.* See Isa. 5: 22.

68. 27, note *w* 'Drunk people do many things of which they are ashamed afterwards when sober.' See Seneca, Epistle LXXXIII.

68. 30–2 *It particularly . . . age.* On the consequences of drinking, cf. the Porter in *Macbeth*, II. iii. 28–36.

69. 6, note *y* *Insaniæ . . . ebrietas.* 'Anger is a companion of insanity, and drunkenness is a comrade.' See Plutarch, *Moralia*, 503E, 'De garrulitate', 4 (Loeb, vi. 405). *Corpus onustum . . . prægravat.* 'Clogged with yesterday's excess, the body drags down with itself the mind as well.' See Horace, *Satires*, II. ii. 76–7. *Ebrietas . . . insania.* 'Drunkenness is nothing but a condition of insanity purposely assumed.' See Seneca, Epistle LXXXIII (also commentary to 68. 27, note *w*).

69. 17, note *z* 'It is wine that wounds thee, honey sweet wine, which works harm to others too, if one takes it in great gulps, and drinks beyond measure.' See Homer, *Odyssey*, xxi. 293–4.

69. 18 Josephs *cup*. See Gen. 44: 1–12.

69. 22, note *a* Taylor quotes Philemon from Stobaeus, *Anthologium*, iii. 514, *Florilegium*, xviii. 6: 'No one is a drinker, if you examine the matter, who is not a slave to drinking.'

69. 27–70. 9 Amnon . . . Lot. See 2 Sam. 13: 28–9; 1 Macc. 16: 14–16; Judith 13: 2–3; Gen. 9: 20–4 and 19: 30–6.

70. 1, note *b* 'It was intemperance in drinking, the famous death dealing bowl of Hercules, that laid Alexander low.' From Seneca, Epistle LXXXIII.

71. 8, note *c* See Seneca, Epistle LXXXIII. The Italian proverb, 'He who has drunk the whole sea can still drink a little more', is one of twenty-four scattered throughout *Holy Living*. Except for one of them (85. 17, note *n*), they are all in Gruter, *Florilegium*. The present one is at ii. 2 (p. 211).

71. 8 *aconite*. Deadly poison, specifically, Socrates' hemlock (see *Holy Dying*, 137. 4 and commentary thereto) or, figuratively, any deadly poison.

71. 24, note *d* 'There is no difference between your looking with favour upon a crime and committing it yourself.' The line, wrongly attributed to Seneca, has not been identified.

71. 29–31 *S.* Pauls . . . Salvation. See 1 Thess. 5: 8.

71. 33 *the sons of* Rechab. A Kenite people who dwelt among the Israelites. Its chief, Jonadab, had placed it under a strict rule of life, which included total abstinence. See Jer. 35: 5–10.

72. 22–4 All things . . . Paul. See 1 Cor. 6: 12.

72. 26 smoke. Tobacco. Taylor joins the opposition to tobacco on grounds of its intemperate use and habit-forming properties. King James had raised economic objections (among others) in his *Counterblast to Tobacco* (1604), remarking that some gentlemen spend three or four hundred pounds a year 'upon this precious stink'. Robert Burton speaks on both sides of the controversy in *The Anatomy of Melancholy* (1st edn., 1621): 'Tobacco, divine, rare, superexcellent tobacco, which goes far beyond all the panaceas, potable gold, and philosophers' stones, a sovereign remedy to all diseases. A good vomit, I confess, a virtuous herb, if it be well qualified, opportunely taken, and medicinally used; but as it is commonly abused by most men, which take it as tinkers do ale, 'tis a plague, a mischief, a violent purger of goods, lands, health; hellish, devilish, and damned tobacco, the ruin and overthrow of body and soul' (Part II; IV. ii. 1, ed. H. Jackson (London: Dent, 1932), ii. 228, 'Everyman's Library').

73. 20–1 *circumcision* . . . naughtinesse. See Deut. 10: 16; Jer. 4: 4, 9; Rom. 2: 29; and Jas. 1: 21.

74. 10, note *f* 'Virginity is a preparation in the corruptible flesh for perpetual incorruption': from St Augustine, *De sancta virginitate*, 13 (*PL*, xl. 401).

74. 11 *enamel.* Any smooth and lustrous surface colouring (*OED*).

75. 18, note *i* 'Vile affections'; see Rom. 1: 26.

75. 22, note *k* 'The desire for fornication breeds anxiety; the satiety of the desire breeds regret.' Taylor probably saw the quotation and the attribution to Jerome in Caussin, *The Holy Court*, I. ii. 9, where it appears as a marginal note (p. 99).

75. 23–4 *amazements.* Overwhelming fears or apprehensions.

75. 28–9 Lucifer . . . *Heaven.* See Rev. 12: 4.

76. 2, note *m* 'Destructive agents or principles'; see Aristotle, *Nicomachean Ethics*, vi. 5.

76. 3, note *n* See Ps. 51: 12: 'Uphold me with thy free spirit', or 'Confirm me in the principal spirit.'

76. 6 *he prayed to God.* See 2 Sam. 12: 13.

76. 30, note *q* See St Gregory the Great, *Moralia in Job*, xxxi. 45 (*PL*, lxxxvi. 623).

76. 36 *unprejudicate.* Unprejudiced.

77. 2, note *r* See St Cyprian, *De disciplina et bono pudicitiae*, 11 (*PL*, iv. 858).

77. 7–8 Abimelech . . . *wife of* Isaac. See Gen. 26: 11 and 38: 24. *Meddle* (in l. 8) is an archaic term for sexual intercourse).

77. 8 *Judah . . . Thamar.* See Gen. 38: 24.

77. 12–13 *Egyptian Law.* See Diodorus Siculus, i. 78 (Loeb, i. 271).

77. 14 *Locrians.* See Aelianus, *Varia Historia*, xiii. 24.

77. 15 *Germanes.* See Tacitus, *Dialogues, Agricola and Germania*, 19.

77. 17 *Gortinaeans.* See Aelianus, loc. cit.

77. 18 *Cumani.* See Plutarch, 'Quaestiones Graecae', 2 (in *Moralia*, 291F; Loeb, iv. 177), whence note *t*: 'she who rode on an ass'.

77. 23, note *u* See Concilium Triburense (AD 895), canon 46; and Concilium Aureliense (AD 511), canon 1. See Mansi, xviii. 154; viii. 350–1.

77. 24, note *v* See the *Digestorum seu pandectarum*, xlviii. 5, in *Corpus juris civilis*; and the *Codex Theodosianus*, 9, title 7. 3, 'Ad legem Juliam de Adulteriis', in *Theodosiani Libri*, XVI, ed. T. Mommsen and P. M. Meyer (2 vols., Berlin, 1905), trans. C. Pharr (Princeton, 1952).

78. 1 *defensative.* Defence, protection.

78. 2, note *w* St Augustine quotes Marcus Aurelius in 'De incompetentibus nuptiis', ii. 8 (*PL*, xl. 475); Taylor also cites Plutarch, *Moralia*, 144F, 'Conjugalia præcepta', 47 (Loeb, ii. 335–6).

78. 7 *disinherisons.* Disinheritances.

78. 25, note *x* 'To love, at least with hollow enjoyment, that which is impossible to obtain.' Taylor is quoting the last two lines (23–4) of a work by Apuleius, beginning 'Amare liceat, si potiri non licet'; see *Pœtae Latini Minores*, iv. 104.

78. 28, note *y* 'Isidorus says the eyes are the platters of lechery, and someone else says [the eyes are] the sorrows of men': from a marginal note in

Caussin, *The Holy Court*, I. iii. 23 (p. 168). The Greek expresion is apparently derived from Herodotus's phrase ἀλγηδόνας ὀφθαλμῶν, meaning 'torment of the eyes' or 'eye torture' (v. 18). The passage from St Augustine occurs in his *Ennaratio in Psalmum L*, 3 (*PL*, xxxvi–xxxvii. 587): 'Fear to see from whence you can fall, and do not become secure in perverse simplicity.'

78. 30 Look not . . . after her. See Matt. 5: 28.

79. 12, note *z* 'Minucius Pontifex admonished Postumias that she should not use words that do not measure up to the chastity of life' (that is, she should use chaste words); from Plutarch, *Moralia*, 89F, 'De capienda ex inimicis utilitate', 6 (Loeb, ii. 25).

80. 27 vidual. Belonging to widowhood.

80. 28 *fontinel* (or *fontanelle, fontanel*). Outlet. See 259. 27 and commentary thereto.

81.13, note *b* 'The home's foundation being wrongly laid, / The offspring needs must be unfortunate.' See Euripides, *Hercules Furens*, i. 1261; quoted by Plutarch, *Moralia*, 1B, 'De liberis educandis', 2 (Loeb, i. 5).

81. 23, note *c* 'We must not use the same person both as a friend and as a flatterer, nor the same woman as a wife and a whore.' See Plutarch, *Moralia*, 142C, 'Conjugalia praecepta', 29 (Loeb, ii. 321).

81. 32–4 Onan . . . *punished him.* See Gen. 38: 8–10.

82. 1, note *d* 'Herodotus was not right in saying that a woman lays aside her modesty when she takes off her clothes. She who is modest is modest even when her clothes are off, for modesty clothes her instead of her dress. Spouses use the greatest modesty towards each other as a token of their love.' See Plutarch, *Moralia*, 139C, 'Conjugalia praecepta', 10 (Loeb, ii. 305).

82. 26–34 and note *e* Socrates . . . *chastity.* Taylor summarizes a passage from Plutarch's *Moralia*, 141D, 'Conjugalia praecepta', 25 (Loeb, ii. 317).

83. 9, note *g* 'Tertullian also says this in the manner of Christians when he counsels Christian women not to marry unbelievers: "Who will bear without anxiety [a wife's] absence all night long at the Paschal solemnities?" Tertullian, *Ad uxorem*, ii. 4; [see *PL*, i. 1407] And in the manner of Gentiles too, Plutarch says that we must take care, if we are to obey the laws of the state, not to approach the temples and the sacrifices if we have only a short while previously engaged in sexual intercourse. And he says that it is better to let a sufficient interval come in between and then rise again, clean and pure, with (as Democritus says) "new thoughts for the new day".' See Plutarch, *Moralia*, 655C–D, 'Quæstiones convivales', iii. 6 (Loeb, viii. 257).

83. 29, note *h* The first passage is from St Augustine, Sermon 293: 'Take flight against the temptation to lust if you wish to obtain victory' (*PL*, xxxix. 2301). The second passage is a proverb: 'In the war of love he who flees, wins' (from Gruter, *Florilegium*, i. 2 (p. 164)).

84. 3–6 *S.* Hierome . . . *contention.* See St Jerome, *Adversus Jovinianum*, i. 41 (*PL*, xxiii. 82–5).

84. 18, note *i* 'Whoever at the outset has resisted and routed love, has been safe and a conqueror, but whoso by dalliance has fed the sweet torment, too late refuses to bear the accepted yoke.' See Seneca, *Hippolytus*, 132–5.

84. 21 *cockatrice.* Fabulous serpent, often identified with the basilisk, which kills with a glance. It was supposed to be hatched from a cock's egg.

84. 32–3 Moses . . . Amalek. See Exod. 17: 8–12.

85. 2–3 *Saint* Pauls . . . under. See 1 Cor. 9: 27.

85. 4 and note *j* The story of the man who spits out his tongue into the courtesan's face is told in St Jerome's *Life of St Paul the First Hermit* (*PL*, xxii. 17). Cf. Taylor's sermons on 'The Flesh and the Spirit' (*Works*, iv. 121–2) and 'The Foolish Exchange' (*Works*, iv. 558). Another source is Nicephorus Callistus (758?–829?), *Ecclesiasticæ historiæ* (Paris, 1630), vii. 13.

85. 9, note *k* 'Benedict rolled himself in thorns [see St Gregory, *Dialogues*, ii. 2, in *PL*, lxvi. 132]. St Martin burnt his face and his hands. St John called the Good pushed sharp needles between the nails and flesh of his fingers. St Theoctistes lived in the forest in the manner of wild animals lest he become tainted among the Arabs' (see Surius, *Historiæ seu vitæ sanctorum*, i. 76 and iv. 238).

85. 11, note *l* 'Once while weaving a garland / I found Eros among the roses / and, catching him by the wings, / I dipped him into the wine and, / taking up the wine, I drank it. / Even within my limbs / he tickles me with his wings.' Taylor says that this is by Julian (d. 363), but I have not been able to locate this passage in his works. The line attributed to Libanius (d. *c.* 393) seems to be a translation of an unidentified passage from one of his orations to Julian: 'Venus loves the rose because of the fable which it recites.'

85. 13–14 *starings . . . singers.* See Ecclus. 9: 4–8.

85. 16, note *m* 'The stomach that is full of wine quickly foams over into lust.' See St Jerome, Epistle LXIX. 9 (*PL*, xxii. 663).

85. 17, note *n* 'I do not want the fire that warms me to burn me.' This is the only one of the Italian proverbs not in Gruter; I have not found Taylor's source.

85. 18 *condited.* Preserved or pickled.

85. 24–6. *like the Sun . . . close about her.* A variation on the ancient fable of the sun and the wind. Taylor may have found a suggestion for this in Plutarch, *Moralia*, 139D, 'Conjugalia praecepta', 12 (Loeb, ii. 307): 'The Sun won a victory over the North Wind. For the wind tried by force to rob a man of his cloak, and blew briskly against him, but the man only drew his garment closer, and held it more tightly together. But when the heat of the sun succeeded the wind, the man began to get warm, and later very hot, and ended by stripping off his shirt as well as his cloak. This is the way most women act.'

86. 1, note *o* 'Do I ever, when my rage is at its worst, ask you for a dame, clad in a *stola*, the offspring of a great consul?' See Horace, *Satires*, I. ii. 69.

86. 18 For this cause . . . thrice. See 2 Cor. 12: 8.

86. 18, note *p* 'It is the mind that makes one shameless, not the body.' See Seneca, *Hippolytus*, ii. 725, where the line reads 'non casus solet' (that is, 'not circumstance').

86. 21 bodily exercises. See 1 Tim. 4: 8.

87. 9, note *q* 'One has to take care that youth are bound by matrimony, which is the most secure bond for them.' See Plutarch, *Moralia*, 13F, 'De liberis educandis', 19 (Loeb, i. 63).

87. 20–1 Learne . . . souls. See Matt. 11: 29.

89. 13, note *r* See Apuleius Madaurensis, *De Deo Socratis*, 4, in *Opera omnia*, ed. G. F. Hildebrand (Hildesheim: Georg Olms, 1968, pp. 122–3.

89. 35 *submissely.* Archaic form of 'submissively'.

90. 10, note *s* The line is from Thomas à Kempis, *De Imitatione Christi*, i. 2 (formerly attributed to Jean Gerson): 'Love to be unknown and to be esteemed for nothing.'

90. 15, note *t* These are two different proverbs, both in Gruter, *Florilegium*, ii. 2: 'The peasant raised to nobility does not recognize his own relatives' (p. 264); 'He who is ashamed of his craft will always live with shame' (p. 223).

90. 20–1 Primislaus . . . *raised.* 'The good *Primislaus* being come from the fortune of a peasant to the Soveraignty of *Bohemia*, caused his country cassock and high shoes to be kept in the Church, and yearly represented to him to renew the memory of his bloud, and thereby cherish his own humility.' See Caussin, *The Holy Court*, I. iii. 31 (p. 182).

90. 21–3 Agathocles . . . *King of* Sicily. See Ausonius, Epigram 2 (Loeb, ii. 157).

91. 5 *like* Moses. See Exod. 34: 29–35.

91. 14, note *u* 'Why, then, do you walk around in our presence as though you had swallowed a spit [that is, strut about ramrod stiff]? "It has always been my wish that those who meet me should admire me and, as they follow me, should exclaim, O the great philosopher!"' From Arrian, *Discourses of Epictetus*, i. 21 (Loeb, I. 143).

91. 21 *suppletories.* 'Supplementaries' or additions.

91. 24, note *v* 'Each of us is enough of an audience for the other; . . . Content with one, content with none at all.' See Seneca, Epistle VII.

91. 28–30 Nebuchodonosor . . . kingdom. See Dan. 4: 30.

92. 25 *chiefest of sinners.* See 1 Tim. 1: 15.

93. 5 *Monitor.* A person who admonishes, or gives advice regarding conduct. Taylor uses the word here in the sense (common in the seventeenth century) of a thing, event, or action which reminds and admonishes by its nature (*OED*).

93. 17, note *w* 'Love your friends with his defects.' See Gruter, *Florilegium* ii. 2 (p. 198).

93. 21, note *x* 'In debates, boys may avoid getting themselves disliked if they do not strive to obtain victory at all times. For it is a fine thing to under-

stand not only how to be victorious, but to be able to submit to defeat when victory would be harmful.' See Plutarch, *Moralia*, 10A, 'De liberis educandis', 14 (Loeb, i. 47).

93. 31 (*as* Anytus *said to* Alcibiades). Alcibiades took half of Anytus's gold plate. See Plutarch, *Lives*, 'Alcibiades', 4 (Loeb, iv. 13).

93. 33, note *y* 'Nothing is so worthy of hate as the behaviour of those who show themselves difficult for those who urge them.' Taylor gives Plutarch as his source, but I have been unable to locate this sentence.

94. 19–20 *one fly . . . ointment.* Cf. Eccles. 10: 1.

94. 31, note *z* 'Who are those people by whom you wish to be admired? Are they not those about whom you are in the habit of saying that they are mad? What then? Do you wish to be admired by the mad?' From Arrian's *Discourses of Epictetus*, i. 21 (Loeb, i. 143).

95. 22, note *a* '"Abstain from beans", said Pythagoras [that is, a man should keep out of politics], "for at one time beans were used to vote upon magistrates' offices."' See Plutarch, *Moralia*, 12F, 'De liberis educandis', 17 (Loeb, i. 61).

95. 36 *reflexe acts.* 'Of acts of thought: Directed or turned back upon the mind itself or its operations' (OED).

96. 24–5 Humility . . . regard. See Ps. 36: 5.

96. 36–7 judge . . . eye. See Matt. 7: 3–5 and Luke 6: 41–2.

98. 13 labour . . . profits not. See Eccles. 1: 3.

98. 36, note *e* 'He commands enough who obeys the wise man': from Gruter, *Florilegium*, ii. 2 (p. 201).

99. 6, note *f* 'Patience shows the truly humble.' The specific reference to St Jerome has not been located.

99. 30, note *g* Εὐσχημοσύνη. 'Propriety', or 'decorum'.

100. 5, note *i* Prov. 25: 27: 'He who examines majesty will be oppressed by its glory.' The Greek passage is from Arrian's *Discourses of Epictetus*, i. 26: 'This, then, is a starting point in philosophy—a perception of the state of one's own governing principle; for when once a man realizes that it is weak, he will no longer wish to employ it upon great matters' (Loeb, i. 169–71). Finally, Taylor quotes Lactantius: 'Occasionally the crowd, which should know as much as is necessary to know, knows more' (from *Divine Institutes*, iii. 5; in *PL*, vi. 359: 'Nam vulgus interdum plus sapit; quia tantum, quantum opus sapit').

100. 16, note *j* 'No eyes on a letter, nor a hand in the pocket, nor an ear in the secrets of others': from Gruter, *Florilegium*, ii. 2 (p. 290).

100. 27–9 *What is it to me . . . expensive.* 'But we, while treating our own affairs with considerable laxity and ignorance and neglect, pry into the pedigrees of the rest of the world: our neighbour's grandfather was a Syrian and his grandmother a Thracian; and so-and-so owes three talents and has not paid the interest. We inquire also into such matters as where so-and-so's wife was coming back from.' See Plutarch, *Moralia*, 516B–C, 'De curiositate', 2 (Loeb, vi. 479).

100. 29 *expensive.* Extravagant.

100. 30 busie-bodies. See 1 Tim. 5: 13 and 1 Pet. 4: 15.

101. 2–27 *But if great things . . . begot curiosity.* Taylor is adapting a passage from Plutarch, *Moralia*, 517D–F, 'De curiositate', 5: 'Direct your curiosity to heavenly things and things on earth, in the air, in the sea. Are you by nature fond of small or of great spectacles? If of great ones, apply your curiosity to the sun: where does it set and whence does it rise? Inquire into the changes in the moon, as you would into those of a human being: . . . Or suppose you have renounced great things. Then turn your curiosity to smaller ones: how are some plants always blooming and green and rejoicing in the display of their wealth at every season, while others are sometimes like these, but at other times, like a human spendthrift, they squander all at once their abundance and are left bare and beggared? Why, again, do some plants produce elongated fruits, others angular, and still others round and globular?

'But perhaps you will have no curiosity about these subjects since there is nothing evil in them. Yet if your zest for meddling must by all means be for ever feeding and dwelling on depraved things, like a maggot on dead matter, let us escort it to history and supply it with an unstinted abundance of evils. For there you will find "The deaths of men, the shufflings off of life", seductions of women, assaults of slaves, slanders of friends, compounding of poisons, envies, jealousies, shipwrecks of households, overthrow of empires. . . .

'But curiosity apparently takes no pleasure in stale calamities, but wants them hot and fresh; it enjoys the spectacle of novel tragedies . . .' (Loeb, vi. 485–7).

101. 28–30 Plutarch . . . *chast or holy.* See Plutarch, *Moralia*, 518C, 'De curiositate', 6. Taylor is further indebted to this source in the remainder of the paragraph. On the meddling physician, Plutarch writes (518D–F, in §7): 'So painful for all of us is the revelation of our own troubles that many die rather than reveal to physicians some hidden malady. Just imagine . . . Asclepius himself . . . calling at one house after another, and inquiring whether a man had an abscess in the anus or a woman a cancer in the womb' (Loeb, vi. 491) And further: 'We are annoyed and displeased with customs officials, not when they pick up those articles which we are importing openly, but when in the search for concealed goods they pry into baggage and merchandize which are another's property.' Taylor concludes his discussion in the next paragraph (101. 40–102. 14), basing it on sections from 'De curiositate', 3, 8, 9.

101. 36–7 *Searchers and Publicans.* Customs officers and tax gatherers.

102. 15, note *k* 'A sense of shame'.

102. 35, note *l* 'God does not show the public the faults of the man whom he covers with the veil of modesty.' See Maimonides (1135–1204), *Canones ethici* [ed.] G. Gentius (Amsterdam, 1640), iii. 83, 'De verecundia'. The Greek is from Antonius the Monk, *Melissa* (1546), chap. 19: 'The first of good things is to be without sin, and the second to have a sense of shame.'

103. 3, note *m* 'From Chione at least, or from Ias learn modesty: for dirty drabs even tombs are hiding places.' See Martial, *Epigrams*, I. xxxiv. 7–8. 'The first thing is to wish to resist, and to wish not to fall from the right path; the second is to have a limit in transgressing': from Seneca, *Hippolytus*, i. 140.

103. 15, note *o* 'Decorum, propriety'; 'orderly behaviour'; 'comeliness, decency'.

103. 31–2 rejoyce . . . weep. See Rom. 12: 15.

104. 13 *that law.* See Lev. 18 and 20.

104. 23, note *q* 'But a harlot repels a witness both by curtain and bolt, and barely a chink gapes in the archway under the walls': from Martial, *Epigrams*, I. xxxiv. 5–6.

104. 33, note *r* See Ovid, *Ars amatoria*, iii. 239–42 (containing advice to women on dressing and make-up): 'Let the tiring woman be safe; I hate her who tears with her nails her handmaid's face, or seizing a needle stabs her arms. That maid curses, as she touches it, her mistress's head, and weeps the while, bloodstained, over the hated locks.'

105. 16 *relations, Theatres.* Relations = narrations, accounts, or idle, gossip-filled stories. Theatres = things displayed for the sake of curiosity.

105. 17, note *u* 'It was . . . curiosity which involved Oedipus in the greatest calamities.' See Plutarch, *Moralia*, 522B, 'De curiositate', 14 (Loeb, vi. 511). See also the previous section in Plutarch.

105. 28 *body of* Epiphanius. The saint objected with his dead body to an inquisitive person. See Surius, *Vitæ sanctorum*, ii. 165; also *Holy Dying*, chap. 5, sect. 8, and Commentary to 229. 40–230. 1.

105. 32–3 He that despiseth . . . little. See Ecclus. 19: 1.

106. 30, note *v* 'No injury is done to you, unless you so pretend.' See Plutarch, *Moralia*, 599C, 'De exilio', 1 (from the *Epitrepontes* of Menander) (Loeb, vii. 519).

108. 18, note *y* 'This is the law which God has ordained, and He says, "If you wish any good thing, get it from yourself."' See Arrian's *Discourses of Epictetus*, i. 29 (Loeb, i. 187).

109. 2–8 *The old Stoicks . . . other times.* See Arrian's *Discourses*, loc. cit., iv. 7, i. 1, and i. 29 (Loeb, ii. 361–75; i. 7–15, 187–205). These chapters treat 'Of freedom from fear', 'Of the things which are under our control', and 'Of steadfastness', respectively.

109. 13, note *a* 'He who can[not] endure both good or bad cannot attain high office': from Gruter, *Florilegium*, i. 2 (p. 131).

109. 13–16 *playing at Tables . . . wickedly.* Cf. Plutarch, *Moralia*, 467A, 'De tranquillitate animi', 5: 'Plato . . . compared life to a game of dice in which we must try, not only to throw what suits us best, but also, when we have thrown, to make good use of whatever turns up' (Loeb, vi. 181).

109. 26, note *b* 'Everything rational is endurable': from Arrian's *Discourses of Epictetus*, i. 2 (Loeb, i. 15).

110. 7–8 The Ox . . . surest. Cf. St Jerome, Epistle CXII (*PL*, xxii. 831), for the probable source of this proverb.

110. 15 Thasus. An island in the Aegean, off the coast of Thrace. Cf. Livy, xxxiii. 30, and Herodotus, ii. 44.

110. 22 Zeno Citiensis. The example of Zeno occurs, for example, in Plutarch, *Moralia*, 467D, 'De tranquillitate animi', 6 (Loeb, vi. 183).

111. 2 being revenged . . . Philosophers. Cf. Plutarch, loc. cit.

111. 9–20 *son of* Philip . . . *thou beholdest.* Philip's son was Alexander the Great. Pyrrhus, King of Epirus, won his first battle against the Romans at a dreadful cost of life (achieving a 'Pyrrhic victory'). Crassus, one of the triumvirate with Caesar and Pompey, died at the hands of the Parthians. Bajazet was defeated (in 1402), taken captive, and made a spectacle by Tamburlaine (dramatized by Marlowe in 1587–8). Zedekiah's fortune is related in 2 Kgs. 25: 7. Valentinian (in fact, Valerian), Roman emperor, was defeated on an expedition against the Parthians in AD 254, his captor Sapor having ordered him to be flayed alive. Xerxes prepared for an invasion of Greece by building a bridge of boats across the Hellespont and cutting a canal through the isthmus of Athos, concerning which see Plutarch, *Moralia*, 470B–E, 'De tranquillitate animi', 10 (Loeb, vi. 197–201): 'Whenever you account happy, as the man of Hellespont did, that famous Xerxes crossing his bridge, look also upon those who are digging through Athos beneath the lash, and those whose ears and noses are mutilated because the bridge was broken by the current.'

111. 32–3 Absalom *for his beauty.* The variant 'bounty' in the later editions is an obvious mistake. Absalom was better known for his beauty than his bounty; see 2 Sam. 14: 25.

112. 11–20 *If I be overthrown* . . . Athens. See Plutarch, *Moralia*, 469B–F, 'De tranquillitate animi', 8–9 (Loeb, vi. 191–7).

112. 21, note *c* 'Hope is the bread of the poor': from Gruter, *Florilegium*, i. 2 (p. 160). See also Horace, *Odes*, ii. 10; 'If we fare ill today, 'twill not be ever so.'

112. 23, note *d* 'A farmer is always rich until next year.' See Zenobius, *Parœmiographi Græci*, ed. T. Gaisford (Oxford, 1836), ii. 43 (p. 264).

113. 27–30 Aristippus . . . *by one.* See Plutarch, *Moralia*, 469C, 'De tranquillitate)', 8 (Loeb, vi. 193), to which Taylor is also generally indebted for the shape of the discussion which follows in the remainder of the paragraph.

114. 16–17 Nero . . . Poppeas *hairs.* See Tacitus, *Annals*, xv. 23.

114. 18 Lesbias *sparrow.* See Catullus, *Carmina*, 3.

114. 23, note *e* 'Cease to ask what the morrow will bring forth, and set down as gain each day that Fortune grants.' See Horace, *Odes*, I. ix. 13–14; also III. xxix. 29–33: 'With wise purpose does the god bury in the shades of night the future's outcome, and laughs if mortals be anxious beyond due limits. Remember to settle with tranquil heat the problem of the hour'; and Anacreon, Ode XV. 9: 'All my care is for today' (trans. T. Stanley, London, 1893).

115. 7 Sufficient . . . thereof. See Matt. 6: 34.

115. 11–13 *the Ancients . . . finished.* See Plutarch, *Moralia*, 473C–E, 'De tranquillitate animi', 14 (Loeb, vi. 215–17).

115. 26–7 O Death . . . possessions. See Ecclus. 41: 1.

116. 32, note *f* 'Enough is sufficient for him who is not greedy': from Gruter, *Florilegium*, ii. 2 (p. 201).

116. 33–5 *He that would shoot an arrow . . . prey.* 'For he is not unfortunate who wishes to shoot with his plough and hunt the hare with his ox, nor does a malicious destiny oppose him who cannot capture deer or boar with fishing creels or drag-nets; it is through folly and stupidity that such men attempt the impossible.' See Plutarch, *Moralia*, 471D, 'De tranquillitate animi', 12 (Loeb, vi. 205).

117. 6, note *g* *Quanto . . . tophum.* 'How much more near to us would be the spirit of the fountain if its waters were fringed by a green border of grass, and there were no marble to outrage the native tufa!': from Juvenal, *Satires*, iii. 18–20. *me pascunt . . . dones.* 'My fare is the olive, the endive, and the wholesome mallow. Grant me, O Latona's son, to be content with what I have': from Horace, *Odes*, I. xxxi. 15–18. *Amabo . . . doloribus.* Pindar, quoted by Plutarch in *Moralia*, 602F, 'De exilio', 9: 'I shall love the light cypress after I have quitted the fields of Crete. Too little land is given to me, but in the meantime I have no pains' (Loeb, vii. 541).

118. 3, note *h* 'The greatest solace in calamities is to be free of guilt': 'Crantor', quoted by Plutarch in *Moralia*, 114C, 'Consolatio ad Apollonium', 25 (Loeb, ii. 173). Crantor (*c.* 335–*c.* 275 BC) wrote *On Grief*, which Plutarch here recalls.

118. 11–12 Anytus and Melitus . . . hurt me. Socrates' famous saying, as reported by Plato, *Apology*, 18.

119. 1, note *k* 'Happiness depends on right reasoning resulting in a stable frame of mind': from Plutarch, *Moralia*, 611A, 'Consolatio ad Uxorem', 9 (Loeb, vii. 597).

119. 25, note *l* 'O Agamemnon, Atreus did not bring you into the world for happy things only. You were born a mortal and must experience both joy and grief. The gods above have arranged it so, though against your wish.' See Plutarch in *Moralia*, 103C, 'Consolatio ad Apollonium', 5 (Loeb, ii. 115). The lines are from Euripides, *Iphigenia at Aulis*, 29 (here trans. by the ed.).

119. 31 Ahimaaz. One of Joab's messengers to David during Absalom's rebellion. See 2 Sam. 18: 19–32.

120. 2–4 Nero . . . *than he was.* See Lucian, *Nerone*, 9.

120. 4–7 Dionysius . . . *Quarries.* See Plutarch, *Moralia*, 471E, 'De tranquillitate animi', 12 (Loeb, vi. 207).

120. 11–14 *If you covet Learning . . . no leisure at all.* 'Training in rhetoric and the pursuit of mathematics require a quiet life and leisure, while political

functions and the friendship of kings cannot succeed without hard work and the full occupation of one's time.' See Plutarch, *Moralia*, 472B, 'De tranquillitate animi', 13 (Loeb, vi. 209).

120. 16–17 *the most exquisite picture.* See Pliny's account of Zeuxis the painter in *Natural History*, xxxv. 36, and also Cicero's *De inventione*, ii. 1.

120. 28–33 Epaminondas ... *too.* Taylor is again indebted to Plutarch, *Moralia*, 467E, 472D–3B, 'De tranquillitate animi', 6 and 13 (Loeb, vi. 185, 211–15).

120. 33, note *m* 'Aristotle eats when it pleases Philip, Diogenes when it pleases Diogenes.' Diogenes Laertius, quoted by Plutarch in *Moralia*, 604D, 'De exilio', 12 (Loeb, vii. 551).

121. 1–2 Agis ... Alcibiades. See Plutarch's *Life of Alcibiades*, 23 (Loeb, iv. 65).

121. 2–3 Philip ... Galilee. See Josephus, *Antiquities*, xviii. 5.

121. 25, note *n* See Cicero, *Epistulæ ad Familiares*, iv. 5.

121. 33, note *o* *Hic in foro ... nil mihi.* 'He was believed to have been happy in the Forum, / since he was most miserable within his doors. / The wife rules all, orders everything, always fights. / Many things bring pain. Nothing brings him pain. Nothing brings me pain': Menander, quoted by Plutarch, *Moralia*, 471B, 'De tranquillitate animi', 11 (Loeb, vi. 203; trans. by the ed.). *Ferre quam ... recusat.* 'To bear the lot which all endure, none can refuse': from Seneca, *Troades*, iv. 1016.

122. 19, note *p* Taylor quotes Menander from Plutarch's *Moralia*, 103C, 'Consolatio ad Apollonius', 5: 'If you alone, Trophimus, at your birth / Had gained the right to do whate'er you would / Throughout your life, and ever be in luck, / And if some god agreed to this with you, / Then you have right to feel aggrieved' (Loeb, vii. 117).

122. 20–2 Stilpo ... *his misery.* See Plutarch, *Moralia*, 468A, 'De tranquillitate animi', 6 (Loeb, vi. 187).

123. 11–15 Josephs *being sold* ... Egypt. See Gen. 38: 25–8.

123. 17–19 *The case of* Themistocles ... undone. See Plutarch, *Moralia*, 601F, 'De exilio', 7 (Loeb, vii. 535).

123. 30–3 *the fortune of* Theramenes ... *Tyranny.* See Plutarch, *Moralia*, 105B, 'Consolatio ad Apollonium', 6 (Loeb, ii. 125).

124. 11, note *r* Taylor again quotes Menander from Plutarch's *Moralia*, 476D, 'De tranquillitate animi', 19: 'Nobody can refuse to bear what it is necessary to suffer' (Loeb, vi. 235).

125. 6, note *s* 'Great fortune brings high travail': from Gruter, *Florilegium*, ii. 2 (p. 198).

125. 18, note *t* 'Ceremony gives authority to the act': from Gruter, *Florilegium*, ii. 2 (p. 231).

125. 29–126. 4 and note *u* *all our Tragedies ... sad calamity?* Taylor is translating a passage from Arrian's *Discourses of Epictetus*, i. 24. The first sentence of

note *u* reads: 'No poor man fills a tragic role except as a member of the chorus' (Loeb, i. 155). The remainder of the note is from Aeschylus's *Niobe*, quoted by Plutarch in *Moralia*, 603A, 'De exilio', 9: 'The field I sow is twelve days' journey long, | The Berecynthian land . . . My fate, while reaching upward to the skies, | Falls to the earth, and speaks these words to me: | Learn not to honour human things too much' (Loeb, vii. 543).

126. 15, note *v* 'O baneful money, thou hast no temple of thine own; not yet have we reared altars to Money in like manner as we worship Peace.' See Juvenal, *Satires*, i. 113–15.

126. 22–6 and note *w* *Corn . . . them.* See Horace, *Odes*, I. xxxi. 3–8.

126. 26, note *x* See '*Remedies against Covetousnesse*', pp. 240–5.

128. 28–31 *Does not God . . . feeds them.* See Matt. 6: 26; Luke 12: 6, 24; and Job 38: 41.

130. 24–6 *Saint* Peter . . . *provisions.* See Matt. 17: 27 and 1 Kgs. 17: 2–7.

131. 7 *rarely innocent.* Instances of rare innocence.

131. 8 Paulina. Paula Romana. See St Jerome, Epistle LXVI (*PL*, xxii. 639). Cf. *Holy Dying*, 227. 5–7 and 232. 21–2.

132. 9, note *e* Taylor names Seneca in his note, but the passage is from Cicero, *Tusculan Disputations*, I. xxxix. 93: 'The . . . grumblers think that if a small child dies, the loss must be borne calmly; if an infant in the cradle, there must not even be a lament. And yet in this latter case Nature has called in her gift with greater cruelty. . . . But in all other matters this is counted better—to get a part rather than nothing' (Loeb, 111–13).

132. 10–17 *remove thy thoughts . . . at all.* 'Try to carry yourself back in your thoughts and return again and again to the time when this little child [Plutarch and his wife's dead daughter] was not yet born . . . next try to link this present time with that as though our circumstances had again become the same. . . . Yet we must not obliterate the intervening two years from our memory; rather, since they afforded us delight and enjoyment of her, we should credit them to the account of pleasure; and we should not consider the small good a great evil, nor . . . be ungrateful for what was given.' See Plutarch, *Moralia*, 610D, 'Consolatio ad Uxorem', 8 (Loeb, vii. 595–7).

132. 26–31 *And this the wisest . . . uneasy garment.* Taylor is again indebted to Plutarch (*Moralia*, 612A); it is interesting to see how he adapts his source ('Consolatio ad Uxorem', 11): 'Our people do not bring libations to those of their children who die in infancy, nor do they observe in their case any of the other rites that the living are expected to perform for the dead. . . . For the laws forbid us to mourn for infants, holding it impiety to mourn for those who have departed to a dispensation and a region too that is better and more divine' (Loeb, vii. 605).

133. 17, note *f* Taylor cites Menander, from Plutarch, who quotes him in *Moralia*, 119E, 'Consolatio ad Apollonium', 34: 'He whom the gods love dies young' (Loeb, ii. 201).

134. 14 *lost his head.* Was beheaded.

134. 22–5 *there are many Kings . . . greatnesse.* Cf. Plutarch, *Moralia*, 467E, 'De tranquillitate animi', 6 (Loeb, vi. 185), and Tacitus, *Annals*, i. 3 (Loeb, ii. 247).

134. 33, note *g* Taylor quotes Epictetus, *Enchiridion*, 12: 'Better for your slave-boy to be bad than for you to be unhappy' (Loeb, ii. 493).

135. 1–2 *wilde* Americans . . . Dodonaim. This reference to the Americans (presumably, native Indians) is puzzling; but the general import is clear, for it expresses the tradition of ascribing Old Testament ancestors to every race of people. The Dodonaim were the descendants of Dodanim (or Rodanim), who was the fourth son of Javan (see Gen. 10: 4).

135. 4 Solomon . . . Hezekiah. Solomon's son was Rehoboam, from whom ten of the twelve tribes revolted (see 1 Kgs. 12: 1–14: 31, and 2 Chr. 10: 1–12: 16). Manasseh, Hezekiah's successor, undid all his father's work and erected altars to Baal (see 2 Kgs. 21: 1–18 and 2 Chr. 33: 1–20).

135. 10, note *h* 'Let tranquillity suffice for you.' The line has not been identified.

135. 13, note *i* The line is from Pythagoras, as quoted by Plutarch in *Moralia*, 12F, 'De liberis educandis', 17: 'Do not turn back when you have reached the end' (Loeb, i. 61).

135. 21–3 Fannius . . . *throat.* See Martial, *Epigrams*, ii. 80 and i. 42. The death of Cato of Utica in 46 BC, the 'conscience of Rome', is the subject of various panegyrics and literary celebrations, by authors such as Livy, Cicero, and Lucan.

135. 24, note *j* 'Not death is dreadful, but a shameful death.' See Arrian's *Discourses of Epictetus*, ii. 1. The Loeb translator (W. A. Oldfather) notes that the line is from 'an unknown tragic poet', but is 'included also among the *Monostichs* of Menander, 504' (Loeb, i. 217 and cf. Nauck, Fr 88).

139. 24–5 *What is man . . . regardest him.* See Ps. 8: 4 and Heb. 2: 6.

141. 4–5 Whatsoever yee would . . . do to them. See Matt. 7: 12.

141. 5–6 commutative justice. The kind of justice 'that is corrective between man and man' (Aristotle, *Nicomachean Ethics*, v. 4. See also Aquinas, *Summa Theologica*, IIa–IIae, Quæst. 61, *commutativa justitia*.

141. 19 obnoxious. 'Open to, or liable to be affected by, harm, injury, or evil of any kind' (*OED*)

141. 25 *justice . . .* distributive. The kind of justice that consists in the distribution of something in shares proportionate to the deserts of each among several parties (cf. Aquinas's term in *Summa*, cited above).

142. 14 Render to Cæsar . . . Cæsars. See Matt. 22: 21 and Rom. 13: 7.

143. 17, note *i* 'Custom's gained control over our very laws. . . . Laws are slaves of custom.' See Plautus, *Trinummus*, iv. 1037, 1043.

143. 23, note *j* 'A rule of justice may be settled one way or the other indifferently, though having once been settled it is not indifferent.' See Aristotle *Nicomachean Ethics*, v. 7.

146. 9–12 He that despiseth you ... ordained of God. See Luke 10: 16; Num. 16: 11; and Rom. 13: 1.

147. 10–11 *For the crime ... his people.* See Exod. 32: 25–8.

147. 18 Rebellion ... Witchcraft. See 1 Sam. 15: 23.

147. 25, note *m* 'It does not become a ruler of men, who is charged with the welfare of the people and the good of the state, to sleep through the night': from Homer, *Iliad*, ii. 24–5.

147. 35–8 Obey them ... for you. See Heb. 13: 17.

148. 4 *Son of God ...* his Father. See John 4: 34.

150. 10, note *o* Tacitus, *Annals*, iii. 53 (from a letter of the emperor Tiberius to the senate about an unenforced law): 'Leave vigorous and full-blown vices alone, rather than force matters to an issue which might only inform the world with what abuses we were powerless to cope.'

150. 18 *Communalty.* Commonalty, here signifying the generality of persons.

150. 23, note *p* Aristotle, *Nicomachean Ethics*, v. 10: 'The equitable consists in a correction of the law where the law is defective because of its generality.'

150. 27–31 *the people ... by the Law.* See 1 Sam. 14: 45.

151. 10, note *q* 'The greed of kings is the ruin of kingdoms': from Gruter, *Florilegium*, ii. 2 (p. 131).

151. 11–12 *lost ... Tribes of Israel.* See 1 Kgs. 12: 1–16.

151. 15 *imbecilled.* Obsolete form of 'imbezilled', or 'embezzled'.

151. 29, note *r* 'The man who buys the office, it is inevitable that he will sell justice': from Gruter, *Florilegium*, ii. 2 (p. 131).

152. 8, note *s* 'A [civil] law does not owe to itself alone a sure sense of its own justice; it owes it to those from whom it expects obedience': from Tertullian, *Apologeticum*, iv. 13.

152. 21–9 *Tutor of* Cyrus ... *bought it.* See Xenophon, *Cyropædia*, i. 3.

153. 21, note *u* 'I should give my vote for virtuous living in preference to even supreme excellence of speaking': from Quintilian, *Institutio oratoria*, x. ii. 3.

153. 27, note *v* See Plutarch, *Moralia*, 9B, 'De liberis educandis', 6 (Loeb, i. 43).

154. 5–6 a laying up for the Children. See 2 Cor. 12: 14.

154. 18, note *x* This long note, apart from the quotations, is by Taylor. He begins by commenting on his own text: 'Without consent of the parents, children ought not to marry. Andromache in Euripides, when she was solicited for marriage, answers that it is a father's business to take care of the marriage of his children: "My marriage—'tis my father shall take thought / Thereof: herein decision is not mine" (Euripides, *Andromache* [not *Electra*], 987–8); "I was given to you by Tyndareus, weighty of counsel both for his life and for his years; the grandsire was arbiter of the grandchild's fate" (Ovid, *Heroides*, viii. 31–2). And Achilles in Homer did not marry the daughter of a king without his father's consent: "For if the gods preserve me, and I reach my home,

Peleus methinks will thereafter of himself seek me a wife" (*Iliad*, ix. 393–4). And the emperor Justinian says that natural and civil reasons coincide, that sons do not take wives against parental authority [see *Corpus juris civilis*, i. 10, 'De nuptiis', i. 41]. Terence's Simo prepares a disinheritance because Pamphilus has married a wife secretly [*Andria*, i]. Marriages of that kind are unlawful unless the parents consent; but many cautions and dangers persuade one not to break up those marriages hastily if they have been consummated. Children, however, if they enter into secret marriages, as long as they are not independent, according to the laws of their country, sin against the Fifth Commandment, and secondly against the law of nature. Properly speaking, parents, in fact, do not have *potestas*, but *authoritas*; they have the right to approve or prohibit, but not to make unlawful. And moreover that *authoritas* derives from equality and goodness; it is evident that he should not be a fretful and unbearable father. The mother, indeed, scarcely has any right except the one that derives from love and gratitude. If, however, the father had not found a place for his daughter before her twenty-fifth year, the daughter had the ability to marry whomever she wished, according to Roman law [see *Theodosian Code*, III. vii. 1, 'De nuptiis', p. 70]. The authority of fathers, in fact, is either greater or lesser according to the laws of the country, and usually extends up to a fixed age, and then expires as far as the ability to give in marriage is concerned; and it is greater with respect to daughters than to sons. [See] Numbers 30.'

155. 1, note *y* 'Wherefore it is becoming for a wife to worship and to know only the gods that her husband believes in, and to shut the front door tight upon all queer rituals and outlandish superstitions. For with no god do stealthy and secret rites performed by a woman find any favour': Plutarch, *Moralia*, 140D, 'Conjugalia præcepta', 19 (Loeb, ii. 311). 'We summon the young wife and look for her expression' (see Gen. 24: 57).

155. 7 *Coleworts.* Any plant of the cabbage variety.

155. 13, note *z* See Homer, *Odyssey*, vi. 180–5, where Odysseus is speaking to Nausicaa: 'May the gods grant . . . a husband and a home may they grant thee, and oneness of heart—a goodly gift. For nothing is greater or better than this, when man and wife dwell in a home in one accord, a great grief to their foes and a joy to their friends; but they know it best themselves.'

155. 14, note *a* 'There is one genuine love-philtre—considerate dealing. By this the woman is apt to sway her man.' See Menander, *Fragments*, ed. A. Körte (Leipzig: Teubner, 1959), ii. 186, Fr 571. Taylor quotes also from Homer's *Iliad*, ix. 340–3: 'Do they alone of mortal men love their wives, these sons of Atreus? Nay, for whoso is a true man and sound of mind, loveth his own and cherisheth her, even as I too loved her with all my heart, though she was but the captive of my spear.'

155. 16 *complicated.* Intertwined, or combined intricately.

155. 23–156. 3 and note *b* *S.* Basil *commended . . . all that.* Basil (in what

recent scholarship has shown to be a spurious homily) develops this theme, but in words different from Taylor's quotation: 'The woman having thieved good thefts without her husband did good deeds' (see *PG*, xxx. 36A, 'De hominis structura', i. 22). The statement, in witty, but rather inelegant, Greek, is evidently Taylor's own.

156. 4–5 Abigail . . . Nabal *had refused it.* See 1 Sam. 25: 18–31.

156. 13, note *c* 'The command of the husband must be cheerful and courteous. . . . For he is to her a father and brother and venerable mother; it does not diminish the dignity of a man if his wife calls him her teacher, philosopher, and master.' See Plutarch, *Moralia*, 142E, 145C, 'Conjugalia præcepta', 15, 48 (Loeb, ii. 309; 337–9). Cf. Taylor's discussion of Plutarch (who adapts some phrases from the *Iliad*, vi. 429) in his sermon on 'The Marriage Ring', part II (*Works*, iv. 219–33).

156. 8 and note *d* *the old philosopher.* Aristotle. Taylor's statement (in the text and note) is a partial summary of Aristotle's argument in *Nicomachean Ethics*, IX. 12: 'Living together is, as it were, an application of good will.' See also Plutarch, *Moralia*, 140F, 'Conjugalia præcepta', 20 (Loeb, ii. 313).

156. 13, note *e* See Apollonides, Fr 1 (in Nauck, p. 825): 'Neither gold nor kingly power, nor the luxury of wealth offers pleasures so various as the right judgement of a noble man and of a pious woman—one who also thinks her husband's thoughts.' The lines appear in Stobaeus, *Anthologium*, xxii. 3 (Hense ed., iv. 494–5), where Taylor would have seen them. See Martial, *Epigrams*, viii. 12: 'Let the matron be subject to her husband, Priscus [*Sextus* in Taylor's note]; in no other way do woman and man become equal.'

156. 21–2 *S.* Paul's *oeconomie . . . minority.* See Gal. 4: 1.

157. 8–9 *S.* Paul . . . Master in Heaven. See Eph. 6: 9.

159. 12, note *f* 'Goods don't need friends or relatives': see Gruter, *Florilegium*, i. 2 (p. 163).

159. 33, note *g* Taylor quotes from Seneca's 'De beneficiis', iv. 39: 'I will arise from my table because I have promised to attend a betrothal, although I have not digested my food; but not so if I have a fever. . . . There is understood, I say, the unexpressed reservations: "If I can, if I ought, if things remain so-and-so". When you exact fulfilment, see to it that the situation is the same as it was when I promised; then, if I fail, I shall be guilty of fickleness. If something new has happened, put everything back as it was, and I shall be as I was.'

160. 19 and note *h* Taylor retells the story which is in Brassavolus, *Examen omnium simplicium medicamentorum* (Lyons, 1537), esp. the section 'De succis prædensis, et concretis liquoribus, quorum in officinis usus est'.

160. 25, note *i* The account of Lysimachus and the salt is in Cælius Rhodiginus, *Lectionum antiquarum libri triginta* ([Basil], 1599), ix. 12 (p. 401G–H). The story of Antigonus is told in Athenaeus, *Deipnosophists*, iii. 73 (Loeb, i. 319).

161. 12, note *l* 'He who does not want to give should not take': see Gruter, *Florilegium*, ii. 2 (p. 226).

161. 25, note *m* 'If any damage was caused by your fault, you must give satisfaction for it.' The statement has not been identified; but it is possibly a note of Taylor's own, not a quotation at all.

162. 9, note *o* See Procopius, *History of the Wars*, vii. 25. Totila, king of the Goths, is addressing his soldiers: 'For he who praises the man who has done a deed becomes himself the agent of the deed no less than the other' (Loeb, vi. 373). See also Ulpian, *Digestorum seu pandectarum*, IX. iii. 1: 'He who praises a fugitive servant should be held in custody, for it is not fitting that evil deeds be increased through being praised' (in *Corpus juris civilis*, i. 183).

162. 10, note *p* 'A fire is the responsibility of the one who started it, but also of the one who is able to put it out but is totally unwilling to do so.' See Nicetas Choniates, 'Manuel Comnenus', *Historia Byzantina*, ii. 3 (*PG*, cxxxix. 388). The second statement is from Plutarch, in *Lives*, 8, 'Cimon' (Loeb, ii. 427): 'So the Syrians were penalized through the judgement of the Amphyctions because they did not prohibit piracy when they could.'

163. 4, note *q* Taylor quotes from the Elder Seneca, *Controversiæ*, v. 5: 'You did not intend one part of the loss: but if you intended the other part, you are liable for the whole as if you had caused it purposely; a man who defends himself by a plea of non-intention must not have intended the act even in part' (Loeb, i. 487). 'An involuntary act arising from a voluntary act is considered to be voluntary': this is probably a note of Taylor's own, not a quotation.

163. 10–15 and note *r* Ariarathes . . . *the damage.* See Strabo, *Geography*, xii. 2 (Loeb, v. 363–5).

163. 17, note *s* 'He who does not help with money because of his lack of generosity is not to be called greedy': from Aristotle, *Nicomachean Ethics*, v. 2.

164. 12–15 Philip *of* Macedon . . . *his own dominions.* See Aelius Aristides ed. W. Dindorf (Leipzig, 1829; rept. 1964), *Orations*, 38.

164. 33, note *t* 'No one comes to his fall for another's deed.' See Arrian's *Discourses of Epictetus*, i. 28 (Loeb, i. 183).

164. 34, note *u* Plato (*Sophists*, 228C) is here quoted in Arrian's *Discourses of Epictetus*, i. 28: 'For every soul is unwillingly deprived of the truth' (Loeb, i. 179). For the reference to Maimonides, see his *Canones ethici*, ii. 6: 'Nonnunquam bonum esse extremum, cujus affert rationem' ('It is not permitted to steal a mind secretly, even the Samaritan's').

165. 19–20 Hercules . . . *his children.* See Diodorus Siculus, *Library of History*, iv. 31.

165. 20, note *v* 'For what the wife or children or relatives of a slain man receive, has in a way been given to the man himself.' Taylor quotes from Michael Ephesius's commentary on Book v of Aristotle's *Nicomachean Ethics* (see the edition of Eustratius, which includes this commentary on the *Ethics* (Venice, 1536), f. 64). Mulct = a fine or penalty.

165. 21, note *w* 'So Vivianus smacked of an unjust accusation': in Cassiodorus, *Historia Ecclesiastica Tripartita*, ed. W. Jacob and R. Hanslik (*CSEL*, lxxi 1952), iv. 41.

174. 14 *duties of the first Table.* That is, religious, as distinguished from moral duties, the division being based on the 'two tables of stone' (Exod. 31: 18).

175. 4, note *c* The reference is to St Augustine, Epistle CXXXVII. 2 (not *City of God*, but see commentary to 178. 35, note *i*): 'Let us assume that God can do something which we have to admit we cannot investigate' (*PL*, xxxiii. 519).

176. 22, note *d* See St Jerome, 'Dialogus contra Luciferianos', 14 (*PL*, xxiii. 178).

177. 10 *momentany.* Obsolete form of 'momentary'.

177. 15 *S.* James's *signe.* See Jas. 2: 18.

177. 17–21 Fedinando *of Arragon* . . . *Faith.* Christopher Columbus (1451–1506) was determined to realize his dream of discovering the new world in his 'Enterprise of the Indies', and the story of his efforts to convince reluctant supporters is familiar. Richard Hakluyt (1553–1616) pleads the English attitude in his *Principall Navigations, Voiages and Discoveries of the English Nation* (1589): 'Christopher Columbus of famous memorie, the first instrument to manifest the great glory and mercie of Almightie God in planting the Christian faith, in those so long unknowen regions, having in purpose to acquaint (as he did) that renoumed Prince, the Queenes Majesties grandfather King Henry the seventh, with his intended voyage for the Westerne discoveries, was not onely derided and mocked generally, even here in England, but afterward became a laughing stocke to the Spaniards themselves, who at this day (of all other people) are most bounden to laude and prayse God, who first stirred up the man to that enterprise. . . . But the sequele thereof hath since awaked out of dreames thousands of soules to knowe their Creator, being thereof before that time altogether ignorant: And hath since made sufficient proofe, neither to be fantasticke nor vainely imagined.' See *Voyages* (London: Dent, 1907), vi. 47, 'Everyman's Library'.

177. 21–2 He that forgives . . . forgiven. See Luke 6: 37.

178. 35, note *i* 'The final reason for believing in miracles is the omnipotence of the Creator.' See St Augustine, *City of God*, xxi. 7. Taylor is citing the chapter heading (Loeb, vii. 41).

179. 35, note *j* See St Augustine, *Enchiridion*, 8 (*PL*, xl. 234).

181. 9–12 Herod *the Sophister* . . . *letters perfectly.* See Philostratus and Eunapius, *Lives of the Sophists*, ii. 10 (Loeb, p. 165).

181. 35 *Reed of* Egypt. Proverbial for its fragility. Cf. 2 Kgs. 18: 21.

182. 10, note *l* 'Do not [try to] experience things that are beyond belief': from Gruter, *Florilegium*, ii. 2 (p. 234).

182. 19–21 *The men of* Bethulia . . . *came at last.* See Judith 7: 30–12: 20.

182. 30, note *m* 'Small-souled people are prone to sorrow.' The source of the statement has not been unidentified. Taylor may have coined the second of the Greek words, since it does not appear in any of the standard lexicons.

183. 1, note *n* 'Hopes, and yon Fortune, a firm farewell! I have found the right path: for no longer do I find pleasure in your ways. You are very deceptive among mortals: you toss illusions, as in sleep, among us which appear real

though they are not. Begone, evil puppets, full of grief; begone both of you. May you find and twirl about many others who cannot think rightly and who are less wise than I.' The lines are not Homer's; but see Brunck's *Anthologia* (13 vols., Leipzig, 1794–1814), iii. 143, where they are attributed to Palladas of Alexandria; see also *The Greek Anthology* (Loeb, iii. §172).

185. 11–12 and note *p* God hath placed . . . portions of Hell. See the Venerable Bede, *The Ecclesiastical History of the English People*, ed. B. Colgrave and R. A. B. Mynors (Oxford, 1969), i. 7 (pp. 30–1). Taylor is quoting from Bede's account of St Alban's martyrdom.

186. 4–6 *S.* Bernard . . . *performance.* See St Bernard, 'Pro Dominica V post Pentecosten' (*PL*, clxxxiii. 344, Sermon 3).

186. 9–10 Experience . . . ashamed. See Rom. 5: 3–4.

186. 30–1 *band of perfection.* See Col. 3: 14.

187. 35–7 and note *q* *our vices . . . but in God.* See St Augustine, *Confessions*, ii. 6. The reference is to the title of the chapter: 'All those things which under the shew of Good invite us unto sin, are in God alone, to be found True and perfect' (Loeb, i. 83).

189. 6, note *s* 'He who truly feels the sting of love': from Plutarch, *Moralia*, 77C, 'Quomodo quis suos in virtute sentiat profectus', 4 (Loeb, i. 413).

189. 12 *disproves.* Disapproves.

189. 24, note *t* 'Quoting a poem about his Apollo, Plutarch adds [something] from Herodotus as though it were from his own work: "From speaking of that my mouth should abstain".' See Plutarch, *Moralia*, 607C, 'De exilio', 17 (Loeb, vii. 569).

192. 1–2 Hezekiah . . .before the Lord. See 2 Kgs. 19: 14.

192. 20, note *u* 'So Jesus said to St Carpo according to Dionysius's letter to Demophilos.' See Dionysius the Areopagite, Epistle VIII. 6 (*PG*, iii. 1100).

192. 25 *the Sugar-canes of* India. See Pliny, *Natural History*, xii. 17. Cf. Plutarch's cane simile in *Moralia*, 77B, 'Quomodo quis suos in virtute sentiat profectus', 4 (Loeb, i. 411).

192. 36 no man . . . than this. See John 15: 13.

193. 12 *excrescencies, and suckers.* The imagery is botanical; Taylor is referring to the shoots that are thrown out from the base of a tree or other plant which help in its propagation.

193. 18, note *v* See Gal. 4: 18: 'But it is good to be zealously affected always in a good thing.'

193. 25–9 Elijah . . . *the first.* See 1 Kgs. 19: 9–12 and Exod. 32: 19.

194. 9–13 *Zealots . . . Synagogue.* See *The Mishna*, 'Sanhedrin', ix. 6.

194. 28, note *x* 'Work as if you have to get your living all the time; pray as if you have to die right away': from Gruter, *Florilegium*, i. 2 (p. 161).

195. 31 bodily exercise. See 1 Tim. 4: 8.

196. 7 Whoremongers . . . judge. See Heb. 13: 4.

196. 26–7 Be not drunk . . . excesse. See Eph. 5: 18.

197. 2–4 Thou shalt not . . . so to them. See Exod. 20: 13; Eph. 5: 18, 25; Col. 3: 19; and Matt. 7: 12 (Luke 6: 31).

198. 4–10 *When the word of God . . . service of God.* Taylor echoes a number of phrases in the collect for the second Sunday in Advent (*BCP*): 'Blessed Lord, who hast caused all Holy Scriptures to be written for our learning: Grant that we may in such wise hear them, read, mark, learn, and inwardly digest them, that by patience, and comfort of thy holy Word, we may embrace, and ever hold fast the blessed hope of everlasting life. . . .'

198. 23 *remark.* Observe and carefully take notice.

198. 31–34 *I can better be comforted . . . divine instrument.* Cf. *The Great Exemplar*, iii. 15, in *Works*, ii. 663: 'We feel a pleasure when a friendly hand lays upon our wound the plaster which ourselves have made, and applies such instruments and considerations of comfort, which we have in notion and an ineffective habit, but cannot reduce them to act, because no man is so apt to be his own comforter.'

199. 29–31 *Thus the Jews . . . sixth hour.* Cf. Josephus, *De vita sua*, 54: 'The sixth hour . . . it is our custom on the Sabbath to take our midday meal' (Loeb, i. 105). See also Acts 2: 13–15.

200. 17 *milk-meats.* Food made with or from milk.

200. 22–4 Take heed . . . unawares. See Luke 21: 34.

200. 24, note *e* 'Fasting without alms is like a lamp without oil': from St Augustine, Sermon 142 (*PL*, xxxix. 2024).

201. 33, note *f* 'He who eats badly fasts a good deal': from Gruter, *Florilegium*, i. 2 (p. 128).

201. 37 *assoon.* Even more quickly.

202. 2, note *g* 'He who fasts and does not do any other good acts, saves [sparagna, *obsolete* = spares] the bread and goes to hell': from Gruter, *Florilegium*, iii. 2 (p. 275).

202. 3–4 *substraction.* Subtraction.

203. 18 *nicenesse and curiosity.* Fastidiously careful and scrupulous.

203. 18, note *h* See St Basil, *Constitutiones monasticæ* ('Monastic rules'), iv. 6 (*PG*, xxxi. 1345). The statement is St Basil's: 'Lest through the cause of necessity we come to the point where we serve pleasure.' The second reference is to Cassian, *Collationes*, xxi. 22, 'Concerning continence' (*PL*, xlix. 1195–8, and cf. 25. 8–10, note *j*).

203. 25, note *i* 'Guarding the day'. Taylor attributes this phrase to St Gregory Nazianzen; but, in fact, it comes from St Basil, 'De jejunio', Sermon i. 10 (*PG*, xxxi. 181).

204. 3 *maigrenesse.* Meagreness, leanness, or emaciation. Cf. 'maigre-days', days on which, in the Roman Catholic Church, abstinence from flesh is enjoined.

204. 5–7 *Saint* Basil . . . *wrath of God.* See 'De jejunio', Sermon II. 2 (*PG*, xxxi. 185).

204. 29 *Creature.* Creation.

205. 10–13 *the Jew in* Synesius . . . *great storm.* See Synesius, Epistle IV (*PG*, lxvi. 1332).

206. 30–1 God is to be worshipped . . . truth. See John 4: 23.

207. 39–40 Christian liberty . . . bondage. Cf. Gal. 5: 1.

209. 26 *president.* Precedent, or one who is both exemplary and first.

214. 7–9 For this cause . . . *half a night.* See 2 Cor. 12: 8.

215. 6, note *u* See Arrian's *Discourses of Epictetus*, ii. 16: 'And then we say, "O Lord God, how may I escape anxiety?" Fool, have you not hands? Did not God make them for you? Sit down now and pray forsooth that the mucus in your nose may not run! Nay, rather wipe your nose' (Loeb, i. 325).

215. 12–13 work . . . of need. See Eph. 4: 28.

215. 26, note *v* 'Amid rites and vows, abstain from profane words': from Tacitus, *Annals*, iv. 70.

217. 19 Jacobs *vow.* See Gen. 28: 20–1.

217. 28, note *y* '"Do not wear a tight ring," said Pythagoras. That is, one should live an unhampered life and not be subject to any bond': from Plutarch, *Moralia*, 12E, 'De liberis educandis', 17 (Loeb, i. 59). 'So Novatus forced his novices to swear that they would never return to the Catholic bishops': from Eusebius, *Ecclesiastical History*, vi. 43.

223. 27–8 It is appointed . . . judgement. See Heb. 9: 27.

223. 31, note *z* Taylor means to refer to Discourse XV, 'Of the excellency, ease, reasonableness, and advantages of bearing Christ's yoke, and living according to His institution' (see *Works*, ii. 515–46).

224. 9–10 it is better . . . fall away. See Luke 8: 13.

224. 25–6 Thamars *Midwife* . . . *distinguish them.* See Gen. 38: 27–30.

224. 26 *threed.* Thread.

226. 1, note *c* See Martial, *Epigrams*, i. 36: 'Now would there be proud rivalry of love betwixt you twain, for each would wish to be the first to die for his brother.'

226. 14, note *f* From the *History of Apollonius, King of Tyre*, chap. 33; 'The girl said, throwing herself at his feet: "Have pity, O Lord, on my virginity and do not prostitute this body under a shameful title."' See *Historia Apollonii Regi Tyri*, ed. Josef Raith (Munich, 1956), p. 23.

226. 17, note *g* 'Conduct praised among the ancients: "Speedily and skilfully he brings to an end even a great quarrel."' See Hesiod, *Theogony*, 87.

227. 2, note *h* See St Gregory the Great, *Epistles*, IX. 106, 'Ad Sygarium Ætherium, Virgilium et Desiderium, Episcopos' (*PL*, lxxvii. 1030): 'For indeed it is not to be accounted almsgiving if that be dispersed to the poor which is got by unlawful dealings' (trans. J. Barmby, *Selected Epistles*, in *The Nicene and Post-Nicene Fathers* (New York, 1905), viii. 24).

227. 8, note *i* 'Let them exhibit pity so that justice is preserved': from St Augustine, Sermon 113 (2) (*PL*, xxxviii. 649).

227. 17 *escheats.* In feudal law, lands given up to the lord on the death of the tenant without heir.

227. 27, note *k* See the Decretals of Gregory IX, in *Corpus juris canonici*, ii. 752.

228. 6, note *l* 'A gift is naked if it is not dressed in consent.' See the *Digestorum seu pandectarum*, in *Corpus juris civilis*, i. 56.

228. 16–17 that our light . . .before men. See Matt. 5: 16.

228. 18, note *m* 'Let the giver of a benefit hold his tongue; let the recipient talk.' See Seneca, 'De beneficiis', ii. 11 (Loeb, iii. 69).

228. 35, note *p* 'One does not sift oats for a horse that does not carry a saddle': from Gruter, *Florilegium*, iii. 2 (p. 269).

229. 1, note *q* 'You do a beggar a bad service by giving him food and drink; you lose what you give and prolong his life for more misery': from Plautus, *Trinummus*, II. ii. 339–40.

229. 10, note *r* See Ps. 41: 1 (40: 2 in the Vulgate): 'Blessed is he that considereth the poor and needy.' The Italian proverb is from Gruter, *Florilegium*, ii. 2 (p. 192): 'In order to give and to keep, it is necessary to have the ability.'

229. 31, note *s* 'I forewarn you to pity others in such a way as not to let others pity you.' See Plautus, *Trinummus*, II. ii. 61.

229. 32 He that hath . . . hath none. See Luke 3: 11.

231. 10–12 *S.* Martin . . . *beggers.* See Sulpicius Severus, *Life of St. Martin* (New York: Fathers of the Church, 1949), iii. 106–9. See also de Voragine, *The Golden Legend*, 'St Martin' (p. 664).

231. 12–14 *A Father . . .himself.* See Palladius, *Historia Lausiaca*, 116 (*PG*, xxxiv. 1220).

231. 15–18 *S.* Paulinus . . . *impudently.* For Paulinus, see St Gregory the Great, *Dialogues*, iii. 1 (*PL*, lxxvii. 217); for Katherine, see Surius, *Vitæ sanctorum*, ii. 366–85 (29 April).

232. 11, note *t* 'He who gives you a bone would not wish you dead': from Gruter, *Florilegium*, ii. 2 (p. 218).

233. 18, note *a* In *Holy Dying*, Taylor cites the same passage from St Jerome, there translating it as follows: 'I do not remember to have read that ever any charitable person died an evil death' (see Commentary to *Holy Dying*, 63. 5–6 and note *v*, and *PL*, xxii. 527).

233. 27–8 Give almes . . . unto you. See Luke 11: 41.

233. 34–234. 2 *S.* Chrysostome . . . poor. See *PG*, lx. 9, 'De pœnitentia' ['Concerning penitence'].

234. 10–235. 8 *Against Envy. . . repents of.* This passage is largely based on St Cyprian's *On Jealousy and Envy*, chaps. 7–8. See *The Treatises of Cyprian*, trans. A. Roberts and J. Donaldson, in *The Ante-Nicene Fathers*, vol. 5 (Buffalo, 1886), p. 493.

234. 20, note *d* 'No one envies the virtue of another if he has sufficient trust in his own. Cicero against Marcus Antonius': from Cicero, *The Phillipics*, 10 (Loeb, p. 423).

234. 33, note *e* Taylor writes: 'Homer, describing the bad behaviour of

Thersites, added, as the greatest of his sins, that he was the enemy of Pelides and of Ulysses' (cf. *Iliad*, ii. 211–20).

234. 33 *Cantharides.* Spanish fly. Cf. *Holy Dying*, 103. 13–16 and commentary thereto.

235. 24, note *f* See Sappho, quoted by Plutarch in *Moralia*, 456E, 'De cohibenda ira', 7: 'When rapid anger fills my breast, / I command my tongue to refrain / from futile barking and boasting about vain things' (Loeb, vi. 115). Ps. 77: 4: 'I am so troubled that I cannot speak.' Taylor's reference is to the Vulgate.

235. 25–7 *It is good* in a fever . . . in anger. Cf. Plutarch, *Moralia*, 456E, 'De cohibenda ira', 7: 'Just as it is a good thing in a fever, so it is an even better thing in anger, to keep the tongue soft and smooth' (Loeb, vi. 133–5).

236. 26–9 *For as* Phocion . . . as today. Cf. Plutarch, *Moralia*, 459F, 'De cohibenda ira', 11 (Loeb, vi. 133).

236. 34, note *g* 'The day when I slew Amphidamus's son in my folly, I willed it not, but was angered over a dice game.' See Homer, *Iliad*, xxiii. 87–8.

237. 2–7 and note *h* *But they . . . anger.* 'Those who need but little are not disappointed of much': from Plutarch, *Moralia*, 461C, 'De cohibenda ira', 13 (Loeb, vi. 141). These lines of the text, as well as the note, are indebted to the same source.

237. 34, note *i* Taylor's unspecified reference to Homer is elusive, for the translation is probably an echo, making it difficult to assign it to a specific place. It may be intended to recall some line(s) of the *Iliad* following the death of Patroclus.

238. 19, note *j* See Euripides, *Medea*, 1078–9: 'And I understand, to be sure, what evils I intend to do: but my passion is stronger than my reason.' (See Loeb text, iv. 366; trans. by the ed.)

238. 32, note *k* 'Passion is a cause of murders, a companion of disaster, a helper of lust and dishonour, a destroyer of property, and still an initiation of ruin.' Taylor cites Aristotle, perhaps in error. The quotation remains unidentified.

238. 32–239. 25 *It makes . . . hath it.* Taylor draws on Plutarch for his description of the results of anger. See *Moralia*, 454–6, 461–2, 'De cohibenda ira', 3, 6, 8, 13, 14 (Loeb, vi. 101–3, 109, 117, 141–5, 147–9).

239. 7, note *l* 'Can you say what is more unpleasant than this supper?': from Homer, *Odyssey*, xx. 392, quoted in Plutarch, *Moralia*, 461C, 'De cohibenda ira', 13 (Loeb, vi. 143).

239. 28, note *m* 'Those who purge bitter bile with bitter drugs': from Sophocles, Fr 770 in Nauck, quoted by Plutarch, *Moralia*, 463F, 'De cohibenda ira', 16 (Loeb, vi. 155).

240. 4, note *n* See Plutarch, *Moralia*, 537E, 'De invidia et odio', 5 (Loeb, vii. 101).

240. 14, note *o* 'What matters it, then, how spacious are the colonnades

which tire out his horses, how large the shady groves in which he drives, how many acres near the Forum, how many palaces, he has bought? No bad man can be happy': from Juvenal, *Satires*, iv. 5–8.

240. 17–19 *for what* Hippomachus ... reach it. See Plutarch, *Moralia*, 523C–D, 'De cupiditate divitiarum', 1 (Loeb, vii. 7).

240. 30–3 and note *p* *but when* ... vanity. See Plutarch, *Moralia*, 528B, 'De cupiditate divitiarum', 10 (Loeb, vii. 37).

241. 6–242. 2 *And certainly* ... *desires.* See Plutarch, *Moralia*, 523C–4D, 'De cupiditate divitiarum', 1–3 (Loeb, vii. 9–11).

241. 28, note *q* 'Life's anguish hath no pause! / Thou money art the cause; / Through thee on death's untimely road we speed': from Propertius, *Elegies*, iii. 7 (trans. E. H. W. Meyerstein (London: Oxford Univ. Press, 1935), p. 102).

242. 4–7 *well said of* Aristippus ... *to be filled.* See Plutarch, *Moralia*, 524B, 'De cupiditate divitiarum', 3 (Loeb, vii. 11).

242. 10–17 *Give to a poor man* ... *what he hath.* See Plutarch, *Moralia*, 524D, 'De cupiditate divitiarum', 3 (Loeb, vii. 13).

242. 25–245. 15 *No man* ... *almes.* Paragraphs 5–7 of this section are indebted to Plutarch, *Moralia*, 524–5, 'De cupiditate divitiarum', esp. 3–7 (Loeb, vii. 11–23). In many instances, Taylor has done little more than work Plutarch into his own context.

243. 22–3 Covetousnesse is Idolatry. See Col. 3: 5.

243. 25, note *r* 'Love of money is the mother of all evil. Gold and silver is ever a trap for men. O gold, initiator of evils, life destroying, all crushing, would that you were not a desired trouble for men; because of you, battles arise and thefts and murders; and children become hostile to their parents and brethren to their kin': from Phocylides, ll. 42–7, in *Anthologia Lyrica Græca*, ed. E. Diehl (Leipzig: Teubner, 1950), p. 95, fasc. 2.

244. 1–2 *Mice of* Africa. Plutarch refers in *Moralia*, 526, 'De cupiditate divitiarum', 7, to these 'mice that eat the gold ore in the mines, [which] ... cannot be had until they are dead and laid open' (Loeb, vi. 23).

244. 17, note *s* 'So that clever poverty may provoke the tardy souls and make them gradually explore the remote path of things': from Claudian, *The Rape of Proserpine*, iii. 30–1 (Loeb, ii. 347; trans. by the ed.).

244. 25, note *t* 'To be old and noble has long since become as good as a prodigy': from Juvenal, *Satires*, iv. 96–7.

244. 26, note *u* 'And you will there have a little garden, with a shallow well from which you can easily draw water, without need of a rope, to bedew your weakly plants. There make your abode, a friend of the mattock, tending a trim garden fit to feast a hundred Pythagoreans. It is something, in whatever spot, however remote, to have become the possessor of a single lizard': from Juvenal, *Satires*, iii. 226–31.

244. 31 *5 l.* Five pounds (£5).

245. 10 *pepper-corns.* Insignificant, trivial things.

245. 22–3 with whom . . . shadow of change. See Jas. 1: 17.

247. 37, note *w* See Hugo of St-Victor (d. 1142), 'De sacramentis', II. iv. 2 (*PL*, clxxvi. 555).

248. 36, note *z* 'It is necessary to confess sins to those who are entrusted with the stewardship of the mysteries of God.' See St Basil, *Regulæ brevis tractatæ*, 288 (*PG*, xxxi. 1284); trans. W. K. Clark, *Ascetic Works of St Basil* (London, 1925), p. 340. See Concilium Laodicenum (AD 367), canon 2; and Concilium Quinsextum (AD 692), canon 102, in Mansi, ii. 564, xii. 54. See Tertullian, 'De pœnitentia', 9 (*PL*, i. 1354–5).

249. 22 *Vulgar Latin.* The Vulgate.

249. 23–8 Climacus *reports* . . . *incouraged.* See St John Climacus (*c.* 570–649), *Scala Paradisi* (Cologne, 1624), Gradus IV, 'De obedientia', p. 43, and the translation (as *The Ladder of Paradise* (London, 1959)) by Archimandrite Lazarus Moore: 'Having earnestly observed the activities of the brother in charge of the refectory, I saw that he always had in his belt a small book, and I learnt that he wrote his thoughts in it each day and showed them all to the shepherd. And I saw that not only he, but also very many of the brethren there did the same' (p. 81). The work appears in *PG*, lxxxviii. 585–1248.

249. 31, note *d* '"Good wishes!" That's a useless phrase without good actions': from Plautus, *Trinummus*, II. iv. 439.

250. 10 *Relative* . . . *Correspondent.* A thing standing in some inevitable or congruous relation to another.

251. 5, note *e* 'One must give time to repentance': from Tacitus, *Histories*, i. 32 (where the text reads: 'daret malorum penitentiæ' ('give time to the disloyal to repent')).

251. 11, note *f* 'Sins and debts are always more than one believes they are': from Gruter, *Florilegium*, i. 2 (p. 153).

251. 18, note *g* 'What reinforcements, then, is it possible to find with which to oppose habit? Why, the contrary habit': from Arrian's *Discourses of Epictetus*, i. 27 (Loeb, i. 173).

251. 33, note *h* 'No one welcomes [death] cheerfully, except the man who has long since composed himself for death.' See Seneca, Epistle XXX.

252. 1, note *i* See Arrian's *Discourses of Epictetus*, i. 15, which Taylor translates in the text (Loeb, i. 107).

254. 27 anathema *or* devoted thing. See 1 Cor. 16: 22.

255. 32, note *m* See Martial, *Epigrams*, v. vi. 10–12: 'You know the seasons when Jove's brow is unruffled, when he beams with that calm look, all his own, that is wont to deny suppliants naught.'

255. 34 *his Fathers* well-beloved . . . well pleased. See Mark 12: 6.

256. 7, note *n* 'Pure vessels for divine service': adapted from Plautus, *Captivi*, II. ii. 289–91.

256. 10–11 *the hand* . . . *Table.* See Luke 22: 21.

256. 31 put off the old man . . . lusts. See Eph. 4: 22; Rom. 8: 29 and 12: 2.

256. 36 *communicate.* Receive Holy Communion.

257. 4–6 *dust . . . rot.* See Num. 5, esp. 17 and 22.

259. 12, note *o* 'Depart from the altars; you, to whom Venus gave joy last night': from Tibullus, *Elegies*, II. i. 11–12 (ed. J. P. Postgate (Oxford, 1915), Scriptorum Classicorum Bibliotheca Oxoniensis).

259. 13 *counsel of Saint* Paul. See 1 Cor. 7: 5.

259. 23, note *p* 'We stick close to the cross, we suck His blood, and fasten our tongue between the very wounds of our Redeemer': from 'De cœna Domini', a work attributed to St Cyprian, Bishop of Carthage. Taylor refers a number of times in his works to this tract by the 'pseudo-Cyprian', esp. in *The Real Presence and Spiritual of Christ in the Blessed Sacrament* (1654), vi. 146–7, and 135, where he gives the translation quoted above. This is from a text thought by Taylor and his contemporaries to be by Cyprian, but in fact it is by Arnold of Bonneval, whose works were published for a while under the name of Cyprian. See G. Macy, *The Ecclesiastical Approach to the Eucharist* (Oxford, 1983), p. 124 and note on p. 211, with references (to which should be added *Dictionnaire d'histoire et de géographie ecclesiastique*, iv [1930], 422–3).

Cf. Donne's well-known conclusion to 'Deaths Duell': 'There wee leave you in that *blessed dependancy*, to *hang* upon *him* that *hangs* upon the *Crosse* . . . there *suck* at his *woundes*, and *lye downe in peace* in his *grave* . . .' (*Sermons*, ed. Evelyn M. Simpson and George R. Potter (Berkeley: Univ. of California Press, 1962), x. 248). Cf. also Richard Hooker's use of Cyprian in the great Eucharistic passage in Book v of the *Ecclesiastical Polity* (chap. 67, sects. 11–13; in The Folger Library Edition of the Works, ed. W. S. Hill (Cambridge, Mass.: Harvard Univ. Press, 1977), ii. 338–43). In the text, Taylor echoes the Exhortations before Holy Communion in the *BCP*, especially the following: 'For as the benefit is great, if with a true penitent heart and living faith we receive that holy Sacrament; . . . so is the danger great, if we receive the same unworthily. For then we are guilty of the Body and Blood of Christ our Saviour; we eat and drink our own condemnation, not discerning the Lord's Body. . . .'

259. 27 *fontinel.* Fountain, outlet. The word appears earlier; see 80. 28 and commentary thereto.

260. 27 *Supper of the Lambe.* See Rev. 19: 9.

260. 39 a perfect man in Christ Jesus. See Eph. 4: 13.

262. 13–34 and note *q* *They . . . purities.* This lovely passage really marks the conclusion of *Holy Living*; what remains is an appendix of prayers 'for all sorts of Men'. Taylor is indebted in this passage to 'the Bishop of Geneva', St Francis de Sales (1567–1622), whose *Introduction to the Devout Life* (1608), ii. 21, he follows closely (see trans. by J. K. Ryan (New York: Image, 1955), pp. 114–15). Cf. Richard Hooker's praise of Eucharistic devotion: 'Why should any cogitation possesse the minde of a faithfull communicant but this, *O my God thou art true, O my soule thou art happie?*' (*Ecclesiastical Polity*, loc. cit., ii. 343).

270. 21 respersed. Dispersed, scattered.

272. 19–21 *Have mercy . . . my sin.* See Pss. 51: 1 and 38: 18.

272. 24–5 But . . . great. See Ps. 25: 11.

274. 9 Miserable man . . . body of sin? See Rom. 7: 24.

275. 17 indifferently. Without difference, equally well.

275. 23 Ex Liturgia . . . magna ex parte. 'Based on the Liturgy of St Basil to a great extent'. Much of what follows (275. 24–279. 34) is indebted to the Euchologion, or book of liturgical offices of the Eastern Orthodox Church. It contains the texts and rubrics of the Eucharistic rites of St Chrysostom and St Basil, and the Liturgy of the Pre-sanctified. Taylor also adapts material from the Euchologion in *Holy Dying*; see 218. 19–26 and commentary thereto.

276. 35 O that men would therefore praise the Lord. See Ps. 107: 8.

278. 22–3 O give thanks . . . for ever. See Ps. 106: 1.

278. 24–7 O all ye angels. . . magnifie him for ever. From the Benedicite, or the 'Song of the Three Children' in the addition to Dan. 3. The full version is also given as a canticle for Morning Prayer in the *BCP*.

279. 12–13 I will give thanks . . . in the congregation. See Ps. 111: 1.

280. 33–281. 18 *We praise thee . . . never be confounded.* Amen. This is the 'Te Deum Laudamus', found in the Office of Morning Prayer in the *BCP*.

283. 22 *preventing.* Anticipating.

284. 31–288. 24 A form . . . Amen. Taylor recalls the various events of the Passion recorded in the Gospels, especially Matt. 27 and John 18–19.

285. 9–10 What is man . . . him. See Ps. 8: 4 and Heb. 2: 6.

290. 24 *temporals.* Possessions.

291. 31 clefts of the rock. See Isa. 2: 21 and 1 Cor. 10: 4.

292. 13–294. 6 For all estates . . . Amen. This prayer is based on The Great Litany in the *BCP*.

299. 18–19 the hand of him . . . on the Table. See Luke 22: 21.

299. 28 He that glorieth . . . in the Lord. See 1 Cor. 1: 30, 31.

BIBLIOGRAPHY

Except where otherwise noted, Greek and Latin texts are in the Loeb Classical Library.

Aelianus, Claudius. *Varia historia: libri XIII.* Lyons: Gazeium [1558]. Trans. Thomas Stanley, London, 1665. Cf. ed. M. R. Dilts, Leipzig: Teubner, 1974.

Anthologia Latina. Ed. A. Riese and F. Bücheler. 2 vols. Leipzig: Teubner, 1894, 1906.

Aristophanes. Trans. B. B. Rogers. 3 vols. 1924.

Aristotle. *The Nicomachean Ethics.* Trans. H. Rackham. 1926, rev. 1934.

Arrian. See Epictetus.

Athenaeus. *The Deipnosophists.* Trans. C. B. Gulick. 7 vols. 1927.

Augustine. *Confessions.* Trans. W. Watts. 2 vols. 1912.

— *City of God.* Trans. W. G. Green. 7 vols. 1957–72.

Ausonius. *Works.* Trans. H. G. Evelyn-White. 2 vols. 1919, 1921.

Boethius. *Theological Tractates.* Trans. H. F. Stewart and E. K. Rand. 1918.

Camerarius. *The Living Library, Meditations and Observations Historical, Natural, Moral, Political, and Poetical.* Trans. John Molle. 2nd edn. London: Adam Islip, 1625.

Catullus. Ed. R. A. B. Mynors. Oxford Classical Texts, 1958.

Caussin, Nicolas. *The Holy Court in Three Tomes.* Written in French by Nicolas Caussin. Trans. Sir T. H[awkins]. Third Tome now first published in English, the first and second newly reviewed and much augmented according to the last Edition of the Authour. [Rouen:] Coustourier, 1634.

Cicero. *De inventione.* Trans. H. M. Hubbell. 1949.

— *De officiis.* Trans. W. Miller. 1921.

— *De senectute.* Trans. W. Falconer. 1923.

— *Letters to His Friends.* Trans. W. G. Williams. 3 vols. 1927.

— *The Phillipics.* Trans. W. C. A. Ker. 1926.

— *Tusculan Disputations.* Trans. J. E. King. 1927, rev. 1960.

Claudian. *Works.* Trans. M. Platnauer. 2 vols. 1922.

Corpus juris canonici. Ed. Aemilius Friedberg. 2 vols. Graz: Akademische Druck- u. Verlagsanstalt, 1959.

Corpus juris civilis. Ed. Paul Krueger and Theodore Mommsen. 3 vols. Berlin: Weidmann, 1954.

Cosin, John. *A Collection of Private Devotions.* Ed. P. G. Stanwood. Oxford: Clarendon Press, 1967.

Diodorus Siculus. *Library of History.* Trans. C. H. Oldfather *et al.* 12 vols. 1933.

Diogenes Laertius. *Lives of Eminent Philosophers.* Trans. R. D. Hicks. 2 vols. 1925.

Epictetus. *The Discourses as reported by Arrian.* Trans. W. A. Oldfather. 2 vols. 1925.

Euripides. *Works.* Trans. A. S. Way. 4 vols. 1912.

Eusebius. *Ecclesiastical History.* Trans. K. Lake and J. E. L. Oulton. 2 vols. 1926, 1932.

Golden Legend. See de Voragine, Jacobus.

The Greek Anthology. Trans. W. R. Paton. 5 vols. 1916–18.

Gruter, Janus. *Florilegium Ethico-Politicum nunquam antehac editum; nec non P. Syriac L. Senecae Sententiae Aureae.* [2 vols.] Frankfurt, 1610.

—— *Lampas, sive fax artium liberalium, hoc est Thesaurus Criticus, in quo infinitis locis theologorum, Jurisconsultorum, Medicorum, Philosophorum, Oratorum, Historicorum, Poetarum, Grammaticorum, scripta supplentur, corriguntur, illustrantur, notantur.* 7 vols. Frankfurt, 1602–34.

Herodotus. *The Histories.* Trans. A. D. Godley. 4 vols. 1924–8.

Hesiod and the Homeric Hymns. Trans. H. G. Evelyn-White. 1964.

Homer. *Iliad.* Trans. A. T. Murray. 2 vols. 1925.

—— *Odyssey.* Trans. A. T. Murray. 2 vols. 1919.

Horace. *Odes and Epodes.* Trans. C. E. Bennett. 1914.

—— *Satires, Epistles and Ars Poetica.* Trans. H. R. Fairclough. 1926.

Isocrates. *Works.* Trans. G. Norlin and L. van Hook. 3 vols. 1928–45.

Josephus. *Works.* Trans. H. St. J. Thackeray *et al.* 9 vols. 1926–65.

Juvenal and Persius. *Works.* Trans. G. G. Ramsay. 1918.

Livy. *History.* Trans. B. O. Foster *et al.* 14 vols. 1926.

Lucan. *Pharsalia.* Trans. J. D. Duff. 1929.

Lucian. *Works.* Trans. A. M. Harmon and M. D. Macleod. 8 vols. 1913.

Lucretius. *De rerum natura.* Trans. and ed. W. H. D. Rouse and M. F. Smith. Rev. 1975.

Martial. *Epigrams.* Trans. W. C. A. Ker. 2 vols. 1919.

Minor Latin Poets. Trans. J. W. Duff and A. M. Duff. 2 vols. 1934, rev. 1935.

The Mishna. Trans. Herbert Danby. 1933; rept. London: Oxford University Press, 1950.

Ovid. *The Art of Love, and Other Poems.* Trans. J. H. Mozley. 1929, rev. 1939.

—— *Ex Ponto.* Trans. A. L.Wheeler. 1924.

—— *Heroides and Amores.* Trans. F. J. Miller. 2 vols. 1956.

—— *Metamorphoses.* Trans. F. J. Miller. 2 vols. 1956.

Petronius. *Satyricon.* Trans. M. Heseltine. 1913, rev. 1961. Includes also

—— *Poems* (from the edition by A. Baehrens, in *Poetæ Latini Minores*, vol. 4, 1882).

Philostratus and Eunapius. *Lives of the Sophists.* Trans. W. C. Wright. 1922.

Plato. *Phaedo.* Trans. H. N. Fowler. 1914.
Plautus. *Works.* Trans. Paul Nixon. 5 vols. 1938.
Pliny. *Natural History.* Trans. H. Rackham *et al.* 10 vols. 1940–62.
Plutarch. *Moralia.* Trans. F. C. Babbitt *et al.* 15 vols. 1926.
—— *Parallel Lives.* Trans. B. Perrin. 11 vols. 1926.
Poetæ Latini Minores. Ed. A. Baehrens. 5 vols. Leipzig: Teubner, 1879–83.
Procopius. *History of the Wars.* Trans. H. B. Dewing. 7 vols. 1914.
Pythagoras. *I Versi Aurei di Pitagora.* Ed. Antonio Farina. Naples: Libreria Scientifica Editrice, 1962.
Quintilian. *Institutes.* Trans. H. E. Butler. 4 vols. 1920.
Seneca. *Ad Lucilium epistulæ morales.* Trans. R. M. Gummere. 3 vols. 1917–25.
—— *Moral Essays.* Trans. J. W. Basore. 3 vols. 1925.
—— *Tragedies.* Trans. F. J. Miller. 2 vols. 1917.
Seneca, The Elder. *Controversies.* Trans. M. Winterbottom. 2 vols. 1974.
Sophocles. *Electra.* Trans. F. Storr. 1913.
Stobaeus, Johannes. *Anthologium.* Ed. Otto Hense. 3 vols. Berlin: Weidmann, 1894–1912.
—— *Dicta poetarum.* Ed. Hugo Grotius. Paris, 1623.
Strabo. *Geography.* Trans. H. L. Jones. 8 vols. 1928.
Suetonius. *Lives.* Trans. J. C. Rolfe. 2 vols. 1914.
Surius, Laurentius. *Historiæ seu vitæ sanctorum.* 12 vols. Cologne, 1617–18.
Tacitus. *Dialogus, Agricola and Germania.* Trans. W. Peterson and M. Hutton. 1914, rev. 1970.
—— *Histories and Annals.* Trans. C. H. Moore and J. Jackson. 4 vols. 1937.
Tertullian. *Apology, De spectaculis.* Trans. T. R. Glover. 1931.
The Theodosian Code. Trans. Clyde Pharr. Princeton: Princeton University Press, 1952.
Valerius Maximus. *Factorum et dictorum memorabilium libri IX.* Ed. C. Kempf. Stuttgart: Teubner, 1966.
Virgil. *Aeneid and Minor Poems.* Trans. H. R. Fairclough. 2 vols. 1930.
Voragine, Jacobus de. *The Golden Legend of Jacobus de Voragine.* Trans. Granger Ryan and Helmut Ripperger. New York: Longmans, Green, 1941.
Xenophon. *Cyropædia.* Trans. W. Miller. 2 vols. 1914.

INDEX

The Index gives Taylor's sources by citing page numbers of the text and the corresponding Commentary, with bracketed numbers showing the frequency. Italicized page numbers indicate references that appear in the text only, the Scriptural citations being excluded from this rule.